CGI/Perl

Diane Zak

**COURSE
TECHNOLOGY**
™
THOMSON LEARNING

Australia • Canada • Mexico • Singapore • Spain • United Kingdom • United States

COURSE TECHNOLOGY
★
TM
THOMSON LEARNING

CGI/Perl
is published by Course Technology.

Senior Product Manager:
Jennifer Muroff

Development Editor:
Amanda Brodkin

Cover Designer:
Peter Karpick, Black Fish Design

Managing Editor:
Jennifer Locke

Editorial Assistant:
Janet Aras

Compositor:
GEX Publishing Services

Senior Acquisitions Editor:
Christine Guivernau

Production Editor:
Daphne Barbas

Manufacturing Coordinator:
Alexander Schall

Disclaimer
Course Technology reserves the right to revise this publication and make changes from time to time in its content without notice.

ISBN 0-619-03440-8

BRIEF
Contents

TABLE OF
Contents

Preface

One of the key strengths of the Web is its ability to provide users customized data in the form they seek it. One way this can be accomplished is through the use of a CGI script. CGI scripts provide the speed and adaptability required by Web programmers to develop powerful, customized Web pages in response to user requests. The most widely used language for creating CGI scripts is the Practical Extraction and Report Language, known simply as Perl. Perl is powerful, yet easy to learn, and is available free of charge.

Users of both UNIX- and Windows-based systems can use *CGI/Perl* to learn how to create, modify, and debug CGI scripts using the Perl language. You will learn to add functionality to your Web pages using features such as hyperlinks, forms, data files, and databases. Subroutines, string manipulation, cookies, hidden fields, and redirects give you the power to create truly interactive Web applications.

THE INTENDED AUDIENCE

CGI/Perl is intended for the individual who wants to create interactive Web pages that provide customized data in response to visitor requests or collect data from site visitors. An overview of scripts is provided; however, readers should have some familiarity with general programming concepts and also should have some experience with the HTML markup language. You need to be familiar with either the UNIX or Windows operating system and have a basic understanding of how to use the Internet. No prior experience with databases is required. The book emphasizes the necessity of planning for multiple scenarios, encouraging the reader to thoroughly prepare for the various options that Web page visitors might require in using a site.

THE APPROACH

To facilitate the learning process, this book presents content and theory integrated with sample exercises that help you conceptualize and build CGI scripts. Each chapter introduces a separate scripting topic, and also provides a sample case for which the user creates topic-related scripts and Web pages in step-by-step instructions. The chapters build on one another, allowing readers to combine concepts to create more sophisticated Web pages using multiple scripting features. Each chapter includes a Chapter Summary, Review Questions, Hands-on Projects, and Case Projects that highlight the major concepts that were presented, allowing readers to apply their knowledge. The Hands-on Projects are guided activities that let you practice and reinforce the techniques and skills you learn within the chapter and build on the techniques and skills you learned in previous chapters. These Hands-on Projects enhance your learning experience by providing additional ways to apply your knowledge in new situations. At the end of each chapter, there are two Case Projects that allow you to use the skills that you have learned in the chapter to create CGI scripting solutions from the ground up.

OVERVIEW OF THIS BOOK

The examples, steps, projects, and cases in this book will help you achieve the following objectives:

- Understand the role of a CGI script in creating interactive Web sites
- Create scripts that allow users to interact with Web sites
- Understand how Web pages can provide responses to site user requests for data
- Use scripts to collect data from Web page visitors
- Learn how to use scalar, array, and hash variables in a script
- Include the selection and repetition structures in a script
- Save data to a data file and a database
- Use Perl's string manipulation features
- Send e-mail using a script

Chapter 1 introduces you to scripting technologies in general and CGI and Perl in particular. You learn how to create, run, and debug CGI scripts. In **Chapter 2**, you learn how to create a hyperlink to a CGI script, append data to a URL, parse data, and access data using the `param` function. In **Chapter 3** you learn how to send data using an online form. You also learn how to use variables in CGI scripts and avoid undeclared variables in CGI scripts. **Chapter 4** covers arrays and hashes, and you learn how to code the repetition structure for use in CGI scripts. In **Chapter 5** you learn how to use a CGI script to open files for writing and reading. You also learn how to separate fields and use counters. **Chapter 6** covers the use of the selection structure, comparison operators, and logical operators in CGI scripts. You also learn how to determine the size of an array. In **Chapter 7**, you learn how to use user-defined functions, and you learn more about the repetition structure. This chapter also covers environment variables. In **Chapter 8**, you learn about various string manipulation options, including pattern matching, case conversion, and locating, replacing, or inserting text. **Chapter 9** introduces you to DBM databases and covers DBM database creation and adding records to a DBM database as well as record modification and deletion. You also learn how to concatenate strings and use "here" documents. In **Chapter 10** you learn how to create a form using a CGI script and pass information between scripts using hidden fields. You also learn how to send an e-mail message using a script. **Chapter 11** covers the use of cookies in CGI scripts, including how to create cookies and how to access the information stored in a cookie. Finally, in **Chapter 12**, you learn how to redirect a Web page visitor's browser to a different URL using the Location and Refresh script headers.

Each chapter in *CGI/Perl* includes the following elements to enhance the learning experience:

- **Chapter Objectives:** Each chapter in this book begins with a list of the important concepts to be mastered within the chapter. This list provides you with a quick reference to the contents of the chapter.

- **Step-By-Step Methodology:** As new concepts are presented in each chapter, step-by-step instructions allow you to actively apply the concepts you are learning. In each chapter, you build scripts and pages for a different application.

- **Tips:** Chapters contain Tips designed to provide you with practical advice and proven strategies related to the concept being discussed. Tips also provide suggestions for resolving problems you might encounter while proceeding through the chapters.

- **Chapter Summaries:** Each chapter's text is followed by a summary of chapter concepts. These summaries provide a helpful way to recap and revisit the ideas covered in each chapter and are a useful study aid.

- **Review Questions:** End-of-chapter assessment begins with a set of approximately 20 review questions that reinforce the main ideas introduced in each chapter. These questions ensure that you have mastered the concepts and understand the information you have learned.

Hands-on Projects: Along with conceptual explanations and step-by-step instructions, each chapter provides Hands-on Projects related to each major topic aimed at providing you with practical experience. Some of the Hands-on Projects provide detailed instructions, while as the book progresses, others provide less detailed instructions that require you to apply the materials presented in the current chapter with less guidance. As a result, the Hands-on Projects provide you with practice implementing scripting in real-world situations.

Case Projects: Two Case Projects are presented at the end of each chapter. These Case Projects are designed to help you apply what you have learned in the chapter to real-world situations. They give you the opportunity to independently synthesize and evaluate information, examine potential solutions, and make recommendations, much as you would in an actual business situation.

TEACHING TOOLS

The following supplemental materials are available when this book is used in a classroom setting. All of the teaching tools available with this book are provided to the instructor on a single CD-ROM.

Electronic Instructor's Manual. The Instructor's Manual that accompanies this textbook includes:

- Additional instructional material to assist in class preparation, including suggestions for lecture topics.
- Solutions to the Review Questions, Hands-on Projects, and Case Projects.

ExamView® This textbook is accompanied by ExamView, a powerful testing software package that allows instructors to create and administer printed, computer (LAN-based), and Internet exams. ExamView includes hundreds of questions that correspond to the topics covered in this text, enabling students to generate detailed study guides that include page references for further review. The computer-based and Internet testing components allow students to take exams at their computers, and also save the instructor time by grading each exam automatically.

PowerPoint Presentations. This book comes with Microsoft PowerPoint slides for each chapter. These are included as a teaching aid for classroom presentation, to make available to students on the network for chapter review, or to be printed for classroom distribution. Instructors can add their own slides for additional topics they introduce to the class.

Data Files. Data files, containing all of the data necessary for steps within the chapters and the Hands-On Projects, are provided through the Course Technology Web site at **www.course.com**, and are also available on the Teaching Tools CD-ROM.

Solution Files. Solutions to end-of-chapter Review Questions, Hands-on Projects, and Case Projects are provided on the Teaching Tools CD-ROM and may also be found on the Course Technology Web site at **www.course.com**. The solutions are password protected.

Distance Learning. Course Technology is proud to present online courses in WebCT and Blackboard, as well as at MyCourse.com, Course Technology's own course enhancement tool, to provide the most complete and dynamic learning experience possible. When you add online content to one of your courses, you're adding a lot: self tests, links, glossaries, and, most of all, a gateway to the 21st century's most important information resource. We hope you will make the most of your course, both online and offline. For more information on how to bring distance learning to your course, contact your local Course Technology sales representative.

ACKNOWLEDGMENTS

I truly want to thank both Jennifer Muroff and Amanda Brodkin for their help, enthusiasm, and patience during this project. Thank you, Jennifer, for your encouraging words and for always anticipating my needs. And thank you, Amanda, for being such a great Development Editor and for working above and beyond to keep this project on schedule. I also want to thank John Bosco for agreeing to QA the book, and for his suggestions on ways to improve the book. Thank you also to Daphne Barbas for her fine attention to detail. Last, but certainly not least, I especially want to thank the following reviewers for their invaluable ideas and comments: Chris Davis, Baker College; Marty Loughlin, Terra Community College; Peter B. MacIntyre; Jim Newtown, Baker College; W. J. Patterson, Sullivan University; Deborah Rowden, Baker College; Mark Terwilliger, Lake Superior State University; Lou Tinaro, Tidewater Community College; and Kevin Wishart.

Diane Zak

Read This Before You Begin

TO THE USER

Data Files

To complete the steps and projects in this book, you will need data files that have been created for this book. Your instructor will provide the data files to you. You also can obtain the files electronically from the Course Technology Web site by connecting to **www.course.com**, and then searching for this book title.

Each chapter in this book has its own set of data files that typically include HTML files and CGI script files. The HTML files for each chapter are stored in a separate chapter directory within the public_html directory. For example, the HTML files for Chapter 2 are stored in the public_html/chap02 directory. Similarly, each chapter's CGI script files are stored in a separate chapter directory within the cgi-bin directory. The CGI script files for Chapter 2, for example, are stored in the cgi-bin/chap02 directory. Throughout this book, you will be instructed to open files from or save files to these directories.

You can use a computer in your school lab or your own computer to complete the chapters, Hands-on Projects, and Case Projects in this book.

Using Your Own Computer

To use your own computer to complete the chapters, Hands-on Projects, and Case Projects in this book, you will need the following:

- **A 486-level or higher personal computer running Windows 2000 Professional or UNIX.** Please note that all references to UNIX in this book also include the different flavors of UNIX, such as Linux and FreeBSD. This book was tested using Red Hat Linux 7.

- **Netscape Communicator or Microsoft Internet Explorer browser software.** If you do not have either program, you can download them for free from **www.netscape.com** or **www.microsoft.com**, respectively.

- **Perl interpreter.** The Perl interpreter is part of the standard UNIX distribution. If you are using a Windows system, you will need to obtain a copy of the Perl interpreter. You can obtain a free copy of Perl from the ActiveState Web site at **www.activestate.com** or the Perl Web site at **www.perl.com**. Please note that this book was tested with Perl version 5.6.0 built for i386 Linux, and ActiveState ActivePerl version 5.6.0.623 for Windows.

■ **The Mail::Sendmail module.** You will need the Mail::Sendmail module to complete Chapter 10. You can obtain a free copy of the Mail::Sendmail module from the CPAN (Comprehensive Perl Archive Network) Web site at **www.perl.com/CPAN-local/ authors/id/M/MI/MIVKOVIC/**. Please note that this book was tested with Mail::Sendmail version 0.78. Instructions for installing Perl modules on UNIX and Windows systems can be found at **theoryx5.uwinnipeg.ca/CPAN/perl/pod/ perlmodinstall.html**. You also can use the following tables as a guide when installing the Mail::Sendmail module. The first table contains the instructions for installing the Mail::Sendmail module on a UNIX system. The second table contains the instructions for installing the Mail::Sendmail module on a Windows system.

Installing Mail::Sendmail on a UNIX system
1. Create a directory named **mail** in the /usr/lib/perl5/5.6.0 directory.
2. Download the Mail-Sendmail-0.78.tar.gz file into the mail directory.
3. At the UNIX command prompt, type **gzip -dc Mail-Sendmail-0.78.tar.gz	tar -xof -** (be sure to type a space and the hyphen after -xof) and press **Enter**.
4. Make the mail directory the current directory.
5. At the UNIX command prompt, type **perl Makefile.PL** and press **Enter**.
6. Type **make** and press **Enter**.
7. Type **make test** and press **Enter**.
8. Type **make install** and press **Enter**.

Installing Mail::Sendmail on a Windows system
1. Download the Mail-Sendmail-0.78.tar.gz file.
2. Open the Mail-Sendmail-0.78.tar.gz file in WinZip. (You can obtain a free evaluation copy of WinZip from **www.winzip.com**.) When the message "Archive contains one file: Mail-Sendmail-0.78.tar. Should WinZip decompress it to a temporary folder and open it?" appears, click **Yes**.
3. Use WinZip to extract the module files into the perl/lib directory.
4. Open the perl/lib directory. Change the Mail-Sendmail-0.78 folder's name to Mail.

■ **Data files**. You will not be able to complete the chapters and projects in this book using your own computer unless you have the data files. You can get the data files from your instructor, or you can obtain the data files electronically from the Course Technology Web site by connecting to **www.course.com**, and then searching for this book title. If you are using a UNIX system, the files should be placed in your home directory. If you are using a Windows system, the files should be placed in the C:/inetpub/wwwroot directory.

■ **A Web server that allows you to create, save, and execute CGI scripts.** You can test your Perl scripts from the command line without using a Web server. However, you will need a Web server to test the scripts using your Web browser. The Web server can be located at your school or at your Internet Service Provider. You also can use your personal computer as a Web server, as long as you have the appropriate Web server software, such as IIS or Apache. The chapters and projects in this book were tested using IIS 5.0 (which comes with Windows 2000 Professional) and Apache (which comes with Red Hat Linux 7). You can use the instructions in the following two tables as a guide when setting up your computer as a personal Web server. The first table contains the instructions for configuring Apache in Red Hat Linux 7, and the second table contains the instructions for installing and configuring IIS (Internet Information Services) 5.0 in Windows 2000 Professional. (If you are using your computer as a personal Web server, you will not need access to the Internet to complete the chapters and projects in this book. The only exception to this is in Chapter 10, where you learn how to send e-mail from a script.)

Configuring Apache in Red Hat Linux 7

1. Modify the httpd.conf file, which typically is located in the etc/httpd/conf directory, as follows:
   a. If necessary, remove the # symbol from the beginning of the `ServerName localhost` line.
   b. Change the `DocumentRoot "/var/www/html"` line to `DocumentRoot` **"/home/**_yourUserName_**/public_html"**, where _yourUserName_ is your user name.
   c. Insert the line **Alias /public_html/ "/home/**_yourUserName_**/public_html/"** in the Aliases section of the file.
   d. Change the `ScriptAlias /cgi-bin/ "/var/www/cgi-bin/"` line to **ScriptAlias /cgi-bin/ "/home/**_yourUserName_**/cgi-bin/"**.
   e. Change the `<Directory "/var/www/cgi-bin">` line to **<Directory "/home/**_yourUserName_**/cgi-bin">**.
   f. If necessary, remove the # symbol from the beginning of the `AddHandler cgi-script .cgi` line.
   g. Insert the line **AddType application/x-httpd-cgi .cgi** in the `AddType` section of the file.
   h. Save the file.
2. The file permissions for your home directory, the public_html directory, the cgi-bin directory, and all chapter directories should be set to 755.

Installing and configuring IIS 5.0 in Windows 2000 Professional

Note: IIS 5.0 is not installed on Windows 2000 Professional by default. However, if you _upgraded_ to Windows 2000, IIS 5.0 will be installed by default if Personal Web Server (PWS) was installed on your previous version of Windows.

1. To install IIS 5.0:
   a. Log on as Administrator.
   b. Click **Start**, point to **Settings**, click **Control Panel** and start the **Add/Remove Programs** application.
   c. Select **Add/Remove Windows Components**.
   d. Select the **Indexing Service** and **Internet Information Services (IIS)** options.
   e. Click **Next**. Insert the Windows CD when prompted, then click **OK**.
   f. Click **Finish** when prompted, then click **Exit**.
   g. Close the Add/Remove Programs box, then close Control Panel.

Installing and configuring IIS 5.0 in Windows 2000 Professional

2. To set the properties of the cgi-bin folder so that you can run the scripts contained in the folder:
   a. Download or copy the data files that come with this book to the inetpub/wwwroot directory. The cgi-bin folder is part of these files.
   b. In Explorer, right-click the **cgi-bin** folder, then click **Properties**.
   c. Click the **Web Sharing** tab.
   d. Click the **Share this Folder** option button.
   e. Leave cgi-bin as the alias.
   f. Select the **Read**, **Script Source Access** check boxes and **Scripts** option button.
   g. Click **OK**, then click **OK** again.

3. To associate the CGI extension with the Perl interpreter so that you can run the scripts from the DOS command line:
   a. In Explorer, click the **C drive**. Click **Tools**, then click **Folder Options**.
   b. Click the **File Types** tab.
   c. Click **New**. Type **CGI** as the File Extension, then click the **Advanced >>** button.
   d. Scroll the Associated File type box until you see Perl File.
   e. Click **Perl File**, then click **OK**, then click **Close**.
   f. Close Explorer.

4. To associate the .cgi extension with the Perl interpreter so that you can run the scripts from the browser, and also identify the Perl program as the script engine for .pl and .cgi files:
   a. Click **Start**, point to **Settings**, and then click **Control Panel**.
   b. Double-click **Administrative Tools**, then double-click **Computer Management**.
   c. Expand the **Services and Applications** folder, then expand the **Internet Information Services** folder.
   d. Expand the **Default Web Site** folder.
   e. Right-click the **cgi-bin** folder, then click **Properties**.
   f. Click the **Virtual Directory** tab if necessary, then click the **Configuration...** button.
   g. Scroll until you see the .pl extension information.
   h. Click the **.pl** extension. Click the **Edit** button, then select the **Script Engine** option. Also deselect the **Check that file exists** option, if necessary. Click **OK**.
   i. Click the **Add** button. In the Executable box, type **C:\Perl\bin\Perl.exe "%s" %s**
   j. In the Extension box, type **.cgi**
   k. Select the **Limit to** button, then type **GET,HEAD,POST**
   l. If necessary, select the **Script Engine** option.
   m. If necessary, unselect the **Check that file exists** option.
   n. Click **OK**.
   o. Click **OK** to close the Application Configuration window.
   p. Click **OK** to close the cgi-bin properties window.
   q. Close the Computer Management and Administrative Tools windows.

Figures

You can run your Perl CGI scripts on various systems (such as UNIX, Windows, and Macintosh). You also can use various Web browsers (such as Netscape Communicator and Microsoft Internet Explorer) to display your Web pages. Many of the figures in this book reflect how your screen will look if you are using a UNIX system and Netscape

Communicator. Your screen will look similar to these figures if you are using a Windows system and Microsoft Internet Explorer.

Using a Windows Text Editor and a UNIX Server

If you are using a Windows text editor (such as Notepad) to create your script, and then uploading the script to a UNIX server, you will need to convert the script from a DOS file to a UNIX file, because DOS uses a different set of control characters at the end of each line. To convert a DOS file to a UNIX file, type the command **perl -pi -e "s/\cM//g"** *filename* at the UNIX command prompt, where *filename* is the name of the file to convert, and then press Enter.

Visit Our World Wide Web Site

Additional materials designed especially for you might be available for your course on the World Wide Web. Go to **www.course.com**. Periodically search this site for more details.

TO THE INSTRUCTOR

To complete the chapters in this book, your users must use a set of data files. These files are included in the Instructor's Resource Kit. They also may be obtained electronically through the Course Technology Web site at **www.course.com**. Follow the instructions in the Help file to copy the data files to your server or standalone computer. You can view the Help file using a text editor such as WordPad or Notepad.

Once the files are copied, you should instruct your users how to copy the files to their own computers or workstations. If a user is using a UNIX system, the files should be copied to his or her home directory. If a user is using a Windows system, the files should be copied to the C:/inetpub/wwwroot directory.

The chapters and projects in this book were tested using Windows 2000 Professional with IIS 5.0 as the Web server and ActiveState's ActivePerl version 5.6.0.623 for Windows as the Perl interpreter. They also were tested using Red Hat Linux 7 with Apache as the Web server and Perl version 5.6.0 built for i386 Linux as the Perl interpreter. You will need to install the Mail::Sendmail module on your Web server. You can obtain a free copy of the Mail::Sendmail module from the CPAN (Comprehensive Perl Archive Network) Web site at **www.perl.com/CPAN-local/authors/id/M/MI/MIVKOVIC/**. Please note that this book was tested with Mail::Sendmail version 0.78. Instructions for installing Perl modules on UNIX and Windows systems can be found at **theoryx5.uwinnipeg.ca/CPAN/ perl/pod/perlmodinstall.html**.

Course Technology Data Files

You are granted a license to copy the data files to any computer or computer network used by individuals who have purchased this book.

AN INTRODUCTION TO CGI AND PERL

In this chapter, you will:

♦ Review basic Internet terminology
♦ Learn about the CGI protocol
♦ Create a CGI script using the Perl language
♦ Run a CGI script from the command line and Web browser
♦ Debug a CGI script

To do business on the Web, a company must be able to interact with customers through its Web site. The Web site should allow customers to submit inquiries, select items for purchase, provide shipping information, and submit payment information. It also should allow the company to track customer inquiries and process customer orders.

In this chapter, you learn about a technology that allows you to create interactive Web sites, CGI scripts. You create a simple CGI script using the Perl scripting language. Before doing so, however, you review some basic Internet terminology.

INTERNET TERMINOLOGY

The **Internet** is the world's largest computer network, connecting millions of computers located all around the world. Every computer that is connected to the Internet has a unique identifying number called an IP (Internet Protocol) address. An **IP address** is a set of four numbers between 0 and 255 that are separated by periods. For example, 216.148.218.195 is the IP address for a computer at Red Hat Inc., a company that distributes a UNIX-like operating system named Linux. Numeric IP addresses are difficult for people to remember, so an IP address also can be represented by a name, called a **domain name**. Unlike numeric IP addresses, domain names are easy to remember, because they have meaning to people. For example, it is much easier to remember Red Hat Inc.'s domain name, which is www.redhat.com, than it is to remember its numeric IP address.

One of the most popular features of the Internet is the **World Wide Web**, often referred to simply as **WWW** or the **Web**. The Web consists of documents called **Web pages** that are written in **HTML (Hypertext Markup Language)** and stored on Web servers in files having an .htm or .html extension. A **Web server** is a computer that contains special software that "serves up" Web pages in response to requests from Web browsers. A **Web browser**, or simply **browser**, is a program that allows you to access and view Web pages. Currently, the two most popular browsers are Netscape Communicator and Microsoft Internet Explorer.

Every Web document has a unique address that indicates its location on the Web. The address is called a **URL**—an acronym for **Uniform Resource Locator**. To view a Web document, you simply enter the document's URL in the location or address box of a Web browser. Entering the URL shown in Figure 1-1, for example, displays the "Retrieve Forms and Instructions" Web page located on the United States Treasury Department's Web site.

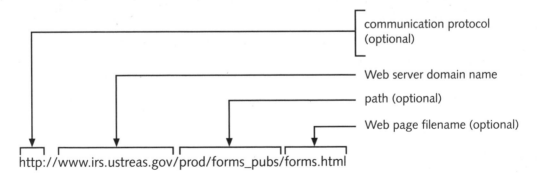

communication protocol (optional)

Web server domain name

path (optional)

Web page filename (optional)

http://www.irs.ustreas.gov/prod/forms_pubs/forms.html

Figure 1-1   Example of a URL for a Web page

As Figure 1-1 indicates, a URL consists of four parts. The first part of the URL shown in Figure 1-1, http://, refers to the **HTTP communication protocol**, which is the protocol used to transmit Web pages on the Web. A **protocol** is simply an agreement between a sender and a receiver regarding how data are sent and interpreted. If you do not enter the communication protocol in a URL, Web browsers by default assume the HTTP protocol.

 You can find more information about the HTTP protocol by visiting the Web Developer's Virtual Library Web site at www.wdvl.com/Internet/Protocols/HTTP or the WhatIs.com Web site at www.whatis.com.

The second part of the URL is the domain name of the Web server where the document resides. You also can use the Web server's numeric IP address in a URL, rather than its domain name. In Figure 1-1, the Web server's domain name is www.irs.ustreas.gov.

The third part of the URL is the **path**, which specifies the location of the document on the Web server. Figure 1-1 indicates that the document is located in the prod/forms_pubs directory on the www.irs.ustreas.gov server. It is important that the path you enter in the URL is exact; otherwise, the browser will not be able to locate the document. If you do not specify a path, the Web server assumes that the document is contained in a default location on the server. The network administrator defines the default location when the Web server is configured.

 The prod/forms_pubs path shown in Figure 1-1 indicates that the forms.html document is contained in the forms_pubs directory, which is a subdirectory of the prod directory on the www.irs.ustreas.gov server.

The last part of the URL specifies the name of the document—in this case, forms.html. If you do not specify the name, most Web servers send a default home page to the Web browser. Default home pages usually have names such as home.html, default.html, or index.html. The default home page for the United States Treasury Department, for example, is named index.html; you can view the page using either the URL http:// www.irs.ustreas.gov/index.html or, more simply, the URL http://www.irs.ustreas.gov.

When you request a Web page using your Web browser, the browser looks for the Web server specified in the URL. If the browser is able to locate the server, it opens a connection between the server and your computer, and then submits your request to the server. How the Web server handles the request depends on whether the Web page you are requesting is static or dynamic.

STATIC AND DYNAMIC WEB PAGES

A **static Web page** is an HTML document whose content is established at the time the page is created. Any time you access a static Web page, the same information appears. The information changes only when someone—typically the document's creator or a Web programmer—manually updates the HTML file stored on the server. Static Web pages are useful for displaying information that does not change often and information that must be updated by hand, such as a college catalog or a list of the current exhibits at a museum.

One drawback of static Web pages is that they are not interactive. The only interaction that can occur between a static Web page and the user is through links that allow the user to "jump" from one Web page to another. Despite this limitation, most Web pages are static.

When a Web server receives a request for a static Web page, the server locates the file, opens it, and then transfers its contents to the browser. The browser interprets the HTML instructions it receives and renders the Web page. Figure 1-2 illustrates the process by which a static Web page is requested and delivered.

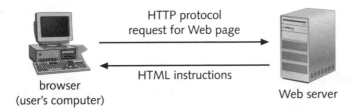

HTTP protocol
request for Web page

HTML instructions

browser
(user's computer)

Web server

Figure 1-2   Process used to request and deliver a static Web page

Unlike a static Web page, a **dynamic Web page** is interactive; it can accept information from the user and also retrieve information for the user. If you have ever completed an online form—say, for example, to purchase merchandise or submit a resume—then you have used a dynamic Web page.

Whereas a static Web page is simply an HTML document, a dynamic Web page usually requires both an HTML document and either a program or script. **Programs** and **scripts** are sets of instructions, written in a programming or scripting language, that tell a computer how to perform a task. The programs or scripts associated with dynamic Web pages, for example, tell the computer how to process the data submitted by or retrieved for the user.

The difference between a program and a script is that a program is compiled and a script is interpreted. A compiled program is converted into machine code—the 0s and 1s the computer can understand—once and doesn't need to be converted each time the program is run. The instructions in a script, on the other hand, are converted into machine code line by line as the script is running—a process referred to as interpreting. A script must be interpreted each time the script is run. Compiled programs run faster than scripts, because they already are in a more efficient format that the computer can understand. However, scripts are easier to create, debug, and modify. The biggest advantage scripts have over programs is that scripts can be ported to, or run on, different platforms (such as UNIX, Windows, and Macintosh), usually requiring little (if any) modification to do so. Programs, on the other hand, need to be compiled for each different platform.

Several technologies are available for creating dynamic Web pages; examples include CGI, Active Server Pages (ASP), and Java applets. In this book, you use CGI, because it is one of the most popular technologies available, and is supported by all of the major Web servers.

CGI

CGI stands for **Common Gateway Interface** and is the protocol that allows a Web server to communicate with CGI scripts. **CGI scripts** are scripts that follow the standards specified by the CGI protocol.

Some Web servers require you to store files containing CGI scripts in a special directory named cgi-bin; otherwise, the server will not recognize the file as a CGI script file. Other Web servers require CGI script filenames to have either a .cgi or .pl extension. In this book, you store the files containing your CGI scripts in the cgi-bin directory, and you append the .cgi extension to their names.

For discussion purposes, assume that your Web server requires you to store CGI scripts in the cgi-bin directory. When your server receives a URL from your browser, it examines the URL to see if the cgi-bin directory appears in the path. If it does, the server goes to the cgi-bin directory and runs the script whose name is specified in the URL. For example, the URL http://yourservername/cgi-bin/regForm.cgi tells your server to run the regForm.cgi script, which is located in the cgi-bin directory on the server.

While a script is running, it can send information to and retrieve information from databases and other files on the same or a different server. When the script has finished running, it sends its output—typically HTML—to the server. The server transmits the HTML to your browser, which renders the Web page. Figure 1-3 (on the next page) illustrates the process by which dynamic Web pages are requested and delivered.

You can write CGI scripts using various scripting languages, such as Perl, AppleScript, or a UNIX shell. In this book, you use the Perl language, because it is the most widely used language for creating CGI scripts. The popularity of Perl can be attributed to the fact that it is powerful, yet easy to learn, and is available free of charge. (You can obtain a free copy of Perl from the ActiveState Web site at www.activestate.com or the Perl Web site at www.perl.com.)

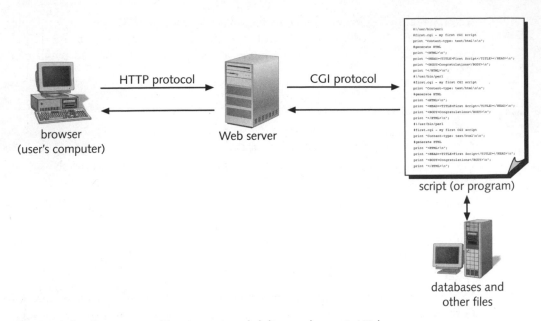

Figure 1-3   Process used to request and deliver a dynamic Web page

 You also can create CGI programs. You do so using a programming language rather than a scripting language. C, C++, and Visual Basic are examples of programming languages that you can use to create CGI programs.

Next, you learn how to use Perl to write a simple CGI script.

Writing Your First CGI Script in Perl

Before you create your first CGI script in Perl, you should determine the location of the Perl interpreter on your server. You need to enter the location in any CGI script written in Perl and running on a UNIX server. Typically, Windows servers do not require you to enter the Perl interpreter's location in a CGI script. However, if you intend to write CGI scripts that eventually will be run on a UNIX server, it is a good idea to get in the habit of entering the location, even if it is not entirely necessary.

On a UNIX system, the Perl interpreter is named perl; on a Windows system, it is named perl.exe.

 Most CGI scripts are run on UNIX servers. Recall from the Read This Before You Begin section that references to UNIX in this book also include the different flavors of UNIX, such as Linux and FreeBSD.

To determine where the Perl interpreter resides on your server:

1. *If you are using a UNIX system,* log on to UNIX. If necessary, open a terminal window. A screen similar to the one shown in Figure 1-4 appears. Your screen might look different, but it should show a UNIX command prompt; in this case, it shows a dollar sign ($). (The command prompt might be different on your system.)

    If you are using a Windows system, skip to Step 2.

---

zakdiane@coursetech: /home/zakdiane

File   Edit   Settings   Help

[zakdiane@coursetech zakdiane]$ ▮

— UNIX command prompt

Figure 1-4   Screen showing a UNIX command prompt

2. *If you are using a UNIX system,* type **whereis perl** after the UNIX command prompt and then press **Enter**. Be sure to type the entire command using lowercase letters, as UNIX commands are case-sensitive. Typical responses from this command include /usr/bin/perl and /usr/local/bin/perl.

    If you are using a Windows system, click **Start**, point to **Search**, and then click **For Files or Folders**. Type **perl.exe** in the Search for files or folders named text box, and then click the **Search Now** button. The path to the Perl interpreter—typically C:\Perl\bin—appears in the Search Results window. When entering the interpreter's location in a Perl script, you append the interpreter's name (perl.exe) to the path, and you replace the backslashes (\) with forward slashes (/), like this: C:/Perl/bin/perl.exe. (In Perl, you use the forward slash, rather than the backslash, to separate the directories in a path.) Close the Search Results window.

If you do not get a response from the UNIX whereis perl command, or if the location of the Perl interpreter does not appear in the Search Results window in Windows, the Perl interpreter might not be installed on your system. You will need to check with your technical support person.

The first CGI script you write in Perl creates a Web page that contains the word "Congratulations". You can use any text editor to enter the Perl instructions for your script. For example, you can use pico, vi, or gedit in UNIX, and Notepad or WordPad in Windows.

To create a Perl CGI script:

1. Open a text editor, and then enter the text shown in Figure 1-5. Be sure to type each line exactly as shown, as Perl commands are case sensitive. If necessary, modify the first line to reflect the location of the Perl interpreter on your system.

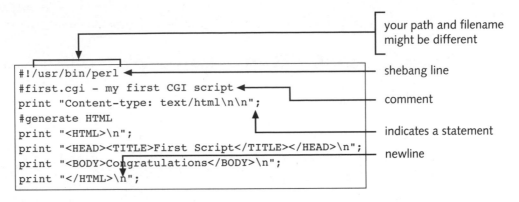

```
#!/usr/bin/perl
#first.cgi - my first CGI script
print "Content-type: text/html\n\n";
#generate HTML
print "<HTML>\n";
print "<HEAD><TITLE>First Script</TITLE></HEAD>\n";
print "<BODY>Congratulations</BODY>\n";
print "</HTML>\n";
```

your path and filename might be different

shebang line

comment

indicates a statement

newline

Figure 1-5   Perl CGI script

2. Save the script in the cgi-bin/chap01 directory using the name **first.cgi**.

Study closely each line in the script shown in Figure 1-5. The first line, `#!/usr/bin/perl`, is called the **shebang line**, simply because it begins with a sharp symbol (#) followed by an exclamation point (!), referred to as the **bang symbol**. Immediately after the bang symbol, you enter the location of the Perl interpreter on your system. The location is /usr/bin/perl in Figure 1-5, but might be different on your system. The shebang line is required in Perl CGI scripts run on a UNIX system, and it must be the first line in the script. The shebang line is optional in Perl CGI scripts run on a Windows system.

On a UNIX system, the shebang line tells the operating system which interpreter to use to convert the script instructions into machine code. The shebang line is not required on most Windows systems, because Windows allows you to associate the script filename extension with the appropriate interpreter. For example, you can associate the .cgi filename extension with the perl.exe interpreter in Windows. When you run a script whose filename ends with .cgi, Windows automatically uses the perl.exe interpreter to convert the script instructions into machine code.

The second line in the script, `#first.cgi - my first CGI script`, is a **comment**, which is simply internal documentation. Comments in a Perl script always begin with the sharp symbol (#). The Perl interpreter ignores any text appearing after the sharp symbol on that line. It is a good programming practice to include comments in your scripts as reminders for yourself and others who may have to maintain your script.

Notice that the shebang line also begins with the sharp symbol. The shebang line is treated as a comment on all platforms other than UNIX. Recall that on a UNIX system, the shebang line tells the operating system which interpreter to use to convert the script instructions into machine code.

A CGI script must perform two important tasks. First, the script must specify the type of document it is sending to the browser, and second, the script must output the document. A script uses an HTTP header line, called the **Content-type header**, to perform the first task, and typically uses HTML tags to perform the second task.

Recall that a script does not send information directly to the browser. Rather, it sends information to the server, which then transmits the information to the browser.

The syntax of the Content-type header is shown in Figure 1-6. Notice that Content-type begins with an uppercase letter C. All of the other letters in the Content-type header must be entered using lowercase letters.

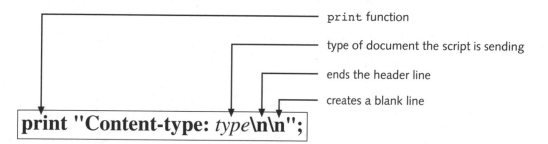

Figure 1-6 Syntax of the Content-type header

The items in **bold** in the syntax are required parts of the Content-type header. The items in *italics* indicate where you must supply information pertaining to the current script.

As Figure 1-6 indicates, a Content-type header begins with the Perl `print` function. The `print` function's task is to send the text enclosed in quotation marks to the browser.

You also can use the `print` function to send information to a disk file rather than to a browser; you learn how to do so in Chapter 5.

In the syntax, *type* is the type of document the script is sending to the browser. Most scripts send an HTML document; therefore, you typically use `text/html` as the *type* in the Content-type header. The Content-type header shown as the third line in the first.cgi script, for example, indicates that the script will send an HTML document to the browser. Other *types* commonly found in the Content-type header include `text/plain` (for sending a text document that does not include HTML tags) and `image/gif` (for sending a gif image).

Notice that \n\n follows the *type* in the Content-type header's syntax. A backslash (\) followed by the letter n is called the **newline character** in Perl, and is used to send a new line to the browser. The newline character creates a new line by inserting a carriage return at the end of the current line. The first newline character in the Content-type header's syntax identifies the end of the Content-type header, and ensures that the header appears on a line by itself. The second newline character inserts a blank line below the header; this signals the browser that it has reached the end of the header information. (A script can contain more than one header.) Both newline characters are necessary; otherwise, the browser will not be able to display the document it receives from the script.

The last character in a Content-type header is the semicolon (;). The Content-type header is considered a **statement**, which is simply an instruction that can be executed by the Perl interpreter. All Perl statements (except selection and looping statements) must end with a semicolon.

The fourth line in the script, `#generate HTML`, is a comment that describes the purpose of the last four lines of code. In this case, the purpose of the code is to generate the HTML that will display the word Congratulations on a Web page. Each of the four lines, you will notice, begins with the Perl `print` function, which sends the text enclosed in quotation marks to the browser. The lines end with a semicolon, because they are considered Perl statements.

Look closely at the four statements that generate the HTML. The statement `print "<HTML>\n";` sends the <HTML> tag, which denotes the beginning of a Web page, and a newline character to the browser. Although the newline character is not required when entering HTML, it will make the HTML code generated by the CGI script easier to read when the code is viewed in a browser. You will observe the effect of the newline character later in this chapter.

The next statement in the script, `print "<HEAD><TITLE>First Script </TITLE></HEAD>\n";`, sends the beginning and ending HEAD and TITLE tags, along with the title (which will appear in the browser's title bar) and a newline character. The next statement, `print "<BODY>Congratulations</BODY>\n";`, sends the beginning and ending BODY tags, together with the text to display on the Web page and a newline character. The last statement in the script, `print "</HTML>\n";`, sends the </HTML> tag and a newline character to the browser. The </HTML> tag denotes the end of the Web page.

 HTML tags usually are used in pairs that consist of an opening and a closing tag.

In the next section, you learn how to test a script from both the command line and browser.

Testing a Script

Before testing a script from a browser, it is a good idea to test it from the command line to verify that it does not contain any syntax errors. The term **syntax** refers to the rules of a language. A syntax error occurs when you fail to follow one or more of the rules.

To test a Perl script from the command line:

1. *If you are using a UNIX system*, skip to Step 2.

   If you are using a Windows system, click **Start**, point to **Programs**, point to **Accessories**, and then click **Command Prompt**. A Command Prompt window opens and displays the MS-DOS command prompt, as shown in Figure 1-7.

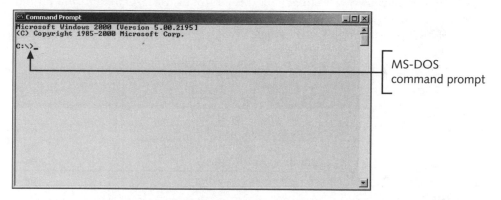

Figure 1-7   Command Prompt window showing the MS-DOS command prompt

2. Now make the cgi-bin/chap01 directory the current directory.

   If you are using a UNIX system, type **cd** *path* after the UNIX command prompt, where *path* is the path to the cgi-bin/chap01 directory. Press **Enter**.

   If you are using a Windows system, type **cd** *path* after the MS-DOS command prompt, where *path* is the path to the cgi-bin\chap01 directory. (Be sure to use the backslash as the directory separator, as MS-DOS requires it.) Press **Enter**.

3. Type **perl –c first.cgi** after the UNIX or MS-DOS command prompt and press **Enter**. (Be sure to enter the –c using a lowercase letter c.) The word perl in the command starts the Perl interpreter. The –c, referred to as an option or switch, tells the Perl interpreter to check for syntax errors in the first.cgi script, and then exit without executing the script.

If you typed the script instructions correctly, the Perl interpreter responds with the message "first.cgi syntax OK." (In the next section, "Debugging a Perl Script," you introduce an error in the first.cgi script so that you can view a sample message produced by the -c switch.)

> If the Perl interpreter displays an error message, an instruction in the script is probably mistyped and needs to be corrected. Usually, the error message includes a line number that indicates which instruction is causing the error. You can compare the instruction you entered with the corresponding instruction shown in Figure 1-5. Look for a missing semicolon, or a word entered using the wrong case. If you cannot find an error in the instruction, look at the instructions that precede it in the script. After correcting the error, try Step 3 again.

Now run the script again. This time, use the -w switch, which tells the Perl interpreter to check for errors and also execute the script.

4. Type **perl -w first.cgi** after the UNIX or MS-DOS command prompt and press **Enter**. *If you are using a UNIX system*, your screen will look similar to Figure 1-8. *If you are using a Windows system*, your screen will look similar to Figure 1-9.

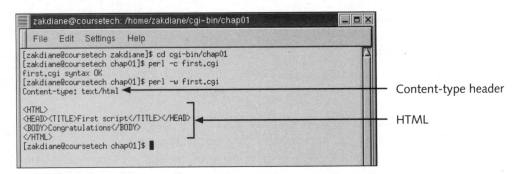

Figure 1-8   UNIX screen showing the result of the -c and -w switches

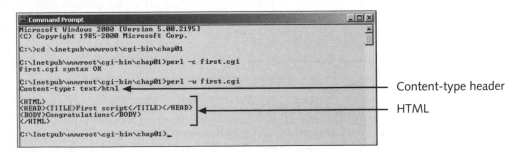

Figure 1-9   Command Prompt window showing the result of the -c and -w switches

Notice that the screen displays the information contained in each of the print functions in the script. For example, it displays the Content-type header line, followed by a blank line. (Recall that the Content-type header contains two newlines: the first ensures that the header will appear on its own line, and the second inserts a blank line below the header.) The screen also displays the HTML entered in the script.

Now that you know that the script does not contain any errors, and you have some idea what the script's output will look like, you can test the script using your browser.

To test the script using a browser:

1. *If you are using a UNIX system*, change the file permissions for the first.cgi file to **755**.

 Appendix A explains that you use the chmod command to change file permissions. For example, to change the file permissions for the first.cgi file, you type chmod 755 first.cgi after the UNIX command prompt.

2. Open your browser.

   Now type the first.cgi script's URL in the address box of the browser. The address box is labeled Location in Netscape Communicator; it is labeled Address in Internet Explorer.

3. In the address box, type **http://*yourservername*/cgi-bin/chap01/first.cgi**. Be sure to replace "yourservername" with the name of your server (for example, www.microsoft.com). If necessary, change the path to reflect the location of the first.cgi file on your system.

4. Press **Enter**. The browser submits the URL to the server, which goes to the cgi-bin/chap01 directory and runs the first.cgi script, using the Perl interpreter to convert the instructions into machine code. When the script is finished running, it sends its output to the server. The server sends the output to the browser, which renders the Web page. Figure 1-10 shows the output in a Netscape Communicator window. The output will look similar if you are using Internet Explorer.

title

type your server name here

body

Figure 1-10 Output from the first.cgi script

Next, view the source code used to create the Web page. The source code is the HTML code generated by the first.cgi script.

5. Click **View** on the browser's menu bar, and then click **Page Source** (Netscape Communicator) or **Source** (Internet Explorer). The HTML code generated by the first.cgi script appears in the browser window, as shown in Figure 1-11.

```
Netscape: Source of: http://localhost/cgi-bin/chap01/first.cgi
<HTML>
<HEAD><TITLE>First script</TITLE></HEAD>
<BODY>Congratulations</BODY>
</HTML>
```

Figure 1-11   HTML code generated by the first.cgi script

Compare the HTML code shown in Figure 1-11 with the `print` statements shown in Figure 1-5. Notice that each statement appears on a separate line in Figure 1-11. This happens because you included a newline character (\n) in each `print` statement. Without the newline character, the HTML code would appear on one line in the browser window and would be difficult to read.

6. Close the window containing the source code, then minimize your browser window.

Next, you introduce an error in the first.cgi script. This will allow you to view a sample error message produced by the -c switch.

Debugging a Perl Script

It is extremely easy to make a typing error when entering instructions in a Perl script. A typing error typically results in a syntax error, because the Perl interpreter is not able to understand the instruction. As you learned earlier, you can use the -c switch to tell the Perl interpreter to check a script for syntax errors. If the interpreter finds an error in the script, it displays a message that describes the error and also gives the error's location (by line number) in the script. You will see how this works in the next set of steps.

To introduce a syntax error in the first.cgi script, and then use the -c switch to locate the error:

1. Return to the first.cgi script in your text editor.

2. Delete the semicolon that appears at the end of the instruction `print "<BODY>Congratulations</BODY>\n";`. The instruction should now be `print "<BODY>Congratulations</BODY>\n"`.

3. Save the script.

4. Return to the UNIX or MS-DOS command prompt. *If you are using a UNIX system*, type **clear** to clear the contents of the screen. *If you are using a Windows system*, type **cls** to clear the contents of the Command Prompt window.

5. Type **perl –c first.cgi** after the command prompt and press **Enter**. The Perl interpreter displays a syntax error message similar to the one shown in Figure 1-12. (Figure 1-12 shows the message on a UNIX system. The message on a Windows system will be similar.)

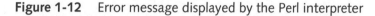

```
zakdiane@coursetech: /home/zakdiane/cgi-bin/chap01
 File   Edit   Settings   Help
[zakdiane@coursetech chap01]$ perl -c first.cgi
syntax error at first.cgi line 8, near "print"          ◄──── error message
first.cgi had compilation errors.
[zakdiane@coursetech chap01]$ █
```

Figure 1-12   Error message displayed by the Perl interpreter

The message indicates that the error is on line 8 in the script, near the `print` function. However, line 8 contains the statement `print "</HTML>\n";`, which is correct. If you cannot find an error in the line identified in the error message, look at the line that precedes it in the script. In this case, the error is actually in the statement entered on the preceding line—line 7; recall that you deleted the semicolon from the statement.

6. Return to the first.cgi script in your text editor. Enter the missing semicolon at the end of the `print "<BODY>Congratulations</BODY>\n"` statement.

7. Save the script.

8. Close your browser and any other open windows.

CHAPTER SUMMARY

❏ Web pages are either static or dynamic.

❏ A static Web page's content is established when the page is created. Static Web pages are stored on Web servers. When a Web server receives a request for a static Web page, the server locates the file, opens it, and then transfers its contents to the browser. The browser interprets the HTML instructions it receives and renders the Web page.

❏ A dynamic Web page can accept information from the user and also retrieve information for the user. Dynamic Web pages typically require the use of an HTML document and either a program or script.

❏ The CGI protocol defines how a server communicates with CGI scripts (or CGI programs).

❏ UNIX and Perl commands are case-sensitive.

❑ Perl CGI scripts running on a UNIX system must begin with the shebang line. The shebang line begins with #! followed by the location of the Perl interpreter on the system. The shebang line is optional in a Perl CGI script running on a Windows system.

❑ To send HTML output to a browser, a script must contain the header line print `"Content-type: text/html\n\n";`.

❑ The newline character is `\n`.

❑ The command `perl -c scriptname` tells the Perl interpreter to check for syntax errors in a script, but not run the script. The command `perl -w scriptname` tells the Perl interpreter to check for errors in a script and then run the script.

❑ Perl statements must end with a semicolon (;).

REVIEW QUESTIONS

1. Every computer connected to the Internet is identified by a numeric _____ address.

   a. AP

   b. CGI

   c. IP

   d. URL

2. A _____ is an agreement between a sender and a receiver regarding how data is sent and interpreted.

   a. program

   b. protocol

   c. script

   d. None of the above.

3. If you omit the communication protocol from a URL, Web browsers use the _____ protocol.

   a. CGI

   b. Content-type

   c. HTTP

   d. Script

4. CGI stands for _____.

   a. Cool Gateway Interface

   b. Common Gateway Interface

   c. Common Gateway Internet

   d. Content Gateway Interface

5. The _____ protocol allows a Web server to communicate with a script.

   a. CGI

   b. GCI

   c. HTTP

   d. None of the above.

6. The shebang line begins with the two characters _____.

   a. @!

   b. !#

   c. &!

   d. #!

7. Which of the following is the newline character?

   a. \n

   b. /n

   c. !n

   d. #n

8. If the intended output of a Perl script is an HTML page, then the Content-type header must contain the *type* _____.

   a. html

   b. html/text

   c. text

   d. text/html

9. Which of the following commands tells the Perl interpreter to check for syntax errors in the sample.cgi script and then exit without executing the script?

   a. `perl -c sample.cgi`

   b. `perl -w sample.cgi`

   c. `perl -x sample.cgi`

   d. None of the above.

10. Which of the following is the bang symbol?

   a. @

   b. !

   c. &

   d. #

11. The name associated with a computer connected to the Internet is called a
    _____ .

12. A _____ is a computer that "serves up" Web pages to Web browsers.

13. What are the four parts of a URL?

14. A comment in Perl must begin with the _____ symbol.

15. Perl statements must end with a _____ .

16. A dynamic Web page typically requires an HTML document and either a
    _____ or _____ .

17. Write the command to run a CGI script named item.cgi from the command line.
    The command also should check for errors in the script.

18. Every Web document has a unique address, called a _____ , that indi-
    cates its location on the Web.

19. What is the purpose of the Content-type header?

20. Some Web servers require you to store files containing CGI scripts in a special
    directory named _____ .

HANDS-ON PROJECTS

Project 1

In this project, you create a CGI script that displays your name on a Web page.

a. Use a text editor to create the script shown in Figure 1-13. If necessary, change
   the shebang line to reflect the location of the Perl interpreter on your system.
   Save the script in the cgi-bin/chap01 directory and name it c01ex1.cgi. (The
   c01ex1 stands for chapter 01, exercise 1.)

```
#!/usr/bin/perl
#c01ex1.cgi - displays a name
print "Content-type: text/html\n\n";
#generate HTML
print "<HTML>\n";
print "<HEAD><TITLE>My Name</TITLE></HEAD>\n";
print "<BODY>enter your name here</BODY>\n";
print "</HTML>\n";
```

Figure 1-13

b. Make the cgi-bin/chap01 directory the current directory.

c. *If you are using a UNIX system*, use the **chmod 755 c01ex1.cgi** command to
   change the file permissions.

1

d. Use the `perl -c c01ex1.cgi` command to test for syntax errors in the script.

e. Use the `perl -w c01ex1.cgi` command to run the script from the command line.

f. Open your Web browser. Enter the script's URL in the location or address box. Your name appears on a Web page.

Project 2

In this project, you create a CGI script that displays a message on a Web page.

a. Use a text editor to create the script shown in Figure 1-14. If necessary, change the shebang line to reflect the location of the Perl interpreter on your system. Save the script in the cgi-bin/chap01 directory and name it c01ex2.cgi.

```
#!/usr/bin/perl
#c01ex2.cgi - displays a message
print "Content-type: text/html\n\n";
#generate HTML
print "<HTML>\n",
print "<HEAD><TITLE>Message</TITLE></HEAD>\n";
print "<BODY>Perl statements \n";
print "end with a semicolon.</BODY>\n";
print "</HTML>\n";
```

be sure to include a space after the letter s

Figure 1-14

b. Make the cgi-bin/chap01 directory the current directory.

c. *If you are using a Unix system*, use the `chmod 755 c01ex2.cgi` command to change the file permissions.

d. Use the `perl -c c01ex2.cgi` command to test for syntax errors in the script.

e. Use the `perl -w c01ex2.cgi` command to run the script from the command line.

f. Open your Web browser. Enter the script's URL in the location or address box. The message "Perl statements end with a semicolon." appears on a Web page. (Notice that the message prints on one line, even though the script contains two `print` statements.)

Project 3

In this project, you create a CGI script that displays three lines of text on a Web page.

   a. Use a text editor to create the script shown in Figure 1-15. If necessary, change the shebang line to reflect the location of the Perl interpreter on your system. Save the script in the cgi-bin/chap01 directory and name it c01ex3.cgi.

```
#!/usr/bin/perl
#c01ex3.cgi - displays a message
print "Content-type: text/html\n\n";
#generate HTML
print "<HTML>\n";
print "<HEAD><TITLE>Message</TITLE></HEAD>\n";
print "<BODY>Perl is powerful.<BR>\n";
print "Perl is easy to learn.<BR>\n";
print "Perl is free.</BODY>\n";
print "</HTML>\n";
```

Figure 1-15

   b. Make the cgi-bin/chap01 directory the current directory.

   c. *If you are using a Unix system*, change the c01ex3.cgi file permissions to 755.

   d. Test for syntax errors in the script.

   e. Run the script from the command line.

   f. Open your Web browser. Enter the script's URL in the location or address box. Three lines of text appear on a Web page.

2

SENDING DATA USING A HYPERLINK

In this chapter, you will:

♦ Create a hyperlink to a CGI script
♦ Append data to a URL
♦ Use the CGI.pm module to parse data
♦ Access data using the `param` function

In Chapter 1, you learned that the Web contains both static and dynamic pages. Recall that the contents of a static Web page cannot change without human intervention. Changes to a static Web page occur only when someone—usually the page's creator or a Web programmer—updates the HTML file stored on the server. In contrast, the contents of a dynamic Web page can change automatically in response to information you send it through your Web browser. You can send the information using a hyperlink or a form. In this chapter, you learn how to use a hyperlink to send information to a dynamic Web page. You learn how to send information using a form in Chapter 3.

CREATING A LINK TO A SCRIPT

Most Web pages, like the Jackson Elementary School Web page shown in Figure 2-1, contain text, images, and hyperlinks.

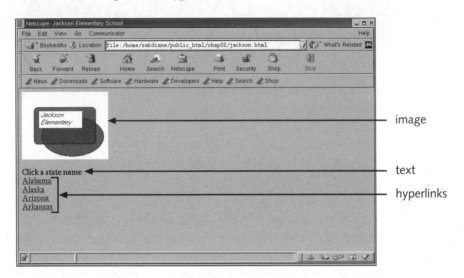

Figure 2-1   Jackson Elementary School Web page

Hyperlinks, or links, typically appear on a Web page as different colored or underlined text or as clickable images. Hyperlinks allow you to navigate the Internet, moving from one resource on the Internet to another. Examples of Internet resources include HTML documents, images, video files, and CGI scripts.

You create a link using the HTML anchor tag (<A>) together with the anchor tag's HREF property. The HREF property, short for Hypertext Reference, indicates the location to link to. For example, to create a text link to a CGI script, you use a tag that follows the syntax **<A HREF=**_URL_**>**_hyperlinkText_**</A>**. In the syntax, _URL_ is the URL of the script, and _hyperlinkText_ is the word or phrase that you click to activate the link. The syntax for creating an image link to a CGI script is **<A HREF=**_URL_**><IMG SRC=**_imageFile_**></A>**, where _URL_ is the URL of the script, and _imageFile_ is the path and name of the image file. (You can omit the path if the image file is stored in the same directory as the Web page that contains the link.)

The Jackson Elementary School Web page, which you will create in the next set of steps, will allow you to observe how a text link to a CGI script works. You will link each of the four state names on the Web page to a CGI script named jackson.cgi, which you will create later in the chapter.

As you learned in Chapter 1, you can use any text editor to create HTML documents and Perl scripts.

To create the Jackson Elementary School Web page, which is shown in Figure 2-1:

1. Open a new document in a text editor, and then enter the HTML code shown in Figure 2-2. Replace yourservername in the four URLs with the name of your server. For example, if your server's name is www.course.com, then replace yourservername with www.course.com. Similarly, if your server's name is localhost, then replace yourservername with localhost.

```
<!jackson.html>
<HTML>
<HEAD><TITLE>Jackson Elementary School</TITLE><BASEFONT SIZE=5></HEAD>
<BODY>
<IMG SRC="jackson.gif"><BR><BR>
Click a state name<BR>
<A HREF="http://yourservername/cgi-bin/chap02/jackson.cgi">Alabama</A><BR>
<A HREF="http://yourservername/cgi-bin/chap02/jackson.cgi">Alaska</A><BR>
<A HREF="http://yourservername/cgi-bin/chap02/jackson.cgi">Arizona</A><BR>
<A HREF="http://yourservername/cgi-bin/chap02/jackson.cgi">Arkansas</A><BR>
</BODY>
</HTML>
```

Figure 2-2   HTML code for the Jackson Elementary School Web page

2. Save the document in the public_html/chap02 directory using the name **jackson.html**.

Now view the document in your Web browser.

3. Start your Web browser. Use the File menu on the browser's menu bar to open the jackson.html file. A Web page similar to the one shown in Figure 2-1 appears in the browser window.

4. Minimize the browser window.

Before you can test the four links on the Jackson Elementary School Web page, you need to create the jackson.cgi script. The script will create a dynamic Web page that displays the message "You have linked to the jackson.cgi script."

To begin creating the jackson.cgi script:

1. Open a new document in your text editor.

First enter the shebang line and a comment that includes the script's name and purpose.

2. Type **#!/usr/bin/perl** (or the location of the Perl interpreter on your system) and press **Enter**, then type **#jackson.cgi – creates a dynamic Web page** and press **Enter**.

Recall that the shebang line is required in Perl CGI scripts run on a UNIX system, and it must be the first line in the script. The shebang line is optional in Perl CGI scripts run on a Windows system.

As you learned in Chapter 1, the output of a CGI script—typically HTML—is sent to the Web browser through the Web server. You alert the browser that it will be receiving HTML by including the statement `print "Content-type: text/html\n\n";` in the script.

3. Type **print "Content-type: text/html\n\n";** and press **Enter** twice. Be sure to type the statement exactly as shown.

4. Save the document in the cgi-bin/chap02 directory using the name **jackson.cgi**.

A CGI script written in Perl can use various methods to generate HTML output. Examples of these methods include the `print` and `printf` functions and "here" documents. In this chapter, you learn how to use the `print` function. The `printf` function and "here" documents are covered in Chapter 3 and Chapter 9.

The `print` Function

You can use the Perl **print function** to generate a script's output. To do so, you use the `print` function in a Perl statement that follows the syntax **print** *output*;, where *output* is the expression, or a list of expressions separated by commas, that you want the script to output. *Output* can include items such as strings, functions, and variables. Figure 2-3 shows examples of using the `print` function to output HTML tags and messages, which are strings. (Later in this chapter, you learn how to include a function in the *output*. You learn how to include a variable in the *output* in Chapter 3.)

Examples	Results
`print "<HTML>\n";`	outputs the <HTML> tag and a newline character
`print "</BODY></HTML>\n";`	outputs the </BODY> and </HTML> tags and a newline character
`print "</BODY>", "</HTML>", "\n";`	same as above
`print "Good morning!\n";`	outputs the message "Good morning!" and a newline character
`print "Good ", "morning!", "\n";`	same as above

Figure 2-3   Examples of using the `print` function in a Perl statement

As you learned in Chapter 1, the \n that appears in each statement shown in Figure 2-3 is the newline character. The newline character makes the HTML code generated by the CGI script easier to read when the code is viewed in a browser.

The first statement shown in Figure 2-3, `print "<HTML>\n";`, outputs the <HTML> tag and a newline character. The second and third examples output the same information: the </BODY> and </HTML> tags followed by a newline character. Notice that the second example contains one string, whereas the third example contains three strings; a comma separates the strings in the third example. The fourth and fifth examples shown in

Figure 2-3 output the message "Good morning!" and a newline character. Here again, the fourth example contains one string, and the fifth example contains a comma-separated list of three strings.

Now you will complete the jackson.cgi script by using the `print` function to generate the script's HTML output.

To complete the jackson.cgi script, then test the script from the command line:

1. Enter the comment and `print` statements shaded in Figure 2-4.

```
#!/usr/bin/perl
#jackson.cgi - creates a dynamic Web page
print "Content-type: text/html\n\n";

#create Web page
print "<HTML>\n";
print "<HEAD><TITLE>Jackson Elementary School</TITLE><BASEFONT SIZE=5></HEAD>\n";
print "<BODY>\n";
print "You have linked to the jackson.cgi script.\n";
print "</BODY>\n";
print "</HTML>\n";
```

Figure 2-4   Completed jackson.cgi script

 Although most of the popular browsers allow you to omit the HTML, HEAD, and BODY tags from your HTML code, it is a good practice to include these tags for browsers that require them.

2. Save the document.

3. *If you are using a UNIX system*, open a terminal window, if necessary. Make the cgi-bin/chap02 directory the current directory, and then change the jackson.cgi file permissions to **755**. (Changing the file permissions to 755 allows the script to be executed when called from a browser.)

   If you are using a Windows system, open a Command Prompt window, and then make the cgi-bin\chap02 directory the current directory.

4. Type **perl –c jackson.cgi** and press **Enter**. Recall that the –c switch checks the script for syntax errors, but does not execute the script. If necessary, correct any syntax errors in the script before continuing to the next step.

5. Type **perl –w jackson.cgi** and press **Enter**. Recall that the –w switch checks the script for errors and also executes the script. If necessary, correct any errors in the script before continuing to the next step.

 The -c switch checks the script for syntax errors only. However, not all errors in a script are syntax errors. The -w switch checks the script for errors that surface only when the script is executed.

Now that you have created the jackson.cgi script, you can test the four links contained on the Jackson Elementary School Web page.

To test the four links contained on the Jackson Elementary School Web page:

1. Restore the browser window, which you minimized in an earlier set of steps.

2. Click **Alabama** on the Jackson Elementary School Web page. The browser passes the URL of the jackson.cgi script to the server. The server runs the script and sends the script's output—HTML—to the browser, which renders the dynamic Web page shown in Figure 2-5. Notice that the script's URL appears in the address box in the browser window.

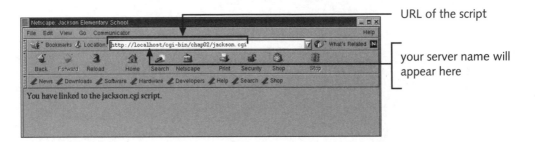

URL of the script

your server name will appear here

Figure 2-5   Dynamic Web page created by the jackson.cgi script

Next, view the dynamic Web page's source code, which is the HTML code generated by the jackson.cgi script and used to create the Web page.

3. Click **View** on the browser's menu bar, and then click **Page Source** (Netscape Communicator) or **Source** (Internet Explorer). The HTML code generated by the jackson.cgi script appears in the browser window, as shown in Figure 2-6.

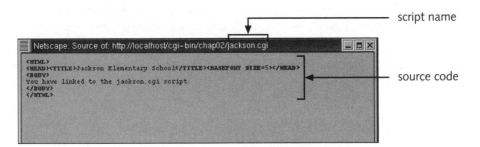

script name

source code

Figure 2-6   HTML code generated by the jackson.cgi script

4. Compare the HTML code shown in Figure 2-6 with the `print` statements shown in Figure 2-4. Notice that the string in each `print` statement appears on a separate line in Figure 2-6. This happens because you included a new-line character (\n) at the end of each `print` statement. Without the newline

character, the HTML code would appear on one line in the browser window and would be difficult to read.

5. Close the window containing the source code, then click the **Back** button to return to the Jackson Elementary School Web page.

6. On your own, verify that the Alaska, Arizona, and Arkansas links display the Web page shown in Figure 2-5.

7. Return to the Jackson Elementary School Web page, then minimize the browser window.

Now that you know how to create a link to a CGI script, you can learn how to use the link to send information to a script.

SENDING ONE ITEM OF DATA USING A LINK

Currently, the jackson.cgi script creates a dynamic Web page that displays the message "You have linked to the jackson.cgi script." Assume you want to change the message to "You selected *state*.", where *state* is the name of the state whose link you selected on the Jackson Elementary School Web page. For the script to display such a message, each link on the Web page will need to send the script the appropriate state name. For example, the Alabama link should send the state name Alabama, the Alaska link should send the state name Alaska, and so on.

To send data using a link, you simply append the data to the link's URL, which is specified in the anchor tag's HREF property. You can send one or more items of data to a script; however, in this section you learn how to send one item only. You learn how to send multiple items later in the chapter.

Figure 2-7 shows the syntax and three examples of sending one item of data using a link. The data sent to the script is shaded in each example. Notice that you use a question mark (?) to separate the URL from the data.

Syntax
<A HREF=_URL_**?**_key=value_**>**_hyperlinkText_**</A>**
Examples
<A HREF="http://yourservername/cgi-bin/chap02/jackson.cgi?state=Alabama">Alabama</A>
<A HREF="http://yourservername/cgi-bin/chap02/jackson.cgi?cap=Montgomery">Alabama</A>
<A HREF="http://yourservername/cgi-bin/chap02/jackson.cgi?number=22">Alabama</A>

Figure 2-7   Syntax and examples of sending one item using a link

Each item of data passed to a script has a *key* and a *value*. The *key* is simply a one-word name that you assign to the *value*. In Figure 2-7, for example, `state` is the *key* (name) assigned to the *value* `Alabama`. The *key* allows you to refer to the *value* in a CGI script. For instance, to refer to the *value* `Alabama` in a script, you use its *key*, which is `state`. Notice that you use an equal sign (=) to separate the *key* from the *value*.

In the next set of steps, you modify the links on the Jackson Elementary School Web page so that each sends the appropriate state name to the jackson.cgi script.

To send the state name using a link:

1. Open the jackson.html file, which is contained in the public_html/chap02 directory, in your text editor. Modify the four URLs so that each passes the appropriate state name to the jackson.cgi script. The modifications you should make to the URLs are shaded in Figure 2-8.

```
<!jackson.html>
<HTML>
<HEAD><TITLE>Jackson Elementary School</TITLE><BASEFONT SIZE=5></HEAD>
<BODY>
<IMG SRC="jackson.gif"><BR><BR>
Click a state name<BR>
<A HREF="http://yourservername/cgi-bin/chap02/jackson.cgi?state=Alabama">Alabama</A><BR>
<A HREF="http://yourservername/cgi-bin/chap02/jackson.cgi?state=Alaska">Alaska</A><BR>
<A HREF="http://yourservername/cgi-bin/chap02/jackson.cgi?state=Arizona">Arizona</A><BR>
<A HREF="http://yourservername/cgi-bin/chap02/jackson.cgi?state=Arkansas">Arkansas</A><BR>
</BODY>
</HTML>
```

modify the four URLs

Figure 2-8   Modified URLs shown in the jackson.html document

2. Save the document.

3. Restore the browser window. Click the **Reload** button (Netscape Communicator) or **Refresh** button (Internet Explorer) to reopen the jackson.html file in your browser.

4. Click **Alabama**. See Figure 2-9. Notice that, in addition to the script's URL, the data passed to the script—in this case, `state=Alabama`—also appears in the address box of the browser window. The data is sent using the format *key=value*.

script URL

data sent to the script

You have linked to the jackson.cgi script.

Figure 2-9   Address box showing the script's URL and the data passed to the script

2

5. Click the **Back** button to return to the Jackson Elementary School Web page.

6. On your own, verify that the Alaska, Arizona, and Arkansas links send the appropriate state name to the script.

7. Return to the Jackson Elementary School Web page, then minimize the browser window.

Before a script can use the data sent to it, it must parse the data. The term **parse** refers to the process of splitting the data's *key* from its *value*.

PARSING DATA

The Perl code needed to parse a script's incoming data is fairly complex and especially difficult to understand when you are first learning Perl. Fortunately, many Perl programmers have written parsing routines that you can use—for free—in your CGI scripts. One such parsing routine is contained in a Perl module named CGI.pm. A **module** is simply a collection of prewritten code stored in a file. Module filenames in Perl usually end with *pm*, which stands for *perl module*.

 The CGI.pm module was created by Lincoln Stein and is part of the standard Perl distribution. The module also contains routines for other tasks commonly performed by CGI scripts, such as creating cookies, generating HTML, and uploading files.

 You can determine whether your system contains the CGI.pm module by entering `whereis cgi.pm` at the UNIX command prompt, or by right-clicking the Windows Start button, then clicking Search, then typing CGI.pm in the Search for files or folders named text box, and then clicking the Search Now button. If necessary, you can download the CGI.pm module from the Web site http://www.genome.wi.mit.edu/ftp/pub/software/WWW/cgi_docs.html.

To use the CGI.pm module to parse a script's incoming data, you simply enter the statement `use CGI qw(:standard);` in a script. The `qw` in the statement is a Perl function and stands for *quote words*. The **qw function** tells the Perl interpreter to treat the word within the parentheses that follow the function as though the word were entered in single quotation marks. In other words, the statement `use CGI qw(:standard);` is equivalent to the statement `use CGI (':standard')`, but the former statement is more commonly used by Perl programmers.

Notice that you do not include the ".pm" part of the module name in the use statement.

The :standard part of the use CGI qw(:standard); statement is called an **import tag**. The :standard import tag tells the Perl interpreter to import (make available to the script) only the standard features of the CGI.pm module; for most scripts, the standard features are sufficient.

 You can learn about other import tags by typing perldoc CGI.pm after the UNIX or MS-DOS (Windows) command prompt.

Typically, the use CGI qw(:standard); statement is entered at the beginning of the script, below the Content-type statement.

To use the CGI.pm module's standard features in the jackson.cgi script:

1. Open the jackson.cgi file in your text editor. The file is contained in the cgi-bin/chap02 directory.

2. Position the insertion point in the blank line below the Content-type statement, then press **Enter**.

3. Type **use CGI qw(:standard);** and press **Enter**. Be sure to type CGI using uppercase letters. Also be sure to type the colon after the opening parentheses, and the semicolon at the end of the statement.

The CGI.pm module automatically parses the data sent to a script. In other words, the module splits the data's *key* from its *value*. You then can use the **param function**, which is one of the features provided by the :standard import tag, to access the *value* associated with a *key*. For example, you can use the **param** function to access the state name passed to the jackson.cgi script; recall that the state name *value* is associated with the **state** *key*.

The syntax of the **param** function is **param(***key***)**, where *key* is enclosed in either single or double quotation marks. In other words, you can use either param('state') or param("state") to access the state name associated with the **state** *key*. However, single quotation marks are more commonly used in the **param** function, and this is the convention you will follow in this book.

Recall that you want the jackson.cgi script to create a dynamic Web page that displays the message "You selected *state*.", where *state* is the state name passed to the script. You will make the appropriate modifications to the script in the next set of steps.

To modify the message displayed by the jackson.cgi script, then test the script:

1. Change the
   print "You have linked to the jackson.cgi script.\n";
   statement to **print "You selected ", param('state'), ".\n";**, as shown in Figure 2-10.

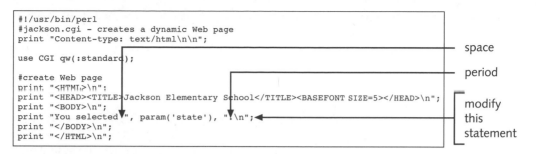

```
#!/usr/bin/perl
#jackson.cgi - creates a dynamic Web page
print "Content-type: text/html\n\n";

use CGI qw(:standard);

#create Web page
print "<HTML>\n";
print "<HEAD><TITLE>Jackson Elementary School</TITLE><BASEFONT SIZE=5></HEAD>\n";
print "<BODY>\n";
print "You selected ", param('state'), ".\n";
print "</BODY>\n";
print "</HTML>\n";
```

— space

— period

modify
this
statement

Figure 2-10　Modified jackson.cgi script

2. Save the document.

3. *If you are using a UNIX system*, return to the UNIX command prompt. Type **clear** after the UNIX command prompt and then press **Enter** to clear the previous commands and output from the screen.

   If you are using a Windows system, return to the Command Prompt window. Type **cls** after the command prompt and then press **Enter** to clear the previous commands and output from the screen.

4. The cgi-bin/chap02 (UNIX) or cgi-bin\chap02 (Windows) directory should be the current directory. Type **perl -c jackson.cgi** and press **Enter**. If necessary, correct any syntax errors in the script before continuing to the next step.

   As you observed earlier in Figure 2-9, the browser sends data to the script using the format *key=value*. When testing a script from the command line, you also use the *key=value* format to send data to the script. You can include the data on the same line as the command that executes the script, as shown in Step 5.

5. Type **perl -w jackson.cgi state=Alabama** and press **Enter**. (Be sure to type a space after the script's name, but do not type any spaces before or after the equal sign.) See Figure 2-11.

```
zakdiane@coursetech: /home/zakdiane/cgi-bin/chap02                         _ □ ×
 File  Edit  Settings  Help
[zakdiane@coursetech chap02]$ perl -c jackson.cgi
jackson.cgi syntax OK
[zakdiane@coursetech chap02]$ perl -w jackson.cgi state=Alabama
Content-type: text/html

<HTML>
<HEAD><TITLE>Jackson Elementary School</TITLE><BASEFONT SIZE=5></HEAD>
<BODY>
You selected Alabama.
</BODY>
</HTML>
[zakdiane@coursetech chap02]$ █
```

— input data

Figure 2-11　Result of including the data on the same line as the -w switch

If you have a lot of data to pass to a script, you might find it more convenient to send each item of data on a separate line, rather than on the same line as the command that executes the script. This is shown in Step 6.

Important note: Some versions of the CGI.pm module require you to include the **–debug** pragma in the `use CGI qw(:standard);` statement, like this: `use CGI qw(:standard -debug);`. A **pragma** is simply a special type of Perl module. The **–debug** pragma tells the CGI.pm module to pause the execution of a script to allow you to enter information from the keyboard. If the instruction you enter in Step 6 does not produce the results shown in Figure 2-12, then be sure to read the Tip section that follows the figure. The Tip instructs you to enter the **–debug** pragma in your script.

6. Type **perl -w jackson.cgi** and press **Enter**. The message "(offline mode: enter name=value pairs on standard input)" appears on the screen, as shown in Figure 2-12. (Standard input refers to the keyboard.)

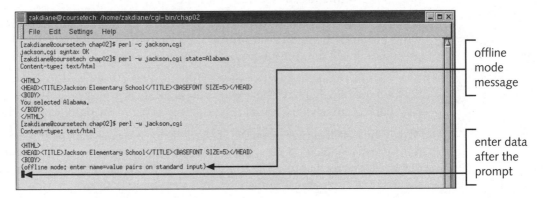

Figure 2-12   Screen showing the offline mode message

If the offline mode message does not appear on your screen, open the jackson.cgi script in your text editor, if necessary. Change the `use CGI qw(:standard);` statement to `use CGI qw(:standard -debug);`, then save the script and repeat Step 6.

7. Type **state=Alabama** and press **Enter**.

You indicate that you have finished entering the input data by pressing Ctrl+d (UNIX) or Ctrl+z (Windows).

8. *If you are using a UNIX system*, press and hold down the **Ctrl** key as you type the letter **d**, then release the **Ctrl** key. See Figure 2-13.

If you are using a Windows system, press and hold down the **Ctrl** key as you type the letter **z**, then release the **Ctrl** key. ^Z appears on the screen. Press **Enter**. See Figure 2-13.

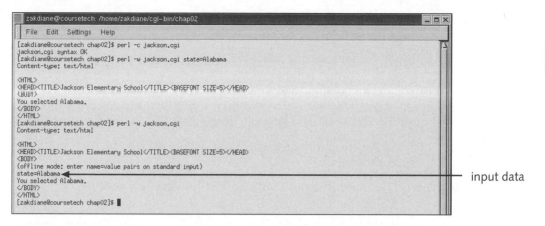

Figure 2-13   Screen showing input data entered on a separate line

Now test the script by clicking the state name links on the jackson.html Web page.

To test the jackson.cgi script from the jackson.html Web page:

1. Restore the browser window. Click **Alabama** on the jackson.html Web page. The jackson.cgi script creates the dynamic Web page shown in Figure 2-14. Notice that the Web page contains the state name passed to the script.

data sent to the script

input data

Figure 2-14   Dynamic Web page showing the state name

Now view the dynamic Web page's source code.

2. Click **View** on the browser's menu bar, then click **Page Source** (Netscape Communicator) or **Source** (Internet Explorer). See Figure 2-15.

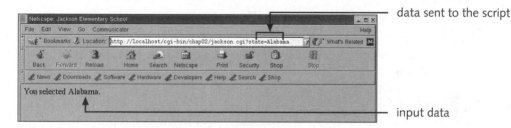

Figure 2-15   Source code for the dynamic Web page

Notice that the source code contains the name of the state passed to the script; in this case, it contains Alabama.

3. Close the source code window.

4. Return to the Jackson Elementary School Web page.

5. On your own, verify that the Alaska, Arizona, and Arkansas links display the appropriate state name on the dynamic Web page.

6. Return to the Jackson Elementary School Web page, then minimize the browser window.

Next, learn how to send more than one item of data to a script.

SENDING MULTIPLE ITEMS OF DATA USING A LINK

Assume that, rather than displaying the message "You selected *state*." on a Web page, you want the jackson.cgi script to display the message "The capital of *state* is *capital*.", where *state* is the name of the state whose link you clicked and capital is the name of the state's capital. For the script to display such a message, each link on the Web page will need to send the script two items of data: the name of the state and the name of the state's capital. For example, the Alabama link should send the state name Alabama together with the capital name Montgomery, the Alaska link should send the state name Alaska together with the capital name Juneau, and so on.

As you learned earlier, you send data using a link by simply appending the data to the link's URL. Recall that the syntax for sending one item of data is **<A HREF=** *URL?key=value>hyperlinkText***</A>**. To send more than one item of data, you use the syntax **<A HREF=***URL?key1=value1&key2=value2…&keyN=valueN>hyperlinkText* **</A>**. Notice that you use an ampersand (&) to separate one data item (*key* and *value* pair) from the next. You can send as many data items as desired, but keep in mind that some browsers limit the amount of data that can be attached to a URL.

Now you will modify the jackson.html file so that each link on the Jackson Elementary School Web page sends the name of the state and the name of the state's capital. You also will modify the jackson.cgi file to display the message "The capital of *state* is *capital*."

To modify the jackson.html and jackson.cgi files:

1. Open the jackson.html file in your text editor, then modify the four URLs as shaded in Figure 2-16. The figure shows each URL on two lines, but you should keep each URL on one line.

   Notice the plus sign (+) between the word "Little" and the word "Rock". If you are sending a *value* that contains more than one word, you replace the space that separates the words with a plus sign.

2

```
<!jackson.html>
<HTML>
<HEAD><TITLE>Jackson Elementary School</TITLE><BASEFONT SIZE=5></HEAD>
<BODY>
<IMG SRC="jackson.gif"><BR><BR>
Click a state name<BR>
<A HREF="http://yourservername/cgi-bin/chap02/jackson.cgi
    ?state=Alabama&cap=Montgomery">Alabama</A><BR>
<A HREF="http://yourservername/cgi-bin/chap02/jackson.cgi
    ?state=Alaska&cap=Juneau">Alaska</A><BR>
<A HREF="http://yourservername/cgi-bin/chap02/jackson.cgi
    ?state=Arizona&cap=Phoenix">Arizona</A><BR>
<A HREF="http://yourservername/cgi-bin/chap02/jackson.cgi
    ?state=Arkansas&cap=Little+Rock">Arkansas</A><BR>
</BODY>
</HTML>
```

modify
the four
URLs

plus sign

Figure 2-16   jackson.html document showing the modified URLs

2. Save the document.

3. Open the jackson.cgi script in your text editor. Change the
   `print "You selected ", param('state'), ".\n";` statement to
   print "The capital of ", param('state'), " is ", param('cap'), ".\n";, as
   shown in Figure 2-17.

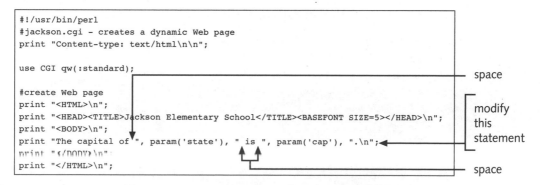

```
#!/usr/bin/perl
#jackson.cgi - creates a dynamic Web page
print "Content-type: text/html\n\n";

use CGI qw(:standard);

#create Web page
print "<HTML>\n";
print "<HEAD><TITLE>Jackson Elementary School</TITLE><BASEFONT SIZE=5></HEAD>\n";
print "<BODY>\n";
print "The capital of ", param('state'), " is ", param('cap'), ".\n";
print "</BODY>\n";
print "</HTML>\n";
```

space

modify
this
statement

space

Figure 2-17   jackson.cgi document showing modified `print` statement

4. Save the document.

5. *If you are using a UNIX system*, return to the UNIX command prompt. Type
   clear after the command prompt and press **Enter**.

   If you are using a Windows system, return to the Command Prompt window.
   Type **cls** after the command prompt and press **Enter**.

6. Type **perl –c jackson.cgi** and press **Enter**. If necessary, correct any syntax
   errors in the script before continuing to the next step.

7. Type **perl –w jackson.cgi** and press **Enter**. When the message "(offline mode: enter name=value pairs on standard input)" appears, type **state=Alabama** and press **Enter**, then type **cap=Montgomery** and press **Enter**.

8. Press **Ctrl+d** (UNIX), or press **Ctrl+z** and then press **Enter** (Windows), to indicate that you are finished entering the input data. See Figure 2-18.

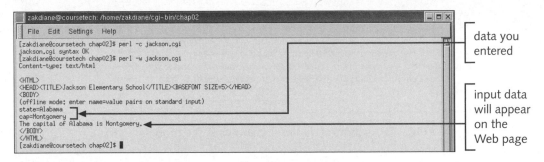

data you entered

input data will appear on the Web page

Figure 2-18   Screen showing the names of the state and capital

Now test the script by clicking the state name links on the jackson.html Web page.

To test the jackson.cgi script from the jackson.html Web page:

1. Restore the browser window. Click the **Reload** button (Netscape Communicator) or **Refresh** button (Internet Explorer) to reopen the jackson.html file.

2. Click **Alabama**. The message "The capital of Alabama is Montgomery." appears on a Web page, as shown in Figure 2-19.

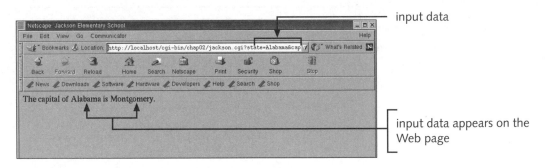

input data

input data appears on the Web page

Figure 2-19   State and capital names displayed on the Web page

Notice that, in addition to the script's URL, the data passed to the script—in this case, `state=Alabama&cap=Montgomery`—also appears in the address box of the browser window. (You will need to scroll the address box to view the entire entry.)

3. Click the **Back** button to return to the Jackson Elementary School Web page.

4. On your own, verify that the Alaska, Arizona, and Arkansas links display the appropriate state and capital names on the dynamic Web page.

5. Close the browser and all open windows.

CHAPTER SUMMARY

❐ The syntax for creating a text link to a CGI script is **<A HREF=***URL***>** *hyperlinkText***</A>**. In the syntax, *URL* is the URL of the script, and *hyperlinkText* is the word or phrase that you click to activate the link.

❐ The syntax for creating an image link to a CGI script is **<A HREF=***URL***><IMG SRC=***imageFile***></A>**, where *URL* is the URL of the script, and *imageFile* is the path and name of the image file.

❐ You can use the **print** function in a Perl script to generate HTML instructions to send to a Web browser through a Web server. The **print** function's syntax is **print** *output***;**, where *output* is the expression, or a list of expressions separated by commas, that you want the script to output.

❐ To pass one item of data to a script using a link, you use the syntax **<A HREF=** *URL***?***key***=***value***>***hyperlinkText***</A>**, where *key* is the name of the *value* you are sending.

❐ To pass more than one item of data to a script using a link, you use the syntax **<A HREF=***URL***?***key1***=***value1***&***key2***=***value2***…&***keyN***=***valueN***>***hyperlinkText***</A>**.

❐ To use a link to pass a value that contains a space, replace the space with a plus sign (+).

❐ You can use the CGI.pm module to automatically parse the data passed to a CGI script. To do so, you simply include the statement **use CGI qw(:standard);** in the script.

❐ When testing a script from the command line, you enter the data that you want sent to the script using the format *key=value.* You can enter the data on the same line as the command that executes the script. You also can enter each item of data on a separate line. However, to do so, some versions of the CGI.pm module require you to include the **–debug** pragma in the **use** statement, like this: **use CGI qw(:standard -debug);**.

❐ You can use the CGI.pm module's **param** function to access the *value* portion of each item of data passed to a script. The syntax of the **param** function is **param(***key***)**, where *key* is enclosed in either single or double quotation marks.

REVIEW QUESTIONS

1. You can create a link to a CGI script using the HTML anchor tag (<A>) together with the tag's _____ property.

   a. ALINK

   b. AREF

   c. HREF

   d. HLINK

2. Which of the following links the phrase "Click here" to the city.cgi script?

   a. `<A HREF="http://yourservername/cgi-bin/chap02/city.cgi">`
      `Click here</A>`

   b. `<A LINK="http://yourservername/cgi-bin/chap02/city.cgi">`
      `Click here</A>`

   c. `<A HLINK="http://yourservername/cgi-bin/chap02/city.cgi">`
      `Click here</A>`

   d. `<A HREF="http://yourservername/cgi-bin/chap02/city.cgi>`
      `Click here"</A>`

3. The output of a CGI script is usually HTML.

   a. true

   b. false

4. Which of the following statements indicates that a script's output is HTML?

   a. `print "Content text/html";`

   b. `print 'Content-type html/text\n\n";`

   c. `print "Content-type text/html\n";`

   d. None of the above.

5. Which of the following passes the number 1980 to the age.cgi script?

   a. `<A HREF="http://yourservername/cgi-bin/chap02/`
      `age.cgi&year=1980">Click here</A>`

   b. `<A HREF="http://yourservername/cgi-bin/chap02/`
      `age.cgi?year=1980">Click here</A>`

   c. `<A HREF="http://yourservername/cgi-bin/chap02/`
      `age.cgi/year=1980">Click here</A>`

   d. None of the above.

6. Which of the following can be used in a script to send the BODY tag to the browser?

   a. `print <BODY>\n`

   b. `print <BODY>\n;`

   c. `print "<BODY>\n;"`

   d. `print "<BODY>\n";`

7. You use the statement _____ to import the standard features of the CGI.pm module.

   a. `use CGI.pm qw(:standard);`

   b. `use CGI qw(standard);`

   c. `use CGI "(standard)";`

   d. None of the above.

8. When an item of data is sent to a script, the _____ character separates the item's *key* from its *value*.

    a. ampersand (&)

    b. equal sign (=)

    c. plus sign (+)

    d. question mark (?)

9. When using a link to send data to a script, you use the _____ character to separate the URL from the data.

    a. ampersand (&)

    b. equal sign (=)

    c. plus sign (+)

    d. question mark (?)

10. When sending multiple items of data to a script, the _____ character separates one item from the next item.

    a. ampersand (&)

    b. equal sign (=)

    c. plus sign (+)

    d. question mark (?)

11. Each item of data sent to a script contains two elements: a _____ and a _____.

12. If you are using a link to send a value that contains a space, you replace the space with a _____.

13. The _____ module contains a routine that automatically parses the data received by a script.

14. Assume an HTML document contains the tag `<A HREF="http://yourservername/cgi-bin/chap02/pay.cgi">Click here<BR>`. Modify the tag so that it passes a pay rate to the script. Use "pay" as the *key* and 5.75 as the *value*.

15. Modify the HTML tag from Question 14 so that it also passes the department name. Use "dept" as the *key* and "Accounting" as the *value*.

16. Modify the HTML tag from Question 15 so that it passes the value "Accounting Department" rather than "Accounting".

17. The process of splitting the data's *key* from its *value* is called _____.

18. The _____ pragma tells the CGI.pm module to pause the execution of a script to allow you to enter information from the keyboard.

19. The _____ function tells the Perl interpreter to treat the word within the parentheses that follow the function as though the word were entered in single quotation marks.

20. You use the CGI.pm module's _____ function to access the *value* associated with a *key*.

HANDS-ON PROJECTS

Project 1

In this project, you include another link in the jackson.html Web page, which you created in the chapter.

   a. Open the jackson.html file in a text editor. The file is contained in the public_html/chap02 directory.

   b. Change the filename in the first line from jackson.html to c02ex1.html. Save the document as c02ex1.html.

   c. Add another link to the Web page. Use the state name "North Carolina" as the *hyperlinkText*. Pass the state name (North Carolina) and capital name (Raleigh) to the jackson.cgi script. Save the c02ex1.html document.

   d. Open the c02ex1.html file in your Web browser. Click the North Carolina link. The message "The capital of North Carolina is Raleigh." should appear on a Web page.

Project 2

In this project, you include another link in the jackson.html Web page, which you created in the chapter. You also create a CGI script that displays a message on a Web page.

   a. Open the jackson.html file in a text editor. The file is contained in the public_html/chap02 directory.

   b. Change the filename in the first line from jackson.html to c02ex2.html. Save the document as c02ex2.html.

   c. Create an image link by changing the `<IMG SRC="jackson.gif"><BR><BR>` instruction to `<A HREF="http://`*yourservername*`/cgi-bin/chap02/c02ex2.cgi">` `<IMG SRC="jackson.gif"></A><BR><BR>`.

   d. Modify the image link so that it passes the school's name (Jackson Elementary School) to the c02ex2.cgi script.

   e. Save the c02ex2.html document.

   f. Open a new document in your text editor. Create a script that displays the school's name on a dynamic Web page. (If necessary, include the **-debug** pragma in the **use CGI qw(:standard);** statement.)

   g. Save the script in the cgi-bin/chap02 directory and name it c02ex2.cgi.

   h. *If you are using a UNIX system*, change the c02ex2.cgi file permissions to 755.

   i. Test the script from the command line.

   j. Open the c02ex2.html file in your Web browser. Click the image link. The school's name should appear on a Web page.

Project 3

In this project, you modify the links contained on the jackson.html Web page, which you created in the chapter. Each link will now send three items of data to the script: the state name, the capital name, and an ordinal number (such as 1st, 2nd, and so on) that indicates the state's U.S. Constitution signing order. You also modify the message displayed by the jackson.cgi script, as shown in Figure 2-20.

Figure 2-20

a. Open the jackson.html file in a text editor. The file is contained in the public_html/chap02 directory.

b. Change the filename in the first line from jackson.html to c02ex3.html. Modify the URLs so that each refers to the c02ex3.cgi file, and each passes the appropriate data. (Alaska was the 49th state to sign the Constitution, Arizona was the 48th state, and Arkansas was the 25th state.)

c. Save the document as c02ex3.html.

d. Open the jackson.cgi file in your text editor. The file is contained in the cgi-bin/chap02 directory.

e. Change the filename in the second line from jackson.cgi to c02ex3.cgi. Modify the script appropriately, then save the document as c02ex3.cgi.

f. If you are using a UNIX system, change the c02ex3.cgi file permissions to 755.

g. Test the script from the command line.

h. Open the c02ex3.html file in your Web browser. Verify that each link displays the appropriate Web page.

Project 4

In this project, you modify the links in an existing HTML document so that each link passes a word to a script. You also create a script that displays the word passed to it.

a. Open the spanish.html file in a text editor. The file is contained in the public_html/chap02 directory.

b. Change the filename in the first line from spanish.html to c02ex4.html. The file contains five English words that should be defined as links. Complete the HREF property for each link; each should pass both the English word (Hello, Good-bye,

Love, Cat, and Dog) and its Spanish equivalent (Hola, Adios, Amor, Gato, and Perro) to the c02ex4.cgi script. Modify the URLs appropriately, then save the document as c02ex4.html.

c. Open the spanish.cgi file in your text editor. The document is contained in the cgi-bin/chap02 directory.

d. If necessary, change the shebang line to reflect the location of the Perl interpreter on your system.

e. Change the filename in the second line from spanish.cgi to c02ex4.cgi. The script should display the message "The Spanish word for <display the English word here> is <display the Spanish word here>." Complete the script's code appropriately, then save the script as c02ex4.cgi.

f. *If you are using a UNIX system*, change the c02ex4.cgi file permissions to 755.

g. Test the script from the command line.

h. Open the c02ex4.html file in your Web browser. Verify that each link displays the appropriate Web page.

CASE PROJECTS

1. Create an HTML document and a script for Jackson Elementary School. Name the HTML document c02case1.html and save it in the public_html/chap02 directory. Name the script c02case1.cgi and save it in the cgi-bin/chap02 directory. The HTML document should display a Web page that lists the numbers 1 through 10; each number should be a link to the c02case1.cgi script. Each link should pass to the script the name of the president that corresponds to the number. For example, the number 1 link should pass the name "George Washington", the number 2 link should pass the name "John Adams", and so on. The script should display a Web page that contains the data passed to the script. (The third through tenth presidents were Thomas Jefferson, James Madison, James Monroe, John Quincy Adams, Andrew Jackson, Martin Van Buren, William Henry Harrison, and John Tyler.)

2. Create an HTML document and a script for Jackson Elementary School. Name the HTML document c02case2.html and save it in the public_html/chap02 directory. Name the script c02case2.cgi and save it in the cgi-bin/chap02 directory. The HTML document should display a Web page that lists the 12 months in a year; each month should be a link to the c02case2.cgi script. Each link should pass to the script the name of the month and a message that indicates the number of days in the month. For example, the January link should pass "January" and the message "31 days". The February link should pass "February" and the message "28 or 29 (leap year) days", and so on. The script should display a Web page that contains the data passed to the script.

3

SENDING DATA USING AN ONLINE FORM

In this chapter, you will:

♦ Plan and create a CGI script that processes form data

♦ Learn how to prevent Perl from creating undeclared variables in a script

♦ Declare (create) scalar variables in a script

♦ Use assignment statements to assign values to existing variables

♦ Send form data to a script using GET and POST

♦ Improve the appearance of numbers displayed on a Web page

In Chapter 2, you used a hyperlink to send information to a CGI script named jackson.cgi. Recall that the script displayed the information it received—the state and capital names—on a dynamic Web page. In addition to using a hyperlink, you also can use an online form to send information to a CGI script.

An online form is created with HTML and is the electronic equivalent of a paper form that you fill out by hand. As you can with paper forms, you can use online forms to purchase products or services, submit inquiries, or respond to surveys. However, unlike paper forms which you typically send back through the mail, online forms are sent back by clicking a special button, referred to as a submit button. Usually, the submit button is located at the bottom of the form and labeled "Submit", "Send", or something similar.

When you click a form's submit button, the data entered on the form is typically given to a CGI script for processing. In most cases, the script outputs a dynamic Web page that contains an appropriate response to the person submitting the form—such as an acknowledgment of an order or an answer to an inquiry. In this chapter, you learn how to use an online form to send information to a CGI script. You also learn how to plan and create a CGI script that processes the form data it receives.

PROCESSING FORM DATA

Assume that your Web browser displays a Bonus Calculator form that allows you to enter your name, sales amount, and bonus rate. An example of a completed Bonus Calculator form is shown in Figure 3-1.

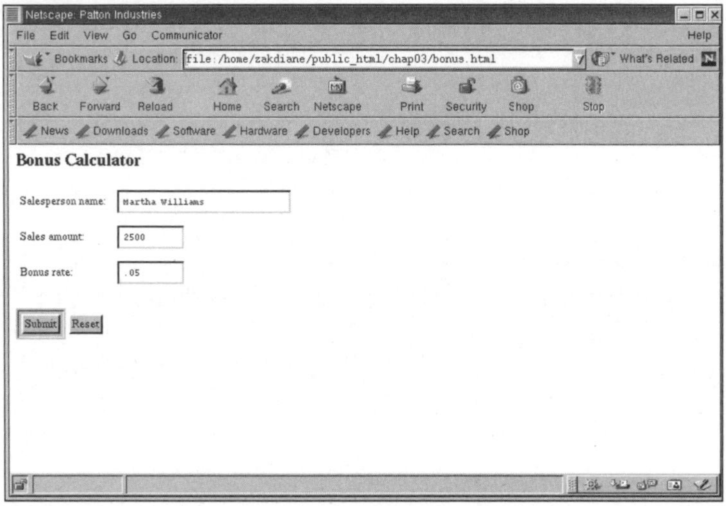

Figure 3-1   Completed Bonus Calculator form

After entering your information, you click the form's Submit button. Almost immediately, the browser displays a personalized Web page that contains the information you entered on the form and the amount of your bonus, as shown in Figure 3-2.

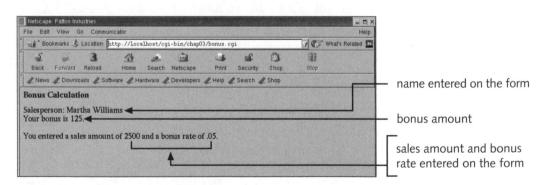

name entered on the form

bonus amount

sales amount and bonus rate entered on the form

Figure 3-2   Personalized Web page

Did you ever wonder what happens to the data you enter on a form when the form is submitted, or how a personalized Web page is created? The answer to both questions can be found in the form processing procedure shown in Figure 3-3.

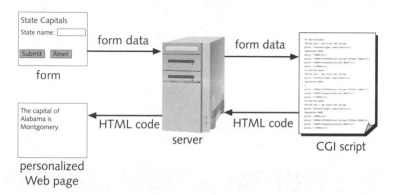

Figure 3-3   Form processing procedure

When you click the Submit button (or a similarly named button) on a form, the browser sends the form data to the server. In the case of the Bonus Calculator form, for example, the browser sends the name, sales amount, and bonus rate that you entered on the form. If the form is associated with a CGI script, the server forwards the form data to the script for processing. The amount and type of processing a script performs varies with each script and is determined by the programmer. Examples of tasks performed by CGI scripts include making calculations, saving data to and retrieving data from a database, and preparing output (typically HTML code) to send to the server. The CGI script associated with the Bonus Calculator form, for example, calculates the bonus amount and prepares the HTML code for the personalized Web page shown in Figure 3-2.

When a CGI script has finished processing, it sends its output—in this case, HTML code—to the server. The server transfers the HTML code to the browser, which renders the personalized Web page on the screen.

In the next section, you learn the steps involved in planning a CGI script that processes form data.

PLANNING THE BONUS CALCULATOR SCRIPT

Most CGI scripts are not as simple as the ones that you created in Chapters 1 and 2; most perform many more tasks and contain many more instructions. CGI scripts that perform more than one task, or those that contain more than a few lines of code, should be planned before they are created. The importance of planning cannot be stressed enough. If you do not take the time to plan a script, the script likely will contain errors that are difficult to find and expensive to correct.

When planning a script, you first determine the script's input and output. The input for a script that processes form data is the form data itself. The Bonus Calculator script's input, for example, is the name, sales amount, and bonus rate entered on the Bonus Calculator form.

A script's output is the purpose for writing the script. The Bonus Calculator script's output is the personalized Web page shown earlier in Figure 3-2. Notice that the Web page contains the three input items: name, sales amount, and bonus rate. It also contains a bonus amount, which is calculated by multiplying the sales amount by the bonus rate.

After determining the script's input and output, you list the steps the script will need to follow to transform the input into the output. The list of steps, referred to as an **algorithm**, is typically written in either pseudocode or flowchart form. Figure 3-4 shows the input, output, and algorithm (written in pseudocode) for the Bonus Calculator script.

Input	Output
name sales amount bonus rate	Web page containing the name, sales amount, bonus rate, and bonus amount
Algorithm	
1. assign input items to variables 2. calculate the bonus amount by multiplying the sales amount by the bonus rate 3. create a dynamic Web page that displays the name, sales amount, bonus rate, and bonus amount	

Figure 3-4   Input, output, and algorithm for the Bonus Calculator script

 An algorithm is simply a set of step-by-step instructions that solve a problem. Pseudocode consists of short English statements. A flowchart, on the other hand, is composed of standardized symbols.

As its algorithm indicates, the Bonus Calculator script first will assign the three input items (name, sales amount, and bonus rate) to variables. The script then will calculate the bonus amount by multiplying the sales amount by the bonus rate. Finally, the script will create a dynamic Web page that displays the name, sales amount, bonus rate, and bonus amount.

After planning a script, you then code the script's algorithm using a language that the computer can understand—such as the Perl scripting language. However, before you can begin coding the algorithm shown in Figure 3-4, you need to learn about variables in Perl.

VARIABLES IN PERL

A **variable** is a location (within the computer's internal memory) where a script can temporarily store data. The data may come from a form, or it may be read in from a file, or it may be the result of a calculation made by the computer.

Every variable has a data type, which determines the kind of data the variable can store. Perl provides three basic data types for variables: scalar, array, and hash. A **scalar variable**, which you learn about in this chapter, can store precisely one value—typically a number or a string. Array and hash variables, on the other hand, store lists or sets of values. You will learn much more about the array and hash data types in Chapter 4.

 Unlike many programming languages, Perl does not have separate data types for integers, floating-point numbers, and strings.

3

In addition to a data type, every variable also has a name. The name of a scalar variable must begin with a dollar sign ($) followed by a letter and then, optionally, one or more letters, numbers, or underscores. Examples of valid names for scalar variables include $city, $income2002, and $inc_tax. Keep in mind that variable names in Perl are case sensitive; so the names $city, $CITY, and $City do not refer to the same location in the computer's internal memory. It is important to use the exact capitalization of a name throughout the entire Perl script; otherwise, the script will not work correctly.

 The dollar sign ($) indicates the variable's data type: scalar. An easy way to remember that scalar variable names begin with a dollar sign ($) is to associate the $ with the letter "S" in the word "Scalar".

 Although variable names can include both uppercase and lowercase letters, most Perl programmers use lowercase letters when naming variables.

You should assign a descriptive name to each variable the script will use. The name should help you remember the purpose of the variable—in other words, the meaning of the value stored therein. For example, the names $length and $width are much more meaningful than are the names $x and $y, because $length and $width remind you that the amounts stored in the variables represent a length and width measurement, respectively.

Unlike many programming languages, Perl does not require you to explicitly declare the variables used in a script. By default, variables in Perl are created "on the fly" and spring into existence upon their first use in a script. It is considered a good programming practice to prevent a programming language from creating variables "on the fly"—in other words, from creating variables that you have not explicitly declared. You prevent Perl from creating undeclared variables using the statement **use strict;**. The use strict; statement typically is entered near the beginning of the script, before any statements that declare variables.

To explicitly declare one or more variables, you use a statement that follows the syntax **my** (*variablelist*);, where *variablelist* is a comma-separated list of variable names. When you declare a variable, the computer creates the variable in its internal memory. For example, the statement my ($hours, $gross, $sales); declares (creates) three scalar variables named $hours, $gross, and $sales. Typically, variable declaration statements are entered below the **use strict;** statement in a script.

If you have only one variable to declare, you can omit the parentheses in the declaration statement. For example, you can use either the statement `my ($hours);` or the statement `my $hours;` to declare the `$hours` variable.

After declaring a variable, you can use an assignment statement to assign a value to the variable.

Assignment Statements

You can use an assignment statement to assign a value to or change the value stored in an existing variable. The syntax of an assignment statement is *variable = value;*, where *variable* is the variable's name and *value* is the number or string you want stored in the variable. Figure 3-5 shows examples of assignment statements that assign values to scalar variables.

Assigning numeric values	Results
`$hours = 40;`	assigns the number 40 to the $hours variable
`$gross = $hours * 8;`	assigns the number 320 (40 * 8) to the $gross variable
Assigning double-quoted strings	**Results**
`$first = "Jim";`	assigns the string "Jim" to the $first variable
`$msg = "His name is $first.";`	assigns the string "His name is Jim." to the $msg variable
Assigning single-quoted strings	**Results**
`$first = 'Jim';`	assigns the string 'Jim' to the $first variable
`$msg = 'His name is $first.';`	assigns the string 'His name is $first.' to the $msg variable

Figure 3-5   Examples of assignment statements

The first two examples shown in Figure 3-5 assign a number to a scalar variable: the first example assigns the number 40 to the `$hours` variable, and the second example assigns the result of a calculation—in this case, the number 320—to the `$gross` variable. The 320 is calculated by multiplying the contents of the `$hours` variable (40) by the number 8.

The third and fourth examples shown in Figure 3-5 assign a double-quoted string to a scalar variable. The third example assigns the string "Jim" (without the double quotation marks) to the `$first` variable. The fourth example assigns the string "His name is Jim." to the `$msg` variable. Notice that the variable name (`$first`) in the fourth example is replaced with the contents of the variable (Jim) before the string is assigned to the `$msg` variable. When the name of a variable appears within double quotation marks in a statement, Perl replaces the variable's name with the variable's contents—a process referred to as **interpolation**.

Any statement that contains a variable's name enclosed in double quotation marks is subject to interpolation. You will see more examples of interpolation later in this chapter.

3

The last two statements shown in Figure 3 5 assign a single-quoted string to a scalar variable Unlike double quotation marks, single quotation marks indicate that no interpolation should be performed in the string; rather, the string should be treated verbatim. For example, the fifth statement shown in the figure, `$first = 'Jim';`, assigns the string 'Jim' (without the single quotation marks) to the `$first` variable. Notice that the statement produces the same result as the statement `$first = "Jim";`, which is the third statement shown in the figure; this is because neither statement contains the name of a variable. However, notice that the statement `$msg = 'His name is $first.';` (the last example) does not produce the same result as the statement `$msg = "His name is $first.";` (the fourth example). Unlike the latter statement, the former statement does not replace the variable name (`$first`) with its contents; rather, it assigns the string 'His name is $first.' verbatim.

Now that you have learned about variables, you can begin coding the Bonus Calculator script.

CODING THE BONUS CALCULATOR SCRIPT

The Bonus Calculator script will use four scalar variables: three to store the input items (name, sales amount, and bonus rate) and one to store the bonus amount. You will name the variables `$name`, `$sales`, `$rate`, and `$bonus`. Before entering the statement to declare the variables, you will enter the `use strict;` statement to stop Perl from creating variables "on the fly."

To prevent Perl from creating undeclared variables, and then declare the variables in the Bonus Calculator script:

1. Open the bonus.cgi file in a text editor. The file is contained in the cgi-bin/chap03 directory. Figure 3-6 (on the next page) shows the partially completed bonus.cgi document. **Important Note**: If you are using a Windows system, the shebang line will say `#!C:/Perl/bin/perl.exe`.

2. If necessary, change the shebang line to reflect the location of the Perl interpreter on your system.

3. In the blank line below the comment `#prevent Perl from creating undeclared variables`, type **use strict;** and press **Enter**.

4. In the blank line below the comment `#declare variables`, type **my ($name, $sales, $rate, $bonus);** and press **Enter**.

```
#!/usr/bin/perl
#bonus.cgi - calculates a bonus amount and creates a dynamic Web page
#that contains form data and a bonus amount
print "Content-type: text/html\n\n";

#prevent Perl from creating undeclared variables

#declare variables

#assign values to variables

#calculate bonus amount

#create Web page
print "<HTML>\n";
print "<HEAD><TITLE>Patton Industries</TITLE><BASEFONT SIZE=5></HEAD>\n";
print "<H1>Bonus Calculation</H1>\n";
print "<BODY>\n";

print "</BODY>\n";
print "</HTML>\n";
```

if necessary, change the shebang line to reflect the location of the Perl interpreter on your system

Figure 3-6   Partially completed bonus.cgi document

The first step in the Bonus Calculator script's algorithm, shown earlier in Figure 3-4, is to assign the input items (name, sales amount, and bonus rate) to variables. Recall that the script will receive the input items from an online form. When you first are creating a script, it is helpful to assign sample values to the input variables rather than worrying about assigning the form values themselves; doing this allows you to test the script without the form. When the script is working correctly, you then replace the sample values with the form values. In this case you will assign "Martha Williams" to the $name variable, 2500 to the $sales variable, and .05 to the $rate variable.

To assign sample values to the input variables:

1. In the blank line below the comment #assign values to variables, type the three assignment statements shaded in Figure 3-7.

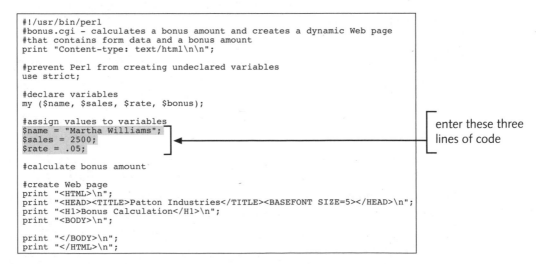

```
#!/usr/bin/perl
#bonus.cgi - calculates a bonus amount and creates a dynamic Web page
#that contains form data and a bonus amount
print "Content-type: text/html\n\n";

#prevent Perl from creating undeclared variables
use strict;

#declare variables
my ($name, $sales, $rate, $bonus);

#assign values to variables
$name = "Martha Williams";
$sales = 2500;
$rate = .05;

#calculate bonus amount

#create Web page
print "<HTML>\n";
print "<HEAD><TITLE>Patton Industries</TITLE><BASEFONT SIZE=5></HEAD>\n";
print "<H1>Bonus Calculation</H1>\n";
print "<BODY>\n";

print "</BODY>\n";
print "</HTML>\n";
```

enter these three lines of code

Figure 3-7   Assignment statements entered in the bonus.cgi script

2. Save the bonus.cgi document.

Step 2 in the script's algorithm is to calculate the bonus amount by multiplying the sales amount by the bonus rate. Figure 3-8 lists the arithmetic operators that you can use to perform calculations in a Perl statement, along with their precedence numbers. The precedence numbers indicate the order in which Perl performs the arithmetic operations in an expression. Operations with a precedence number of 1 are performed before operations with a precedence number of 2, which are performed before operations with a precedence number of 3, and so on. However, you can use parentheses to override the order of precedence, because operations within parentheses always are performed before operations outside parentheses.

Operator	Operation	Precedence number
()	override normal precedence rules	1
**	exponentiation	2
-	negation	3
*, /, %	multiplication, division, and modulus arithmetic	4
+, −	addition and subtraction	5

Figure 3-8   Perl arithmetic operators and their order of precedence

The difference between the negation and subtraction operators shown in Figure 3-8 is that the negation operator is unary, whereas the subtraction operator is binary. *Unary* and *binary* refer to the number of operands required by the operator. Unary operators require one operand. For example, the negative number −3 contains the negation operator (−), which is unary, and one operand—the number 3. Unlike unary operators, binary operators require two operands. For example, the expression 4 * 3 contains the multiplication operator (*), which is binary, and two operands: the number 4 and the number 3.

Notice that some operators shown in Figure 3-8 have the same precedence number. For example, both the addition and subtraction operator have a precedence number of 5. If an expression contains more than one operator having the same priority, those operators are evaluated from left to right. In the expression 3 + 12 / 3 − 1, for instance, the division (/) is performed first, then the addition (+), and then the subtraction (−). In other words, the computer first divides 12 by 3, then adds the result of the division (4) to 3, and then subtracts 1 from the result of the addition (7). The expression evaluates to 6.

You can use parentheses to change the order in which the operators in an expression are evaluated. For example, the expression 3 + 12 / (3 − 1) evaluates to 9, not 6. This is because the parentheses tell the computer to subtract 1 from 3 first, then divide the result of the subtraction (2) into 12, and then add the result of the division (6) to 3.

One of the arithmetic operators listed in Figure 3-8, the modulus arithmetic operator (%), might be less familiar to you. The modulus arithmetic operator is used to divide two integers, and results in the remainder of the division. For example, 211 % 4 (read 211 mod 4) equals 3, which is the remainder of 211 divided by 4. One use for the modulus operator is to determine if a year is a leap year—one that has 366 days rather than 365 days. As you may know, if a year is a leap year, then its year number is evenly divisible by the number 4—in other words, if you divide the year number by 4 and the remainder is 0 (zero), then the year is a leap year. You can determine if the year 2004 is a leap year by using the expression 2004 % 4. This expression evaluates to 0 (the remainder of 2004 divided by 4), so the year 2004 is a leap year. Similarly, you can determine if the year 2005 is a leap year by using the expression 2005 % 4. This expression evaluates to 1 (the remainder of 2005 divided by 4), so the year 2005 is not a leap year.

Years ending in 00 are only leap years if they also are evenly divisible by 400.

The appropriate operator to use in the bonus amount calculation is the multiplication operator, the asterisk (*). You will store the result of the calculation in the $bonus variable.

To calculate the bonus amount and assign the result to a variable:

1. In the blank line below the comment #calculate bonus amount, type **$bonus = $sales * $rate;** and press **Enter**.

2. Save the bonus.cgi document.

The last step in the script's algorithm is to create the dynamic Web page shown earlier in Figure 3-2. Recall that the Web page displays the name, sales amount, bonus rate, and bonus amount. The bonus.cgi document already contains most of the HTML code for the dynamic Web page. You complete the code in the next set of steps.

To finish creating the dynamic Web page, then test the script:

1. Position the insertion point in the blank line below the statement print "<BODY>\n";.

   First display a message that contains the salesperson's name. Recall that the name is stored in the $name variable.

2. Type **print "Salesperson: $name
\n";** and press **Enter**. This statement will display the string "Salesperson: Martha Williams" on a Web page. As you learned earlier, when the name of a variable appears within double quotation marks in a statement, Perl replaces the variable's name with the variable's contents—a process referred to as interpolation.

 is the line break tag in HTML.

Next, display a message that contains the bonus amount, which is stored in the $bonus variable.

3. Type **print "Your bonus is $bonus.

\n";** and press **Enter**.

Finally, display a message that contains the sales amount and bonus rate, which are stored in the **$sales** and **$rate** variables.

4. Type the two lines of code shaded in Figure 3-9.

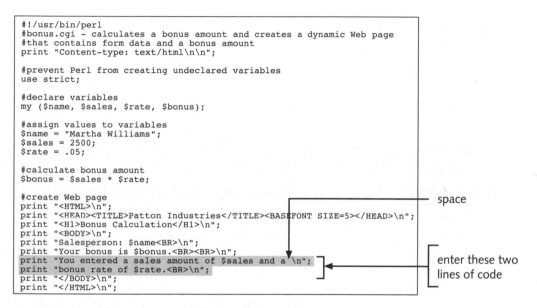

```
#!/usr/bin/perl
#bonus.cgi - calculates a bonus amount and creates a dynamic Web page
#that contains form data and a bonus amount
print "Content-type: text/html\n\n";

#prevent Perl from creating undeclared variables
use strict;

#declare variables
my ($name, $sales, $rate, $bonus);

#assign values to variables
$name = "Martha Williams";
$sales = 2500;
$rate = .05;

#calculate bonus amount
$bonus = $sales * $rate;

#create Web page
print "<HTML>\n";
print "<HEAD><TITLE>Patton Industries</TITLE><BASEFONT SIZE=5></HEAD>\n";
print "<H1>Bonus Calculation</H1>\n";
print "<BODY>\n";
print "Salesperson: $name<BR>\n";
print "Your bonus is $bonus.<BR><BR>\n";
print "You entered a sales amount of $sales and a \n";
print "bonus rate of $rate.<BR>\n";
print "</BODY>\n";
print "</HTML>\n";
```

space

enter these two lines of code

Figure 3-9   Additional code entered in the bonus.cgi script

5. Save the bonus.cgi document.

6. *If you are using a UNIX system*, open a terminal window, if necessary. Make the cgi–bin/chap03 directory the current directory, and then change the bonus.cgi file permissions to **755**.

If you are using a Windows system, open a Command Prompt window, and then make the cgi–bin\chap03 directory the current directory.

7. Type **perl –c bonus.cgi** and press **Enter** to check the script for syntax errors. If necessary, correct any syntax errors in the script before continuing to the next step.

8. Type **perl –w bonus.cgi** and press **Enter** to execute the bonus.cgi script. See Figure 3-10.

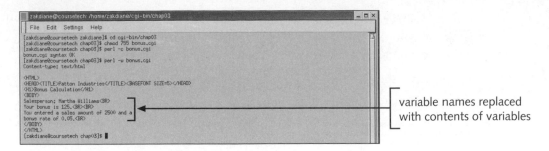

variable names replaced
with contents of variables

Figure 3-10   Result of using the -w switch

Notice that Perl replaces the variable names in the `print` statements with the contents of the variables.

Now that you know the script is working correctly, you can replace the sample values with the values received from the online form.

Accessing the Values Received from an Online Form

As you learned in Chapter 2, each item of data passed to a script by a hyperlink has a *key* and a *value*. Online forms also use *keys* and *values* to pass data to a script. The *key* is simply a one-word name that you assign to the *value*. In the case of a hyperlink, recall that you append the *key* and *value* to the link's URL, which is specified in the anchor tag's HREF property. In the case of an online form, the *key* is the name of the form element containing the *value* entered by the user. Figure 3-11 shows the *keys* (names) assigned to the three text boxes on the Bonus Calculator form.

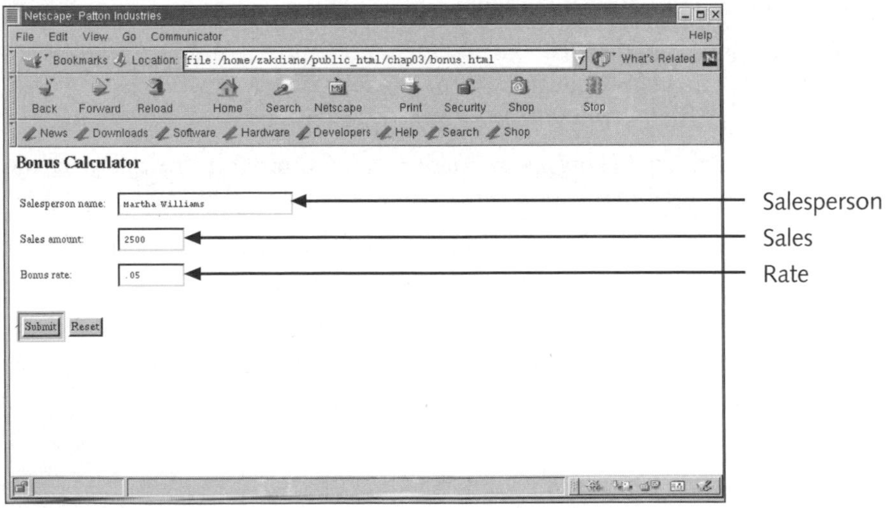

Figure 3-11   *Keys* assigned to the text boxes on the Bonus Calculator form

Later in this chapter, you will view the HTML code for the Bonus Calculator form. At that time, you will see how the text boxes were named.

Form *keys* and *values* are passed automatically to a script when you click the form's submit button. For example, when you click the Submit button on the Bonus Calculator form, the *keys* (Salesperson, Sales, and Rate) along with their *values* (Martha+Williams, 2500, and .05) will be sent to the bonus.cgi script.

Just as you do when sending multiple words using a hyperlink, the browser replaces the space that separates two words with a plus sign (+) when sending the data to a script.

As is true of data sent using a hyperlink, data sent using an online form must be parsed by the script when it is received. You can use the parsing routine contained in the CGI.pm module to parse the data. Recall that to do so, you first enter the statement `use CGI qw(:standard);` or the statement `use CGI qw(:standard -debug);` in the script. You then use the **param** function, whose syntax is **param(***key***)**, to access the parsed data.

To parse the data sent by the Bonus Calculator form, then test the script:

1. Return to the bonus.cgi document in your text editor. In the blank line below the Content-type statement, type either the statement **use CGI qw(:standard);** or the statement **use CGI qw(:standard -debug);**. Press **Enter**.

As you learned in Chapter 2, some versions of the CGI.pm module require you to include the –debug pragma in the `use CGI qw(:standard);` statement. If you needed to include the –debug pragma in the scripts you created in Chapter 2, then you will need to include it in all of the scripts you create in this book.

Now use the **param** function to access the form values.

2. Replace the sample values assigned to the input variables with the values received from the form, as indicated in Figure 3-12.

3

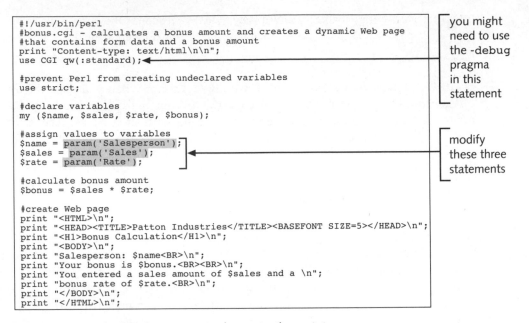

```
#!/usr/bin/perl
#bonus.cgi - calculates a bonus amount and creates a dynamic Web page
#that contains form data and a bonus amount
print "Content-type: text/html\n\n";
use CGI qw(:standard);

#prevent Perl from creating undeclared variables
use strict;

#declare variables
my ($name, $sales, $rate, $bonus);

#assign values to variables
$name = param('Salesperson');
$sales = param('Sales');
$rate = param('Rate');

#calculate bonus amount
$bonus = $sales * $rate;

#create Web page
print "<HTML>\n";
print "<HEAD><TITLE>Patton Industries</TITLE><BASEFONT SIZE=5></HEAD>\n";
print "<H1>Bonus Calculation</H1>\n";
print "<BODY>\n";
print "Salesperson: $name<BR>\n";
print "Your bonus is $bonus.<BR><BR>\n";
print "You entered a sales amount of $sales and a \n";
print "bonus rate of $rate.<BR>\n";
print "</BODY>\n";
print "</HTML>\n";
```

you might need to use the -debug pragma in this statement

modify these three statements

Figure 3-12   Modified statements shown in the script

3. Save the bonus.cgi document.

4. *If you are using a UNIX system*, return to the UNIX command prompt. Type **clear** after the command prompt and press **Enter**.

   If you are using a Windows system, return to the Command Prompt window. Type **cls** after the command prompt and press **Enter**.

5. Type **perl –c bonus.cgi** and press **Enter**. If necessary, correct any syntax errors in the script before continuing to the next step.

6. Type **perl –w bonus.cgi** and press **Enter**. When the offline mode message appears, type **Salesperson=Martha+Williams** and press **Enter**, then type **Sales=2500** and press **Enter**, and then type **Rate=.05** and press **Enter**.

7. *If you are using a UNIX system*, press **Ctrl+d** to indicate that you have finished entering data. See Figure 3-13.

   If you are using a Windows system, press **Ctrl+z** and then press **Enter** to indicate that you have finished entering data. See Figure 3-13.

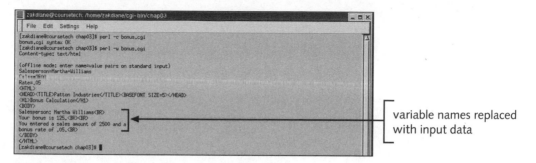

Figure 3-13 Input data displayed on the screen

Notice that Perl replaces the variable names in the **print** statements with the input data.

Next you view the HTML code that creates the Bonus Calculator form, and then you learn how to associate the form with the bonus.cgi script.

THE BONUS CALCULATOR FORM

The Bonus Calculator form was shown earlier in Figure 3-11. In the next set of steps, you view the partially completed HTML code used to create the form, and you begin completing the code.

To view the partially completed HTML code for the Bonus Calculator form, and then begin completing the code:

   1. Open the bonus.html file in a text editor. The file is contained in the public_html/chap03 directory. Figure 3-14 shows the partially completed bonus.html document.

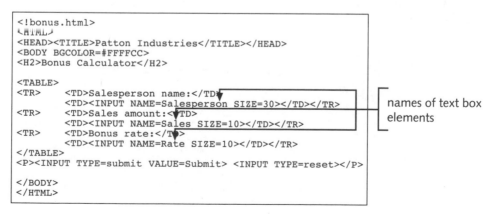

Figure 3-14 Partially completed bonus.html document

Notice the names of the text boxes: Salesperson, Sales, and Rate. Recall that these are the names you used in the `param` function in the bonus.cgi script.

The <FORM> and </FORM> tags, which are necessary to create a form, are missing from the bonus.html document. The <FORM> tag marks the beginning of the form, and the </FORM> tag marks the end of the form.

2. In the blank line below the <H2> tag, type **<FORM>**. Then, in the blank line above the </BODY> tag, type **</FORM>**.

The <FORM> tag provides two properties, ACTION and METHOD, that allow you to specify how the form data should be handled. The ACTION property indicates the name of the CGI script that will process the form data, and the METHOD property controls how your Web browser sends the form data to the Web server running the CGI script. The METHOD property can be set to either GET or POST. As you will observe shortly, the GET method, which is the default value for the METHOD property, appends the form data to the end of the URL specified in the ACTION property, and is similar to sending the data using a hyperlink. The server retrieves the data from the URL and stores it in a text string for processing by the CGI script. The POST method, on the other hand, sends the form data in a separate data stream, allowing the Web server to receive the data through what is called "standard input." Because it is more flexible, the POST method is considered the preferred way of sending data to the server. It also is safer, because some Web servers limit the amount of data sent by the GET method and will truncate the URL, cutting off valuable information. You will observe the use of both methods in the next set of steps.

To complete the Bonus Calculator form, then use it to test the Bonus Calculator script:

1. Include the ACTION and METHOD properties in the <FORM> tag, as shown in Figure 3-15. Change yourservername in the ACTION property to the name of your server.

```
<!bonus.html>
<HTML>
<HEAD><TITLE>Patton Industries</TITLE></HEAD>
<BODY BGCOLOR=#FFFFCC>
<H2>Bonus Calculator</H2>
<FORM ACTION="http://yourservername/cgi-bin/chap03/bonus.cgi" METHOD=GET>
<TABLE>
<TR>        <TD>Salesperson name:</TD>
            <TD><INPUT NAME=Salesperson SIZE=30></TD></TR>
<TR>        <TD>Sales amount:</TD>
            <TD><INPUT NAME=Sales SIZE=10></TD></TR>
<TR>        <TD>Bonus rate:</TD>
            <TD><INPUT NAME=Rate SIZE=10></TD></TR>
</TABLE>
<P><INPUT TYPE=submit VALUE=Submit> <INPUT TYPE=reset></P>
</FORM>
</BODY>
</HTML>
```

Figure 3-15   <FORM> tag containing the GET method

2. Save the bonus.html document.

3. Start your browser, then use the browser's File menu to open the bonus.html file.

4. Enter **Martha Williams** as the salesperson name, **2500** as the sales amount, and **.05** as the bonus rate, then click the **Submit** button.

5. Scroll the browser's address box, as shown in Figure 3-16.

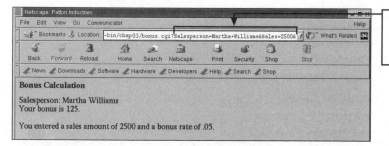

the form data is appended to the URL when using GET

Figure 3-16   Result of using the GET method to send the form data

Notice that the form data is appended to the URL and appears in the browser's address box, just as it does when data is sent using a hyperlink.

Now, see the effect of changing the METHOD property to POST.

6. Return to the bonus.html document in your text editor. Change GET to POST in the <FORM> tag, as shown in Figure 3-17.

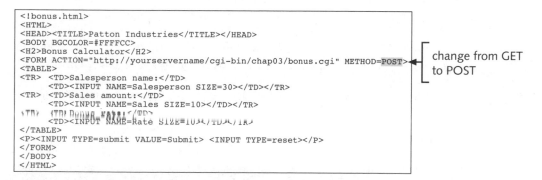

change from GET to POST

```
<!bonus.html>
<HTML>
<HEAD><TITLE>Patton Industries</TITLE></HEAD>
<BODY BGCOLOR=#FFFFCC>
<H2>Bonus Calculator</H2>
<FORM ACTION="http://yourservername/cgi-bin/chap03/bonus.cgi" METHOD=POST>
<TABLE>
<TR>  <TD>Salesperson name:</TD>
      <TD><INPUT NAME=Salesperson SIZE=30></TD></TR>
<TR>  <TD>Sales amount:</TD>
      <TD><INPUT NAME=Sales SIZE=10></TD></TR>
<TR>  <TD>Bonus rate:</TD>
      <TD><INPUT NAME=Rate SIZE=10></TD></TR>
</TABLE>
<P><INPUT TYPE=submit VALUE=Submit> <INPUT TYPE=reset></P>
</FORM>
</BODY>
</HTML>
```

Figure 3-17   <FORM> tag containing the POST method

7. Save the bonus.html document, then close the document.

8. Use your browser's File menu to open the bonus.html file. Enter **Martha Williams** as the salesperson name, **2500** as the sales amount, and **.05** as the bonus rate, and then click the **Submit** button. If a message appears telling you that the information you submit is insecure, click the **Continue Submission** button. See Figure 3-18.

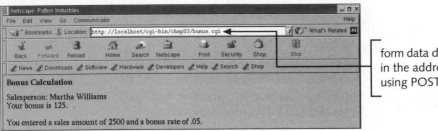

form data does not appear in the address box when using POST

Figure 3-18   Result of using the POST method to send the form data

> Notice that the form data does not appear in the browser's address box when you use the POST method.

9. Click your browser's **Back** button to return to the Bonus Calculator form.

10. Minimize the browser window.

Now that you know that the bonus.cgi script is working correctly, you can begin improving the appearance of the Web page it creates. First, you learn how to include a dollar sign ($) in a number that represents money.

INCLUDING A DOLLAR SIGN IN A NUMBER

Displaying a dollar sign ($) at the beginning of a number makes it obvious that the number represents money. You display a dollar sign in Perl by including a backslash (\) followed by a dollar sign ($) in a `print` statement, as shown in Figure 3-19. The backslash (\) is necessary because the dollar sign ($) has special meaning in Perl. The backslash alerts Perl to ignore the special meaning and simply treat the dollar sign verbatim.

You already learned about the dollar sign's function in creating variables in Perl. You will learn more about using the dollar sign in Chapter 8.

Examples	Results
`print "You earned \$100.\n";`	displays the text "You earned $100."
`print "Price: \$$price\n";`	assuming the $price variable contains the number 35, displays the text "Price: $35"
`print "\$$bill due\n";`	assuming the $bill variable contains the number 150.75, displays the text "$150.75 due"

Figure 3-19   Examples of including a dollar sign in a `print` statement

The first `print` statement shown in Figure 3-19, `print "You earned \$100.\n";`, displays the text "You earned $100." Notice that Perl replaces `\$` in the statement with `$`.

The second `print` statement shown in Figure 3-19 displays the text "Price: $35", and the last `print` statement displays the text "$150.75 due". Here again, Perl replaces `\$` in both statements with `$`. Perl also replaces the variable names (`$price` and `$bill`) with the contents of the variables (35 and 150.75).

In the next set of steps, you include a dollar sign before the bonus and sales amounts in the bonus.cgi script.

To include a dollar sign before the bonus and sales amounts:

1. Open the bonus.cgi file in a text editor. The file is contained in the cgi-bin/chap03 directory.

2. Modify the `print` statements that display the bonus and sales amounts, as shown in Figure 3-20.

```
#!/usr/bin/perl
#bonus.cgi - calculates a bonus amount and creates a dynamic Web page
#that contains form data and a bonus amount
print "Content-type: text/html\n\n";
use CGI qw(:standard);

#prevent Perl from creating undeclared variables
use strict;

#declare variables
my ($name, $sales, $rate, $bonus);

#assign values to variables
$name = param('Salesperson');
$sales = param('Sales');
$rate = param('Rate');

#calculate bonus amount
$bonus = $sales * $rate;

#create Web page
print "<HTML>\n";
print "<HEAD><TITLE>Patton Industries</TITLE><BASEFONT SIZE=5></HEAD>\n";
print "<H1>Bonus Calculation</H1>\n";
print "<BODY>\n";
print "Salesperson: $name<BR>\n";
print "Your bonus is \$$bonus.<BR><BR>\n";
print "You entered a sales amount of \$$sales and a \n";
print "bonus rate of $rate.<BR>\n";
print "</BODY>\n";
print "</HTML>\n";
```

include the \$ in these two places

Figure 3-20   bonus.cgi document showing the modified `print` statements

3. Save the bonus.cgi document.

4. Restore the browser window, which you minimized in an earlier set of steps.

5. Click the **Reset** button to clear the data from the Bonus Calculator form.

6. Enter **Jeff Stein** as the salesperson name, **3550** as the sales amount, and **.03** as the bonus rate, and then click the **Submit** button. If necessary, click the **Continue Submission** button. A dollar sign appears before the bonus and sales amounts on the Web page, as shown in Figure 3-21.

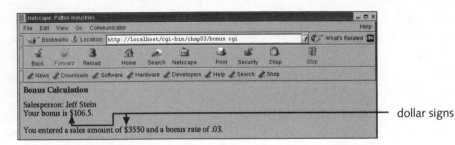

dollar signs

Figure 3-21   Web page showing a dollar sign before the bonus and sale amounts

Notice that the bonus amount ($106.5) contains one decimal place. Most times, a number that represents money is displayed with either zero or two decimal places. You can use the Perl `printf` function to specify the number of decimal places to display in a number.

7. Click the **Back** button to return to the Bonus Calculator form, then minimize the browser window.

Next, you learn about the Perl `printf` function.

USING THE `printf` FUNCTION

In all of the scripts you have created so far, you used the **print function** to display data on a Web page. Perl also provides the **printf function** for displaying data on a Web page. Unlike the `print` function, the `printf` function allows you to format the data it displays. For example, the `printf` function allows you to specify the number of decimal places to include in a number. It also allows you to display a plus sign (+) before positive numbers, and a minus sign (-) before negative numbers.

The syntax of the `printf` function is **printf** *formatstring*, *list*;. In the syntax, *list* is a comma-separated list of items—typically variables—whose values you want to format, and *formatstring* is a string that controls the appearance of each item in the *list*. *Formatstring* can contain text and one or more format fields, as indicated in Figure 3-22. (For now, do not worry about understanding the meaning of the numbers, letters, and symbols that appear in the format fields shown in Figure 3-22. You learn more about format fields later in the chapter.)

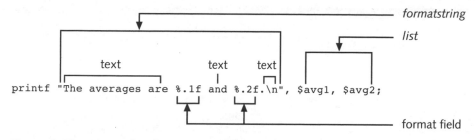

Figure 3-22   Example of a `printf` function

Notice that the *formatstring* shown in Figure 3-22 is enclosed in double quotation marks, and that a comma separates the *formatstring* from the *list*. A comma also is used to separate one item in the *list* from the next. Additionally, notice that the *formatstring* contains two format fields (`%.1f` and `%.2f`), and the *list* contains two items (the variable names `$avg1` and `$avg2`). You should include in the *formatstring* a separate format field for each item in the *list*. The `printf` function uses the first format field in the *formatstring* to format the first item in the *list*, the second format field to format the second item, and so on. In this case, the `printf` function uses the `%.1f` format field to format the value stored in the `$avg1` variable, and it uses the `%.2f` format field to format the value stored in the `$avg2` variable. As you will learn shortly, the `%.1f` format field tells the `printf` function to display the value as a floating-point number (f) with one (1) decimal place. A value of 98, for example, will be displayed as 98.0. Notice that the `printf` function appends the decimal point and a 0 to the end of the number so that the number contains one decimal place.

Similarly, the `%.2f` format field tells the `printf` function to display the value as a floating-point number (f) with two (2) decimal places. A value of 45.3, for example, will be displayed as 45.30.

In the next section, you learn about the parts of a format field.

Parts of a Format Field

Each format field is composed of five parts, three of which are optional. The five parts are described in Figure 3-23.

Parts	Description
%	The percent sign is required. It indicates the beginning of a format field.
modifier	The modifier is optional. The two modifiers most commonly used to display numbers on a Web page are the plus sign (+) and the number 0. The purpose of each modifier is listed below. Modifier Purpose + Display a + sign before a positive number, and a – sign before a negative number 0 Pad the left side of a number with zeros instead of spaces
minimum field width	The minimum field width is optional. When used, it is a number that indicates the minimum number of characters you want displayed in the field.
precision	The precision is optional. When used, it is expressed as a period (.) followed by a number. The precision indicates the number of digits you want displayed to the right of the decimal point in a number.
format type	The format type is required. It indicates the format to use when displaying the field data. The two most commonly used format types are d (decimal number) and f (floating-point number).

Figure 3-23   Parts of a format field

As Figure 3-23 indicates, the first part of a format field is a percent sign (%) and is required; every format field must begin with a percent sign. The second part of the format field, the modifier, is optional. The modifiers most commonly used when displaying numbers on a Web page are the plus sign (+) and the number 0. The plus sign modifier tells the `printf` function to display a plus sign (+) before a positive number, and a minus sign (-) before a negative number. You can use the number 0 modifier to pad the left side of a number with zeros instead of spaces—for example, to display the number 5 as 05.

The third part of a format field is the minimum field width, which is optional. When used, it is a number that indicates the minimum number of characters you want displayed in the field. The fourth part of a format field is the precision, which also is optional. The precision is expressed as a period (.) followed by a number—for example, .4. The precision indicates the number of digits to display to the right of the decimal point in a numeric value. For example, applying a precision of .4 to the number 45.3 results in the number 45.3000.

The last part of a format string is the format type and is required. The most commonly used format types for displaying numeric values are d and f. A format type of d, which stands for *decimal number*, indicates that the numeric value should be displayed as a whole number (a number without any decimal places). A format type of f, which stands for *floating-point number*, indicates that the numeric value should be displayed with zero or more decimal places. Recall that the number of decimal places to display is specified in the precision part of the format field.

The `printf` function also provides the s format type for displaying strings, such as product or employee names. The s stands for *string*. When displaying a string, the precision part of the format field specifies the number of characters you want to display from the string. For example, applying a precision of .4 to the string "Jackie" results in the string "Jack".

The `printf` function is a powerful function that gives you a lot of control over the appearance of data displayed on a Web page. Unfortunately, the function can be difficult to master without a lot of practice. To aid in your learning of the `printf` function, Figure 3-24 shows the function's syntax and several examples of using the function. The format field in each example is shaded in the figure.

Syntax
printf *formatstring, list*;
Examples and results
Example 1
`printf "The price is \$%.2f\n", $price;`
Result
Assuming the `$price` variable contains the number 9.5, the `printf` function will display "The price is $9.50".
Example 2
`printf "The averages are %d and %d.\n", $avg, $tot/3;`
Result
Assuming the `$avg` and `$tot` variables contain the numbers 85.6 and 270, respectively, the `printf` function will display "The averages are 85 and 90."
Example 3
`printf "%04d\n", $num1;` `printf "%04d\n", $num2;`
Result
Assuming the `$num1` and `$num2` variables contain the numbers 7500 and 900, respectively, the `printf` functions will display the following two lines: 7500 0900
Example 4
`printf "Bonus percentage: %.1f%%\n", $rate;`
Result
Assuming the `$rate` variable contains the number 5, the `printf` function will display "Bonus percentage: 5.0%"

to display a percent sign, you must type two percent signs

Figure 3-24   Syntax and examples of the `printf` function

You also can use the Perl `sprintf` function to format numbers. The syntax of the `sprintf` function is similar to the syntax of the `printf` function; it is *variable* = **sprintf** *formatstring, list*;, where *formatstring* and *list* have the same meaning as in the `printf` function. The difference between the two functions is that the `printf` function sends the formatted data to a Web page, whereas the `sprintf` function sends the formatted data to a variable, which then can be printed using a simple `print` statement. You can practice with the `sprintf` function by completing Hands-on Project 4 at the end of this chapter.

The format field shaded in Example 1 (`%.2f`) contains the percent sign (%), precision (.2), and format type (f); it does not contain a modifier or the minimum field width. Recall that the percent sign and format type are required parts of the format field; the precision, modifier, and minimum field width are optional. The format field `%.2f` tells the `printf` function to display the contents of the `$price` variable as a floating-point number with two digits to the right of the decimal point. Assuming the `$price` variable contains the number 9.5, Example 1's `printf` function will display "The price is $9.50". Notice that the `printf` function appends a zero to the end of the number to give the number two decimal places.

The two format fields shaded in Example 2, `%d`, contain only the required parts of a format field: the percent sign and the format type. The `%d` format fields tell the `printf` function to display as decimal (whole) numbers both the contents of the `$avg` variable and the result of dividing the contents of the `$tot` variable by three. Assuming the `$avg` and `$tot` variables contain the numbers 85.6 and 270, respectively, the `printf` function shown in Example 2 will display "The averages are 85 and 90." Notice that the `printf` function truncates (removes or drops off) the decimal portion of the number 85.6 before displaying the number. Also notice that a *list* item can be a calculation, such as `$tot/3`. The `printf` function displays the result of the calculation, rather than the calculation itself.

The two format fields shaded in Example 3 contain the percent sign (%), a modifier (0), the minimum field width (4), and the format type (d). The `%04d` format field tells the `printf` function to display the *list* value as a decimal number containing at least four digits. If the value does not contain four digits, the `printf` function should pad the left side of the value with one or more zeros. Assuming the `$num1` and `$num2` variables contain the numbers 7500 and 900, respectively, the `printf` functions in Example 3 will display the numbers 7500 and 0900, as indicated in the example. Notice that the `printf` function pads the left side of the three-digit number 900 with a zero to give the number four digits.

Example 4 in Figure 3-24 (`printf "Bonus percentage: %.1f%%\n", $rate;`) shows how you can use the `printf` function to display a percent sign at the end of a number. To do so, you must type two percent signs (`%%`) after the format field, as shown in the example.

You will use the `printf` function in the bonus.cgi script to format the numbers displayed on the dynamic Web page.

USING THE `printf` FUNCTION IN THE BONUS CALCULATOR SCRIPT

Although the bonus.cgi script is working correctly, the Web page it creates would look more professional if the bonus and sales amounts included two decimal places, like this: $106.50 and $3550.00. The appearance of the bonus rate also could be improved by displaying the amount as a percentage rather than as a decimal number—in other words, displaying 3.0% rather than .03.

To include the `printf` function in the bonus.cgi script

1. Return to the bonus.cgi document in your text editor.

2. Modify the three statements that display the bonus, sales, and bonus rate amounts, as shown in Figure 3-25. Be sure to change the word `print` to `printf` in each of the three statements.

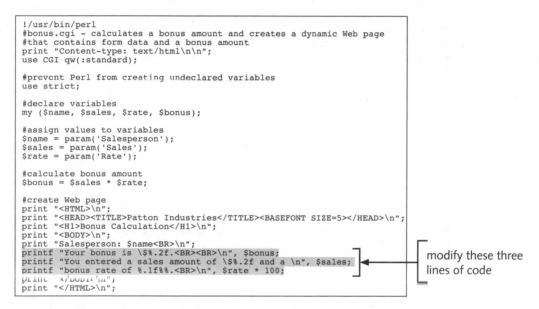

```
!/usr/bin/perl
#bonus.cgi - calculates a bonus amount and creates a dynamic Web page
#that contains form data and a bonus amount
print "Content-type: text/html\n\n";
use CGI qw(:standard);

#prevent Perl from creating undeclared variables
use strict;

#declare variables
my ($name, $sales, $rate, $bonus);

#assign values to variables
$name = param('Salesperson');
$sales = param('Sales');
$rate = param('Rate');

#calculate bonus amount
$bonus = $sales * $rate;

#create Web page
print "<HTML>\n";
print "<HEAD><TITLE>Patton Industries</TITLE><BASEFONT SIZE=5></HEAD>\n";
print "<H1>Bonus Calculation</H1>\n";
print "<BODY>\n";
print "Salesperson: $name<BR>\n";
printf "Your bonus is \$%.2f.<BR><BR>\n", $bonus;
printf "You entered a sales amount of \$%.2f and a \n", $sales;
printf "bonus rate of %.1f%%.<BR>\n", $rate * 100;
print "</BODY>\n";
print "</HTML>\n";
```

modify these three lines of code

Figure 3-25   `printf` statements shown in the bonus.cgi script

3. Save the bonus.cgi document.

4. Return to your browser, which you minimized in an earlier set of steps. The Bonus Calculator form should show Jeff Stein as the salesperson name, 3550 as the sales amount, and .03 as the bonus rate.

5. Click the **Submit** button. If necessary, click the **Continue Submission** button. The script displays the formatted numbers on a Web page, as shown in Figure 3-26.

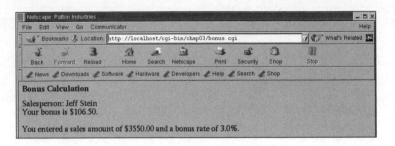

Figure 3-26   Dynamic Web page showing the formatted numbers

6. Close your browser and any open windows.

CHAPTER SUMMARY

❐ When you click the submit button, the browser sends the form data to the server. If the form is associated with a CGI script, the server forwards the form data to the script for processing. When a CGI script has finished processing, it sends its output—typically HTML—to the server, which transfers the output to the browser.

❐ Planning a CGI script involves determining the script's input, output, and algorithm.

❐ A variable is a location (within the computer's internal memory) where a script can temporarily store data. Every variable has a data type and a name.

❐ Perl provides three basic data types for variables: scalar, array, and hash. A scalar variable can store precisely one value—typically a number or a string. Array and hash variables store lists or sets of values.

❐ The name of a scalar variable must begin with a dollar sign ($) followed by a letter and then, optionally, one or more letters, numbers, or underscores. Variable names in Perl are case sensitive.

❐ The statement **use strict;** prevents Perl from creating variables "on the fly" and forces you to declare each variable in the script.

❐ You explicitly declare one or more variables using a statement that follows the syntax **my (***variablelist***);**, where *variablelist* is a comma-separated list of variable names.

❐ The syntax of an assignment statement, which you can use to assign a value to or change the value stored in an existing variable is *variable = value;*, where *variable* is the variable's name and *value* is the number or string you want stored in the variable.

❐ When the name of a variable appears within double quotation marks in a statement, Perl replaces the variable's name with the variable's contents—a process referred to as interpolation.

❐ Single quotation marks around a string indicate that no interpolation should be performed in the string.

❐ You can use the parsing routine contained in the CGI.pm module to parse the data submitted to a script using an online form.

3

❏ You can use the `printf` function to format data displayed on a Web page. The syntax of the `printf` function is **printf** *formatstring,* *list;*, where *list* is a comma-separated list of items whose values you want to format, and *formatstring* is a string that controls the appearance of each item in the *list. Formatstring* can contain text and one or more format fields.

❏ A format field in a `printf` function's *formatstring* is composed of five parts: %, modifier, minimum field width, precision, and format type. Only the % and format type parts are required.

REVIEW QUESTIONS

1. A(n) _____ variable can store precisely one value—typically a number or a string.

   a. array

   b. hash

   c. scalar

   d. singular

2. Names of scalar variables begin with _____.

   a. @

   b. *

   c. &

   d. None of the above.

3. The variable names `$state` and `$State` refer to the same location in the computer's internal memory.

   a. true

   b. false

4. Which of the following statements creates a scalar variable named `$height`?

   a. `my ($height As Scalar);`

   b. `my (Scalar &height);`

   c. `my ($height as scalar);`

   d. None of the above.

5. When the name of a variable appears within double quotation marks in a statement, Perl uses a process referred to as _____ to replace the variable's name with the variable's contents.

   a. interpolation

   b. replacement

   c. substitution

   d. None of the above.

6. Which of the following statements prevents Perl from creating variables "on the fly"?

   a. `declare vars;`

   b. `explicit declare;`

   c. `use explicit;`

   d. `use strict;`

7. Which of the following statements assigns the name "Jack" to the `$employee` variable?

   a. `$employee = Jack;`

   b. `$employee = 'Jack';`

   c. `$employee = "Jack";`

   d. both b and c

8. Which of the following statements assigns the message "Your name is Sue" to the `$msg` variable? (The `$name` variable contains the name "Sue".)

   a. `$msg = Your name is $name;`

   b. `$msg = 'Your name is $name';`

   c. `$msg = "Your name is $name";`

   d. both b and c

9. Which of the following statements displays the message "The total due is $78.50" on a Web page? (Assume that the `$total` variable contains the number 78.5.)

   a. `print "The total due is \$$total\n";`

   b. `printf "The total due is \$%.2f\n, $total";`

   c. `printf "The total due is \$%.2f\n", $total;`

   d. `printf "The total due is \$total\n", %.2f;`

10. Which of the following statements displays the message "Age: 35" on a Web page? (Assume that the `$age` variable contains the number 35.)

    a. `print "Age: $age\n";`

    b. `printf "Age: %d\n", $age;`

    c. `printf "Age: %d, $age\n";`

    d. both a and b

11. What are the three basic data types for Perl variables?

12. Write a variable declaration statement that declares four variables named `$employee`, `$age`, `$payrate`, and `$name`.

13. Write an assignment statement that assigns the number 5.5 to the `$payrate` variable.

14. Write an assignment statement that multiplies the contents of the `$payrate` variable by 2, and then assigns the result to the `$payrate` variable.

15. Write an assignment statement that assigns the contents of the `$employee` variable to the `$name` variable.

16. Write an assignment statement that assigns the message "The employee of the month is " followed by the contents of the `$employee` variable to the `$name` variable.

17. Write an assignment statement that assigns the message "The name is stored in " followed by the variable name `$employee` to the `$name` variable.

18. Assume that a text box included on a form is named Hours. Write an assignment statement that stores the text box value in a scalar variable named `$hours`. (You can assume that the script uses the CGI.pm module to parse the form data.)

19. Write a statement that displays the message "Your gross pay is $650.00." on a Web page. The gross pay amount (650) is stored in the `$gross` variable.

20. Modify the statement that you created in Question 19 so that it displays the message "Your gross pay is $650.00 and your net pay is $615.30." The net pay amount (615.3) is stored in the `$net` variable.

HANDS-ON PROJECTS

Project 1

In this project, you modify the message displayed by the bonus.cgi script created in the chapter.

a. Open the bonus.cgi file in a text editor. The file is contained in the cgi-bin/chap03 directory.

b. Change the filename in the second line from bonus.cgi to c03ex1.cgi.

c. Save the file as c03ex1.cgi.

d. Modify the script to output a Web page similar to the one shown in Figure 3-27.

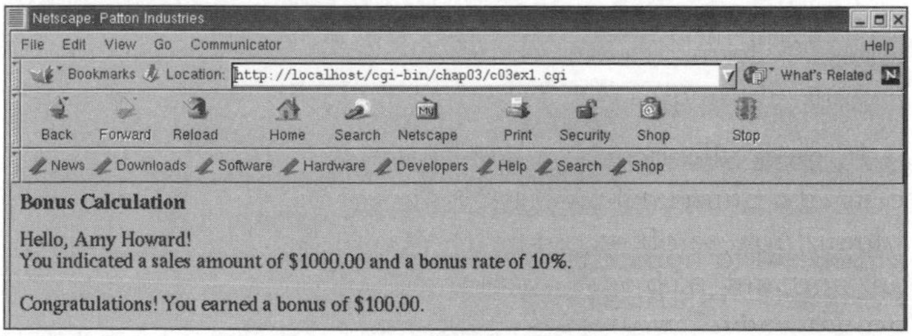

Figure 3-27

e. Save the c03ex1.cgi document.

f. *If you are using a UNIX system*, change the c03ex1.cgi file permissions to 755.

g. Test the script from the command line.

h. Open the bonus.html file in a text editor. The file is contained in the public_html/chap03 directory.

i. Change the filename in the first line from bonus.html to c03ex1.html.

j. Modify the FORM tag to refer to the c03ex1.cgi file, then save the document as c03ex1.html.

k. Open the c03ex1.html file in your Web browser. Enter Amy Howard as the salesperson name, 1000 as the sales amount, and .1 as the bonus rate, then click the Submit button. If necessary, click the Continue Submission button. The browser should display a Web page similar to the one shown in Figure 3-27.

Project 2

In this project, you create a script that processes the data (name, hours, and rate) submitted using an online form. The script calculates the gross pay amount and displays the form data and the gross pay amount on a dynamic Web page.

a. Open the aero.html file in a text editor. The file is contained in the public_html/chap03 directory.

b. Change the filename in the first line from aero.html to c03ex2.html. Save the file as c03ex2.html.

c. The form data will be processed by the c03ex2.cgi script, which you will save in the cgi-bin/chap03 directory. Include the appropriate ACTION and METHOD properties in the <FORM> tag. Use the POST method.

d. Save the c03ex2.html document.

e. Open the aero.cgi file in a text editor. The file is contained in the cgi-bin/chap03 directory. Change the filename in the second line from aero.cgi to c03ex2.cgi. If necessary, change the shebang line to reflect the location of the Perl interpreter on your system.

f. Save the file as c03ex2.cgi.

g. The script should output a Web page similar to the one shown in Figure 3-28. Complete the script appropriately. (You do not have to worry about calculating overtime pay, because all hours worked are paid at the regular pay rate.)

Netscape: AeroDynamics

File Edit View Go Communicator   Help

Bookmarks   Location: http://localhost/cgi-bin/chap03/c03ex2.cgi   What's Related

Back Forward Reload   Home   Search Netscape   Print Security Shop   Stop

News   Downloads   Software   Hardware   Developers   Help   Search   Shop

Gross Pay Calculation

Employee: Jose Gutierez
Hours: 05
Rate: $10.50

Gross pay: $ 52.50

Figure 3-28

h. Save the c03ex2.cgi document.

i. *If you are using a UNIX system*, change the c03ex2.cgi file permissions to 755.

j. Test the script from the command line.

k. Open the c03ex2.html file in your Web browser. Enter Jose Gutierez as the employee name, 5 as the hours, and 10.5 as the pay rate, then click the Submit button. If necessary, click the Continue Submission button. The browser should display a Web page similar to the one shown in Figure 3-28.

Project 3

In this project, you create a script that processes the data (length and width) submitted using an online form. The script calculates the area of a rectangle and displays the form data and the area on a dynamic Web page.

a. Use a text editor to create a Web page similar to the one shown in Figure 3-29. Save the file as c03ex3.html in the public_html/chap03 directory.

Figure 3-29

b. The form data will be processed by the c03ex3.cgi script, which you will save in the cgi-bin/chap03 directory. Include the appropriate ACTION and METHOD properties in the <FORM> tag in the c03ex3.html file. Use the GET method.

c. Save the c03ex3.html document.

d. Use a text editor to create a script that processes the data submitted by the c03ex3.html form, and then displays a Web page similar to the one shown in Figure 3-30 (on the next page). (*Hint*: Display the data using a table. Align the numbers using the <TD> tag's **ALIGN** property.) Name the file c03ex3.cgi and save it in the cgi-bin/chap03 directory.

e. *If you are using a UNIX system*, change the c03ex3.cgi file permissions to 755.

f. Test the script from the command line.

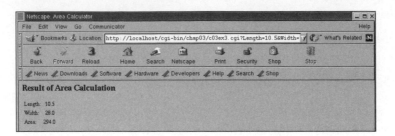

Figure 3-30

   g. Open the c03ex3.html file in your Web browser. Enter 10.5 as the length and 28 as the width. Click the Calculate button. The browser should display a Web page similar to the one shown in Figure 3-30.

Project 4

In this project, you create a script that processes the data (original price and discount rate) submitted using an online form. The script calculates a discount amount and a sale price, and then displays the form data, the discount amount, and the sale price on a dynamic Web page.

   a. Use a text editor to create a Web page similar to the one shown in Figure 3-31. Save the file as c03ex4.html in the public_html/chap03 directory.

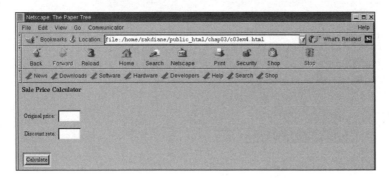

Figure 3-31

   b. The form data will be processed by the c03ex4.cgi script, which you will save in the cgi-bin/chap03 directory. Include the appropriate ACTION and METHOD properties in the <FORM> tag in the c03ex4.html file. Use the POST method.

   c. Save the c03ex4.html document.

   d. Use a text editor to create a script that processes the data submitted by the c03ex4.html form, and then displays a Web page similar to the one shown in Figure 3-32. (*Hint*: Display the data using a table. Align the numbers using the <TD> tag's **ALIGN** property.) Name the file c03ex4.cgi and save it in the cgi-in/chap03 directory.

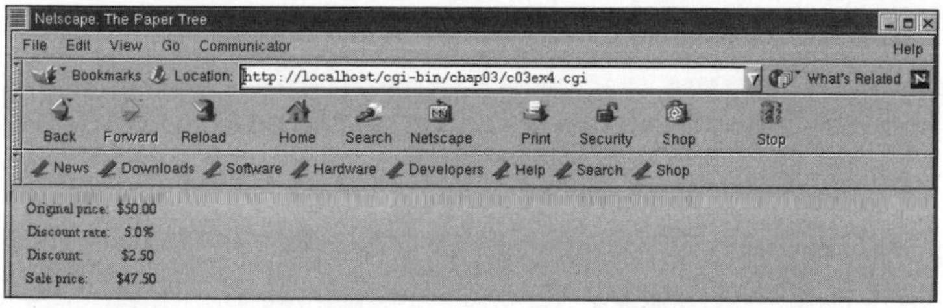

Figure 3-32

e. *If you are using a UNIX system*, change the c03ex4.cgi file permissions to 755.

f. Test the script from the command line using 50 as the original price and .05 as the discount rate.

g. Open the c03ex4.html file in your Web browser. Enter 50 as the original price and .05 as the discount rate. Click the Calculate button. If necessary, click the Continue Submission button. The browser should display a Web page similar to the one shown in Figure 3-32.

h. Press the browser's Back button to return to the Sale Price Calculator form.

i. Enter 50.50 as the original price and .05 as the discount rate. Click the Calculate button. If necessary, click the Continue Submission button. The browser displays a Web page that shows the correct discount amount ($2.53), but an incorrect sale price ($47.98); the sale price should be $47.97. The error occurs because 50.50 multiplied by .05 gives a discount amount of 2.5250, and 50.50 minus 2.5250 results in a sale price of 47.9750. The %.2f format fields in the printf statements that display the discount amount and sale price round the 2.5250 and 47.9750 to two decimal places, giving 2.53 and 47.98. You can use the Perl sprintf function to fix this problem. The syntax of the sprintf function is similar to the syntax of the printf function; it is *variable* = **sprintf** *formatstring, list*;, where *formatstring* and *list* have the same meaning as in the printf function. The difference between the two functions is that the printf function sends the formatted data to a Web page, whereas the sprintf function sends the formatted data to a variable. You will use the sprintf function to round the discount amount to two decimal places before subtracting the amount from the original price.

j. Return to the c03ex4.cgi document in your text editor. Modify the statement that calculates the discount amount as follows: *discount* = sprintf "%.2f", *originalprice* * *discountrate*;, where *discount*, *originalprice*, and *discountrate* are the names of the variables used in your script.

k. Save the c03ex4.cgi script.

l. Return to the Sale Price Calculator form in your browser. Click the Calculate button to calculate the discount amount and sale price based on an original price of 50.50 and a discount rate of .05. If necessary, click the Continue Submission button. The Web page shows $2.53 as the discount amount and $47.97 as the sale price.

Project 5

In this project, you create a script that processes the data (name and number of hours worked during the month) submitted using an online form. The script calculates the number of weeks, days, and hours worked during the month. It then displays the form data and the results of the calculations.

a. Use a text editor to create a Web page for Temp Employers. The Web page should allow the user to enter his or her name and the number of hours he or she worked during the month. Save the file as c03ex5.html in the public_html/chap03 directory.

b. The form data will be processed by the c03ex5.cgi script, which you will save in the cgi-bin/chap03 directory. Include the appropriate ACTION and METHOD properties in the <FORM> tag in the c03ex5.html file. Use the POST method.

c. Save the c03ex5.html document.

d. Use a text editor to create a script that processes the data submitted by the c03ex5.html form. The script should calculate the number of weeks (assume a 40-hour week), days (assume an eight-hour day), and hours worked. For example, if you work 70 hours during the month, then you have worked one week, three days, and six hours. The script should display a Web page that contains the form data and the results of the calculations. (*Hint*: Consider using the modulus arithmetic operator from Figure 3-8.)

e. Name the file c03ex5.cgi and save it in the cgi-bin/chap03 directory.

f. *If you are using a UNIX system*, change the c03ex5.cgi file permissions to 755.

g. Test the script from the command line.

h. Open the c03ex5.html file in your Web browser. Test the script using Jacob Miller as the name and 70 as the number of hours worked during the month. The browser should display the form data and the results of the calculations made by the script.

Project 6

In this project, you create a script that processes the data (item name, number of units in inventory, and number of units that can be packed in a box for shipping) submitted using an online form. The script calculates the number of full boxes that can be packed from the quantity on hand, and the quantity of items left over. It then displays the form data and the results of the calculations on a Web page.

a. Use a text editor to create a Web page for Colfax Industries. The Web page should allow the user to enter the item name, the quantity of the item in inventory, and how many units of the item can be packed in a box for shipping. Save the file as c03ex6.html in the public_html/chap03 directory.

b. The form data will be processed by the c03ex6.cgi script, which you will save in the cgi-bin/chap03 directory. Include the appropriate ACTION and METHOD properties in the <FORM> tag in the c03ex6.html file. Use the POST method.

3

c. Save the c03ex6.html document.

d. Use a text editor to create a script that processes the data submitted by the c03ex6.html form. The script should calculate the number of full boxes that can be packed from the quantity on hand, and the quantity of items left over in inventory. The script should display a Web page that contains the form data and the results of the calculations.

e. Name the file c03ex6.cgi and save it in the cgi-bin/chap03 directory.

f. *If you are using a UNIX system*, change the c03ex6.cgi file permissions to 755.

g. Test the script from the command line.

h. Open the c03ex6.html file in your Web browser. Test the script using Comb as the item name, 78 as the quantity in inventory, and 5 as the number of items that can be packed in a box. The browser should display the form data and the results of the calculations made by the script.

CASE PROJECTS

1. Create an HTML form and a script for Lake College. Name the form c03case1.html and save it in the public_html/chap03 directory. Name the script c03case1.cgi and save it in the cgi-bin/chap03 directory. The form should display a Web page that allows the user to enter a student's name and the number of hours the student is enrolled for the semester. The script should calculate the total due by multiplying the number of hours enrolled by $100 and then adding the room and board fee ($1800) to the result. The script then should display the form data and the total due on a Web page.

2. Create an HTML form and a script for The Paper Tree wallpaper store. Name the form c03case2.html and save it in the public_html/chap03 directory. Name the script c03case2.cgi and save it in the cgi-bin/chap03 directory. The form should display a Web page that allows the user to enter the length, width, and height dimensions of a room; each dimension should be entered in feet. The Web page also should allow the user to enter the number of square feet a single roll of wallpaper will cover. The script should calculate the required number of single rolls of wallpaper the customer will need to purchase to cover the room. The script should display the form data and the required number of single rolls of wallpaper on a Web page. Display the length, width, height, and coverage values with one decimal place. Display the required number of single rolls as a whole number. For example, if you enter 10 as the length, 12 as the width, 8 as the height, and 30 as the coverage, the script should display the numbers 10.0, 12.0, 8.0, and 30.0. It also should display the number 12 as the required number of single rolls of wallpaper.

4

ARRAY AND HASH VARIABLES

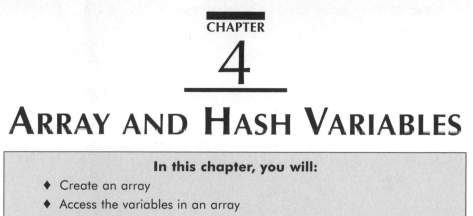

In this chapter, you will:

♦ Create an array
♦ Access the variables in an array
♦ Create a hash
♦ Access the variables in a hash
♦ Learn how to code the repetition structure using the `foreach` and `for` statements

As you learned in Chapter 3, Perl has three data types for its variables: scalar, array, and hash. Recall that a scalar variable can store precisely one value—typically a number or a string. Array and hash variables, on the other hand, store lists or sets of values. You learned how to create and manipulate scalar variables in Chapter 3. In this chapter, you learn how to create and manipulate array and hash variables. You also learn how to use the Perl `foreach` and `for` statements to code the repetition structure.

THE PRODUCT REGISTRATION FORM AND ACKNOWLEDGMENT

Juniper Printers sells three different models of printers; the models are named Laser JX, Laser PL, and ColorPrint XL. Before a customer can take advantage of the technical support provided by the company, the customer must register the printer that he or she purchased. Registration can be accomplished by completing and returning a Product Registration card that is packaged with every printer. Alternatively, the customer can use the online product registration form located on the company's Web site. Figure 4-1 shows a sample of a completed online registration form.

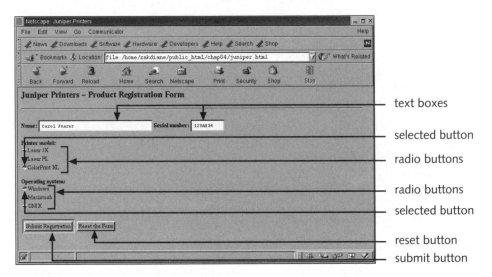

Figure 4-1 Completed online registration form for Juniper Printers

 Most online registration forms require the customer to enter his or her address, phone number, and so on. The additional information is omitted from the Juniper Printers registration form to keep the form simple.

The registration form shown in Figure 4-1 contains two text boxes. The first text box allows the customer to enter his or her name, and the second text box allows him or her to enter the printer's serial number. The form also contains two sets of three radio buttons: the first set is used to select the printer model, and the second set to select the computer's operating system. The form also contains a submit button and a reset button. Now view the HTML code used to create the registration form.

To view the HTML code used to create the Juniper Printers registration form:

1. Open the juniper.html file in a text editor. The file is contained in the public_html/chap04 directory. Figure 4-2 shows the contents of the file.

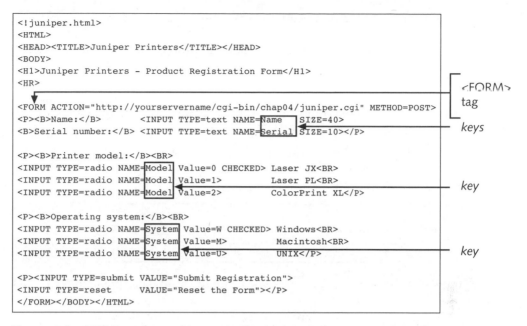

```
<!juniper.html>
<HTML>
<HEAD><TITLE>Juniper Printers</TITLE></HEAD>
<BODY>
<H1>Juniper Printers - Product Registration Form</H1>
<HR>

<FORM ACTION="http://yourservername/cgi-bin/chap04/juniper.cgi" METHOD=POST>
<P><B>Name:</B>          <INPUT TYPE=text NAME=Name  SIZE=40>
<B>Serial number:</B> <INPUT TYPE=text NAME=Serial SIZE=10></P>

<P><B>Printer model:</B><BR>
<INPUT TYPE=radio NAME=Model Value=0 CHECKED> Laser JX<BR>
<INPUT TYPE=radio NAME=Model Value=1>         Laser PL<BR>
<INPUT TYPE=radio NAME=Model Value=2>         ColorPrint XL</P>

<P><B>Operating system:</B><BR>
<INPUT TYPE=radio NAME=System Value=W CHECKED> Windows<BR>
<INPUT TYPE=radio NAME=System Value=M>         Macintosh<BR>
<INPUT TYPE=radio NAME=System Value=U>         UNIX</P>

<P><INPUT TYPE=submit VALUE="Submit Registration">
<INPUT TYPE=reset      VALUE="Reset the Form"></P>
</FORM></BODY></HTML>
```

Figure 4-2 HTML code used to create the Juniper Printers registration form

2. Change yourservername in the ACTION property of the <FORM> tag to the name of your server, then save the juniper.html file.

The <FORM> tag's ACTION property indicates that the juniper.cgi script will process the form data. The tag's METHOD property directs the browser to use the POST method when sending the form data to the server. The form data in this case is the customer name, printer serial number and model, and computer operating system.

Recall that each item of data sent to a server has both a *key* and a *value*. The *keys* associated with form data are the names of the form elements whose *values* will be passed to the server. For example, Name and Serial are the *keys* (names) for the two text boxes on the Juniper Printers registration form. The browser will pass the Name and Serial *keys*, along with the text entered in the text boxes, to the server.

As Figure 4-2 indicates, Model is the *key* (name) associated with the first set of radio buttons on the registration form. Notice that the same *key* is used for each of the three radio buttons in the set. The browser will pass the Model *key* along with the *value* assigned to the VALUE property of the selected radio button. For example, if the Laser JX radio button is selected, the browser passes the *value* 0. However, if the Laser PL radio button is selected, the browser passes the *value* 1. The *value* 2 is passed if the ColorPrint XL radio button is selected.

Figure 4-2 also indicates that System is the *key* (name) associated with the second set of radio buttons on the registration form. Here again, the same *key* is used for each of the three radio buttons in the set. The browser will pass the System *key* along with the *value* assigned to the VALUE property of the selected radio button. In this case, if the customer selects the Windows radio button, the *value* W is passed to the server. If the customer selects the Macintosh radio button, the *value* M is passed. The *value* U is passed if the customer selects the UNIX radio button.

Figure 4-3 shows how the form data entered in Figure 4-1 will be sent to the server when the user clicks the Submit Registration button.

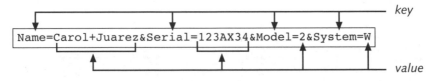

Figure 4-3   *Keys* and *values* associated with the form data shown in Figure 4-1

Notice that the Name and Serial *key*s are sent along with the contents of their respective text boxes. Also sent are the Model *key* and the *value* assigned to the ColorPrint XL radio button (2), which is selected in Figure 4-1. Additionally, the System *key* and the *value* assigned to the Windows radio button (W), which also is selected in Figure 4-1, is sent.

3. Close the juniper.html file.

When a customer clicks the Submit Registration button on the Juniper Printers registration form, a dynamic Web page similar to the one shown in Figure 4-4 should appear on the screen. Notice that the Web page acknowledges the receipt of the form and contains the customer's name, the printer's serial number and model name, and the name of the customer's operating system.

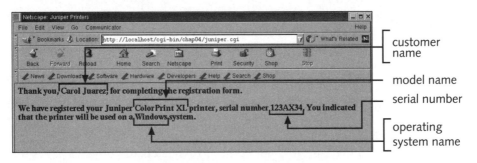

Figure 4-4   Dynamic Web page acknowledgment

Now that you know what information will be passed to the server and what information to include on the Web page acknowledgment, you can complete the juniper.cgi script, which will process the form data.

PLANNING AND CODING THE JUNIPER PRINTERS SCRIPT

As you learned in Chapter 3, CGI scripts that perform more than one task, or those that contain more than a few lines of code, should be planned before they are created. When planning a script, you first determine the script's input and output. You then list the steps the script must follow to transform the input into the output. Recall that the list of steps is referred to as an algorithm. Figure 4-5 shows the input, output, and algorithm for the Juniper Printers script.

Input	Output
customer name printer serial number printer model number (0, 1, or 2) operating system letter (W, M, or U)	Web page containing the customer name, printer serial number, printer model name, and operating system name
Algorithm	
1. assign input items to variables 2. create a dynamic Web page that displays the customer name, printer serial number, printer model name, and operating system name	

Figure 4-5   Input, output, and algorithm for the Juniper Printers script

Important note: In most cases, the information entered on a registration form is saved in a file. You learn how to save information to a file in Chapter 5.

As Figure 4-5 indicates, the script's input is the data submitted using the registration form: customer name, printer serial number, printer model number (0, 1, or 2), and operating system letter (W, M, or U). Only two of the four input items—the customer name and printer serial number—appear in the script's output. The remaining two input items—printer model number and operating system letter—do not appear in the output; rather, the output includes the printer model name and operating system name. You learn how to convert the model number and system letter into the model name and system name later in the chapter. First, you complete a script that assigns the four input items to variables and then displays the items on a dynamic Web page.

To begin completing the juniper.cgi script:

1. Open the juniper.cgi file in a text editor. The file is contained in the cgi-bin/chap04 directory.

2. If necessary, change the shebang line to reflect the location of the Perl interpreter on your system.

3. If necessary, add the **-debug** pragma to the use CGI qw(:standard); statement.

   First, declare the necessary variables. The Juniper Printers script will use four scalar variables to store the four input items.

4. In the blank line below the comment #declare variables, type **my ($name, $serial, $modnum, $sysletter);** and press **Enter**.

The first step in the algorithm shown in Figure 4-5 is to assign the input items to variables.

5. In the blank line below the comment #assign input items to variables, type the following four assignment statements:

$name = param('Name');
$serial = param('Serial');
$modnum = param('Model');
$sysletter = param('System');

Now enter the code to display the four input items on a dynamic Web page.

6. Enter the six lines of code shaded in Figure 4-6.

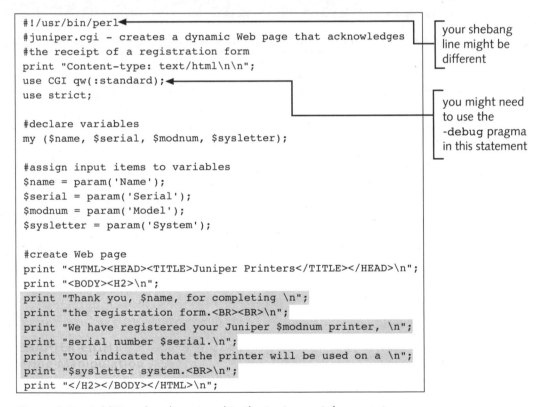

```
#!/usr/bin/perl                                              your shebang
#juniper.cgi - creates a dynamic Web page that acknowledges  line might be
#the receipt of a registration form                          different
print "Content-type: text/html\n\n";
use CGI qw(:standard);                                       you might need
use strict;                                                  to use the
                                                             -debug pragma
#declare variables                                           in this statement
my ($name, $serial, $modnum, $sysletter);

#assign input items to variables
$name = param('Name');
$serial = param('Serial');
$modnum = param('Model');
$sysletter = param('System');

#create Web page
print "<HTML><HEAD><TITLE>Juniper Printers</TITLE></HEAD>\n";
print "<BODY><H2>\n";
print "Thank you, $name, for completing \n";
print "the registration form.<BR><BR>\n";
print "We have registered your Juniper $modnum printer, \n";
print "serial number $serial.\n";
print "You indicated that the printer will be used on a \n";
print "$sysletter system.<BR>\n";
print "</H2></BODY></HTML>\n";
```

Figure 4-6 Additional code entered in the juniper.cgi document

7. Save the juniper.cgi document.

Now test the juniper.cgi script to make sure that it is working correctly.

To test the juniper.cgi script:

1. *If you are using a UNIX system*, open a terminal window, if necessary. Make the cgi-bin/chap04 directory the current directory, and then change the juniper.cgi file permissions to **755**.

    If you are using a Windows system, open a Command Prompt window, and then make the cgi-bin\chap04 directory the current directory.

2. Type **perl –c juniper.cgi** and press **Enter** to check the script for syntax errors. If necessary, correct any syntax errors in the script before continuing to the next step.

3. Type **perl –w juniper.cgi** and press **Enter** to execute the script. When the offline mode message appears, type **Name=Carol+Juarez** and press **Enter**, then type **Serial=123AX34** and press **Enter**. Type **Model=2** and press **Enter**, then type **System=W** and press **Enter**.

4. *If you are using a UNIX system*, press **Ctrl+d** to indicate that you are finished entering the input data. See Figure 4-7.

    If you are using a Windows system, press **Ctrl+z** and then press **Enter** to indicate that you are finished entering the input data. See Figure 4-7.

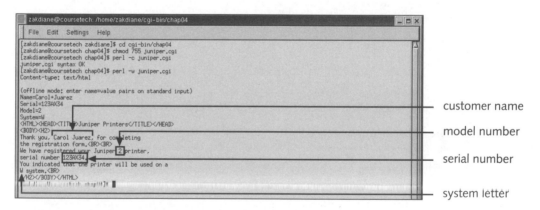

Figure 4-7   Result of using the -c and -w switches

Before you can replace the model number and system letter in the dynamic Web page with the model name and system name, respectively, you need to learn about array and hash variables in Perl. First, learn about array variables.

ARRAY VARIABLES

An **array variable**, more commonly called an **array**, is simply a group of related scalar variables, each one having the same name. You distinguish one scalar variable in an array from another scalar variable in the same array by a unique number, referred to as an **index**. The computer assigns the index to each of the scalar variables when it creates the array in memory. The first scalar variable in an array is assigned an index of 0, the next scalar variable in the array is assigned an index of 1, and so on.

An index also is referred to as a subscript.

Typically, you declare (or create) an array using a statement that follows the syntax **my** *arrayname* = (*list*);. In the syntax, *arrayname* is the name of the array; the name must begin with an at sign (@) followed by a letter and then, optionally, one or more letters, numbers, or underscores. *List* is a comma-separated list of values that will be stored in the array. Figure 4-8 shows two statements that declare an array.

```
my @sales = (25000, 35000, 10000);

my @cities = ("Boston", "Chicago", "Detroit", "San Diego");
```

Figure 4-8   Statements that declare an array

The at sign (@) indicates the variable's data type: array. An easy way to remember that array names begin with an at sign is to associate the @ with the letter "a" in the word "array".

The first statement shown in Figure 4-8 declares an array named `@sales` that contains three scalar variables. The statement stores the number 25000 in the first scalar variable in the array, 35000 in the second scalar variable, and 10000 in the third scalar variable, as shown in Figure 4-9.

Array name: `@sales`

Scalar variable names:

        `$sales[0]` —— 25000
        `$sales[1]` —— 35000
        `$sales[2]` —— 10000

Figure 4-9   Illustration of the `@sales` array in memory

As Figure 4-9 indicates, you use the array name to refer to a scalar variable contained in an array, but you replace the @ in the name with a $, and you follow the name with the scalar variable's index enclosed in square brackets ([ ]). For example, `$sales[0]` refers to the first scalar variable contained in the `@sales` array, `$sales[1]` refers to the second scalar variable, and `$sales[2]` refers to the third scalar variable.

Recall that the $ at the beginning of a variable's name indicates that the variable is a scalar variable.

A scalar variable that belongs to an array can be used in the same manner as any scalar variable. For example, to print the contents of the first scalar variable in the @sales array, you use the statement print "$sales[0]";. To calculate a 5% bonus on the sales amount stored in the $sales[1] variable, you use the assignment statement $bonus = $sales[1] * .05;.

The second statement shown earlier in Figure 4-8, my @cities = ("Boston", "Chicago", "Detroit", "San Diego");, declares an array named @cities that contains four scalar variables. The scalar variables are named $cities[0], $cities[1], $cities[2], and $cities[3]. The statement assigns the string "Boston" to the $cities[0] variable, the string "Chicago" to the $cities[1] variable, and so on.

You will use an array to store the printer model names in the juniper.cgi script.

Using an Array in the Juniper Printers Script

Recall that when the customer clicks the Submit Registration button on the Juniper Printers registration form, the browser sends, among other things, the printer model number to the server. The model number—either 0, 1, or 2—indicates which radio button was selected in the Printer model section of the form. In other words, it indicates which printer model—either Laser JX, Laser PL, or ColorPrint XL—the customer purchased. Notice that the number 0 is associated with the Laser JX model, the number 1 with the Laser PL model, and the number 2 with the ColorPrint XL model. To convert the model number to the model name, you first will store the model names in an array named @models, as shown in Figure 4-10.

```
$models[0] ———— Laser JX
$models[1] ———— Laser PL
$models[2] ———— ColorPrint XL
```

Figure 4-10   @models array

You then will use the model number, which is passed to the server, to select the appropriate name from the array; in other words, you will use the model number as the index. Recall that the model number is stored in the $modnum variable in the juniper.cgi script. If the $modnum variable contains the number 0, then $models[$modnum] refers to the first model name in the @models array: Laser JX. If the $modnum variable contains the number 1, then $models[$modnum] refers to the second model name in the @models array: Laser PL. Finally, if the $modnum variable contains the number 2, then $models[$modnum] refers to the third model name in the @models array: ColorPrint XL.

To use an array to convert the model number to the model name, and then test the script:

1. Return to the juniper.cgi document in your text editor. In the blank line below the statement my ($name, $serial, $modnum, $sysletter);, type my @models = ("Laser JX", "Laser PL", "ColorPrint XL"); and press Enter.

   Next, modify the statement that displays the model number so that it now displays the model name. Recall that the appropriate model name to display is stored in the $models[$modnum] variable.

2. Modify the print statement shaded in Figure 4-11.

```
#!/usr/bin/perl
#juniper.cgi - creates a dynamic Web page that acknowledges
#the receipt of a registration form
print "Content-type: text/html\n\n";
use CGI qw(:standard);
use strict;

#declare variables
my ($name, $serial, $modnum, $sysletter);
my @models = ("Laser JX", "Laser PL", "ColorPrint XL");

#assign input items to variables
$name = param('Name');
$serial = param('Serial');
$modnum = param('Model');
$sysletter = param('System');

#create Web page
print "<HTML><HEAD><TITLE>Juniper Printers</TITLE></HEAD>\n";
print "<BODY><H2>\n";
print "Thank you, $name, for completing \n";
print "the registration form.<BR><BR>\n";
print "We have registered your Juniper $models[$modnum] printer, \n";
print "serial number $serial.\n";
print "You indicated that the printer will be used on a \n";
print "$sysletter system.<BR>\n";
print "</H2></BODY></HTML>\n";
```

Figure 4-11   Script showing the modified print statement

3. Save the juniper.cgi document.

   Now test the script.

4. *If you are using a UNIX system*, return to the UNIX command prompt. The cgi-bin/chap04 directory should be the current directory. Type **clear** after the command prompt and press **Enter**.

   If you are using a Windows system, return to the Command Prompt window. The cgi-bin\chap04 directory should be the current directory. Type **cls** after the command prompt and press **Enter**.

5. Type **perl –c juniper.cgi** and press **Enter**. If necessary, correct any syntax errors in the script before continuing to the next step.

6. Type **perl –w juniper.cgi** and press **Enter**. When the offline mode message appears, type **Name=Carol+Juarez** and press **Enter**, then type **Serial=123AX34** and press **Enter**. Type **Model=2** and press **Enter**, then type **System=W** and press **Enter**.

7. Press **Ctrl+d** (UNIX), or press **Ctrl+z** and then press **Enter** (Windows), to indicate that you are finished entering data. The printer model name, rather than the model number passed to the script, appears in the output, as shown in Figure 4-12.

4

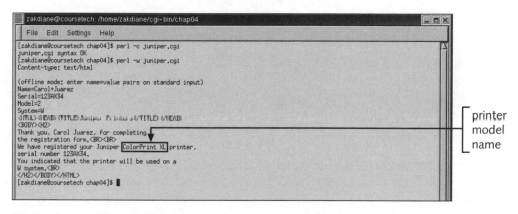

printer model name

Figure 4-12   Output showing the printer model name

Next, you learn about hash variables.

HASH VARIABLES

Similar to an array variable, a **hash variable**, more commonly called a **hash**, is a collection of related scalar variables. However, unlike the scalar variables contained in an array, the scalar variables contained in a hash are distinguished from one another by a *key* (name) rather than by an index (number). The *keys* are assigned to the scalar variables when the hash is created in memory.

A hash also is referred to as an associative array.

You can declare (or create) a hash using a statement that follows the syntax **my** *hashname* = **(***key1*, *value1*, *key2*, *value2*,…*keyn*, *valuen***)**;, where *hashname* is the name of the hash. Hash names must begin with a percent sign (%) followed by a letter and then, optionally, one or more letters, numbers, or underscores. Figure 4-13 shows two statements that create a hash.

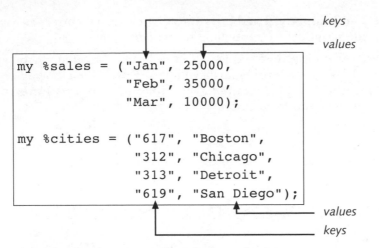

Figure 4-13   Statements that declare a hash

 The percent sign (%) indicates the variable's data type: hash. One way to remember that hash names begin with a percent sign is to associate the two circles on either side of the slash with the *key/value* pairs in a hash. You also can associate the slash (/) that appears in the percent sign with the word *hash*.

 You can enter the statement to declare a hash on the same line in a script. You do not need to enter each *key/value* pair on a separate line, as shown in Figure 14-13. However, doing so helps ensure that the statement contains the same number of *keys* as *values*. It also makes it easier to distinguish the *keys* and their corresponding *values*.

The first statement shown in Figure 4-13 creates a hash named %sales that contains three scalar variables. The statement assigns the *key* "Jan" to one of the scalar variables in the hash, and it stores the *value* 25000 in the variable. The statement assigns the *keys* "Feb" and "Mar" to the remaining two scalar variables in the hash, and it stores the *values* 35000 and 10000, respectively, in the variables. Unlike the scalar variables in an array, the scalar variables in a hash are stored in no particular order in the computer's memory, as illustrated in Figure 4–14.

Hash name: %sales

Scalar variable names:

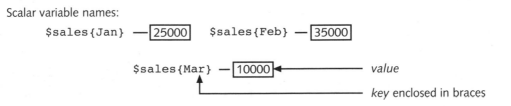

Figure 4-14   Illustration of the %sales hash in memory

As Figure 4-14 indicates, you also use the hash name to refer to a scalar variable contained in a hash, but you replace the % in the name with a $, and you follow the name with the scalar variable's *key* enclosed in braces ({ }). For example, `$sales{Jan}` refers to the scalar variable associated with the Jan *key* in the `%sales` hash, `$sales{Feb}` refers to the scalar variable associated with the Feb *key*, and `$sales{Mar}` refers to the scalar variable associated with the Mar *key*.

 If a *key* contains a space, you will need to enclose the *key* in either single or double quotation marks within the braces. For example, you use either `$state{'New Mexico'}` or `$state{"New Mexico"}` to refer to a scalar variable whose *key* is "New Mexico".

A scalar variable that belongs to a hash can be used in the same manner as any scalar variable. For example, to print the contents of the scalar variable associated with the Jan *key* in the `%sales` hash, you use the statement `print "$sales{Jan}";`. To calculate a 5% bonus on the sales amount stored in the `$sales{Feb}` variable, you use the assignment statement `$bonus = $sales{Feb} * .05;`. Finally, to increase the sales amount stored in the `$sales{Mar}` variable by 10%, you use the assignment statement `$sales{Mar} = $sales{Mar} * 1.1;`.

The second statement shown earlier in Figure 4-13, `my %cities = ("617", "Boston", "312", "Chicago", "313", "Detroit", "619", "San Diego");`, declares a hash named `%cities` that contains four scalar variables. The *key* assigned to each variable is an area code, and the *value* stored in each variable is the name of the city associated with the area code. You can display the name of the city whose area code is 312 using the statement `print "$cities{312}";`. In this case, the statement will display the city name, Chicago.

You will use a hash to store the operating system names in the juniper.cgi script.

Using a Hash in the Juniper Printers Script

Recall that when the customer clicks the Submit Registration button on the Juniper Printers registration form, the browser sends to the server a letter that indicates the radio button selected in the Operating system section of the form. If the Windows radio button is selected, the letter W is passed to the server. If the Macintosh radio button is selected, the letter M is passed. Finally, if the UNIX radio button is selected, the letter U is passed. To convert the operating system letter to the operating system name, you first will store the system names in a hash named `%systems`, as shown in Figure 4-15 (on next page).

You then will use the system letter passed to the server as the *key* to select the appropriate *value* (system name) from the hash. Recall that the system letter is stored in the `$sysletter` variable in the juniper.cgi script. The appropriate system name, therefore, can be found in the `$systems{$sysletter}` variable in the `%systems` hash.

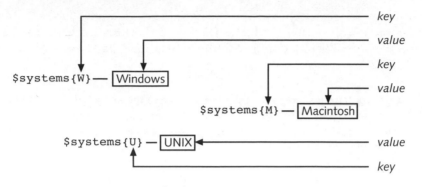

Figure 4-15 `%systems` hash

To use a hash to convert the system letter to the system name, and then test the script:

1. Return to the juniper.cgi document in your text editor. Type the additional statement shaded in Figure 4-16. Also modify the statement that displays the system letter so that it now displays the system name. The modified statement also is shaded in the figure.

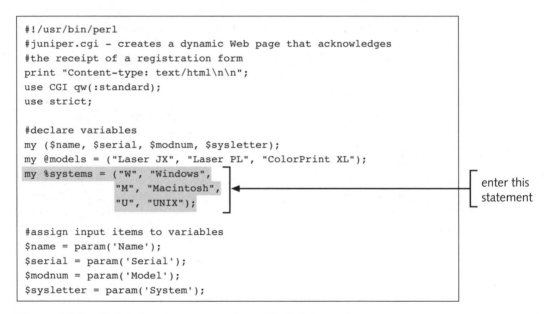

```perl
#!/usr/bin/perl
#juniper.cgi - creates a dynamic Web page that acknowledges
#the receipt of a registration form
print "Content-type: text/html\n\n";
use CGI qw(:standard);
use strict;

#declare variables
my ($name, $serial, $modnum, $sysletter);
my @models = ("Laser JX", "Laser PL", "ColorPrint XL");
my %systems = ("W", "Windows",
               "M", "Macintosh",
               "U", "UNIX");

#assign input items to variables
$name = param('Name');
$serial = param('Serial');
$modnum = param('Model');
$sysletter = param('System');
```

enter this statement

Figure 4-16 Script showing new and modified statements

```
#create Web page
print "<HTML><HEAD><TITLE>Juniper Printers</TITLE></HEAD>\n";
print "<BODY><H2>\n";
print "Thank you, $name, for completing \n";
print "the registration form.<BR><BR>\n";
print "We have registered your Juniper $models[$modnum] printer, \n";
print "serial number $serial.\n";
print "You indicated that the printer will be used on a \n";
print "$systems{$sysletter} system.<BR>\n";
print "</H2></BODY></HTML>\n";
```

modify this statement

Figure 4-16   Script showing new and modified statements (continued)

2. Save the juniper.cgi document.

   Now test the script.

3. *If you are using a UNIX system*, return to the UNIX command prompt. The cgi-bin/chap04 directory should be the current directory. Type **clear** after the command prompt and press **Enter**.

   If you are using a Windows system, return to the Command Prompt window. The cgi-bin\chap04 directory should be the current directory. Type **cls** after the command prompt and press **Enter**.

4. Type **perl –c juniper.cgi** and press **Enter**. If necessary, correct any syntax errors in the script before continuing to the next step.

5. Type **perl –w juniper.cgi** and press **Enter**. When the offline mode message appears, type **Name=Jason+Wong** and press **Enter**, then type **Serial=34TU78** and press **Enter**. Type **Model=1** and press **Enter**, then type **System=U** and press **Enter**.

6. Press **Ctrl+d** (UNIX), or press **Ctrl+z** and then press **Enter** (Windows), to indicate that you are finished entering data. The operating system name, rather than the system letter passed to the script, appears in the output, as shown in Figure 4-17.

operating system name

Figure 4-17   Output showing operating system name

Now test the script from your browser.

7. Start your Web browser, then use the browser's File menu to open the juniper.html file.

8. Type **Jason Wong** as the customer name and **34TU78** as the serial number. Select the **Laser PL** and **UNIX** radio buttons. Click the **Submit Registration** button. If necessary, click the **Continue Submission** button. A Web page similar to the one shown in Figure 4-18 appears on the screen.

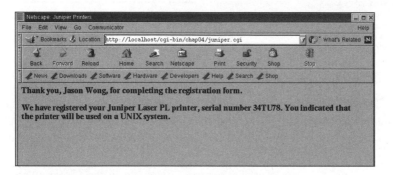

Figure 4-18   Web page acknowledgment

In the remaining sections of this chapter, you modify the Juniper Printers registration form to allow the customer to select more than one operating system. You also modify the Juniper Printers script to accommodate the change made to the form.

MODIFYING THE JUNIPER PRINTERS FORM AND SCRIPT

To allow the customer to select more than one operating system on the registration form, you will change the radio buttons that appear in the Operating system section of the form to check boxes. Unlike radio buttons, where only one button in a group can be selected at any one time, any number of check boxes on a form can be selected at the same time.

To include check boxes on the Juniper Printers registration form:

1. Open the juniper.html file in a text editor. The file is located in the public_html/chap04 directory.

2. Change the filename in the first line from juniper.html to **juniper2.html**.

3. Change the filename in the <FORM> tag's ACTION property from juniper.cgi to **juniper2.cgi**.

4. Change the TYPE property for the three elements in the Operating system section from radio to **checkbox**. The changes you made to the original HTML code are shaded in Figure 4-19.

```
<!juniper2.html>
<HTML>
<HEAD><TITLE>Juniper Printers</TITLE></HEAD>
<BODY>
<H1>Juniper Printers - Product Registration Form</H1>
<HR>

<FORM ACTION="http://yourservername/cgi-bin/chap04/juniper2.cgi" METHOD=POST>
<P><B>Name:</B>          <INPUT TYPE=text NAME=Name   SIZE=40>
<B>Serial number:</B> <INPUT TYPE=text NAME=Serial SIZE=10></P>

<P><B>Printer model:</B><BR>
<INPUT TYPE=radio NAME=Model Value=0 CHECKED> Laser JX<BR>
<INPUT TYPE=radio NAME=Model Value=1>         Laser PL<BR>
<INPUT TYPE=radio NAME=Model Value=2>         ColorPrint XL</P>

<P><B>Operating system:</B><BR>
<INPUT TYPE=checkbox NAME=System Value=W CHECKED> Windows<BR>
<INPUT TYPE=checkbox NAME=System Value=M>         Macintosh<BR>
<INPUT TYPE=checkbox NAME=System Value=U>         UNIX</P>

<P><INPUT TYPE=submit VALUE="Submit Registration">
<INPUT TYPE=reset      VALUE="Reset the Form"></P>
</FORM></BODY></HTML>
```

Figure 4-19   Changes made to the original HTML code

Notice that the three check boxes have the same *key*, System. If the Windows check box is selected when the customer submits the registration form, the System *key* and the *value* W are passed to the server, like this: System=W. However, if both the Windows and UNIX check boxes are selected, System=W&System=U is passed. And if all three check boxes are selected, System=W&System=M&System=U is passed. Notice that more than one *value* for the same *key* might be sent to the server. When more than one *value* is sent, an ampersand (&) separates one *key* and *value* pair from the next. You will need to modify the Juniper Printers script so that it can accept more than one *value* for the System *key*.

5. Save the document as **juniper2.html**, then close the document.

6. Return to your browser, then use the browser's File menu to open the juniper2.html file. A Web page similar to the one shown in Figure 4-20 appears on the screen.

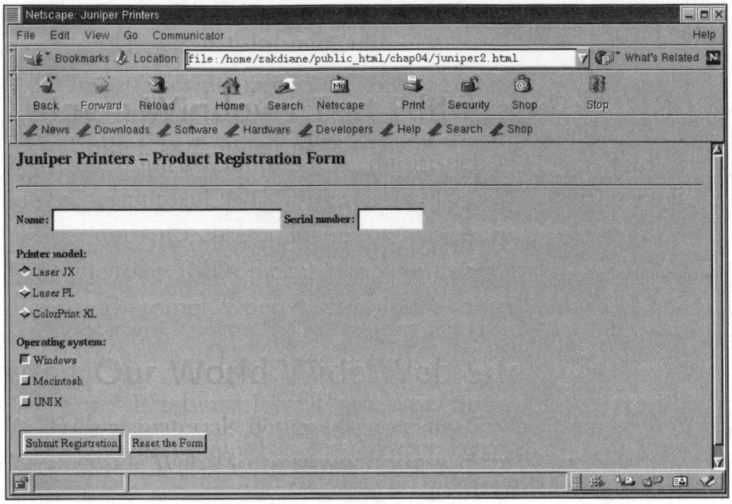

Figure 4-20   Modified registration form

Now you need to modify the Juniper Printers script so that it can store more than one value for the System *key*.

To begin modifying the Juniper Printers script:

1. Open the juniper.cgi script in a text editor. The file is located in the cgi-bin/chap04 directory.

2. Change the filename in the second line from juniper.cgi to **juniper2.cgi**.

3. Save the document as **juniper2.cgi**.

   Currently, the Juniper Printers script uses the statement `$sysletter = param('System');` to store the *value* of the System *key* in a scalar variable. A scalar variable was used because the script expected the System *key* to have only one *value*. Only one *value* was expected because the Operating system section contained radio buttons, and you can select only one operating system radio button at a time. Now that you have changed the radio buttons in the Operating system section to check boxes, it is possible that the `param('System')` function will return more than one value. Therefore, you will need to store the result of the `param('System')` function in an array rather than in a scalar variable.

4. Change `$sysletter` in the statement `my ($name, $serial, $modnum, $sysletter);` to **@sysletter**.

5. Change the statement `$sysletter = param('System');` to **@sysletter = param('System');**.

6. Save the juniper2.cgi document.

Next, you need to modify the HTML code in the script so that it displays the contents of the `@sysletter` array. Before doing so, however, you learn about the `foreach` and `for` statements in Perl.

The foreach and for Statements

All scripts, no matter how simple or how complex, are written using one or more of three basic structures: sequence, selection, and repetition. These structures are called control structures or logic structures, because they control the flow of a script's logic. You used the sequence structure in the scripts you created in previous chapters. Recall that the script instructions were processed, one after another, in the order in which each appeared in the script. You use the selection structure to make a decision or comparison and then, based on the result of that decision or comparison, select one of two paths. You learn about the selection structure in Chapter 6. In this chapter, you learn how to include the repetition structure in a script. You use the **repetition structure**, also called a **loop**, to instruct the computer to repeat a block of instructions either a specified number of times or until some condition is met.

Perl provides several statements that you can use to code a loop: `foreach`, `for`, `while`, and `until`. You learn how to use the `foreach` and `for` statements in this chapter. The `while` and `until` statements are covered in Chapter 7.

Figure 4-21 shows the syntax of the `foreach` and `for` statements, along with an example of using each syntax.

foreach **statement**	

<u>Syntax</u>
foreach *element* (*group*) {
        one or more statements to be processed for each element in the group
}	

<u>Example</u> `my ($num, @numbers);` `@numbers = (5000, 200, 100, 3);` `foreach $num (@numbers) {` `print "$num \n";` `}`	<u>Result</u> 5000 200 100 3

for **statement**	

<u>Syntax</u>
for (*initialization*; *loop condition*; *update*) {
        one or more statements to be processed as long as the loop condition is true
}	

<u>Example</u> `my $num;` `for ($num = 1; $num < 4; $num = $num + 1) {` `print "$num \n";` `}`	<u>Result</u> 1 2 3

Figure 4-21   Syntax and examples of the `foreach` and `for` statements

You use the `foreach` statement to repeat one or more instructions for each element in a group—such as for each scalar variable in an array. You can use the `foreach` statement shown in Figure 4-21, for example, to print each number stored in the `@numbers` array. When the statement is processed, it assigns the first value from the `@numbers` array—the number 5000—to the `$num` variable. The `print "$num<BR>\n";` statement within the loop then prints the number 5000. Next, the `foreach` statement assigns the second number in the `@numbers` array—the number 200—to the `$num` variable, and the `print` statement prints the number 200. This process will be followed for each number contained in the `@numbers` array. The `foreach` statement will stop processing when it has processed each number in the array.

You use the `for` statement to repeat one or more statements as long as the *loop condition* is true. The `for` statement begins with the `for` clause, which contains three arguments, separated by two semicolons. In most `for` clauses, the *initialization* argument initializes a variable, referred to as a **counter variable**, which is used by the `for` statement to keep track of the number of times the loop instructions are processed. The second argument in the `for` clause, *loop condition*, specifies the condition that must be true for the loop to continue processing its instructions. The *loop condition* must be a Boolean expression, which is an expression that evaluates to either true or false. The loop stops when the *loop condition* evaluates to false. The third argument in the `for` clause, *update*, usually contains an expression that updates the counter variable specified in the *initialization* argument.

The example of the `for` statement included in Figure 4-21 shows how you can print the numbers 1 through 3 on a Web page. The *initialization* argument in the example, `$num = 1`, initializes the `$num` variable to the number 1. The *loop condition* argument, `$num < 4`, instructs the computer to repeat the loop's instructions as long as the `$num` variable contains a number that is less than the number 4. Unlike the *initialization* argument, which is processed only once, the *loop condition* argument is processed with each repetition, or iteration, of the loop. The example's *update* argument, `$num = $num + 1`, instructs the computer to add the number 1 to the value stored in the `$num` variable. Like the *loop condition* argument, the *update* argument is processed with each repetition of the loop.

You will use the `foreach` statement in the Juniper Printers script to print the contents of the `@sysletter` array on a Web page.

To complete the juniper2.cgi script, then test the script:

1. Change the statement `my ($name, $serial, $modnum, @sysletter);` to **my ($name, $serial, $modnum, @sysletter, $key);**. You will use the `$key` variable in the `foreach` statement to keep track of each element in the `@sysletter` array.

2. Make the additional changes shaded in Figure 4-22, which shows the completed juniper2.cgi script.

3. Save the juniper2.cgi script.

```perl
#!/usr/bin/perl
#juniper2.cgi - creates a dynamic Web page that acknowledges
#the receipt of a registration form
print "Content-type: text/html\n\n";
use CGI qw(:standard);
use strict;

#declare variables
my ($name, $serial, $modnum, @sysletter, $key);
my @models = ("Laser JX", "Laser PL", "ColorPrint XL");
my %systems = ("W", "Windows",
               "M", "Macintosh",
               "U", "UNIX");

#assign input items to variables
$name = param('Name');
$serial = param('Serial');
$modnum = param('Model');
@sysletter = param('System');

#create Web page
print "<HTML><HEAD><TITLE>Juniper Printers</TITLE></HEAD>\n";
print "<BODY><H2>\n";
print "Thank you, $name, for completing \n";
print "the registration form.<BR><BR>\n";
print "We have registered your Juniper $models[$modnum] printer, \n";
print "serial number $serial.\n";
print "You indicated that the printer will be used on the \n";
print "following systems:<BR><BR>\n";
foreach $key (@sysletter) {
     print "$systems{$key}<BR>\n";
}
print "</H2></BODY></HTML>\n";
```

be sure to declare the $key variable

Figure 1-22   Completed juniper2.cgi script

4. *If you are using a UNIX system*, return to the UNIX command prompt. Change the juniper2.cgi file permissions to **755**. Type **clear** after the command prompt and press **Enter**.

   If you are using a Windows system, return to the Command Prompt window. Type **cls** after the command prompt and press **Enter**.

5. Type **perl –c juniper2.cgi** and press **Enter**. If necessary, correct any syntax errors in the script before continuing to the next step.

6. Type **perl –w juniper2.cgi** and press **Enter**. When the offline mode message appears, type **Name=Paul+Yahiro** and press **Enter**, then type **Serial=22SS67** and press **Enter**, and then type **Model=2** and press **Enter**. Now enter two operating system letters. Type **System=W** and press **Enter**, and then type **System=U** and press **Enter**.

7. Press **Ctrl+d** (UNIX), or press **Ctrl+z** and then press **Enter** (Windows), to indicate that you are finished entering data. Notice that both operating system names appear in the output, as shown in Figure 4-23.

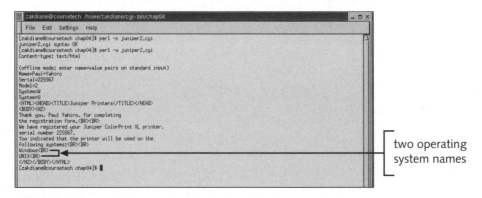

two operating system names

Figure 4-23   Output showing both operating system names

8. Return to the juniper2.html document in your browser.

9. Enter **Paul Yahiro** as the name and **22SS67** as the serial number. Select the **ColorPrint XL** radio button and the **UNIX** check box. The Windows check box should already be selected. Click the **Submit Registration** button. If necessary, click the **Continue Submission** button. A Web page similar to the one shown in Figure 4-24 appears on the screen.

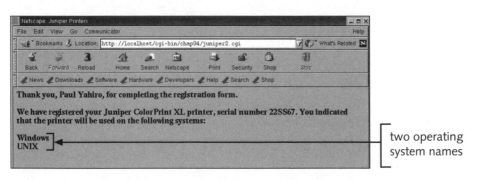

two operating system names

Figure 4-24   Web page showing registration information

10. Close your browser and any open windows.

CHAPTER SUMMARY

◻ The *keys* associated with form data are the names of the form elements whose *values* will be passed to the server. If a form element is a text box, the *value* is the text entered in the text box. If a form element is a radio button or check box, the *value* is the value assigned to the VALUE property of the selected radio button or check box.

◻ An array variable, or array, is a group of related scalar variables. Each scalar variable in an array has the same name, but a unique index number. The first scalar variable in an array has an index of 0.

◻ You can declare (or create) an array using a statement that follows the syntax **my** *arrayname* = **(***list***)**;, where *arrayname* is the name of the array and *list* is a comma-separated list of values to store in the array.

◻ The name of an array must begin with an at sign (@) followed by a letter and then, optionally, one or more letters, numbers, or underscores.

◻ You use the array name to refer to a scalar variable contained in the array, but you replace the @ in the name with a $, and you follow the name with the scalar variable's index enclosed in square brackets ([ ]).

◻ A hash variable, or hash, is a group of related scalar variables. Each scalar variable in a hash has the same name, but a unique *key*. Unlike the scalar variables in an array, the scalar variables in a hash are not stored in any particular order in the computer's internal memory.

◻ You can declare (or create) a hash using a statement that follows the syntax **my** *hashname* = **(***key1, value1, key2, value2,...keyn, valuen***)**;, where *hashname* is the name of the hash.

◻ The name of a hash must begin with a percent sign (%) followed by a letter and then, optionally, one or more letters, numbers, or underscores.

◻ You use the hash name to refer to a scalar variable contained in the hash, but you replace the % in the name with a $, and you follow the name with the scalar variable's *key* enclosed in braces ({ }).

◻ You use the repetition structure, also called a loop, to instruct the computer to repeat a block of instructions either a specified number of times or until some condition is met.

◻ You use the **foreach** statement to repeat one or more instructions for each element in a group.

◻ You use the **for** statement to repeat one or more statements as long as a condition, referred to as the *loop condition*, is true.

4

REVIEW QUESTIONS

1. The <FORM> tag's _____ property indicates the name of the script that will process the form data.

   a. ACTION

   b. METHOD

   c. SCRIPT

   d. VALUE

2. The *keys* associated with form data are the names of the form elements whose *values* will be passed to the server.

   a. true

   b. false

3. Assume that the California radio button is selected on a form. The value passed to the script is contained in the radio button's _____ property.

   a. ACTION

   b. SELECTED

   c. TEXT

   d. VALUE

4. Which of the following statements assigns the string "Monday" to the second variable contained in the @days array?

   a. @days{1} = "Monday";

   b. @days[1] = Monday;

   c. $days[1] = "Monday";

   d. None of the above.

5. Which of the following statements assigns the number 25600 to the variable associated with the FirstQtr *key* in the %sales hash?

   a. %sales['FirstQtr'] = 25600;

   b. %sales{'FirstQtr'} = 25600;

   c. %sales('FirstQtr') = 25600;

   d. None of the above.

6. You distinguish one scalar variable in an array from another scalar variable in the same array by the variable's _____.

   a. index

   b. key

   c. value

   d. None of the above.

7. You distinguish one scalar variable in a hash from another scalar variable in the same hash by the variable's _____.

a. index

b. key

c. value

d. None of the above.

8. Which of the following statements will print the contents of the @names array on a Web page?

a.
```
foreach $x (@names) {
     print "@names[$x]<BR>\n";
}
```

b.
```
foreach ($x in @names) {
     print "$x<BR>\n";
}
```

c.
```
for each ($x in @names) {
     print "$names[$x]<BR>\n";
}
```

d.
```
foreach $x (@names) {
     print "$x<BR>\n";
}
```

9. Which of the following statements will print the numbers 10 through 15 on a Web page?

a.
```
for ($x = 10, $X < 16, $x = $x + 1) {
     print "$x<BR>\n";
}
```

b.
```
for ($x = 10; $x <= 15; $x = $x + 1) {
     print "$x<BR>\n";
}
```

c.
```
for ($x = 10: $x <= 15: $x = $x + 1) {
     print "$x<BR>\n";
}
```

d.
```
for $x = 10 to 15 {
     print "$x<BR>\n";
}
```

10. Assume that the *key* for the California, Illinois, and Massachusetts check boxes is State. The *values* associated with the three check boxes are CA, IL, and MA, respectively. If the California and Illinois check boxes are selected, the browser passes _____ to the server.

   a. State=CA&State=IL

   b. State=CA&IL

   c. CA&IL

   d. None of the above.

11. Write a Perl statement that declares an array named @states and assigns the following state codes to the array: CA, IL, MA.

12. How do you refer to the second state name in the @states array?

13. The three basic data types for variables in Perl are _____, _____, and _____.

14. Assume that an array named @payrate contains four pay rates: 5, 6.5, 8.75, and 10. Write a Perl statement that multiplies the 8.75 pay rate by the number 40, and then assigns the result to the $grosspay variable.

15. What is a hash?

16. What is an array?

17. Write a Perl statement that declares a hash named %states. The statement should assign the following state codes as the *keys*: CA, IL, MA. It also should store the following *values* in the hash: California, Illinois, Massachusetts.

18. How do you refer to the state name associated with the CA *key* in the %states hash?

19. Assume that a hash named %payrate contains four *keys* and *values*, as follows: "A", 5, "B", 6.5, "C", 8.75, "D", 10. Write a Perl statement that multiplies the 8.75 pay rate by the number 40, and then assigns the result to the $grosspay variable. The appropriate *key* is stored in the $jobcode variable.

20. Write a foreach statement that prints the contents of the @states array on a Web page.

HANDS-ON PROJECTS

Project 1

In this project, you modify the Juniper Printers registration form so that it passes the printer model codes JX, PL, and XL (rather than the printer model numbers 0, 1, and 2) to the server. You also modify the Juniper Printers script so that it stores the printer model codes and names in a hash.

   a. Open the juniper.html file in a text editor. The file is contained in the public_html/chap04 directory.

b. Change the filename in the first line from juniper.html to c04ex1.html.

c. Modify the <FORM> tag to refer to the c04ex1.cgi script.

d. Modify the document so that it assigns the codes JX, PL, and XL to the VALUE property of the printer model radio buttons.

e. Save the document as c04ex1.html.

f. Open the juniper.cgi file in a text editor. The file is contained in the cgi-bin/chap04 directory.

g. Change the filename in the second line from juniper.cgi to c04ex1.cgi, then save the document as c04ex1.cgi.

h. Modify the script so that it stores the printer model codes and names in a hash. Also modify the statement that displays the printer model name.

i. Save the c04ex1.cgi document.

j. *If you are using a UNIX system,* change the c04ex1.cgi file permissions to 755.

k. Test the script from the command line.

l. Open the c04ex1.html file in your Web browser. Enter Kevin Williams as the customer name and C78DX as the serial number. Select the Laser PL and UNIX radio buttons. Click the Submit Registration button. If necessary, click the Continue Submission button. The Web page should display the appropriate printer model name.

Project 2

In this project, you modify the Juniper Printers registration form so that it passes the operating system numbers 0, 1, and 2 (rather than the operating system letters W, M, and U) to the server. You also modify the Juniper Printers script so that it stores the operating system names in an array.

a. Open the juniper.html file in a text editor. The file is contained in the public_html/chap04 directory.

b. Change the filename in the first line from juniper.html to c04ex2.html.

c. Modify the <FORM> tag to refer to the c04ex2.cgi script.

d. Modify the document so that it assigns the numbers 0, 1, and 2 to the VALUE property of the operating system radio buttons.

e. Save the document as c04ex2.html.

f. Open the juniper.cgi file in a text editor. The file is contained in the cgi-bin/chap04 directory.

g. Change the filename in the second line from juniper.cgi to c04ex2.cgi, then save the document as c04ex2.cgi.

h. Modify the script so that it stores the operating system names in an array. Also modify the statement that displays the operating system name.

i. Save the c04ex2.cgi document.

j. *If you are using a UNIX system*, change the c04ex2.cgi file permissions to 755.

k. Test the script from the command line.

l. Open the c04ex2.html file in your Web browser. Enter Jacob Stein as the customer name and K23BW as the serial number. Select the Macintosh radio button. Click the Submit Registration button. If necessary, click the Continue Submission button. The Web page should display the appropriate operating system name.

Project 3

In this project, you modify the Juniper Printers form so that it displays the primary use for the printer. You also modify the Juniper Printers script so that it stores the values associated with the primary use radio buttons in an array.

a. Open the printer.html file in a text editor. The file is contained in the public_html/chap04 directory.

b. Change the filename in the first line from printer.html to c04ex3.html.

c. The <FORM> tag indicates that the form data will be processed by the c04ex3.cgi script, which you will save in the cgi-bin/chap04 directory. Change yourservername in the <FORM> tag's ACTION property to the name of your server.

d. Notice that the HTML document includes four radio buttons that allow the customer to select the primary use for the printer he or she is registering. The radio buttons are named Use. The c04ex3.cgi script that will process the form data will store the different uses ("Home", "Business", "Educational", and "Other) in an array. Assign the appropriate *values* to the VALUE property of the Use radio buttons.

e. Save the document as c04ex3.html.

f. Open the juniper.cgi file in a text editor. The file is contained in the cgi-bin/chap04 directory.

g. Change the filename in the second line from juniper.cgi to c04ex3.cgi.

h. Save the file as c04ex3.cgi.

i. Modify the script so that it creates an array named @uses. The @uses array should contain four strings: "Home", "Business", "Educational", and "Other".

j. Modify the script so that it stores the *value* of the Use *key* in a scalar variable named $use.

k. Modify the script so that it displays the sentence "The primary use for this printer is: *primary use*." as the last sentence on the dynamic Web page.

l. Save the c04ex3.cgi file.

m. *If you are using a UNIX system*, change the c04ex3.cgi file permissions to 755.

n. Test the script from the command line.

o. Open the c04ex3.html file in your Web browser. Enter Helen Jacoby as the customer name and TW98Q as the serial number. Select the Laser PL, UNIX, and Business radio buttons. Click the Submit Registration button. If necessary, click the Continue Submission button. The Web page should display the sentence "The primary use for this printer is: Business."

Project 4

4

In this project, you modify the Juniper Printers form and script from Exercise 3. The form will pass different *values* for the Use *key*, and the script will use a hash to store the *keys* and *values* associated with the Use radio buttons.

a. Open the c04ex3.html file in a text editor. The file is contained in the public_html/chap04 directory.

b. Change the filename in the first line from c04ex3.html to c04ex4.html.

c. Modify the <FORM> tag to refer to the c04ex4.cgi script.

d. The c04ex4.cgi script that will process the form data will store the different uses ("Home", "Business", "Educational", and "Other") in a hash. Change the *values* assigned to the Use radio buttons to H, B, E, and O.

e. Save the document as c04ex4.html.

f. Open the c04ex3.cgi file in a text editor. The file is contained in the cgi-bin/chap04 directory.

g. Change the filename in the second line from c04ex3.cgi to c04ex4.cgi.

h. Save the document as c04ex4.cgi.

i. Change the @uses array to a hash, then modify the statement that displays the primary use on the dynamic Web page.

j. Save the c04ex4.cgi file.

k. *If you are using a UNIX system*, change the c04ex4.cgi file permissions to 755.

l. Test the script from the command line.

m. Open the c04ex4.html file in your Web browser. Enter Stan Kozlowski as the customer name and TT123R as the serial number. Select the ColorPrint XL radio button. (The Windows and Home radio buttons should already be selected.) Click the Submit Registration button. If necessary, click the Continue Submission button. The Web page should display the sentence "The primary use for this printer is: Home."

Project 5

In this project, you modify the Juniper Printers form and script from Exercise 3. The form will use check boxes rather than radio buttons for the primary use options, and the script will store the primary use *values* in an array.

a. Open the c04ex3.html file in a text editor. The file is contained in the public_html/chap04 directory.

b. Change the filename in the first line from c04ex3.html to c04ex5.html.

c. Modify the <FORM> tag to refer to the c04ex5.cgi script.

d. Change the Use radio buttons to check boxes.

e. Save the document as c04ex5.html.

f. Open the c04ex3.cgi file in a text editor. The file is contained in the cgi-bin/chap04 directory.

g. Change the filename in the second line from c04ex3.cgi to c04ex5.cgi.

h. Save the document as c04ex5.cgi.

i. Modify the script so that it stores the values received for the Use key in an array named `@primary_uses`. Also modify the script so that it includes the contents of the `@primary_uses` array on the Web page.

j. Save the c04ex5.cgi file.

k. *If you are using a UNIX system*, change the c04ex5.cgi file permissions to 755.

l. Test the script from the command line.

m. Open the c04ex5.html file in your Web browser. Enter John Doe as the customer name and AB123Z as the serial number. Select the ColorPrint XL radio button. Deselect the Home check box, then select the Business and Educational check boxes. Click the Submit Registration button. If necessary, click the Continue Submission button. The Web page should display the two primary uses, Business and Educational.

Project 6

In this project, you create a script that will process the data entered on the Patton Industries Bonus Calculator form. The script will display a bonus amount calculated at various rates.

a. Open the patton.html file in a text editor. The file is contained in the public_html/chap04 directory.

b. Change the filename in the first line from patton.html to c04ex6.html.

c. The <FORM> tag indicates that the form data will be processed by the c04ex6.cgi script, which you will save in the cgi-bin/chap04 directory. Change yourservername in the <FORM> tag's ACTION property to the name of your server.

d. Save the document as c04ex6.html.

e. Create a script that will process the form data entered on the Patton Industries form. Name the script c04ex6.cgi and save it in the cgi-bin/chap04 directory. The script should create a Web page similar to the one shown in Figure 4-25.

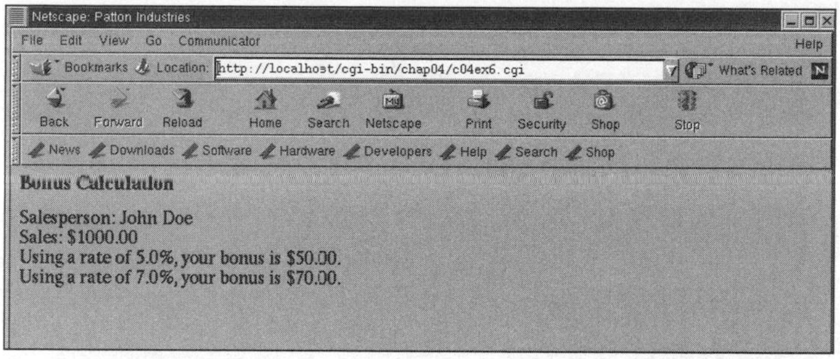

Figure 4-25

f. *If you are using a UNIX system*, change the c04ex6.cgi file permissions to 755.

g. Test the script from the command line.

h. Open the c04ex6.html file in your Web browser. Enter John Doe as the salesperson name and 1000 as the sales amount. Select the 5% and 7% check boxes. A Web page similar to the one shown in Figure 4-25 should appear on the screen.

CASE PROJECTS

1. Create an HTML form and a script for the Political Action Committee. Name the form c04case1.html and save it in the public_html/chap04 directory. Name the script c04case1.cgi and save it in the cgi-bin/chap04 directory. The form should display a Web page similar to the one shown in Figure 4-26. Assume that the CGI script that processes the form data will store the values associated with each set of radio buttons in a separate array. The script should create a Web page similar to the one shown in Figure 4-27.

Figure 4-26

Figure 4-27

2. Open the c04case1.html file, which you created in Case Project 1, in a text editor. Change the filename in the <FORM> tag from c04case1.cgi to c04case2.cgi. Assume that the c04case2.cgi script will store the values associated with each set of radio buttons in a separate hash rather than in a separate array. Make the appropriate modifications to the form, then save the form as c04case2.html. Open the c04case1.cgi file, which you created in Case Project 1, in a text editor. Modify the script so that it uses hashes rather than arrays, then save the script as c04case2.cgi.

5

DATA FILES

In this chapter, you will:

♦ Open a file

♦ Use the `die` function to exit a script when a file cannot be opened

♦ Write records to a file using the `print` function

♦ Read records from a file

♦ Remove the newline character using the `chomp` function

♦ Separate fields using the `split` function

♦ Initialize and update counters

♦ Learn how to use the `keys` and `sort` functions

Most times, you will want to save the data entered on a form to a file for future reference. For example, the data entered on the Juniper Printers registration form in Chapter 4 needs to be saved to a file so that the company can keep track of the customers who registered their printers. Similarly, the data entered on a survey form—such as the Super Bowl form that you use in this chapter—needs to be saved to a file so that the data can be used to calculate the survey statistics. In this chapter, you learn how to create and manipulate a file in a Perl script.

THE SUPER BOWL FORM AND ACKNOWLEDGMENT

For Super Bowl Sunday, WKRK-TV added a new Web page to the television station's Web site. The Web page—an online form—is shown in Figure 5-1.

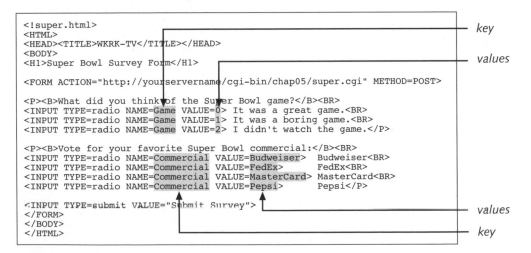

Figure 5-1   Super Bowl form used by WKRK-TV

Notice that the Super Bowl form contains two sets of radio buttons: you use the first set to rate the Super Bowl game, and the second set to vote for your favorite Super Bowl commercial. The form also contains a submit button labeled Submit Survey. Now view the HTML code used to create the form.

To view the HTML code used to create the Super Bowl form:

1. Open the super.html file in a text editor. The file is contained in the public_html/chap05 directory. Figure 5-2 shows the contents of the file. The *keys* and *values* associated with the two sets of radio buttons are shaded in the figure.

```
<!super.html>
<HTML>
<HEAD><TITLE>WKRK-TV</TITLE></HEAD>                          ──────  key
<BODY>
<H1>Super Bowl Survey Form</H1>                              ──────  values

<FORM ACTION="http://yourservername/cgi-bin/chap05/super.cgi" METHOD=POST>

<P><B>What did you think of the Super Bowl game?</B><BR>
<INPUT TYPE=radio NAME=Game VALUE=0> It was a great game.<BR>
<INPUT TYPE=radio NAME=Game VALUE=1> It was a boring game.<BR>
<INPUT TYPE=radio NAME=Game VALUE=2> I didn't watch the game.</P>

<P><B>Vote for your favorite Super Bowl commercial:</B><BR>
<INPUT TYPE=radio NAME=Commercial VALUE=Budweiser>  Budweiser<BR>
<INPUT TYPE=radio NAME=Commercial VALUE=FedEx>      FedEx<BR>
<INPUT TYPE=radio NAME=Commercial VALUE=MasterCard> MasterCard<BR>
<INPUT TYPE=radio NAME=Commercial VALUE=Pepsi>      Pepsi</P>

<INPUT TYPE=submit VALUE="Submit Survey">                    ──────  values
</FORM>
</BODY>                                                      ──────  key
</HTML>
```

Figure 5-2   HTML code used to create the Super Bowl form

The <FORM> tag's ACTION property indicates that the super.cgi script will process the form data.

2. Change your servername in the <FORM> tag's ACTION property to the name of your server, then save the super.html document.

The <FORM> tag's METHOD property directs the browser to use the POST method when sending the form data (*keys* and *values*) to the server. As Figure 5-2 indicates, Game is the *key* associated with the first set of radio buttons on the form. Notice that the *value* 0 is assigned to the "It was a great game." radio button, the *value* 1 to the "It was a boring game." radio button, and the *value* 2 to the "I didn't watch the game." radio button.

Figure 5-2 also indicates that Commercial is the *key* associated with the second set of radio buttons on the form. Notice that the *value* Budweiser is assigned to the Budweiser radio button, the *value* FedEx to the FedEx radio button, and so on.

 The HTML code shown in Figure 5-2 assigns numeric values to the Game radio buttons, and string values to the Commercial radio buttons; this is done to allow you to use both an array and a hash in the super.cgi script. The code also could have assigned string values (such as Great, Boring, and None) to the Game radio buttons, and numeric values (such as 0, 1, 2, and 3) to the Commercial radio buttons. You will make these modifications to the super.html file in Hands-on Project 1 at the end of this chapter.

3. Close the super.html file.

When the user clicks the Submit Survey button on the Super Bowl form, a dynamic Web page similar to the one shown in Figure 5-3 should appear on the screen.

Figure 5-3   Dynamic Web page acknowledgment

Notice that the dynamic Web page contains a message thanking the person for participating in the survey; the message serves to acknowledge receipt of the online form. The Web page also contains the survey statistics—the current number of votes associated with each option on the Super Bowl form. To calculate the statistics, you need to keep track of the game and commercial choices made by each survey participant; you can do so by saving the choices in a file.

Now that you know what information will be passed to the server and what information to include on the dynamic Web page, you can complete the super.cgi script, which will process the form data.

PLANNING AND CODING THE SUPER BOWL SCRIPT

Figure 5-4 shows the input, output, and algorithm for the Super Bowl script.

Input	Output
game rating (0, 1, or 2) commercial vote (Budweiser, FedEx, MasterCard, or Pepsi)	file containing the form data Web page containing an acknowledgment message and the survey statistics
Algorithm	

1. assign input items to variables
2. save form data to a file
   a. open the survey.txt file for append
   b. write a record to the file
   c. close the file
3. calculate total number of votes for each game and commercial choice
   a. open the survey.txt file for input
   b. read the records into an array
   c. close the file
   d. repeat the following for each record stored in the array:
     1) remove the newline character from the end of the record
     2) assign each field in the record to a separate variable
     3) add 1 to the appropriate game counter
     4) add 1 to the appropriate commercial counter
4. create a dynamic Web page that displays an acknowledgment message and the total number of votes for each game and commercial choice	

Figure 5-4   Input, output, and algorithm for the Super Bowl script

As Figure 5-4 indicates, the script's input is the data submitted using the form. The output is a file that contains the form data, and a dynamic Web page that includes an acknowledgment message and the survey statistics. The algorithm shows the steps the computer needs to follow to transform the input into the output.

On your computer's disk is a partially completed script named super.cgi. You begin completing the script in the next set of steps.

To begin completing the super.cgi script:

1. Open the super.cgi file in a text editor. The file is contained in the cgi-bin/chap05 directory.

2. If necessary, change the shebang line to reflect the location of the Perl interpreter on your system.

3. If necessary, add the **-debug** pragma to the **use CGI qw(:standard);** statement.

   Step 1 in the algorithm shown in Figure 5-4 is to assign the input items to variables. Recall that you should declare a variable before assigning a value to it.

4. Enter the three lines of code shaded in Figure 5-5.

```
#!/usr/bin/perl
#super.cgi - saves form data to a file, and creates a dynamic
#Web page that displays a message and survey statistics
print "Content-type: text/html\n\n";
use CGI qw(:standard);
use strict;

#declare variables
my (@game, @commercial);

#assign input items to variables
$game = param('Game');
$commercial = param('Commercial');

#save form data to a file

#calculate survey statistics

#generate HTML acknowledgment
print "<HTML><HEAD><TITLE>WKRK-TV</TITLE></HEAD>\n";
print "<BODY>\n";
print "<H2>Thank you for participating in our survey.</H2>\n";

print "<EM><B>What did you think of the Super Bowl game?</EM></B>\n";
print "<TABLE>\n";
print "<TR><TD>It was a great game.</TD>      <TD></TD></TR>\n";
print "<TR><TD>It was a boring game.</TD>     <TD></TD> /TR>\n";
print "<TR><TD>I didn't watch the game.</TD> <TD></TD></TR>\n";
print "</TABLE><BR>\n";

print "<EM><B>Vote for your favorite Super Bowl commercial:</EM></B>\n";
print "<TABLE>\n";

print "</TABLE>\n";
print "</BODY></HTML>\n";
```

Figure 5-5   Additional code entered in the script

You also can declare a variable and assign a value to it in one statement. For example, you could use the statement my $game = param('Game'); to declare the $game variable and assign the param('Game') value to it.

5. Save the super.cgi document.

Step 2 in the algorithm is to save the form data to a file. As Figure 5-4 indicates, Step 2 involves three tasks, which you learn how to code in the next several sections.

SAVING DATA TO A FILE

Most times, the form data saved to a file is organized into fields and records. A **field** is a single item of information about a person, place, or thing—for example, a Social Security number, a city, or a price. A **record** is one or more related fields that contain all of the necessary data about a specific person, place, or thing. The place where you are employed keeps a record on you. Your employee record might contain your Social Security number, name, address, phone number, starting date, salary or hourly wage, and so on. A collection of related records is called a **data file**. The collection of records for each of the employees at your company forms the employee data file.

The data file associated with the Super Bowl form will contain one record for each survey participant. Each record will be composed of two fields. The first field, called the game field, will contain the *value* passed to the script with the Game *key*. Recall that the *value* associated with the Game *key* indicates the radio button selected in the Game section of the Super Bowl form. The second field, called the commercial field, will contain the *value* passed to the script with the Commercial *key*; this *value* indicates the radio button selected in the Commercial section of the form.

Before you can save data in a file, the file must be created and opened.

Creating and Opening a Data File

You use the **open function** to create and/or open a data file in a Perl script. The syntax of the **open** function is **open**(*filehandle, mode, filename*). In the syntax, *filehandle* is a name that you assign to the data file you want to open; typically, the name is entered using upper-case letters. After a file is opened, you use the *filehandle* to refer to the file. For example, you use the *filehandle* in a statement that writes data to the file or reads data from the file.

The *mode* argument, which is optional in the **open** function's syntax, indicates how the data file is to be opened. Data files can be opened for input, output, or append. Figure 5-6 lists the most commonly used *modes* and describes their meaning.

mode	Description
<	Opens an existing file for input, which allows the script to read the file's contents. This is the default *mode* used to open a file.
>	Opens a file for output, which creates a new, empty file to which data can be written. If the file already exists, its contents are erased before the new data is written.
>>	Opens a file for append, which allows the script to write new data to the end of the existing data in the file. If the file does not exist, the file is created before data is written to it.

Figure 5-6   open function *modes*

The < *mode* tells the computer to open the file for input, which allows a script to read the data stored in the file. The > and >> *modes*, on the other hand, allow a script to write data to a file. You use the > *mode* to open a new, empty file for output. If the file already exists, the computer erases the contents of the file before writing any data to it. You use the >> *mode* when you want to add (append) data to the end of an existing file. If the file does not exist, the computer creates the file for you.

The *filename* argument in the **open** function's syntax is the name of the data file you want to open on the computer's disk. Figure 5-7 shows examples of using the **open** function to open files.

Examples	Results
open(INFILE, "<", "survey.txt");	opens the survey.txt file for input, and assigns the *filehandle* INFILE to the file
open(INFILE, "survey.txt");	opens the survey.txt file for input, and assigns the *filehandle* INFILE to the file
open(OUTFILE, ">", "survey.txt");	opens the survey.txt file for output, and assigns the *filehandle* OUTFILE to the file
open(OUTSUR, ">>", "survey.txt");	opens the survey.txt file for append, and assigns the *filehandle* OUTSUR to the file

Figure 5-7   Examples of using the **open** function to open files

If you are using a UNIX system, the **open** function will create and/or open the data file in the same location as the script file. If you want to create and/or open a data file in another location, you will need to enter the data file's full path in the *filename* argument.

If you are using a Windows system, the **open** function will open the data file in the default directory. When the script is run from the command line, the default directory is the current directory. When the script is run from the browser, the default directory typically is the cgi-bin directory.

It is not necessary to begin *filehandle* names with the two letters IN or the three letters OUT. However, using this naming convention helps to distinguish a script's input files (those from which data will be read) from its output files (those to which data will be written).

As Figure 5-7 indicates, you can use either the statement **open(INFILE, "<", "survey.txt");** or the statement **open(INFILE, "survey.txt");** to open the survey.txt file for input. Notice that the *mode* argument is omitted in the latter statement. If you do not specify the *mode* argument in an **open** function, the computer opens the file for input; in other words, < is the default *mode*.

Figure 5-7 also shows that you can use the statement `open(OUTFILE, ">", "survey.txt");` to open the survey.txt file for output. You can use the statement `open(OUTSUR, ">>", "survey.txt");` to open the survey.txt file for append.

It is possible for the `open` function to fail when attempting to open a file. For example, a file that does not exist cannot be opened for input. Similarly, a file that does not have write permission cannot be opened for append. Unfortunately, unless you direct it otherwise, a script will continue to run even when an `open` function fails. In most cases, you will want to display an error message on the screen and then exit the script when the file you are trying to open cannot be opened; you can use the Perl `die` function to perform these tasks.

Using the `die` Function

The **die function** allows you to display a message and then exit a script when an error occurs. The syntax of the `die` function is **die** *message*, where *message*, which is optional, is the message that you want displayed on the screen. If you do not specify a *message*, the `die` function displays the default *message* "Died at *scriptname* line *linenumber*.", where *scriptname* is the name of the script and *linenumber* is the number of the line of code that contains the `die` function. After displaying the message, the `die` function stops the script immediately.

You can use the `die` function to display a message and then exit a script when a file cannot be opened. To do so, you simply include the `die` function along with the `open` function in a statement that follows the syntax **open(** *filehandle*, *mode*, *filename***) or die** *message*;. Put simply, the syntax tells the computer to open the file or die; in this case, "die" means to stop processing the script. Figure 5-8 shows examples of using the syntax in the super.cgi script to open the survey.txt file for input. The figure also shows the message that the `die` function displays on the screen when the survey.txt file cannot be opened. (You can assume that the `die` function is entered on line 15 in the script.)

The `or` in the syntax is one of the logical operators available in Perl. You will learn more about the Perl logical operators in Chapter 6.

You can enter the `die` function on the same line as the `open` function, as shown in Example 1 in Figure 5-8. Or, you can enter the functions on different lines, as shown in Examples 2 through 5.

Examples and messages displayed by the `die` function
Example 1: `open(INFILE, "<", "survey.txt") or die;`
Message: Died at super.cgi line 15.
Example 2: `open(INFILE, "<", "survey.txt")`   `        or die "Can't open file, stopped";`
Message: Can't open file, stopped at super.cgi line 15.
Example 3: `open(INFILE, "<", "survey.txt")`   `        or die "Can't open file, stopped\n";`
Message: Can't open file, stopped.
Example 4: `open(INFILE, "<", "survey.txt")`   `        or die "Error: $!\n";`
Message: Error: No such file or directory.
Example 5: `open(INFILE, "<", "survey.txt")`   `        or die "Error opening survey.txt. $!, stopped";`
Message: Error opening survey.txt. No such file or directory, stopped at super.cgi line 15.

Figure 5-8   Examples of combining the `die` function with the `open` function

Study closely the `die` function included in each example shown in Figure 5-8. Notice that the `die` function in Example 1 does not specify a *message*; therefore, the function displays the default *message* "Died at super.cgi line 15." when the survey.txt file cannot be opened.

The `die` function in Example 2, on the other hand, specifies the *message* "Can't open file, stopped". In this case, the `die` function displays "Can't open file, stopped at super.cgi line 15." when the survey.txt file cannot be opened. Notice that the `die` function appends the text "at scriptname line linenumber" to the end of the message. You can prevent the `die` function from appending the additional text by including a newline character (\n) at the end of the *message*, as shown in Example 3. Notice that the `die` function in Example 3 displays only the *message* "Can't open file, stopped."

When an `open` function fails, Perl automatically stores the reason for the failure in a special scalar variable named `$!`. You can determine why an `open` function failed by displaying the contents of the `$!` variable; to do so, you simply include the `$!` variable in the `die` function's *message*. For instance, the `die` function shown in Example 4 in Figure 5-8 displays "Error: No such file or directory." when the `open` function cannot locate the survey.txt file.

Most times, you will want to display as much information as possible about the error that occurred in a script. The more information you have, the easier it will be for you to locate and correct the error. To this end, the `die` function shown in Example 5 in

Figure 5-8 displays a *message* that includes the name of the file that the script is trying to open, the reason that the file could not be opened, the name of the script, and the number of the line that contains the `die` function.

Continue coding the super.cgi script by entering a statement that opens the survey.txt file for append. The statement should display an appropriate message and then stop the script if the file cannot be opened.

To instruct the computer to open the survey.txt file for append, and display a message and then exit the script if the file cannot be opened:

1. In the blank line below the comment **#save form data to a file**, type **open(OUTFILE, ">>", "survey.txt")** and press **Enter**.

2. Press **Tab** to indent the line, then type **or die "Error opening survey.txt. $!, stopped";** and press **Enter**.

3. Press **Backspace**, if necessary, to remove the indentation.

4. Save the super.cgi document.

Next you learn how to write records to a data file.

Writing Records to a File

You can use the `print` function, which you learned about in Chapter 2, to write a record to an open file. The syntax to do so is **print** *filehandle data***\n;**, where *filehandle* is the *filehandle* assigned to the file when the file was opened, and *data* is the one or more fields included in each record. To distinguish one record from another in a data file, programmers typically write each record on a separate line in the file. The \n included at the end of the syntax accomplishes this by writing an invisible newline character at the end of each record. The newline character advances the cursor to the next line in the file immediately after a record is written. In other words, the newline character is equivalent to pressing the Enter key.

A common error made when entering the `print` function is to type a comma after the *filehandle*.

When writing to a file a record that contains more than one field, programmers separate each field with a special character, referred to as the **field separator**. Characters commonly used as field separators include the comma, colon (:), ampersand (&), and tab. The **tab character** is represented in Perl by a backslash followed by the letter t (\t) and is equivalent to pressing the Tab key.

Some programmers refer to the field separator as a delimiter.

The following 12 characters have a special meaning in Perl and, therefore, typically are not used as field separators: ^ $ + * ? . | ( ) { \ [. The only exception to this is the pipe symbol (|). You learn how to use the pipe symbol as the field separator in Hands-on Project 4 at the end of this chapter.

You must be sure that the character you use as the field separator does not appear within any of the fields in a record, because the computer will mistake the character within the field for the field separator. For example, do not use a comma as the field separator if it is possible that a field might contain a comma. A name field is an example of a field that might contain a comma; for instance, the field might contain the name "Smith, Mary."

Figure 5-9 shows examples of writing records to the data file whose *filehandle* is OUTFILE. The figure also shows how the records appear in the data file.

Examples	Records contained in the file
`print OUTFILE "$game,$commercial\n";`	0,FedEx 1,Budweiser 0,MasterCard
`print OUTFILE "$game:$commercial\n";`	0:FedEx 1:Budweiser 0:MasterCard
`print OUTFILE "$game&$commercial\n";`	0&FedEx 1&Budweiser 0&MasterCard
`print OUTFILE "$game\t$commercial\n";`	0 FedEx 1 Budweiser 0 MasterCard

Figure 5-9   Examples of writing records to a file

The statements shown in Figure 5-9 tell the computer to write the contents of the $game variable, followed by the field separator, the contents of the $commercial variable, and an invisible newline character to the OUTFILE file. The first statement uses a comma as the field separator; the colon, ampersand, and tab are used as the field separator in the second, third, and fourth statements, respectively. Notice that each record appears on a separate line in the file.

Continue coding the super.cgi script by entering a statement that writes the Super Bowl data to the survey.txt file. Use the comma as the field separator.

To instruct the computer to write the Super Bowl data to the survey.txt file:

1. In the blank line below the **die** function, type **print OUTFILE "$game,$commercial\n";** and press **Enter**. (Be sure you do not enter a space after the comma; otherwise, each field will be separated by a comma and a space, rather than just a comma.)

2. Save the super.cgi document.

To prevent the loss of data, you should close any files opened by a script before the script ends.

Closing a File

You close an open file using the Perl **close function**. The syntax of the **close** function is **close**(*filehandle*), where *filehandle* is the *filehandle* assigned to the file when the file was opened. The statement `close(OUTFILE);`, for example, tells the computer to close the file whose *filehandle* is OUTFILE.

 Although a file will be closed automatically when you exit a script, it is considered a good programming practice to use the `close` function to manually close the file. You should close a file as soon as you are finished using it.

To instruct the computer to close the survey.txt file:

1. In the blank line below the `print OUTFILE "$game,$commercial\n";` statement, type **close(OUTFILE);** and press **Enter**. The three statements associated with Step 2 in the algorithm are shaded in Figure 5-10.

```
#!/usr/bin/perl
#super.cgi - saves form data to a file, and creates a dynamic
#Web page that displays a message and survey statistics
print "Content-type: text/html\n\n";
use CGI qw(:standard);
use strict;

#declare variables
my ($game, $commercial);

#assign input items to variables
$game = param('Game');
$commercial = param('Commercial');

#save form data to a file
open(OUTFILE, ">>", "survey.txt")
     or die "Error opening survey.txt. $!, stopped";
print OUTFILE "$game,$commercial\n";
close(OUTFILE);

#calculate survey statistics
```

Figure 5-10   Statements associated with Step 2 in the algorithm

2. Save the super.cgi document.

Now test the super.cgi script to make sure that the code you entered is working correctly.

To test the super.cgi script:

1. *If you are using a UNIX system*, open a terminal window, if necessary. Make the cgi-bin/chap05 directory the current directory, and then change the super.cgi file permissions to **755**.

If you are using a Windows system, open a Command Prompt window, and then make the cgi–bin\chap05 directory the current directory.

2. Type **perl –c super.cgi** and press **Enter**. If necessary, correct any syntax errors in the script before continuing to the next step.

Now execute the script twice to add two records to the survey.txt file.

3. Type **perl –w super.cgi** and press **Enter**. When the offline mode message appears, type **Game=0** and press **Enter**, then type **Commercial=FedEx** and press **Enter**.

4. Press **Ctrl+d** (UNIX), or press **Ctrl+z** and then press **Enter** (Windows), to indicate that you are finished entering the first record.

The **open** function in the script tells the computer to open the survey.txt file for append. At this point, the survey.txt file does not exist, so the computer creates the file for you and saves it in the cgi–bin/chap05 directory. The `print OUTFILE "$game,$commercial\n";` statement then writes the first record (0,FedEx) to the survey.txt file, and the `close(OUTFILE);` statement closes the file.

5. Type **perl –w super.cgi** and press **Enter**. When the offline mode message appears, type **Game=1** and press **Enter**, then type **Commercial=Budweiser** and press **Enter**.

6. Press **Ctrl+d** (UNIX), or press **Ctrl+z** and then press **Enter** (Windows), to indicate that you are finished entering the second record.

Here again, the **open** function in the script tells the computer to open the survey.txt file for append. At this point, the survey.txt file does exist, so the computer simply opens the file. The `print OUTFILE "$game, $commercial\n";` statement then writes the second record (1,Budweiser) to the survey.txt file, and the `close(OUTFILE);` statement closes the file.

7. Open the survey.txt file, which is contained in the cgi–bin/chap05 directory, in a text editor. The contents of the file are shown in Figure 5-11.

Figure 5-11   Contents of the survey.txt file

Notice that a comma separates the game field from the commercial field in each record, and each record appears on a separate line in the file.

8. Close the survey.txt file.

Step 3 in the algorithm shown earlier in Figure 5-4 is to calculate the total number of votes for each game and commercial choice.

CALCULATING THE SURVEY STATISTICS

Figure 5-12 shows the tasks the computer must perform to calculate the survey statistics, which is Step 3 in the algorithm. (The tasks were shown earlier in Figure 5-4.)

Step 3 in the Super Bowl algorithm

3. calculate total number of votes for each game and commercial choice
   a. open the survey.txt file for input
   b. read the records into an array
   c. close the file
   d. repeat the following for each record stored in the array:
      1) remove the newline character from the end of the record
      2) assign each field in the record to a separate variable
      3) add 1 to the appropriate game counter
      4) add 1 to the appropriate commercial counter

Figure 5-12   Tasks required to calculate the survey statistics

The first task shown in Figure 5-12 is to open the survey.txt file for input. Recall that opening a file for input allows a script to read the file's contents.

To instruct the computer to open the survey.txt for input:

1. Return to the super.cgi document in your text editor. In the blank line below the comment **#calculate survey statistics**, type **open(INFILE, "<", "survey.txt")** and press **Enter**.

2. Press **Tab** to indent the line, then type **or die "Error opening survey.txt. $!, stopped";** and press **Enter**.

3. Press **Backspace**, if necessary, to remove the indentation.

4. Save the super.cgi document.

The second task shown in Figure 5-12 is to read the records (from the file) into an array.

Reading Records into an Array

You use the syntax *arrayname* = <*filehandle*>; to read the records from a file into an array. In the syntax, *arrayname* is the name of the array, and *filehandle* is the *filehandle* assigned to the file when the file was opened. The <> in the syntax is the angle operator in Perl. When used in this manner, the **angle operator** tells the computer to read each record from *filehandle* and store each in a scalar variable within *arrayname*. For example, assuming that INFILE is the *filehandle* assigned to the survey.txt file, the statement @records = <INFILE>; reads each record from the survey.txt file and assigns each to a scalar variable within the @records array. The @records array is illustrated in Figure 5-13.

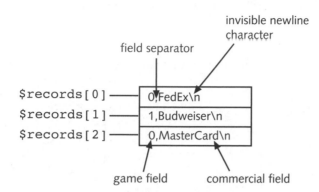

Figure 5-13   Illustration of the @records array in memory

 Be careful to assign only the contents of small files to an array. If a file is large, you should not assign its contents to an array, because it will consume too much of the computer's internal memory. In Chapter 7, you learn how to read the contents of large files.

As Figure 5-13 indicates, each scalar variable within the array contains the game field data, the field separator, the commercial field data, and the invisible newline character. Recall that this is the information written to the file by the `print OUTFILE "$game, $commercial\n";` statement.

You will use the statement `@records = <INFILE>;` in the super.cgi script to read the records from the survey.txt file and assign each to the @records array. Before entering the statement, you need to declare the @records array.

To read the records from the survey.txt file into an array, then close the file:

1. Change the `my ($game, $commercial);` statement, which appears below the comment `#declare variables`, to **my ($game, $commercial, @records);**.

2. In the blank line below the statement that opens the survey.txt file for input, type **@records = <INFILE>;** and press **Enter**.

   The next task listed in Figure 5-12 is to close the file. Recall that you should close a file as soon as you are finished using it. In this case, once the records are read into an array, you no longer need to keep the file opened.

3. Type **close(INFILE);** and press **Enter**.

4. Save the super.cgi document.

Listed next in Figure 5-12 is a repetition structure (loop) that tells the computer to repeat the loop instructions for each record stored in the array. You can use the `foreach` statement, which you learned about in Chapter 4, to code the loop.

More on the `foreach` Statement

Figure 5-14 shows two examples of using the `foreach` statement to code the loop shown in Figure 5-12.

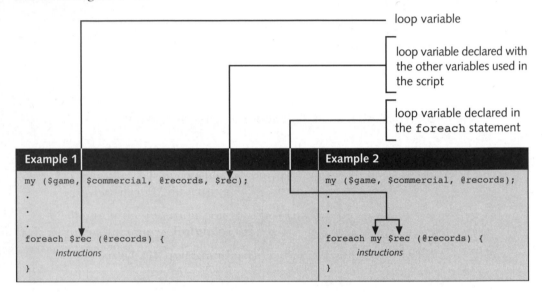

Figure 5-14   Two examples of using the `foreach` statement

As Example 1 indicates, you can declare the loop variable—in this case, `$rec`—in the same statement as the other variables used in the script. This is the way you declared the loop variable, which was named `$key`, in the juniper2.cgi script from Chapter 4. Like the `$key` variable used in the juniper2.cgi script, the `$rec` variable in Example 1 comes into existence when the **my** statement is processed, and it remains in the computer's memory until the script ends.

Rather than including the loop variable in the **my** statement, as shown in Example 1, most programmers declare the loop variable in the **foreach** statement itself, as shown in Example 2. To do so, you simply include the keyword **my** before the variable's name. A variable declared in this manner can be used only by the **foreach** statement and the instructions that appear within the statement's opening and closing braces. The variable comes into existence when the loop begins, which is when the **foreach** statement is first processed. The variable remains in memory until the loop has finished processing, at which time the variable is removed from the computer's memory.

When you declare a variable in a `foreach` (or `for`) statement, instructions entered above or below the statement do not have access to the variable.

To begin coding the loop shown in Figure 5-12:

1. In the blank line below the `close(INFILE);` statement, type **foreach my $rec (@records) {** and press **Enter** twice. Be sure to type the opening brace (`{`) at the end of the line. The code tells the computer to create a scalar variable named `$rec`. Each time the loop is processed, the next record stored in the `@records` array will be assigned to the `$rec` variable.

2. Type **}** (the closing brace), which marks the end of the `foreach` loop.

It is a good programming practice to enter the `foreach` statement's closing brace immediately after entering its opening brace. Forgetting to enter the closing brace is a common error made by programmers.

3. Save the super.cgi document.

The first two instructions in the loop are to remove the newline character (`\n`) from the end of the record, and then assign each field in the record to a separate variable. It is necessary to remove the newline character before making the assignments; otherwise, the newline character will be assigned along with the data in the last field. In this case, for example, the newline character will be assigned along with the commercial field data.

Removing the Newline Character

You can use the Perl **chomp function** to remove the invisible newline character (`\n`) from the end of a record. The syntax to do so is **chomp(***variable***)**, where *variable* is the name of the scalar variable that contains the record. You will use the statement `chomp($rec);` to remove the newline character from the `$rec` variable, which contains the current record.

To remove the newline character from the current record:

1. Position the insertion point in the blank line above the `foreach` statement's closing brace (`}`). Press **Tab** to indent the line, then type **chomp($rec);** and press **Enter**.

2. Save the super.cgi document.

Now assign each field in the current record to a variable. You can use the Perl `split` function to do so.

Using the `split` Function

The Perl **split function** allows you to split (divide) a string of characters into separate parts based on a specific character or characters. The syntax of the `split` function is **split(/***pattern***/,** *string***)**, where *pattern*, which is enclosed in forward slashes (`//`), is the one or more characters that separates one part of the *string* from another part of the *string*. For example, the function `split(/,/, "John,Jane")` tells the computer to split the string "John,Jane" into separate parts based on a *pattern* that consists of one character: a comma. In this case, the computer will separate the string into two parts: "John" and "Jane". Similarly, the function `split(/, /, "Carol, Peter, Carey")` tells the computer to split the string "Carol, Peter, Carey" into separate parts based on a *pattern* that consists of two characters: a comma and a space. In this case, the computer will separate the string into three parts: "Carol", "Peter", and "Carey".

You can assign the values returned by the `split` function to an array, a hash, or a list of individual scalar variables, as shown in Figure 5-15.

Examples and results

Example 1
```
($dad, $mom) = split(/,/, "Roger,Joan");
```

Result
Splits the string into two parts based on the comma. Assigns the first part (Roger) to the `$dad` variable, and the second part (Joan) to the `$mom` variable.

Example 2
```
($boy, $girl) = split(/\t/, "John    Jane");
```

Result
Assuming that a tab separates John from Jane in the string, splits the string into two parts based on the tab character. Assigns the first part (John) to the `$boy` variable, and assigns the second part (Jane) to the `$girl` variable.

Example 3
```
@names = split(/, /, $family);
```

Result
Assuming that the `$family` variable contains the string "John, Jane, Penny", splits the string into three parts based on the comma and space. Assigns the first part (John) to the `$names[0]` variable, the second part (Jane) to the `$names[1]` variable, and the third part (Penny) to the `$names[2]` variable.

Example 4
```
%codes = split(/:/, "1:Personnel:2:Accounting");
```

Result
Splits the string into four parts based on the colon. Assigns the first and second parts (1 and Personnel) as the first *key* and *value* in the `%codes` hash, and assigns the third and fourth parts (2 and Accounting) as the second *key* and *value* in the `%codes` hash.

Figure 5-15   `split` function examples and results

The statement shown in Example 1 assigns the values returned by the `split` function to a comma-separated list of scalar variables; the list must be enclosed within parentheses. In this case, the `split` function splits the string "Roger, Joan" into two parts based on the comma. The statement stores Roger in the `$dad` variable and Joan in the `$mom` variable.

The statement shown in Example 2 also assigns the values returned by the `split` function to a comma-separated list of scalar variables enclosed within parentheses. Assuming that an invisible tab character separates John from Jane in the string "John   Jane", the `split` function splits the string into two parts based on the tab character (\t). The statement stores John in the `$boy` variable, and Jane in the `$girl` variable.

The statement shown in Example 3 assigns the values returned by the `split` function to an array named `@names`. Assuming that the `$family` variable contains the string "John, Jane, Penny", the `split` function splits the string into three parts based on the comma and space. The statement stores John in the `$names[0]` variable, Jane in the `$names[1]` variable, and Penny in the `$names[2]` variable.

The statement shown in Example 4 assigns the values returned by the `split` function to a hash named `%codes`. In this example, the `split` function splits the string "1:Personnel:2:Accounting" into four parts based on the colon. The statement assigns 1 and Personnel as the first *key* and *value*, respectively, in the hash. It assigns 2 and Accounting as the second *key* and *value*, respectively, in the hash.

You will use the `split` function in the super.cgi script to divide each record contained in the `$rec` variable into two fields based on the comma. (Recall that you used a comma to separate the fields when you wrote each record to the survey.txt file.) You will assign the first field to the `$game` variable, and the second field to the `$commercial` variable.

To split the current record into fields, and assign each field to a variable:

1. The insertion point should be positioned in the blank line below the **chomp** function. Press **Tab**, if necessary, to indent the line, then type **($game, $commercial) = split(/,/, $rec);** and press **Enter**.

2. Save the super.cgi document.

The last two tasks associated with calculating the survey statistics are to add the number 1 to the appropriate game and commercial counters.

Using Counters

A **counter** is simply a variable used for counting something—such as the total number of votes cast for the Budweiser commercial. Two tasks are associated with a counter: initializing and updating. **Initializing** means to assign a beginning value to the counter. Although the beginning value usually is zero, counters can be initialized to any number; the initial value you use will depend on the algorithm. **Updating**, also called incrementing, means adding a number to the value stored in the counter. A counter is always incremented by a constant value—typically the number 1.

In addition to using a variable as a counter, you also can use a variable as an accumulator. You would use an accumulator if you needed to accumulate (add together) something—such as the total dollar amount of a customer's online purchase. Like a counter, an accumulator must be initialized and updated. Unlike a counter, however, an accumulator is incremented by an amount that varies.

In the super.cgi script, you will use an array of counters to keep track of the number of votes cast for each game choice on the Super Bowl form. You will use a hash of counters to keep track of the number of votes cast for each commercial choice.

To initialize and update the counters:

1. Enter the initialization and update statements, which are shaded in Figure 5-16.

```
#!/usr/bin/perl
#super.cgi - saves form data to a file, and creates a dynamic
#Web page that displays a message and survey statistics
print "Content-type: text/html\n\n";
use CGI qw(:standard);
use strict;

#declare variables
my ($game, $commercial, @records);
my @game_count = (0, 0, 0);
my %comm_count = ("Budweiser", 0,
                  "FedEx", 0,
                  "MasterCard", 0,
                  "Pepsi", 0);

#assign input items to variables
$game = param('Game');
$commercial = param('Commercial');

#save form data to a file
open(OUTFILE, ">>", "survey.txt")
     or die "Error opening survey.txt. $!, stopped";
print OUTFILE "$game,$commercial\n";
close(OUTFILE);

#calculate survey statistics
open(INFILE, "<", "survey.txt")
     or die "Error opening survey.txt. $!, stopped";
@records = <INFILE>;
close(INFILE);
foreach my $rec (@records) {
     chomp($rec);
     ($game, $commercial) = split(/,/, $rec);
     $game_count[$game] = $game_count[$game] + 1;
     $comm_count{$commercial} = $comm_count{$commercial} + 1;
}

#generate HTML acknowledgment
```

Figure 5-16   Initialization and update statements entered in the script

As you learned in Chapter 4, you enclose an array element's index in square brackets ([ ]), and a hash element's *key* in braces ({ }).

2. Save the super.cgi document.

You now have completed coding Step 3 in the Super Bowl algorithm. Step 4 is the last step you need to code.

COMPLETING THE SUPER BOWL SCRIPT

Step 4 in the Super Bowl algorithm shown earlier in Figure 5-4 is to create a dynamic Web page that displays an acknowledgment message and the total number of votes for each game and commercial choice. The super.cgi script already contains most of the code associated with Step 4. To complete the script, you just need to enter the code that displays the contents of the game and commercial counters. Recall that the game counters are contained in the @game_count array, and the commercial counters are contained in the @comm_count hash. First, enter the code to display the values stored in the @game_count array.

To display the values stored in the @game_count array:

1. Modify the three **print** statements indicated in Figure 5-17. The code you should enter is shaded in the figure.

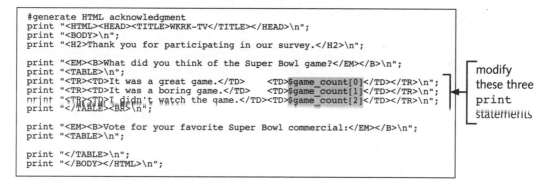

```
#generate HTML acknowledgment
print "<HTML><HEAD><TITLE>WKRK-TV</TITLE></HEAD>\n";
print "<BODY>\n";
print "<H2>Thank you for participating in our survey.</H2>\n";

print "<EM><B>What did you think of the Super Bowl game?</EM></B>\n";
print "<TABLE>\n";
print "<TR><TD>It was a great game.</TD>      <TD>$game_count[0]</TD></TR>\n";
print "<TR><TD>It was a boring game.</TD>      <TD>$game_count[1]</TD></TR>\n";
print "<TR><TD>I didn't watch the game.</TD><TD>$game_count[2]</TD></TR>\n";
print "</TABLE><BR>\n";

print "<EM><B>Vote for your favorite Super Bowl commercial:</EM></B>\n";
print "<TABLE>\n";

print "</TABLE>\n";
print "</BODY></HTML>\n";
```
modify these three print statements

Figure 5-17   Code that displays the contents of the game counters

2. Save the super.cgi document.

Unlike the game counters, the commercial counters are stored in a hash rather than in an array. Figure 5-18 shows examples of code that you can use to display the contents of the commercial counters on a Web page.

5

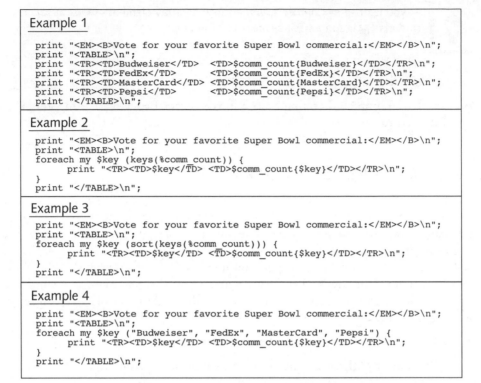

```
Example 1

print "<EM><B>Vote for your favorite Super Bowl commercial:</EM></B>\n";
print "<TABLE>\n";
print "<TR><TD>Budweiser</TD>  <TD>$comm_count{Budweiser}</TD></TR>\n";
print "<TR><TD>FedEx</TD>      <TD>$comm_count{FedEx}</TD></TR>\n";
print "<TR><TD>MasterCard</TD> <TD>$comm_count{MasterCard}</TD></TR>\n";
print "<TR><TD>Pepsi</TD>      <TD>$comm_count{Pepsi}</TD></TR>\n";
print "</TABLE>\n";
```

```
Example 2

print "<EM><B>Vote for your favorite Super Bowl commercial:</EM></B>\n";
print "<TABLE>\n";
foreach my $key (keys(%comm_count)) {
    print "<TR><TD>$key</TD> <TD>$comm_count{$key}</TD></TR>\n";
}
print "</TABLE>\n";
```

```
Example 3

print "<EM><B>Vote for your favorite Super Bowl commercial:</EM></B>\n";
print "<TABLE>\n";
foreach my $key (sort(keys(%comm_count))) {
    print "<TR><TD>$key</TD> <TD>$comm_count{$key}</TD></TR>\n";
}
print "</TABLE>\n";
```

```
Example 4

print "<EM><B>Vote for your favorite Super Bowl commercial:</EM></B>\n";
print "<TABLE>\n";
foreach my $key ("Budweiser", "FedEx", "MasterCard", "Pepsi") {
    print "<TR><TD>$key</TD> <TD>$comm_count{$key}</TD></TR>\n";
}
print "</TABLE>\n";
```

Figure 5-18   Examples of code that you can use to display the contents of the commercial counters

The code shown in Example 1 uses four **print** statements to print the contents of the counters on a Web page. Example 2's code uses a **foreach** loop to do so. The **keys(%comm_count)** that appears in the **foreach** statement is the **keys** function. The syntax of the **keys** function is **keys**(*hash*), where *hash* is the name of a hash. The **keys function** returns an unordered list of the *keys* stored in the *hash*, so the code in Example 2 might not print the commercial choices in the desired order, which, in this case, is the alphabetical order. (As you learned in Chapter 4, the scalar variables in a hash are stored in no particular order in the computer's memory.) You can, however, use the **sort function** to temporarily alphabetize the hash's *keys*. The syntax of the **sort** function is **sort**(*list*), where *list* is the values you want sorted; the **sort** function sorts the values in ascending alphabetical order. The **foreach** loop shown in Example 3 uses the **sort** function to temporarily sort the *keys* stored in the **%comm_count** hash. The code shown in Example 3 will produce the same result as the code shown in Example 1.

You can use the **values** function, whose syntax is **values**(*hash*), to return an unordered list of the *values* stored in a *hash*.

You also can use the sort function to temporarily sort a comma-separated list of values—for example, sort($name1, $name2, $name3). Additionally, you can use the sort function to temporarily sort the contents of an array—for example, sort(@names). To save the array values in sorted order, you simply assign the sort function's return values to either the same or a different array. The statement @names = sort(@names);, for instance, sorts the contents of the @names array and assigns the sorted values back to the array. The statement @sortednames = sort(@names);, on the other hand, sorts the contents of the @names array and assigns the sorted values to the @sortednames array.

5

In some cases, you might want to display a hash's *keys* and/or *values* in a specific order that might not be alphabetical. The code in Example 4 in Figure 5-18 shows how you can control the order in which the *keys* and/or *values* are displayed. Notice that you simply list each *key*, in the desired order, in the parentheses that follow the loop variable in the **foreach** statement. The code shown in Example 4 will produce the same result as the code shown in Examples 1 and 3.

You will use the code shown in Example 4 to complete the super.cgi script. (You will experiment with the code shown in Examples 1 through 3 in Hands-on Project 2 at the end of this chapter.)

To complete the super.cgi script, then save and test the script:

1. Enter the three lines of code shaded in Figure 5-19, which shows the completed script.

```
#!/usr/bin/perl
#super.cgi - saves form data to a file, and creates a dynamic
#Web page that displays a message and survey statistics
print "Content-type: text/html\n\n";
use CGI qw(:standard);
use strict;

#declare variables
my ($game, $commercial, @records);
my @game_count = (0, 0, 0);
my %comm_count = ("Budweiser", 0,
                  "FedEx", 0,
                  "MasterCard", 0,
                  "Pepsi", 0);

#assign input items to variables
$game = param('Game');
$commercial = param('Commercial');

#save form data to a file
open(OUTFILE, ">>", "survey.txt")
     or die "Error opening survey.txt. $!, stopped";
print OUTFILE "$game,$commercial\n";
close(OUTFILE);
```

Figure 5-19   Completed Super Bowl script

```
#calculate survey statistics
open(INFILE, "<", "survey.txt")
     or die "Error opening survey.txt. $!, stopped";
@records = <INFILE>;
close(INFILE);
foreach my $rec (@records) {
     chomp($rec);
     ($game, $commercial) = split(/,/, $rec);
     $game_count[$game] = $game_count[$game] + 1;
     $comm_count{$commercial} = $comm_count{$commercial} + 1;
}

#generate HTML acknowledgment
print "<HTML><HEAD><TITLE>WKRK-TV</TITLE></HEAD>\n";
print "<BODY>\n";
print "<H2>Thank you for participating in our survey.</H2>\n";

print "<EM><B>What did you think of the Super Bowl game?</EM></B>\n";
print "<TABLE>\n";
print "<TR><TD>It was a great game.</TD>    <TD>$game_count[0]</TD></TR>\n";
print "<TR><TD>It was a boring game.</TD>   <TD>$game_count[1]</TD></TR>\n";
print "<TR><TD>I didn't watch the game.</TD><TD>$game_count[2]</TD></TR>\n";
print "</TABLE><BR>\n";

print "<EM><B>Vote for your favorite Super Bowl commercial:</EM></B>\n";
print "<TABLE>\n";
foreach my $key ("Budweiser", "FedEx", "MasterCard", "Pepsi") {
     print "<TR><TD>$key</TD>  <TD>$comm_count{$key}</TD></TR>\n";
}
print "</TABLE>\n";
print "</BODY></HTML>\n";
```

enter
these
three
lines
of
code

Figure 5-19   Completed Super Bowl script (continued)

2. Save the super.cgi document.

3. *If you are using a UNIX system*, return to the UNIX command prompt. Type **clear** after the command prompt and press **Enter**.

   If you are using a Windows system, return to the Command Prompt window. Type **cls** after the command prompt and press **Enter**.

4. Type **perl –c super.cgi** and press **Enter**. If necessary, correct any syntax errors in the script before continuing to the next step.

5. Type **perl –w super.cgi** and press **Enter**. When the offline mode message appears, type **Game=2** and press **Enter**, then type **Commercial=Pepsi** and press **Enter**.

6. Press **Ctrl+d** (UNIX), or press **Ctrl+z** and then press **Enter** (Windows), to indicate that you are finished entering the record. See Figure 5-20.

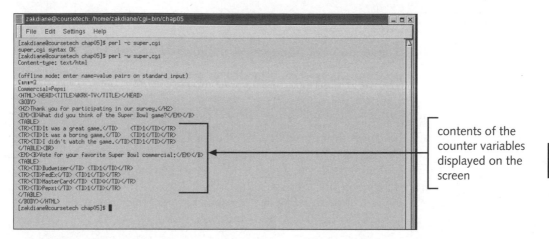

Figure 5-20   Terminal window showing the contents of the counter variables

Now test the script using your Web browser.

7. *If you are using a UNIX system*, change the survey.txt file permissions to **666**.

8. *If you are using a Windows system*, return to the super.cgi document in your text editor. Change "survey.txt" in the two **open** statements to **"chap05/survey.txt"**, then save the super.cgi document.

9. Start your Web browser. Use the browser's File menu to open the super.html file. Click the **It was a great game.** and **Pepsi** radio buttons, then click the **Submit Survey** button. If necessary, click the **Continue Submission** button. A dynamic Web page similar to the one shown in Figure 5-21 appears on the screen.

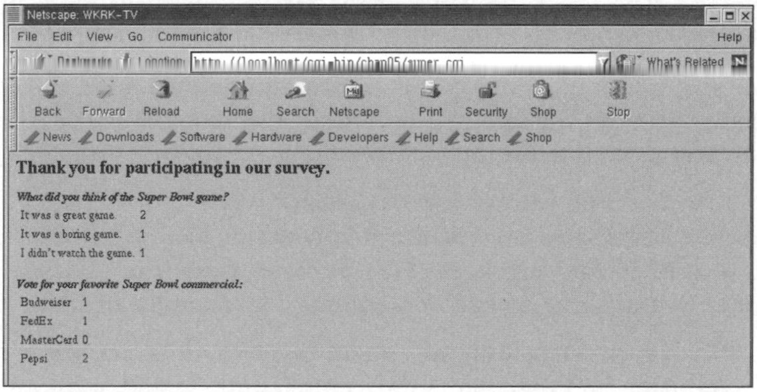

Figure 5-21   Dynamic Web page created by the Super Bowl script

10. Close your browser and any open windows.

CHAPTER SUMMARY

❑ A field is a single item of information about a person, place, or thing.

❑ A record is one or more related fields that contain all of the necessary data about a specific person, place, or thing.

❑ A collection of related records is called a data file.

❑ You use the **open** function to create and/or open a data file in a Perl script. The syntax of the **open** function is **open(***filehandle***, *mode*, *filename***)**. In the syntax, *filehandle* is a name that you assign to the data file you want to open. You use the "<" *mode* to open a file for input, the ">" *mode* to open the file for output, and the ">>" *mode* to open the file for append. The *filename* argument is the name of the file you want to open on the computer's disk.

❑ You use the **die** function to display a message and then exit a script when an error occurs. The syntax of the **die** function is **die** *message*, where *message* is an optional message that you want displayed on the screen.

❑ A description of the error that causes an **open** function to fail is stored in the $! variable.

❑ You can use the **print** function to write a record to an open file. The syntax to do so is **print** *filehandle data*\n;, where *filehandle* is the *filehandle* assigned to the file when the file was opened, and *data* is the one or more fields included in each record. You use a field separator to separate one field from another in a record. The newline character (\n) ensures that every record appears on a separate line in the file.

❑ You use the **close** function, whose syntax is **close(***filehandle***)**, to close an open file. In the syntax, *filehandle* is the *filehandle* assigned to the file when the file was opened.

❑ You use the syntax *arrayname* = <*filehandle*>; to read the records from a file into an array. In the syntax, *arrayname* is the name of the array, *filehandle* is the *filehandle* assigned to the file when the file was opened, and <> is the angle operator.

❑ You use the **chomp** function, whose syntax is **chomp(***variable***)**, to remove the invisible newline character from the end of a record. In the syntax, *variable* is the name of the scalar variable that contains the record.

❑ You use the **split** function, whose syntax is **split(/***pattern***/, *string***)**, to split (divide) a *string* into separate parts based on a *pattern* that contains one or more characters. The *pattern* is enclosed in forward slashes (//). You can assign the values returned by the **split** function to an array, a hash, or a comma-separated list of scalar variables.

❑ A counter is a variable used for counting something, and an accumulator is a variable used to accumulate (add together) something. Counters and accumulators need to be initialized and updated.

❑ You use the **keys** function, whose syntax is **keys(***hash***)**, to return an unordered list of the *keys* stored in a *hash*. You can use the **values** function, whose syntax is **values(***hash***)**, to return an unordered list of the *values* stored in a *hash*.

❐ You use the **sort** function, whose syntax is **sort**(*list*), to temporarily sort the values included in the *list*. The values are sorted in ascending alphabetical order.

REVIEW QUESTIONS

1. Which of the following statements opens the sales.txt file for input?

   a. `open(INF, ">", "sales.txt");`

   b. `open(INF, "<", "sales.txt");`

   c. `open(INF, ">>", "sales.txt");`

   d. None of the above.

2. If a file opened for input does not exist, the computer creates the file for you.

   a. true

   b. false

3. The _____ function tells the computer to display a message and then exit the script when an error has occurred.

   a. `abort`

   b. `die`

   c. `exit`

   d. `stop`

4. When an **open** function fails, Perl stores the reason for the failure in the _____ variable.

   a. `$!`

   b. `!$`

   c. `_$`

   d. `$_`

5. The statement `@cities = split(/,/, "Chicago,Detroit,Atlanta");` will assign the value Atlanta to the _____ variable.

   a. `@cities[2]`

   b. `@cities[3]`

   c. `$cities[3]`

   d. None of the above.

6. When writing a record to a file, you include the _____ character at the end of the **print** function to ensure that the record appears on a separate line in the file.

   a. `$!`

   b. `/n`

   c. `\n`

   d. None of the above.

7. Assume that the `@people` array contains three counters, each initialized to the number 0. Which of the following statements adds the number 1 to the second counter in the array?

   a. `@people[1] = @people[1] + 1;`

   b. `@people[2] = @people[2] + 1;`

   c. `$people[1] = $people[1] + 1;`

   d. `$people[2] = $people[2] + 1;`

8. Assume that the `%states` hash contains the *keys* "ME", "IL", and "TN". Which of the following statements can be used to display the *keys*?

   a. ```
      foreach my $x (keys(%states)) {
          print "$x\n";
      }
      ```

   b. ```
      foreach my $x (sort(keys(%states))) {
          print "$x\n";
      }
      ```

   c. ```
      foreach my $x ("TN", "ME", "IL") {
          print "$x\n";
      }
      ```

   d. All of the above.

9. You can use the _____ function to remove the newline character from the end of a record.

   a. `chomp`

   b. `delete`

   c. `delnew`

   d. `remove`

10. You can use the _____ function to divide a string of characters into separate parts based on a specific character or characters.

    a. `break`

    b. `divide`

    c. `separate`

    d. `split`

11. The angle operator in Perl is _____.

12. Write a `foreach` loop that displays the contents of the `@cities` array, in ascending alphabetical order. Display each city name on a separate line.
      ```

13. Write a statement that opens the employ.txt file for input. Assign the filehandle `INF` to the file. If the file cannot be opened, display the message "Error opening sales.txt" followed by the cause of the error, a comma, the word "stopped", the script name, and the line number of the line that caused the error.

14. Write a statement that opens the employ.txt file for output. Assign the filehandle `OUTEMP` to the file. If the file cannot be opened, display only the message "File error".

15. Write a statement that opens the payroll.txt file for output. Assign the filehandle `OUTFILE` to the file. If the file cannot be opened, display the default message "Died at *scriptname* line *linenumber*."

16. Write a statement that writes the contents of the `$name`, `$hours`, and `$pay` variables to a file whose *filehandle* is `OUTF`. Use the ampersand as the field separator.

17. Write a statement that closes the file whose *filehandle* is `INF`.

18. Write a statement that assigns the contents of the sales.txt file, whose *filehandle* is `INF`, to an array named `@sales`.

19. Write a statement that uses the `split` function to divide the contents of the `$record` variable based on the ampersand (&) character. The statement should assign the values returned by the function to three scalar variables named `$first`, `$middle`, and `$last`.

20. Assume that the `%regions` hash contains three counters, each initialized to the number 0. Write a statement that adds the number 1 to the counter whose *key* is North.

HANDS-ON PROJECTS

Project 1

In this project, you modify the Super Bowl form so that it assigns the *values* 0, 1, 2, and 3 to the commercial choices, and the *values* "Great", "Boring", and "None" to the game choices. You also modify the Super Bowl script so that it uses a hash to keep track of the number of votes for each game choice, and an array to keep track of the number of votes for each commercial choice.

a. Open the super.html file in a text editor. The file is contained in the public_html/chap05 directory.

b. Change the filename in the first line from super.html to c05ex1.html, then save the document as c05ex1.html.

c. Modify the <FORM> tag to refer to the c05ex1.cgi script.

d. Modify the document so that it assigns the *values* 0, 1, 2, and 3 to the VALUE property of the commercial radio buttons.

e. Modify the document so that it assigns the *values* Great, Boring, and None to the VALUE property of the game radio buttons.

f. Save the c05ex1.html document.

g. Open the super.cgi file in a text editor. The file is contained in the cgi-bin/chap05 directory.

h. Change the filename in the second line from super.cgi to c05ex1.cgi, then save the document as c05ex1.cgi.

i. *If you are using a UNIX system*, change the filename argument in the two **open** statements from "survey.txt" to "c05ex1.txt".

   If you are using a Windows system, change the filename argument in the two **open** statements from "chap05/survey.txt" to simply "c05ex1.txt".

j. Change the filename in the two **die** functions from survey.txt to c05ex1.txt.

k. Save the c05ex1.cgi document.

l. Modify the script so that it uses a hash (rather than an array) to keep track of the number of votes for each game choice.

m. Modify the script so that it uses an array (rather than a hash) to keep track of the number of votes for each commercial choice.

n. Modify the statements that display the number of game and commercial votes. (For the game choices, be sure to display the strings "It was a great game.", "It was a boring game.", and "I didn't watch the game." on the Web page.)

o. Save the c05ex1.cgi document.

p. *If you are using a UNIX system*, change the c05ex1.cgi file permissions to 755.

q. Test the script from the command line, using None as the Game choice, and 2 as the Commercial choice.

r. *If you are using a Windows system*, return to the c05ex1.cgi document in your text editor. Change the filename argument in the two **open** statements from "c05ex1.txt" to "chap05/c05ex1.txt", then save the c05ex1.cgi document.

s. *If you are using a UNIX system*, change the c05ex1.txt file permissions to 666.

t. Open the c05ex1.html file in your Web browser. Complete and submit the following four votes:

   I didn't watch the game., Pepsi

   It was a boring game., MasterCard

   It was a great game., Pepsi

   It was a great game., Budweiser

Project 2

In this project, you experiment with different ways of displaying the commercial counters in the Super Bowl script.

a. Open the super.cgi file in a text editor. The file is contained in the cgi-bin/chap05 directory.

b. Change the filename in the second line from super.cgi to c05ex2.cgi, then save the document as c05ex2.cgi.

c. *If you are using a UNIX system*, change the filename argument in the two **open** statements from "survey.txt" to "c05ex2.txt".

   If you are using a Windows system, change the filename argument in the two **open** statements from "chap05/survey.txt" to simply "c05ex2.txt".

d. Change the filename in the two **die** functions from survey.txt to c05ex2.txt.

e. Save the c05ex2.cgi document.

f. Modify the script so that it uses the code shown in Example 1 in Figure 5-18 to display the contents of the commercial counters.

g. Save the c05ex2.cgi document.

h. Test the script from the command line, using 0 as the Game choice, and Pepsi as the Commercial choice.

i. Modify the script so that it uses the code shown in Example 2 in Figure 5-18 to display the contents of the commercial counters.

j. Save the c05ex2.cgi document.

k. Test the script from the command line, using 1 as the Game choice, and MasterCard as the Commercial choice.

l. Modify the script so that it uses the code shown in Example 3 in Figure 5-18 to display the contents of the commercial counters.

m. Save the c05ex2.cgi document.

n. Test the script from the command line, using 2 as the Game choice, and Budweiser as the Commercial choice.

5

Project 3

In this project, you modify the Juniper Printers script that you created in Chapter 4 so that it saves the registration data to a file.

a. Copy the juniper.html file from the public_html/chap04 directory to the public_html/chap05 directory. Rename the file c05ex3.html.

b. Copy the juniper.cgi file from the cgi-bin/chap04 directory to the cgi-bin/chap05 directory. Rename the file c05ex3.cgi.

c. Open the c05ex3.html file in a text editor.

d. Change the filename in the first line from juniper.html to c05ex3.html.

e. Modify the <FORM> tag to refer to the c05ex3.cgi script, which is contained in the cgi-bin/chap05 directory.

f. Save the c05ex3.html document.

g. Open the c05ex3.cgi file in a text editor.

h. Change the filename in the second line from juniper.cgi to c05ex3.cgi. Also insert the text "saves the form data and" before the word "creates".

i. Modify the script so that it saves the registration data to a file named c05ex3.txt. Use the comma as the field separator.

j. Save the c05ex3.cgi document.

k. *If you are using a UNIX system*, change the c05ex3.cgi file permissions to 755.

l. Test the script from the command line. Use Henry+Jones as the name, NN34W as the serial number, 0 (for Laser JX) as the model, and M as the operating system.

m. Open the c05ex3.txt file in a text editor. The record you entered in Step l appears in the file. Close the c05ex3.txt file.

n. *If you are using a Windows system*, return to the c05ex3.cgi document in your text editor. Change the filename argument in the **open** statement from "c05ex3.txt" to "chap05/c05ex3.txt".

o. *If you are using a UNIX system*, change the c05ex3.txt file permissions to 666.

p. Open the c05ex3.html file in your Web browser. Enter Jeremiah Stein as the customer name and LW89W as the serial number. Select the Laser PL and UNIX radio buttons. Click the Submit Registration button. If necessary, click the Continue Submission button.

q. Return to the form. Enter Patty Smith as the customer name and JJ12R as the serial number. Select the ColorPrint XL and Windows radio buttons. Click the Submit Registration button. If necessary, click the Continue Submission button.

r. Open the c05ex3.txt file in a text editor. The file contains the three records you entered.

Project 4

In this project, you modify the script from Project 3 so that it uses the pipe symbol (|) as the field separator.

a. Open the jun.html file in a text editor. The file is contained in the public_html/chap05 directory.

b. Change the filename in the first line from jun.html to c05ex4.html, then save the document as c05ex4.html.

c. The <FORM> tag indicates that the form data will be processed by the c05ex4a.cgi script, which you will save in the cgi-bin/chap05 directory. Modify the <FORM> tag appropriately.

d. The <A> tag's HREF property links the text "View Registration File" to the c05ex4b.cgi script, which you will save in the cgi-bin/chap05 directory. Modify the HREF property appropriately.

e. Save the c05ex4.html document.

f. Open the c05ex3.cgi file in a text editor. The file, which you saved in Project 3, is contained in the cgi-bin/chap05 directory.

g. Change the filename in the second line from c05ex3.cgi to c05ex4a.cgi, then save the document as c05ex4a.cgi.

h. *If you are using a UNIX system*, change the filename argument in the **open** statement from "c05ex3.txt" to "c05ex4.txt".

   If you are using a Windows system, change the filename argument in the **open** statement from "chap05/c05ex3.txt" to simply "c05ex4.txt".

i. Change the filename in the **die** function from c05ex3.txt to c05ex4.txt.

j. Modify the **print** statement that saves the form data to the c05ex4.txt file. The statement should use the pipe symbol (|), rather than the comma, as the field separator.

k. Save the c05ex4a.cgi document.

l. *If you are using a UNIX system*, change the c05ex4a.cgi file permissions to 755.

m. Test the c05ex4a.cgi script from the command line. Use Patel,+Carol (notice the comma after Patel) as the customer name, OP83X as the serial number, 0 as the model, and M as the operating system.

n. Open the c05ex4.txt file in a text editor. The file contains the record you entered in Step m. Close the c05ex4.txt file.

o. *If you are using a Windows system*, return to the c05ex4a.cgi script. Change the filename argument in the **open** statement from "c05ex4.txt" to "chap05/c05ex4.txt".

p. *If you are using a UNIX system*, change the c05ex4.txt file permissions to 666.

q. Open the c05ex4.html file in your Web browser. Enter Barski, John as the customer name and OP56T as the serial number. Select the Laser PL and UNIX radio buttons. Click the Submit Registration button. If necessary, click the Continue Submission button.

r. Open the c05ex4.txt file in a text editor. The file contains the registration data for Carol Patel and John Barski.

s. Create a script named c05ex4b.cgi. The script should display the contents of the c05ex4.txt file on a Web page. Display each record (name, serial number, model number, and operating system letter) on a separate line, with a tab separating each field in the record. You will need to use the *pattern* /\|/ in the `split` function. As you learned in Chapter 3, the backslash alerts Perl to ignore the special meaning of a character and simply treat the character—in this case, the pipe symbol—verbatim.

t. Save the c05ex4b.cgi document.

u. *If you are using a UNIX* system, change the c05ex4b.cgi file permissions to 755.

v. Test the c05ex4b.cgi script from the command line. The registration data for Carol Patel and John Barski appears on the screen.

w. *If you are using a Windows system*, return to the c05ex4b.cgi document in your text editor. Change the filename argument in the `open` statement from "c05ex4.txt" to "chap05/c05ex4.txt", then save the c05ex4b.cgi document.

x. Return to your Web browser. Press the browser's Back button to return to the c05ex4.html form. Click the Reset the Form button.

y. Click the View Registration File link. The registration data for Carol Patel and John Barski appears on a Web page.

Project 5

In this project, you create a script for Seminar Workshop. The script displays, on a Web page, the number of people registering for each of four different seminars. The script also displays the total number of registrants. The registration data is stored in a file named c05ex5.txt.

a. Open the c05ex5.txt file, which is contained in the cgi-bin/chap05 directory, in a text editor. The file contains 10 records. Each record consists of two fields: the registrant's name and a seminar number. (Seminar 1 is the Computer Maintenance seminar, 2 is the Microsoft Office seminar, 3 is the Unix Essentials seminar, and 4 is the CGI/Perl seminar.)

b. *If you are using a UNIX system*, change the c05ex5.txt file permissions to 666.

c. Create a script named c05ex5.cgi that displays a Web page similar to the one shown in Figure 5-22. The Web page displays the number of people registered for each seminar, and the total number of registrants. (*Hint*: Use an array of counters to calculate the number of people registering for each seminar.)

Figure 5-22

d. Test the script from the command line.

e. To test the script from the browser, create an HTML document that links the text View Registration Information to the c05ex5.cgi script. Name the document c05ex5.html and save it in the public_html/chap05 directory.

f. *If you are using a Windows system,* change the filename argument in the **open** statement in the c05ex5.cgi document from "c05ex5.txt" to "chap05/c05ex5.txt", then save the c05ex5.cgi document.

g. Open the c05ex5.html document in your Web browser. Click the View Registration Information link. A Web page similar to the one shown in Figure 5-22 appears on the screen.

Project 6

In this project, you modify the Super Bowl script so that it stores the strings "It was a great game.", "It was a boring game.", and "I didn't watch the game." in an array.

a. Open the super.html file in a text editor. The file is contained in the public_html/chap05 directory.

b. Change the filename in the first line from super.html to c05ex6.html.

c. Modify the <FORM> tag to refer to the c05ex6.cgi script, then save the document as c05ex6.html.

d. Open the super.cgi file in a text editor. The file is contained in the cgi-bin/chap05 directory.

e. Change the filename in the second line from super.cgi to c05ex6.cgi, then save the document as c05ex6.cgi.

f. *If you are using a UNIX system,* change the filename argument in the two **open** statements from "survey.txt" to "c05ex6.txt".

   If you are using a Windows system, change the filename argument in the two **open** statements from "chap05/survey.txt" to simply "c05ex6.txt".

g. Change the filename in the two **die** functions from survey.txt to c05ex6.txt.

h. Save the c05ex6.cgi document.

i. Modify the script so that it stores the strings "It was a great game.", "It was a boring game.", and "I didn't watch the game." in an array named **@messages**.

j. Modify the script so that it uses a loop to display the contents of the game counters. (*Hint*: Use the **for** statement, which you learned about in Chapter 4, to code the loop.)

k. Save the c05ex6.cgi document.

l. *If you are using a UNIX system*, change the c05ex6.cgi file permissions to 755.

m. Test the script from the command line, using 0 as the Game choice, and Pepsi as the Commercial choice.

n. *If you are using a Windows system*, return to the c05ex6.cgi document in your text editor. Change the filename argument in the two **open** statements from "c05ex6.txt" to "chap05/c05ex6.txt", then save the c05ex6.cgi document.

o. *If you are using a UNIX system*, change the c05ex6.txt file permissions to 666.

p. Open the c05ex6.html file in your Web browser. Complete and submit the following three votes:

It was a boring game., MasterCard

It was a great game., Budweiser

It was a great game., MasterCard

CASE PROJECTS

1. Create an HTML form and a script for Jefferson High School. Name the form c05case1.html and save it in the public_html/chap05 directory. Name the script c05case1.cgi and save it in the cgi-bin/chap05 directory. The form should allow the user to select one of three students for class president. The student names are Jeff Stone, Sheima Nadkarni, and Sam Perez. The CGI script that processes the form data should save the votes in a data file named c05case1.txt. The script also should display the number of votes cast for each student.

2. Create an HTML form and a script for Jefferson High School. Name the form c05case2.html and save it in the public_html/chap05 directory. Name the script c05case2.cgi and save it in the cgi-bin/chap05 directory. The form should allow the user to enter his or her name. It also should allow the user to select his or her favorite subject—English, Math, History, Art, or Computer Science. The CGI script that processes the form data should save the form data in a data file named c05case2.txt. The script also should display the number of votes cast for each subject.

6

THE SELECTION STRUCTURE

In this chapter, you will:

♦ Code the selection structure using the Perl `if` statement
♦ Compare data using comparison operators
♦ Include logical operators in an `if` statement's *condition*
♦ Validate data passed to a script
♦ Add items to an array using the push function
♦ Determine the size of an array
♦ Code a multiple-path selection structure

Recall that all scripts, no matter how simple or how complex, are written using one or more of three basic structures: sequence, selection, and repetition. Called control structures or logic structures, they control the flow of a script's logic. You used the sequence structure in the scripts you created in previous chapters. Recall that the script instructions were processed, one after another, in the order in which each appeared in the script. Beginning in Chapter 4, you also used the repetition structure, which instructs the computer to repeat a block of instructions either a specified number of times or until some condition is met. In this chapter, you learn how to include the selection structure in a script. You use the selection structure to make a decision or comparison and then, based on the result of that decision or comparison, select one of two paths.

The Super Bowl Form and Script

Figure 6-1 shows the Super Bowl form from Chapter 5. It also indicates the *key* and *value* associated with each radio button on the form.

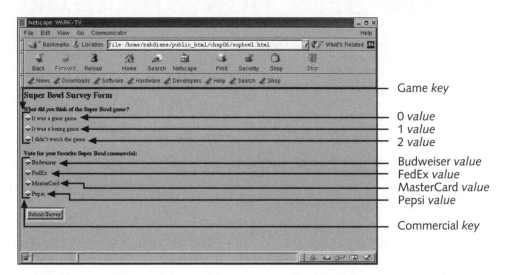

Figure 6-1 Super Bowl form

Notice that Game is the *key* associated with the first set of radio buttons, and Commercial is the *key* associated with the second set. The first set of radio buttons is assigned the *values* 0, 1, and 2. The second set is assigned the *values* Budweiser, FedEx, MasterCard, and Pepsi. Recall that when the user clicks the Submit Survey button, the browser sends to the server the *key* and *value* associated with the radio button selected in each set. The server then conveys the information to the Super Bowl script.

Figure 6-2 shows the Super Bowl script that you created in Chapter 5. (Your Super Bowl script might have a different shebang line. It also might include the **–debug** pragma.)

It is considered a good programming practice for a script to verify that the data received from the server is valid. **Valid data** is data that the script is expecting. The Super Bowl script, for example, expects to receive the *values* 0, 1, or 2 for the Game *key*. It is not expecting to receive the *value* 5, which might be passed to the script by an unscrupulous user calling the script either from his or her own form or with the text **Game=5** appended to the script's URL. Similarly, the Super Bowl script is expecting to receive the *values* Budweiser, FedEx, MasterCard, or Pepsi for the Commercial *key*. It is not expecting to receive an empty *value* (""), which is the *value* sent to the script when the user does not select one of the radio buttons from the Commercial section.

```perl
#!/usr/bin/perl
#super.cgi - saves form data to a file, and creates a dynamic
#Web page that displays a message and survey statistics
print "Content-type: text/html\n\n";
use CGI qw(:standard);
use strict;

#declare variables
my ($game, $commercial, @records);
my @game_count = (0, 0, 0);
my %comm_count = ("Budweiser", 0,
                  "FedEx", 0,
                  "MasterCard", 0,
                  "Pepsi", 0);

#assign input items to variables
$game = param('Game');
$commercial = param('Commercial');

#save form data to a file
open(OUTFILE, ">>", "survey.txt")
     or die "Error opening survey.txt. $!, stopped";
print OUTFILE "$game,$commercial\n";
close(OUTFILE);

#calculate survey statistics
open(INFILE, "<", "survey.txt")
     or die "Error opening survey.txt. $!, stopped";
@records = <INFILE>;
close(INFILE);
foreach my $rec (@records) {
     chomp($rec);
     ($game, $commercial) = split(/,/, $rec);
     $game_count[$game] = $game_count[$game] + 1;
     $comm_count{$commercial} = $comm_count{$commercial} + 1;
}

#generate HTML acknowledgment
print "<HTML><HEAD><TITLE>WKRK-TV</TITLE></HEAD>\n";
print "<BODY>\n";
print "<H2>Thank you for participating in our survey.</H2>\n";

print "<EM><B>What did you think of the Super Bowl game?</EM></B>\n";
print "<TABLE>\n";
print "<TR><TD>It was a great game.</TD>    <TD>$game_count[0]</TD></TR>\n";
print "<TR><TD>It was a boring game.</TD>    <TD>$game_count[1]</TD></TR>\n";
print "<TR><TD>I didn't watch the game.</TD><TD>$game_count[2]</TD></TR>\n";
print "</TABLE><BR>\n";

print "<EM><B>Vote for your favorite Super Bowl commercial:</EM></B>\n";
print "<TABLE>\n";
foreach my $key ("Budweiser", "FedEx", "MasterCard", "Pepsi") {
     print "<TR><TD>$key</TD> <TD>$comm_count{$key}</TD></TR>\n";
}
print "</TABLE>\n";
print "</BODY></HTML>\n";
```

Figure 6-2   Super Bowl script created in Chapter 5

If a script receives data that is not valid, it should display a Web page that directs the user to return to the form and correct any errors. A sample Web page that accomplishes this for the Super Bowl form is shown in Figure 6-3.

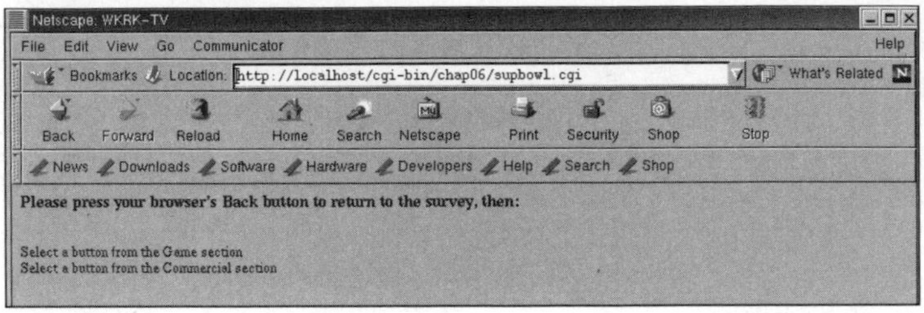

Figure 6-3   Sample corrective Web page for the Super Bowl form

In this chapter, you modify the Super Bowl script so that it validates the data received from the server, and displays a Web page similar to the one shown in Figure 6-3 if the data is incorrect. Figure 6-4 shows the modified output and algorithm for the Super Bowl script. Changes made to the original output and algorithm are shaded in the figure. (The original output and algorithm were shown in Figure 5-4 in Chapter 5.)

Notice that the modified output contains an additional item: a Web page that instructs the user to return to the form to correct the input data. Several changes were made to the original algorithm; the first change appears in Step 2 and indicates that the script will now validate the input data. Two selection structures are required to perform the validation. The first selection structure compares the *value* received for the game rating with the valid *values* for the Game *key* (0, 1, and 2). If the *value* received is not valid, then the script will store the message "Select a button from the Game section" in an array named **@errors**. The second selection structure compares the *value* received for the commercial vote with the valid *values* for the Commercial *key* (Budweiser, FedEx, MasterCard, and Pepsi). If the *value* received is not valid, then the script will store the message "Select a button from the Commercial section" in the **@errors** array.

In the next section, you learn how to code the selection structure in Perl.

Input	Output
game rating (0, 1, or 2) commercial vote (Budweiser, FedEx, MasterCard, or Pepsi)	file containing the form data Web page containing an acknowledgment message and the survey statistics Web page instructing the user to return to the form to correct the input data

Algorithm

1. assign input items to variables
2. validate input data
   a. if (game rating is not 0, 1, or 2)
      1) add "Select a button from the Game section" to @errors array
   b. if (commercial vote is not Budweiser, FedEx, MasterCard, or Pepsi)
      1) add "Select a button from the Commercial section" to @errors array
3. determine the size of the @errors array, which controls whether the input data is processed or the error Web page is displayed
4. process input data or display error Web page
   a. if (the size of the @errors array is equal to 0)
      1) save form data to a file
         (1) open the survey.txt file for append
         (2) write a record to the file
         (3) close the file
      2) calculate total number of votes for each game and commercial choice
         (1) open the survey.txt file for input
         (2) read the records into an array
         (3) close the file
         (4) repeat the following for each record stored in the array:
            (a) remove the newline character from the end of the record
            (b) assign each field in the record to a separate variable
            (c) add 1 to the appropriate game counter
            (d) add 1 to the appropriate commercial counter
      3) create a dynamic Web page that displays an acknowledgment message and the total number of votes for each game and commercial choice
   else
      1) create a dynamic Web page that displays a message instructing the user to return to the form to correct the input data, along with the values stored in the @errors array

Figure 6-4   Modified output and algorithm for the Super Bowl script

CODING THE SELECTION STRUCTURE IN PERL

You use the `if` statement to code the selection structure in Perl. Figure 6-5 shows the syntax of the `if` statement.

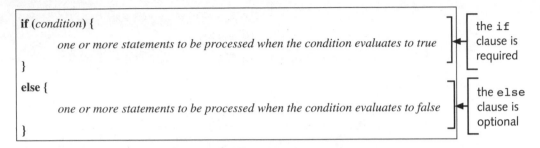

if (*condition*) {
         one or more statements to be processed when the condition evaluates to true
}
else {
         one or more statements to be processed when the condition evaluates to false
}

the `if` clause is required

the `else` clause is optional

Figure 6-5   Syntax of the Perl `if` statement

The `if` statement is composed of two clauses: the `if` clause and the `else` clause. As Figure 6-5 indicates, the `if` clause is required, but the `else` clause is optional.

The items in **bold** in the syntax are essential components of the `if` statement. For example, the keyword `if` and the parentheses that surround the *condition* are required. Also required are the braces ({}) that surround the statements to be processed when the *condition* evaluates to true. If the statement uses the `else` clause, then the keyword `else` and the braces ({}) that surround the statements to be processed when the *condition* evaluates to false also are required.

Items in *italics* in the syntax indicate where you must supply information pertaining to the current script. For instance, you must supply the *condition* to be evaluated. The *condition* must be a Boolean expression, which is an expression that results in a Boolean value (true or false). You also must supply the statements you want the computer to process when the *condition* evaluates to true and, optionally, when it evaluates to false.

The *condition* can contain variables, numbers, strings, functions, arithmetic operators, comparison operators, and logical operators. You already know about variables, numbers, strings, functions, and arithmetic operators. You learn about comparison operators and logical operators in the following sections.

Comparison Operators

Perl has two sets of **comparison operators**, also referred to as **relational operators**: you use one set to compare numeric values and the other to compare string values. Figure 6-6 lists the comparison operators for numeric values. The figure also shows the order of precedence for the operators. The precedence numbers indicate the order in which Perl performs the comparisons in an expression. Comparisons with a precedence number of

1 are performed before comparisons with a precedence number of 2. However, you can use parentheses to override the order of precedence.

Comparison operators for numeric values	Operation	Precedence
<	less than	1
<=	less than or equal to	1
>	greater than	1
>=	greater than or equal to	1
==	equal to	2
!=	not equal to	2
Important note: Notice that four of the operators contain two symbols. When using these operators, do not include any spaces between the symbols. Also be sure you do not reverse the symbols—in other words, use >=, but don't use =>.		

Figure 6-6   Perl comparison operators for numeric values

 Entering a space between the symbols in a comparison operator (for example, entering > = instead of >=) is a syntax error. Reversing the symbols in a comparison operator (for example, entering => instead of >=) also is a syntax error.

Notice that you use two equal signs (==) to test for the equality of two numeric values in Perl. You test for the inequality of two numeric values by using an exclamation point, which stands for *not*, followed by an equal sign (!=).

It is easy to confuse the equality operator (==), which is used to compare numeric values, with the assignment operator (=), which is used to assign a value to a memory location. Keep in mind that you use the Perl statement $num = 100; to assign the number 100 to the $num variable. However, you use the Perl *condition* $num == 100 to compare the contents of the $num variable with the number 100.

Figure 6-7 shows some examples of using the numeric comparison operators in an if statement's *condition*.

6

if statements	Results
| ```
if ($quantity >= 50) {
    $discount = .05;
}
``` | Assigns the number .05 to the $discount variable if the $quantity variable contains a number that is greater than or equal to the number 50. |
| ```
if ($num1 > $num2) {
    $temp = $num1;
    $num1 = $num2;
    $num2 = $temp;
}
``` | Swaps the numbers stored in the $num1 and $num2 variables if the $num1 variable contains a number that is greater than the number stored in the $num2 variable. |
| ```
if ($age < 18) {
    print "You cannot vote";
}
else {
    print "You can vote";
}
``` | Prints the string "You cannot vote" if the $age variable contains a number that is less than the number 18; otherwise, prints the string "You can vote". |
| ```
if ($code == 1) {
    $status = "Salaried";
    $pay = 35000;
}
else {
    $status = "Hourly";
    if($hours <= 40) {
        $pay = $hours * $rate;
    }
    else {
        $pay = $hours * $rate +
        ($hours - 40) * $rate/2;
    }
}
``` | Assigns the string "Salaried" and the number 35000 to the $status and $pay variables, respectively, if the $code variable contains the number 1; otherwise, assigns the string "Hourly" to the $status variable, and then uses a nested if statement to determine the number of hours worked. The nested if statement assigns the result of the regular pay calculation to the $pay variable if the $hours variable contains a number that is less than or equal to 40; otherwise, it assigns the result of the overtime pay calculation to the $pay variable. |

Figure 6-7   if statements that contain numeric comparison operators

 You always should indent the statements within the selection structure's if and else clauses for readability.

The first if statement shown in Figure 6-7 compares the contents of the $quantity variable with the number 50. If the $quantity variable contains a number that is greater than or equal to 50, the if statement assigns the number .05 to the $discount variable.

The second if statement compares the contents of the $num1 variable with the contents of the $num2 variable. The contents of both variables are swapped if the number contained in the $num1 variable is greater than the number contained in the $num2 variable.

Unlike the first two if statements, the third and fourth if statements contain an else clause. The third if statement compares the contents of the $age variable with the number 18. If the $age variable contains a number that is less than 18, the if statement prints the string "You cannot vote"; otherwise, it prints the string "You can vote".

The fourth if statement shown in Figure 6-7 compares the contents of the $code variable with the number 1. If the $code variable contains a number that is equal to 1, the if statement assigns the string "Salaried" and the number 35000 to the $status and $pay variables, respectively. However, if the $code variable does not contain the number 1, the else clause assigns the string "Hourly" to the $status variable, and then uses a nested if statement to compare the contents of the $hours variable with the number 40. If the $hours variable contains a number that is less than or equal to 40, the nested if statement calculates regular pay and assigns the result to the $pay variable; otherwise, it calculates regular pay plus overtime pay and assigns the result to the $pay variable.

 A nested if statement is simply an if statement that is contained (nested) within another if statement.

Figure 6-8 lists the comparison operators used to compare string values in Perl. Notice that each comparison operator is entered using lowercase letters.

Comparison operators for string values	Operation	Precedence
lt	less than	1
le	less than or equal to	1
gt	greater than	1
ge	greater than or equal to	1
eq	equal to	2
ne	not equal to	2
Important note: Be sure to type the operators using lowercase letters.		

Figure 6-8   Perl comparison operators for string values

When used to compare two strings, the string comparison operators compare the ASCII value of each character in the first string to the corresponding character in the second string. Both strings are considered equal if each contains the exact same characters from start to finish. If both strings do not contain the exact same characters, then the first character that differs in both strings determines whether the first string is less than or greater than the second string. If the character in the first string has a lower ASCII value than the character in the second string, then the first string is considered less than the second string. For example, the string "Ace" is considered less than the string "ace", because the character "A" comes before the character "a" in the ASCII coding scheme. Similarly, if the character in the first string has a higher ASCII value than the character in the second string, then the first string is considered greater than the second string.

For example, the string "now" is considered greater than the string "not", because the character "w" comes after the character "t" in the ASCII coding scheme.

 ASCII (pronounced *ASK-ee*) stands for American Standard Code for Information Interchange. The ASCII coding scheme assigns a specific value to each character (letter, number, and symbol) on the keyboard. For example, the uppercase letter A is assigned the ASCII value 65, and the lowercase letter a is assigned the ASCII value 97. The ASCII values assigned to each character on the keyboard are shown in Appendix D.

Figure 6-9 shows some examples of using the string comparison operators in an `if` statement's *condition*.

if statements	Results

`if ($name eq "Mary") {`
`    $msg = "Hello, Mary";`
`}`
	Assigns the string "Hello, Mary" to the `$msg` variable if the string stored in the `$name` variable is equal to "Mary".

`if ($state ge "KY") {`
`    print $state;`
`}`
	Prints the contents of the `$state` variable if the string stored in the variable is greater than or equal to "KY".

`if ($zip ne "") {`
`    print $zip;`
`}`
`else {`
`    print "Missing Zip Code";`
`}`
	Prints the contents of the `$zip` variable if the variable does not contain the empty string (""); otherwise, prints the message "Missing Zip Code".

`if ($age < 18) {`
`    print "You cannot vote";`
`}`
`else {`
`    if ($registered eq "Y") {`
`        print "You can vote";`
`    }`
`    else {`
`        print "Please register";`
`    }`
`}`
	Prints the string "You cannot vote" if the `$age` variable contains a number that is less than the number 18; otherwise, uses a nested `if` statement to compare the contents of the `$registered` variable with the letter "Y". If the string stored in the `$registered` variable is equal to the letter "Y", prints the string "You can vote"; otherwise, prints the string "Please register".

Figure 6-9   `if` statements that contain string comparison operators

The first `if` statement shown in Figure 6-9 compares the string stored in the `$name` variable with the string "Mary". If the string stored in the `$name` variable is equal to "Mary", the `if` statement assigns the message "Hello, Mary" to the `$msg` variable.

The second `if` statement compares the string stored in the `$state` variable with the string "KY". If the string stored in the `$state` variable is greater than or equal to "KY", the `if` statement prints the contents of the `$state` variable.

The third `if` statement compares the string stored in the `$zip` variable with the empty string (""). If the `$zip` variable does not contain the empty string, the `if` statement prints the contents of the `$zip` variable; otherwise, it prints the message "Missing Zip Code".

The fourth `if` statement shown in Figure 6-9 compares the number stored in the `$age` variable with the number 18. If the number stored in the `$age` variable is less than 18, the `if` statement prints the string "You cannot vote"; otherwise, it uses a nested `if` statement to compare the contents of the `$registered` variable with the letter "Y". If the string stored in the `$registered` variable is equal to "Y", the nested `if` statement prints the string "You can vote"; otherwise, it prints the string "Please register".

Be sure that the comparison operator you use matches the type of data you are comparing. In other words, use numeric comparison operators to compare numeric values, and string comparison operators to compare string values; otherwise, your values might not compare correctly. For example, if a string appears on either or both sides of a numeric comparison operator, Perl converts the string to a number before making the comparison. In many cases, the conversion produces the results you are expecting. For example, when evaluating the expression `"5" > "10"`, Perl first converts each string ("5" and "10") to its numeric equivalent (5 and 10), and then compares the two numbers. In this case, the expression correctly evaluates to false, because the number 5 is not greater than the number 10. Sometimes, however, Perl cannot convert a string to its numeric equivalent, simply because a numeric equivalent does not exist. The string "Jan", for example, does not have a numeric equivalent, so Perl converts the string to the number 0. Therefore, the expression `"Jan" == "Ted"` incorrectly evaluates to true, because 0 equals 0.

If you include a numeric value on either or both sides of a string comparison operator, Perl automatically converts the number to a string before making the comparison. Here again, the conversion might or might not produce the results you are expecting. For example, when evaluating the expression `5 lt 6`, Perl first converts the two numbers (5 and 6) to strings ("5" and "6"), and then compares the two strings. Because the string "5" appears before the string "6" in the ASCII coding scheme, the expression correctly evaluates to true; 5 is less than 6. The expression `5 lt 10`, on the other hand, will evaluate incorrectly as false, because the character "5" appears after the character "1" in the ASCII coding scheme.

As you learned earlier, if two strings do not contain the exact same characters, then the first character that differs in both strings determines whether the first string is less than or greater than the second string.

Recall that you also can use logical operators in an `if` statement's *condition*.

Logical Operators

The most commonly used logical operators are **and** and **or**. Logical operators allow you to combine two or more *conditions* into one compound *condition*. When the **and** operator is used to create a compound condition, all of the conditions must be true for the compound condition to be true. However, when the **or** logical operator is used, only one of the conditions needs to be true for the compound condition to be true. The tables shown in Figure 6-10, called truth tables, summarize how Perl evaluates the logical operators in an expression.

Truth table for the and operator		
Value of *condition1*	Value of *condition2*	Value of *condition1* and *condition2*
true	true	true
true	false	false
false	true	false
false	false	false
Truth table for the or operator		
Value of *condition1*	Value of *condition2*	Value of *condition1* or *condition2*
true	true	true
true	false	true
false	true	true
false	false	false

Figure 6-10 Truth tables for the and and or operators

As Figure 6-10 indicates, when you use the **and** operator to combine two conditions (*condition1* **and** *condition2*), the resulting compound condition is true only when both conditions are true. If either condition is false, or if both conditions are false, then the compound condition is false. Compare the **and** operator with the **or** operator. When you combine conditions using the **or** operator, notice that the compound condition is false only when both conditions are false. If either condition is true, or if both conditions are true, then the compound condition is true.

 If you use the and operator to combine two conditions, Perl does not evaluate the second condition if the first condition is false. In this case, there is no need to evaluate the second condition, because both conditions combined with the and operator need to be true for the compound condition to be true. If, on the other hand, you use the or operator to combine two conditions, Perl does not evaluate the second condition if the first condition is true. In this case, there is no need to evaluate the second condition, because only one of the conditions combined with the or operator needs to be true for the compound condition to be true.

Figure 6-11 shows examples of using a logical operator in an **if** statement's condition.

The first `if` statement shown in Figure 6-11 prints the message "Valid status" if the number stored in the `$status` variable is equal to either the number 1 or the number 2; otherwise, it prints the message "Invalid status". The second `if` statement assigns the result of the calculation to the `$bonus` variable if the string stored in the `$state` variable is equal to the string "CA" and, at the same time, the number stored in the `$sales` variable is greater than the number 0. The last `if` statement prints the message "Please enter a correct code" if the `$code` variable contains the empty string (""), or if the variable contains a number that is not equal to the number 1 and also not equal to the number 2.

6

```
if statements/Results
if ($status == 1 or $status == 2) {
    print "Valid status";
}
else
{
    print "Invalid status";
}
```
Result: Prints the message "Valid status" if the number stored in the $status variable is equal to either the number 1 or the number 2; otherwise, prints the message "Invalid status".

```
if ($state eq "CA" and $sales > 0) {
    $bonus = $sales * $rate;
}
```
Result: Assigns the result of the calculation to the $bonus variable if the string stored in the $state variable is equal to "CA" and, at the same time, the number stored in the $sales variable is greater than 0.

```
if ($code eq "" or $code != 1 and $code != 2) {
    print "Please enter a correct code";
}
```
Result: Prints the message "Please enter a correct code" if the $code variable contains the empty string (" "), or if the $code variable contains a number that is not equal to the number 1 and also not equal to the number 2.

Figure 6-11 `if` statements that contain logical operators

Now that you know how to use the `if` statement and the comparison and logical operators, you can begin coding Step 2 in the Super Bowl algorithm.

VALIDATING SCRIPT INPUT DATA

Recall that Step 2 in the Super Bowl algorithm is to validate the input data. The tasks the computer must perform to do so are shown in Figure 6-12.

---

2. validate input data
   a. if (game rating is not 0, 1, or 2)
      1) add "Select a button from the Game section" to @errors array
   b. if (commercial vote is not Budweiser, FedEx, MasterCard, or Pepsi)
      1) add "Select a button from the Commercial section" to @errors array

---

Figure 6-12   Step 2 in the Super Bowl algorithm

As mentioned earlier, Step 2 contains two selection structures; both are used to validate the input data received from the server.

To begin coding Step 2 in the Super Bowl algorithm:

1. Open the supbowl.cgi file in a text editor. The file is contained in the cgi-bin/chap06 directory.

   The supbowl.cgi file is the same as the super.cgi file that you created in Chapter 5, except it contains several additional comments and some of the code has been indented for you.

2. If necessary, change the shebang line to reflect the location of the Perl interpreter on your system.

3. If necessary, add the **-debug** pragma to the use CGI qw(:standard); statement.

   The first selection structure shown in Figure 6-12 should validate the game rating value received from the server. Figure 6-13 shows four different *conditions* that you can use in an **if** statement to accomplish this task.

Test for incorrect values

```
($game ne "0" and $game ne "1" and $game ne "2")
($game eq "" or ($game != 0 and $game != 1 and $game != 2))
```

Test for correct values

```
($game eq "0" or $game eq "1" or $game eq "2")
($game ne "" and ($game == 0 or $game == 1 or $game == 2))
```

Figure 6-13   *Conditions* you can use to validate the game rating value

Notice that you can use a *condition* that tests for either incorrect or correct values. Also notice that you can use either string comparison operators or numeric comparison operators in the *condition*. In this case, Step 2 in the algorithm indicates that you need to check for invalid game rating values. Therefore, you can use either the first or second *condition* shown in Figure 6-13. In the next step, you use the first *condition*. (In Hands-on Project 1 at the end of this chapter, you modify the script so that it uses the second *condition*.)

4. In the blank line below the comment #validate input data, type **if ($game ne "0" and $game ne "1" and $game ne "2") {** and press **Enter**. (Be sure to type the ending parentheses, a space, and the opening brace.)

5. Save the supbowl.cgi document.

According to Step 2 in the algorithm, if the game rating value is not valid, the script should add the message "Select a button from the Game section" to an array named @errors.

Adding Items to an Array

You can use the Perl **push** function to add one or more items to the end of an array. Figure 6-14 shows the syntax of the **push** function and several examples of using the function in a statement. In the syntax, *list* is the one or more items you want added to the *array*. If *list* contains more than one item, you use a comma to separate one item from the next.

Syntax	
push(*array*, *list*)	
Examples	Results
push(@states, "Hawaii");	adds the string "Hawaii" to the end of the @states array
push(@nums, 10, 25);	adds the numbers 10 and 25 to the end of the @nums array
push(@names, @employees);	adds the contents of the @employees array to the end of the @names array

Figure 6-14   Syntax and examples of the push function

You also can add one or more items to the end of an array using a statement that follows the syntax *array = (array, list);*. For example, you could use the statement @nums = (@nums, 10, 25); to add the numbers 10 and 25 to the end of the @nums array.

To insert one or more items at the beginning of an array, you use a statement that follows the syntax *array = (list, array);*. The statement @nums = (10, 25, @nums);, for example, inserts the numbers 10 and 25 at the beginning of the @nums array.

You also can insert items in the middle of an array. Additionally, you can remove items from the beginning, end, and middle of an array. You learn how to accomplish these tasks in Hands-on Project 6 at the end of this chapter.

The statement shown in the first example in Figure 6-14 adds the string "Hawaii" to the end of the @states array. If the @states array contained two elements (Alabama and Wisconsin), it would contain three elements (Alabama, Wisconsin, and Hawaii) after the statement was processed. The statement shown in the second example adds the numbers 10 and 25 to the end of the @nums array. You also can append the contents of one array to the end of another array. The statement shown in the third example in Figure 6-14, for example, adds the contents of the @employees array to the end of the @names array.

To continue coding Step 2 in the Super Bowl algorithm:

1. The insertion point should be positioned in the blank line below the if statement. Press **Tab** to indent the line, then type **push(@errors, "Select a button from the Game section");** and press **Enter**.

2. Press **Backspace**, if necessary, to cancel the indentation, then type **}** (the closing brace) and press **Enter** twice.

   Now declare the @errors array by including its name in the my statement located below the comment #declare variables.

3. Change the my ($game, $commercial, @records); statement to **my ($game, $commercial, @records, @errors);**.

   Now complete Step 2 by entering an if statement that compares the value stored in the $commercial variable with the values "Budweiser", "FedEx", "MasterCard", and "Pepsi". If the $commercial variable does not contain one of these values, then add the message "Select a button from the Commercial section" to the @errors array.

4. Type the additional code shaded in Figure 6-15.

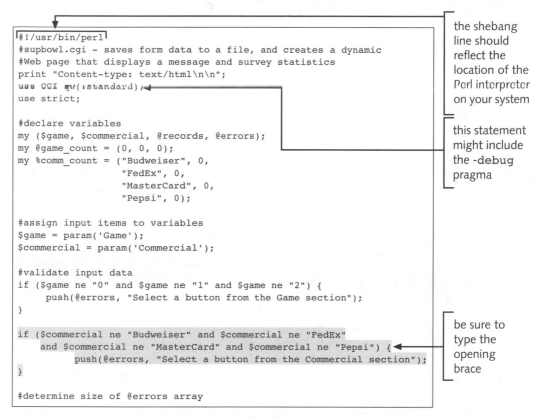

```
#!/usr/bin/perl
#supbowl.cgi - saves form data to a file, and creates a dynamic
#Web page that displays a message and survey statistics
print "Content-type: text/html\n\n";
use CGI qw(:standard);
use strict;

#declare variables
my ($game, $commercial, @records, @errors);
my @game_count = (0, 0, 0);
my %comm_count = ("Budweiser", 0,
                  "FedEx", 0,
                  "MasterCard", 0,
                  "Pepsi", 0);

#assign input items to variables
$game = param('Game');
$commercial = param('Commercial');

#validate input data
if ($game ne "0" and $game ne "1" and $game ne "2") {
    push(@errors, "Select a button from the Game section");
}

if ($commercial ne "Budweiser" and $commercial ne "FedEx"
    and $commercial ne "MasterCard" and $commercial ne "Pepsi") {
        push(@errors, "Select a button from the Commercial section");
}

#determine size of @errors array
```

the shebang line should reflect the location of the Perl interpreter on your system

this statement might include the -debug pragma

be sure to type the opening brace

Figure 6-15   Second `if` statement entered in the script

5. Save the supbowl.cgi document.

Now that you have finished coding Step 2 in the algorithm, you can begin coding Step 3.

DETERMINING THE SIZE OF AN ARRAY

Step 3 in the algorithm is to determine the size of the `@errors` array. The size will control whether the input data is processed or an error Web page is displayed. You can determine the size of an array—in other words, the number of scalar variables contained in the array—simply by assigning the name of the array to a scalar variable. For example, the statement `$size = @errors;` assigns the size of the `@errors` array to the `$size` variable.

You also can determine the size of an array using the `scalar` function, whose syntax is **scalar(*array*);**. For example, the statement `print scalar(@errors);` prints the number of scalar variables contained in the `@errors` array.

To code Step 3 in the algorithm:

1. In the blank line below the comment `#determine size of @errors array`, type **$size = @errors;** and press **Enter**.

   Now declare the `$size` variable by including its name in the **my** statement located below the comment `#declare variables`.

2. Change the `my ($game, $commercial, @records, @errors);` statement to **my ($game, $commercial, $size, @records, @errors);**.

 Some programmers group the variables listed in the my statement by data type, as shown in Step 2. Other programmers list the variable names alphabetically.

3. Save the supbowl.cgi document.

To complete the supbowl.cgi script, you just need to make the modifications indicated in Step 4 in the algorithm.

COMPLETING THE SUPER BOWL SCRIPT

Step 4 in the Super Bowl algorithm is to process the input data or display an error Web page. The tasks the computer must perform to do so are shown in Figure 6-16.

```
4.  process input data or display error Web page
    a.  if (the size of the @errors array is equal to 0)
        1)  save form data to a file
            (1)  open the survey.txt file for append
            (2)  write a record to the file
            (3)  close the file
        2)  calculate total number of votes for each game and commercial choice
            (1)  open the survey.txt file for input
            (2)  read the records into an array
            (3)  close the file
            (4)  repeat the following for each record stored in the array:
                 (a)  remove the newline character from the end of the record
                 (b)  assign each field in the record to a separate variable
                 (c)  add 1 to the appropriate game counter
                 (d)  add 1 to the appropriate commercial counter
        3)  create a dynamic Web page that displays an acknowledgment message and the total
            number of votes for each game and commercial choice
        else
        1)  create a dynamic Web page that displays a message instructing the user to return to
            the form to correct the input data, along with the values stored in the @errors array
```

Figure 6-16 Step 4 in the Super Bowl algorithm

The code for most of Step 4 is already entered in the script. You just need to make the modifications that are shaded in the figure. The first modification uses a selection structure to determine if the @errors array contains any elements. If the size of the array is equal to 0, then no errors were found in the input data, and the script can simply process the input data. However, if the size of the array is not equal to 0, then one or more errors were found in the input data, and the script should display a Web page that lists the errors.

To complete the script:

1. In the blank line below the comment #process input data or display error page, type **if ($size == 0) {** (be sure to type the opening brace) and press **Enter**.

2. Press **Tab** to indent the line, then type **#process input data**.

3. Scroll down to the end of the script. Type a closing brace (}) and the additional lines of code shaded in Figure 6-17, which shows the completed Super Bowl script.

```perl
#!/usr/bin/perl
#supbowl.cgi - saves form data to a file, and creates a dynamic
#Web page that displays a message and survey statistics
print "Content-type: text/html\n\n";
use CGI qw(:standard);
use strict;

#declare variables
my ($game, $commercial, $size, @records, @errors);
my @game_count = (0, 0, 0);
my %comm_count = ("Budweiser", 0,
                  "FedEx", 0,
                  "MasterCard", 0,
                  "Pepsi", 0);

#assign input items to variables
$game = param('Game');
$commercial = param('Commercial');

#validate input data
if ($game ne "0" and $game ne "1" and $game ne "2") {
    push(@errors, "Select a button from the Game section");
}

if ($commercial ne "Budweiser" and $commercial ne "FedEx"
    and $commercial ne "MasterCard" and $commercial ne "Pepsi") {
        push(@errors, "Select a button from the Commercial section");
}

#determine size of @errors array
$size = @errors;
```

Figure 6-17 Completed Super Bowl script

```
#process input data or display error page
if ($size == 0) {
     #process input data
     #save form data to a file
     open(OUTFILE, ">>", "survey.txt")
          or die "Error opening survey.txt. #!, stopped";
     print OUTFILE "$game,$commercial\n";
     close(OUTFILE);

     #calculate survey statistics
     open(INFILE, "<", "survey.txt")
          or die "Error opening survey.txt. $!, stopped";
     @records = <INFILE>;
     close(INFILE);
     foreach my $rec (@records) {
          chomp($rec);
          ($game, $commercial) = split(/,/, $rec);
          $game_count[$game] = $game_count[$game] + 1;
          $comm_count{$commercial} = $comm_count{$commercial} + 1;
     }
     #generate HTML acknowledgment
     print "<HTML><HEAD><TITLE>WKRK-TV</TITLE></HEAD>\n";
     print "<BODY>\n";
     print "<H2>Thank you for participating in our survey.</H2>\n";

     print "<EM><B>What did you think of the Super Bowl game?</EM></B>\n";
     print "<TABLE>\n";
     print "<TR><TD>It was a great game.</TD>     <TD>$game_count[0]</TD></TR>\n";
     print "<TR><TD>It was a boring game.</TD>     <TD>$game_count[1]</TD></TR>\n";
     print "<TR><TD>I didn't watch the game.</TD><TD>$game_count[2]</TD></TR>\n";
     print "</TABLE><BR>\n";

     print "<EM><B>Vote for your favorite Super Bowl commercial:</EM></B>\n";
     print "<TABLE>\n";
     foreach my $key ("Budweiser", "FedEx", "MasterCard", "Pepsi") {
          print "<TR><TD>$key</TD>     <TD>$comm_count{$key}</TD></TR>\n";
     }
     print "</TABLE>\n";
     print "</BODY></HTML>\n";
}
else {
     #display error page
     print "<HTML><HEAD><TITLE>WKRK-TV</TITLE></HEAD>\n";
     print "<BODY>\n";
     print "<H2>Please press your browser's Back button to \n";
     print "return to the survey, then: </H2><BR>\n";
     for(my $x = 0; $x < $size; $x = $x + 1) {
          print "$errors[$x]<BR>\n";
     }
     print "</BODY></HTML>\n";
}
```

enter
these
lines
of
code

Figure 6-17   Completed Super Bowl script (continued)

Recall that you learned about the `for` statement in Chapter 4.

4. Save the supbowl.cgi document

Now test the script from the command line and browser to make sure that the code you entered is working correctly.

To test the supbowl.cgi script:

1. *If you are using a UNIX system*, open a terminal window, if necessary. Make the cgi–bin/chap06 directory the current directory, and then change the supbowl.cgi file permissions to **755**.

   If you are using a Windows system, open a Command Prompt window, and then make the cgi–bin\chap06 directory the current directory.

   First, check the script for syntax errors.

2. Type **perl –c supbowl.cgi** after the command prompt and press **Enter**. If necessary, correct any syntax errors in the script before continuing to the next step.

   Now execute the script and test it using valid input data.

3. Type **perl –w supbowl.cgi** and press **Enter**. When the offline mode message appears, type **Game=1** and press **Enter**, then type **Commercial=FedEx** and press **Enter**.

4. Press **Ctrl+d** (UNIX), or press **Ctrl+z** and then press **Enter** (Windows), to indicate that you have finished entering the record. The script validates the input data. Because both input values are valid, the script processes the input data and displays an acknowledgment message and the survey statistics.

   Now test the script using invalid input data.

5. Type **perl –w supbowl.cgi** and press **Enter**. When the offline mode message appears, type **Game=** (don't type anything after the equal sign; this is equivalent to the user not selecting a button from the Game section) and press **Enter**, then type **Commercial=Visa** and press **Enter**.

6. Press **Ctrl+d** (UNIX), or press **Ctrl+z** and then press **Enter** (Windows) to indicate that you have finished entering the record. The script validates the input data. Because both input values are invalid, the script displays the messages shown in Figure 6-18.

6

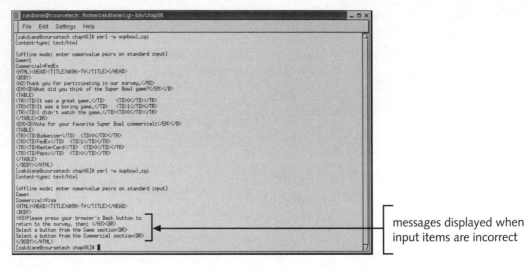

messages displayed when
input items are incorrect

Figure 6-18   Messages displayed when both input values are incorrect

7. On your own, test the script using a valid value for the game rating and an invalid value for the commercial vote—for example, use 1 as the game rating value and Discover as the commercial vote value. Then test the script using an invalid value for the game rating and a valid value for the commercial vote—for example, use 5 as the game rating value and FedEx as the commercial vote value.

Now test the script from your browser.

To test the script from your browser:

1. *If you are using a UNIX system*, change the file permissions for the survey.txt file to **666**.

2. *If you are using a Windows system*, return to the supbowl.cgi script in your text editor. Change the filename argument in both **open** statements from **"survey.txt"** to **"chap06/survey.txt"**, then save the script.

3. Open the supbowl.html file in a text editor. The file is contained in the public_html/chap06 directory. Change yourservername in the <FORM> tag to the name of your server, then save the supbowl.html file.

4. Start your Web browser. Use the browser's File menu to open the supbowl.html file.

5. Click the **It was a great game.** radio button, then click the **Submit Survey** button. Click the **Continue Submission** button, if necessary. The script validates the input data. Because the commercial vote value is incorrect (no button was selected in the Commercial section), the script displays a dynamic Web page similar to the one shown in Figure 6-19.

Figure 6-19   Web page showing messages displayed when the commercial value is incorrect

6. Return to the survey form. Click the **It was a boring game.** and **Pepsi** radio buttons, then click the **Submit Survey** button. Click the **Continue Submission** button, if necessary. The script validates the input data. Because both input values are correct, the script displays a dynamic Web page that contains an acknowledgment message and the survey statistics, as shown in Figure 6-20.

Figure 6-20   Web page showing acknowledgment message and survey statistics

7. Close your browser and any open windows.

Although it is not the case with the Super Bowl script, some scripts require selection structures that are capable of choosing from several alternatives. You can create such selection structures, commonly referred to as **multiple-path selection structures** or **extended selection structures**, using the `if/elsif/else` form of the `if` statement.

USING THE `if/elsif/else` FORM OF THE `if` STATEMENT

At times you might need to create a selection structure that can choose from several alternatives. For example, assume you want to create a script that displays a Web page containing a message. The appropriate message to display is based on a letter grade entered on a form. Figure 6-21 shows the valid letter grades and their corresponding messages.

Letter grade	Message
A	Excellent
B	Above Average
C	Average
D	Below Average
F	Below Average

Figure 6-21   Letter grades and messages

As Figure 6-21 indicates, if the letter grade is an A, then the script should display the message "Excellent." If the letter grade is a B, then the script should display the message "Above Average," and so on. Figure 6-22 shows two versions of the `if` statement that you could use to code the appropriate selection structure. The first version uses the syntax shown earlier in Figure 6-5. The second version uses the `if/elsif/else` form of the `if` statement.

 A common error made when entering the `if/elsif/else` form of the `if` statement is to type `elseif` rather than `elsif`.

Although you can write the selection structure using either of the two methods shown in Figure 6-22, the second version of the code provides a much more convenient way of writing this logic. You experiment with the `if/elsif/else` form of the `if` statement in Hands-on Project 5 at the end of this chapter.

Version 1

```perl
if ($grade eq "A" or $grade eq "a") {
   print "Excellent\n";
}
else {
   if ($grade eq "B" or $grade eq "b") {
      print "Above Average\n";
   }
   else {
      if ($grade eq "C" or $grade eq "c") {
         print "Average\n";
      }
      else {
         if ($grade eq "D" or $grade eq "d"
           or $grade eq "F" or $grade eq "f") {
            print "Below Average\n";
         }
         else {
            print "Error\n";
         }
      }
   }
}
```

Version 2

```perl
if ($grade eq "A" or $grade eq "a") {
    print "Excellent\n";
}
elsif ($grade eq "B" or $grade eq "b") {
    print "Above Average\n";
}
elsif ($grade eq "C" or $grade eq "c") {
    print "Average\n";
}
elsif ($grade eq "D" or $grade eq "d"
      or $grade eq "F" or $grade eq "f") {
    print "Below Average\n";
}
else {
    print "Error\n";
}
```

Figure 6-22   Two versions of the `if` statement

6

CHAPTER SUMMARY

❑ The selection structure allows a script to make a decision or comparison and then, based on the result of that decision or comparison, select one of two paths.

❑ A script should validate the data it receives from the server. Valid data is data that the script is expecting. If a script receives data that is not valid, it should display a Web page that directs the user to return to the form and correct any errors.

❑ You use the `if` statement to code the selection structure in Perl. The `if` statement is composed of two clauses: the `if` clause, which is required, and the `else` clause, which is optional.

❑ The *condition* in an `if` statement can contain variables, numbers, strings, functions, arithmetic operators, comparison (or relational) operators, and logical operators.

❑ The numeric comparison operators in Perl are `<`, `<=`, `>`, `>=`, `==`, and `!=`. The string comparison operators in Perl are `lt`, `le`, `gt`, `ge`, `eq`, and `ne`.

❑ You should use numeric comparison operators to compare numeric values, and string comparison operators to compare string values; otherwise, your values might not compare correctly.

❑ The most commonly used logical operators in Perl are `and` and `or`. When you use the `and` operator to combine two conditions, the resulting compound condition is true only when both conditions are true. When you use the `or` operator to combine two conditions, the resulting compound condition is false only when both conditions are false.

❑ You can use the `push` function to add one or more items to the end of an array. The syntax of the `push` function is **push(***array*, *list***)**, where *list* is the one or more items (separated by commas) that you want added to the *array*.

❑ You can determine the size of an array—in other words, the number of scalar variables contained in the array—simply by assigning the name of the array to a scalar variable.

❑ You can use the `if/elsif/else` form of the `if` statement to code a multiple-path or extended selection structure.

REVIEW QUESTIONS

1. Which of the following `if` statement *conditions* correctly compares the number stored in the `$sales` variable with the number 5000? The *condition* should test for the equality of both numbers.

    a. `($sales = 5000)`

    b. `($sales == 5000)`

    c. `($sales eq 5000)`

    d. `($sales <> 5000)`

2. Which of the following **if** statement *conditions* correctly compares the string stored in the **$city** variable to the string "Detroit"? The *condition* should test for the inequality of both strings.

   a. (**$city != "Detroit"**)

   b. (**$city ne "Detroit"**)

   c. (**$city not "Detroit"**)

   d. (**$city <> "Detroit"**)

3. Assume you want to determine if the **$pay** variable contains a number that is greater than the number stored in the **$max** variable. Which of the following *conditions* should you use in the **if** statement?

   a. (**$pay gr $max**)

   b. (**$pay gt $max**)

   c. (**$pay > $max**)

   d. (**$pay < $max**)

4. Assume you want to determine if the string stored in the **$let1** variable is less than or equal to the string stored in the **$let2** variable. Which of the following *conditions* should you use in the **if** statement?

   a. (**$let1 lt $let2**)

   b. (**$let1 le $let2**)

   c. (**$let1 < $let2**)

   d. (**$let1 <= $let2**)

5. You use _____ to enclose the statements you want processed when an **if** statement's *condition* is true.

   a. braces (**{}**)

   b. brackets (**[ ]**)

   c. parentheses (**( )**)

   d. quotation marks (**" "**)

6. When you compare two strings using a numeric comparison operator, Perl converts the numeric comparison operator to the corresponding string comparison operator before making the comparison.

   a. true

   b. false

7. You can compare two numbers using either a numeric comparison operator or a string comparison operator; the result is the same.

   a. true

   b. false

8. Assume you want to determine if the $item variable contains either the word Chair or the word Desk. Which of the following *conditions* should you use in the if statement?

   a. ($item == "Chair" or $item == "Desk")

   b. ($item == "Chair" and $item == "Desk")

   c. ($item eq "Chair" or $item eq "Desk")

   d. ($item eq "Chair" and $item eq "Desk")

9. Assume you want to determine if the string stored in the $state variable is "MA" and, at the same time, the number stored in the $sales variable is greater than or equal to 10000. Which of the following *conditions* should you use in the if statement?

   a. ($state == "MA" or $sales >= 10000)

   b. ($state == "MA" and $sales >= 10000)

   c. ($state eq "MA" or $sales ge 10000)

   d. None of the above.

10. Which of the following statements can be used to determine the size of the @num array?

   a. $x = @num;

   b. @x = @num;

   c. $x = size(@num);

   d. None of the above.

11. Write an if statement that prints the message "In-range" if the number stored in the $code variable is greater than or equal to 1500.

12. Write an if statement that prints the message "Pass" if the string stored in the $letter variable is equal to either "P" or "p".

13. Modify the if statement you created in Question 12 so that it prints the message "Fail" if the *condition* evaluates to false.

14. Write an if statement that prints the message "Positive number" if the number stored in the $num variable is greater than or equal to 0; otherwise, print the message "Negative number".

15. If the $dept1 variable contains the string "Payroll", and the $dept2 variable contains the string "Advertising", the expression $dept1 > $dept2 evaluates to _____.

16. If the $dept1 variable contains the string "Purchasing", and the $dept2 variable contains the string "Payroll", the expression $dept1 gt $dept2 evaluates to _____.

17. Write an if statement that prints the message "Valid pay rate" if the number stored in the $rate variable is greater than or equal to 5, but less than or equal to 10; otherwise, print the message "Not a valid pay rate".

18. Write a statement that uses the **push** function to append the number 23000 to the end of the **@sales** array.

19. Write a statement that uses the **push** function to append the string "Mary Smith" to the end of the **@names** array.

20. Write an if statement, using the **if/elsif/else** format, that prints the message "The numbers are equal" if the numbers stored in the **$num1** and **$num2** variables are equal. Print the message "The first number is greater than the second number" if the number stored in the **$num1** variable is greater than the number stored in the **$num2** variable. Finally, print the message "The first number is less than the second number" if the number stored in the **$num1** variable is less than the number stored in the **$num2** variable.

6

Hands-on Projects

Project 1

In this project, you modify the *condition* in the **if** statement that validates the game rating value in the Super Bowl script.

a. Open the supbowl.html file in a text editor. The file is contained in the public_html/chap06 directory.

b. Change the filename in the first line from supbowl.html to c06ex1.html. Change the filename in the <FORM> tag from supbowl.cgi to c06ex1.cgi, then save the document as c06ex1.html.

c. Open the supbowl.cgi file in a text editor. The file is contained in the cgi-bin/chap06 directory.

d. Change the filename in the second line from supbowl.cgi to c06ex1.cgi, then save the document as c06ex1.cgi.

e. *If you are using a UNIX system*, change the filename argument in the two **open** statements from "survey.txt" to "c06ex1.txt".

   If you are using a Windows system, change the filename argument in the two **open** statements from "chap06/survey.txt" to simply "c06ex1.txt".

f. Change the filename in the two **die** functions from survey.txt to c06ex1.txt.

g. Change the *condition* in the **if** statement that validates the game rating value to **($game eq "" or ($game != 0 and $game != 1 and $game != 2))**.

h. Save the c06ex1.cgi document.

i. Test the script from the command line, using both valid and invalid data.

j. *If you are using a Windows system*, return to the c06ex1.cgi document in your text editor. Change the filename argument in the two **open** statements from "c06ex1.txt" to "chap06/c06ex1.txt", then save the c06ex1.cgi document.

k. *If you are using a UNIX system*, change the c06ex1.cgi file permissions to 755 and change the c06ex1.txt file permissions to 666.

l. Open the c06ex1.html file in your browser. Test the script using both valid and invalid data.

Project 2

In this project, you validate the data received by the Bonus Calculator script that you created in Chapter 3.

a. Copy the bonus.html file, which is contained in the public_html/chap03 directory, to the public_html/chap06 directory. Rename the file c06ex2.html.

b. Copy the bonus.cgi file, which is contained in the cgi-bin/chap03 directory, to the cgi-bin/chap06 directory. Rename the file c06ex2.cgi.

c. Open the c06ex2.html file in a text editor. Change the filename in the first line from bonus.html to c06ex2.html. Change the <FORM> tag to refer to the c06ex2.cgi file contained in the cgi-bin/chap06 directory, then save the c06ex2.html document.

d. Open the c06ex2.cgi file in a text editor. Change the filename in the second line from bonus.cgi to c06ex2.cgi.

e. Modify the script so that it validates the input data by verifying that the name, sales amount, and bonus rate do not contain the empty string. Also verify that the bonus rate is at least 5% but not greater than 10%. If the input data contains any errors, display a Web page that lists the errors and instructs the user to return to the form to make the corrections.

f. Save the c06ex2.cgi document.

g. Test the script from the command line, using both valid and invalid data.

h. *If you are using a UNIX system*, change the c06ex2.cgi file permissions to 755.

i. Open the c06ex2.html file in your browser. Test the script using both valid and invalid data.

Project 3

In this project, you validate the data received by the Juniper Printers script that you created in Chapter 4.

a. Copy the juniper.html file, which is contained in the public_html/chap04 directory, to the public_html/chap06 directory. Rename the file c06ex3.html.

b. Copy the juniper.cgi file, which is contained in the cgi-bin/chap04 directory, to the cgi-bin/chap06 directory. Rename the file c06ex3.cgi.

c. Open the c06ex3.html file in a text editor. Change the filename in the first line from juniper.html to c06ex3.html. Change the <FORM> tag to refer to the c06ex3.cgi file contained in the cgi-bin/chap06 directory, then save the c06ex3.html document.

d. Open the c06ex3.cgi file in a text editor. Change the filename in the second line from juniper.cgi to c06ex3.cgi.

e. Modify the script so that it validates the input data by verifying that the name and serial number do not contain the empty string. Also verify that the model number and system letter received from the server are valid. (The model number should be 0, 1, or 2. The system letter should be W, M, or U.) If the input data contains any errors, display a Web page that lists the errors and instructs the user to return to the form to make the corrections.

f. Save the c06ex3.cgi document.

g. Test the script from the command line, using both valid and invalid data.

h. *If you are using a UNIX system*, change the c06ex3.cgi file permissions to 755.

i. Open the c06ex3.html file in your browser. Test the script using both valid and invalid data.

Project 4

In this project, you complete a script for the Berrelli Company. The script displays, on a Web page, the names of employees working in a specific department.

a. Open the dept.html file in a text editor. The file is contained in the public_html/chap06 directory. Notice that the document contains four links. Each link passes the **Dept** *key* and department name *value* to the server.

b. Change the filename in the first line from dept.html to c06ex4.html. Change yourservername in the <FORM> tag to the name of your server, then save the document as c06ex4.html.

c. Open the dept.cgi file in a text editor. The file is contained in the cgi-bin/chap06 directory. Change the filename in the second line from dept.cgi to c06ex4.cgi, then save the document as c06ex4.cgi.

d. Study the script's existing code. Notice that the script uses an array to store the department and employee names. (For example, John Montgomery works in the Accounting department, Carol Jefferson works in the Customer Service department, and so on.)

e. Modify the script so that it displays, on a Web page, the names of the employees working in the department whose link was clicked on the c06ex4.html form. (For example, if the user clicks the Accounting link, the script should display the names John Montgomery and Sam Rantini on a Web page.)

f. Save the c06ex4.cgi document.

g. Test the script from the command line.

h. *If you are using a UNIX system*, change the c06ex4.cgi file permissions to 755.

i. Open the c06ex4.html file in your browser. Test each of the form's links.

Project 5

In this project, you complete a script for Thomas Manufacturing. The script displays an employee's telephone extension on a Web page.

   a. Open the phone.html file in a text editor. The file is contained in the public_html/chap06 directory. Study the form's existing code.

   b. Change the filename in the first line from phone.html to c06ex5.html. Change yourservername in the <FORM> tag to the name of your server, then save the document as c06ex5.html.

   c. Open the phone.cgi file in a text editor. The file is contained in the cgi-bin/chap06 directory. Change the filename in the second line from phone.cgi to c06ex5.cgi, then save the document as c06ex5.cgi.

   d. Study the script's existing code. Modify the script so that it displays, on a Web page, the telephone extension for the employee whose name was clicked on the c06ex5.html form. Mary Smith's extension is 1234, Jose Perez's extension is 1122, and Janice Wong's extension is 3345. Use the `if/elsif/else` form of the `if` statement to assign the appropriate extension to the `$ext` variable. Assign the string "Error" to the `$ext` variable if the `Empnum` value passed to the server is invalid.

   e. Save the c06ex5.cgi document.

   f. Test the script from the command line.

   g. *If you are using a UNIX system*, change the c06ex5.cgi file permissions to 755.

   h. Open the c06ex5.html file in your browser. Test each of the radio buttons on the form. Also be sure to reset the form and then click the Submit button.

Project 6

In this project, you learn how to use the Perl `pop`, `shift`, and `splice` functions.

   a. Open the array.cgi file in a text editor. The file is contained in the cgi-bin/chap06 directory. Change the filename in the second line from array.cgi to c06ex6.cgi, then save the document as c06ex6.cgi.

   b. You can use the Perl `pop` function, whose syntax is **pop(***array***)**, to remove the last element from an array. In the blank line below the comment `#remove last element from @names array`, type pop(@names); and press Enter.

   c. Save the c06ex6.cgi document. Execute the script from the command line. Notice that the `pop` function removes the last name, Carl, from the `@names` array.

   d. Return to the script in your text editor. Make the statement you just entered a comment by preceding it with #.

   e. You can use the Perl `shift` function, whose syntax is **shift(***array***)**, to remove the first element from an array. In the blank line below the comment `#remove first element from @names array`, type shift(@names); and press Enter.

f. Save the c06ex6.cgi document. Execute the script from the command line. Notice that the **shift** function removes the first name, Beth, from the **@names** array.

g. Return to the script in your text editor. Make the statement you just entered a comment by preceding it with #.

h. You can use the Perl **splice** function to remove, replace, or insert one or more elements in an array. The syntax of the **splice** function is **splice(***array***,** *offset***,** *length***,** *list***)**, where *array* is the name of the array. The *offset* argument is the starting position (beginning with 0) where elements are to be removed, replaced, or inserted. The *length* argument is the number of elements (from the *offset*) that you want to remove or replace. The *list* argument consists of one or more replacement items, or one or more items that will be inserted. In the blank line below the comment **#remove one or more elements from the @names array**, type splice(@names, 1, 2); and press Enter.

i. Save the c06ex6.cgi document. Execute the script from the command line. Notice that the **splice** function removes the names John and Suman from the **@names** array.

j. Return to the script in your text editor. Make the statement you just entered a comment by preceding it with #.

k. In the blank line below the comment **#splice(@names, 1, 2);**, enter a statement that removes the names Suman, Paula, and Carl from the **@names** array.

l. Save the c06ex6.cgi document. Execute the script from the command line. The **splice** function should remove the names Suman, Paula, and Carl from the **@names** array.

m. Return to the script in your text editor. Make the statement you just entered a comment by preceding it with #.

n. In the blank line below the comment **#replace one or more elements in the @names array**, type splice(@names, 1, 1, "Jonathan"); and press Enter.

o. Save the c06ex6.cgi document. Execute the script from the command line. The **splice** function replaces the name John with the name Jonathan in the **@names** array.

p. Return to the script in your text editor. Make the statement you just entered a comment by preceding it with #.

q. In the blank line below the comment **#splice(@names, 1, 1, "Jonathan");**, enter a statement that replaces the first two names (Beth and John) with the name Archie.

r. Save the c06ex6.cgi document. Execute the script from the command line. The **splice** function replaces the names Beth and John with the name Archie in the **@names** array.

s. Return to the script in your text editor. Make the statement you just entered a comment by preceding it with #.

t. In the blank line below the comment **#insert one or more new elements in the @names array**, type splice(@names, 2, 0, "Zeke"); and press Enter.

6

u. Save the c06ex6.cgi document. Execute the script from the command line. The `splice` function inserts the name Zeke as the third name in the `@names` array.

v. Return to the script in your text editor. Make the statement you just entered a comment by preceding it with #.

w. In the blank line below the comment `#splice(@names, 2, 0, "Zeke");`, enter a statement that inserts the names Jeff and Jim as the fourth and fifth names in the `@names` array.

x. Save the c06ex6.cgi document. Execute the script from the command line. The `splice` function inserts the names Jeff and Jim as the fourth and fifth names in the `@names` array.

CASE PROJECTS

1. Create an HTML form and a script for Professor Johnson at Mountain Community College. Name the form c06case1.html and save it in the public_html/chap06 directory. Name the script c06case1.cgi and save it in the cgi-bin/chap06 directory. The form should allow Professor Johnson to enter a student's name and the points earned by the student on two projects, the midterm, and the final. The CGI script that processes the form data should validate the form data appropriately. Project points must be at least 0 and not more than 50. Midterm and final points must be at least 0 and not more than 100. If the form data contains any errors, the script should list the errors on a Web page. If the form data does not contain any errors, the script should calculate the total points earned by the student, and then save the student's name and his or her total points in a data file named c06case1.txt. The script also should display a Web page informing Professor Johnson that the record (name and total points) was saved.

2. Create a script for Professor Johnson at Mountain Community College. Name the script c06case2.cgi and save it in the cgi-bin/chap06 directory. The script should process the data stored in the c06case2.txt file, which is contained in the cgi-bin/chap06 directory. Open the c06case2.txt file in a text editor. Notice that the file contains five records. Each record contains two fields: a student's name and the total number of points the student earned in Professor Johnson's class. The script should display a Web page that lists each student's name and grade. The grade is based on the total number of points earned, as follows:

Total points	Grade
270 and above	A
240 – 269	B
210 – 239	C
180 – 209	D
Below 180	F

USER-DEFINED FUNCTIONS

In this chapter, you will:

♦ Create and call a user-defined function

♦ Exit a script using the Perl `exit` statement

♦ Pass information to and receive information from a user-defined function

♦ Access the contents of an environment variable

♦ Learn how to code the repetition structure using the Perl `while` and `until` statements

In previous chapters, you learned how to use several of the functions built into the Perl language, such as the **print**, **push**, and **chomp** functions. You also learned how to use the **param** function, which is made available to your script by the CGI.pm module. In addition to including functions that are built into Perl and the CGI.pm module, a script also can include functions that you create, referred to as user-defined functions.

Programmers create user-defined functions for two reasons. First, user-defined functions allow a programmer to avoid writing and testing the same code more than once. If a script needs to perform the same task several times, or if more than one script needs to perform a certain task, it is more efficient to enter the appropriate code once, in a function, and then simply call the function to perform the task when needed. Second, user-defined functions allow large and complex scripts, which typically are written by a team of programmers, to be broken into small and manageable tasks; each member of the team can be assigned one of the tasks to code as a function. When each programmer has completed his or her function, all of the functions can be gathered together to form a complete script.

In this chapter, you learn how to create and call a user-defined function. Before doing so, however, you learn more about functions in general. Also in this chapter, you learn how to access the values stored in environment variables, and how to use the Perl **exit** statement.

FUNCTIONS

A **function**, also called a **subroutine**, is simply a block of code that begins with the Perl keyword `sub`. The code can be contained within the script in which it is used, or it can be contained in a separate file. The code for the `param` function, for example, is stored in the CGI.pm file, and the code for the `push` function is stored in the perl (or perl.exe) file. The code for the functions that you create in this chapter will be stored in the .cgi file that contains the script.

> The keyword `sub` is an abbreviation of the term subroutine, which, in programming terminology, refers to a block of code that performs a specific task and is separate from the main program. The terms *function* and *subroutine* are used interchangeably in Perl. However, in some programming languages, a function differs from a subroutine in that a function returns a value, whereas a subroutine does not. In Perl, all blocks of code created with the `sub` statement return a value.

The code contained in a function is processed only when the function is called, or invoked. You call (invoke) a function by including its name and arguments (if any) in a statement. For example, the statement `$game = param('Game');` calls the `param` function and passes it one argument: the Game *key*. Similarly, the statement `push(@errors, "Select a button from the Game section");` calls the `push` function and passes it two arguments: the `@errors` array and the element to add to the array—in this case, the string `"Select a button from the Game section"`.

Every function performs a specific task that is determined by the function's creator. After completing the task, the function returns a value to the statement that called it. The `param` function, for example, accesses the *value* associated with the function's *key* argument, and returns the *value* to the statement that called the function. The `push` function, on the other hand, adds one or more elements to the end of an array, and then returns the length of the array.

A statement that calls a function can either make use of or ignore the function's return value. The statement `$name = param('Name');`, for example, calls the `param` function and assigns the function's return value to the `$name` variable. Similarly, the `if` statement condition, `if (length($name) > 25)`, calls the `length` function and compares the function's return value, which is the number of characters contained in the `$name` variable, to the number 25. Unlike the two statements just mentioned, the statement `push(@errors, "Select a button from the Game selection");` ignores the value returned by the function it calls. As you may remember, you used the statement in the Super Bowl script that you created in Chapter 6 simply to add an element to the `@errors` array. The value returned by the `push` function was unimportant to the statement.

> The `length` function returns the number of characters stored in a scalar variable. The syntax of the `length` function is **length(*variable*)**, where *variable* is the name of a scalar variable.

Next you learn how to create a user-defined function in Perl.

CREATING A USER-DEFINED FUNCTION

Figure 7-1 shows the syntax used to create a user-defined function in Perl. (You view examples of using the syntax later in the chapter.)

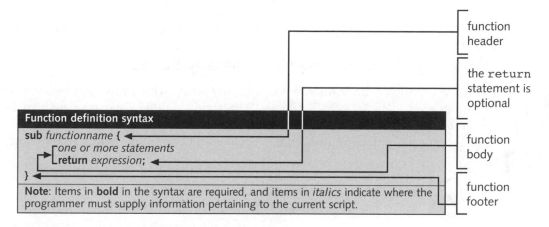

Figure 7-1 showing function header, the return statement is optional, function body, and function footer labels pointing to:

```
Function definition syntax
sub functionname {
    one or more statements
    return expression;
}
```

Note: Items in **bold** in the syntax are required, and items in *italics* indicate where the programmer must supply information pertaining to the current script.

Figure 7-1   Syntax of a function definition in Perl

As Figure 7-1 indicates, a function definition is composed of a function header, function body, and function footer. The **function header** begins with the keyword `sub` followed by a space, the name of the function, another space, and an opening brace ({). The rules for naming user-defined functions are the same as for naming variables. To make your scripts more self-documenting and easier to understand, you should use meaningful names that describe the task the function is to perform. For example, a good name for a function whose task is to calculate a sales tax is `calc_sales_tax`.

A user-defined function ends with the **function footer**, which is simply a closing brace (}). Between the function header and function footer, you enter the instructions the function must follow to perform its assigned task; the instructions are referred to as the **function body**.

As Figure 7-1 indicates, a function body can include a `return` statement. The syntax of the `return` statement is **return** *expression*;, where *expression* represents the value (or values) you want returned to the calling statement. For example, to return the contents of the `$hours` variable, you use the statement `return $hours;`. You also can use the `return` statement to return multiple values to the calling statement. The statement `return $name, $hours, $rate;`, for instance, returns the contents of three variables to the calling statement. Similarly, the statement `return @errors;` returns the contents of the `@errors` array. After returning the appropriate value (or values), the `return` statement terminates the function.

Notice that the `return` statement is optional in a function definition. You include a `return` statement when you want a function to return a specific value or set of values—such as the result of one or more calculations made by the function. When used, the `return` statement typically is the last statement in the function body. If you do not include a `return` statement in a function definition, the function returns the value of the last statement it processes. If the last statement processed is `print "Hello";`, for example, the function will return `true` if the `print` statement was successful; otherwise, it will return `false`.

Next, you view examples of scripts that create and call user-defined functions.

Example 1–The Dombrowski Company Script

Figure 7-2 shows the Dombrowski Company script, which processes two items of form data: a name and an e-mail address. The script includes two user-defined functions named display_error_page and display_acknowledgment. The function definitions and function calls pertaining to both user-defined functions are shaded in the figure.

Many programmers use a comment (such as #*****user-defined functions*****) to separate the code for the main part of the script from the code for the function definitions; this makes the script easier to read.

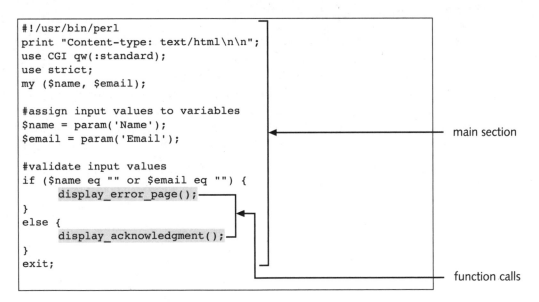

```perl
#!/usr/bin/perl
print "Content-type: text/html\n\n";
use CGI qw(:standard);
use strict;
my ($name, $email);

#assign input values to variables
$name = param('Name');
$email = param('Email');

#validate input values
if ($name eq "" or $email eq "") {
    display_error_page();
}
else {
    display_acknowledgment();
}
exit;
```

main section

function calls

Figure 7-2   The Dombrowski Company script

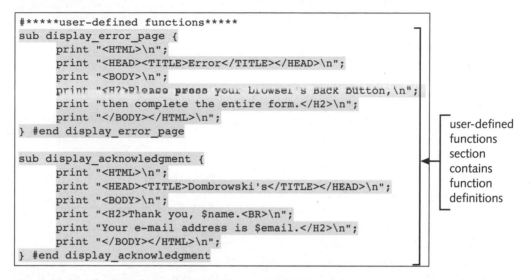

```
#*****user-defined functions*****
sub display_error_page {
     print "<HTML>\n";
     print "<HEAD><TITLE>Error</TITLE></HEAD>\n";
     print "<BODY>\n";
     print "<H2>Please press your browser's Back button,\n";
     print "then complete the entire form.</H2>\n";
     print "</BODY></HTML>\n";
} #end display_error_page

sub display_acknowledgment {
     print "<HTML>\n";
     print "<HEAD><TITLE>Dombrowski's</TITLE></HEAD>\n";
     print "<BODY>\n";
     print "<H2>Thank you, $name.<BR>\n";
     print "Your e-mail address is $email.</H2>\n";
     print "</BODY></HTML>\n";
} #end display_acknowledgment
```

user-defined functions section contains function definitions

7

Figure 7-2   The Dombrowski Company script (continued)

Notice that the script contains two sections: a main section and a user-defined functions section. The main section lists the tasks the Dombrowski Company script will perform. Two of the tasks—`display_error_page();` and `display_acknowledgment();`— are calls to user-defined functions. The tasks performed by both user-defined functions are listed in the user-defined functions section of the script.

Study the code contained in the main section of the Dombrowski Company script. The statement `my ($name, $email);` declares two scalar variables named `$name` and `$email`. The statement `$name = param('Name');` calls the `param` function, which is defined in the CGI.pm file, and assigns the function's return value to the `$name` variable. Likewise, the statement `$email = param('Email');` calls the `param` function and assigns the function's return value to the `$email` variable. The `if` statement in the script compares the contents of the `$name` and `$email` variables with the empty string ("") to determine whether the variables contain data. If either variable contains the empty string, the script calls the `display_error_page` function, which creates a Web page that advises the user to press the browser's Back button and then complete the entire form. Otherwise, the script calls the `display_acknowledgment` function, which creates a Web page that contains the form data. The `display_error_page` and `display_acknowledgment` functions are user-defined functions whose definitions appear in the user-defined functions section of the script.

Notice that you call a user-defined function in exactly the same way as you call a built-in function—by including its name and arguments (if any) in a statement. If you have no arguments to pass to a user-defined function, you enter an empty set of parentheses after the function's name in the calling statement, as shown in the statements `display_error_page();` and `display_acknowledgment();`.

The main section of the Dombrowski Company script ends with the statement `exit;`. The `exit;` statement terminates the script; in other words, it stops the script from processing any further instructions. The Perl interpreter does not require you to use the `exit;` statement to terminate a script. In the Dombrowski Company script, for example, the interpreter will stop processing instructions when it reaches the user-defined functions section. (Recall that the code contained in a function is processed only when the function is called.) However, entering the `exit;` statement as the last statement in the main section indicates, to anyone viewing your script, that processing should end at this point.

Now look closely at the two function definitions shown in Figure 7-2. Both definitions contain a function header that includes the keyword `sub`, the function name, and the opening brace ({). Both definitions also contain a function body that lists the instructions to be processed when the function is called. Lastly, both definitions contain a function footer. In this case, each function footer contains the required closing brace (}) and an optional comment. Although it is not required by the syntax, many programmers include a comment (such as #end *functionname*) in the function footer to make it easier to see where the function ends.

Notice that the function definitions shown in Figure 7-2 do not contain a `return` statement. Recall that when a function definition does not contain a `return` statement, the function returns the value of the last statement it processes. The last statement processed by the `display_error_page` and `display_acknowledgment` functions is `print "</BODY></HTML>\n";`. If the `print` function that appears in the statement is successful—meaning it is able to send the closing BODY and HTML tags to the browser—the function returns `true`; otherwise, it returns `false`. Notice that the statements that call the functions—`display_error_page();` and `display_acknowledgment();`—ignore the value returned by the function.

Next, view an example of a function that receives an argument passed to it.

Example 2–The Temp-Employment Script

Figure 7-3 shows the Temp-Employment script, which processes one item of form data: an hourly rate of pay. The script includes one user-defined function named `display_msg`, whose purpose is to create a Web page that displays one of three different messages. The statements that call the `display_msg` function are shaded in the figure.

Study the code contained in the main section of the Temp-Employment script. The statement `my $hourly_pay;` declares a scalar variable named `$hourly_pay`. The statement `$hourly_pay = param('Pay');` calls the `param` function and assigns the function's return value to the `$hourly_pay` variable. The `if` statement in the script compares the contents of the `$hourly_pay` variable with the number 5.75. If the variable contains a number that is less than 5.75, the script calls the `display_msg` function and passes it one argument: the string "Minimum hourly rate is \$5.75." Otherwise, the nested `if` statement compares the contents of the `$hourly_pay` variable with the number 10.25.

If the variable contains a number that is greater than 10.25, the script calls the display_msg function and passes it the argument "Maximum hourly rate is \\$10.25." If the $hourly_pay variable contains a number that is not less than 5.75 and not greater than 10.25, then the script calls the display_msg function and passes it the argument "The hourly rate is valid."

```perl
#!/usr/bin/perl
print "Content-type: text/html\n\n";
use CGI qw(:standard);
use strict;
my $hourly_pay;

#assign input value to variable
$hourly_pay = param('Pay');

#validate hourly pay
if ($hourly_pay < 5.75) {
    display_msg("Minimum hourly rate is \$5.75.");
}
elsif ($hourly_pay > 10.25) {
    display_msg("Maximum hourly rate is \$10.25.");
}
else {
    display_msg("The hourly rate is valid.");
}
exit;

#*****user-defined functions*****
sub display_msg {
    print "<HTML>\n";
    print "<HEAD><TITLE>Temp_Employment</TITLE></HEAD>\n";
    print "<BODY><H2>\n";
    print "$_[0]\n";       ◄
    print "</H2></BODY></HTML>\n";
} #end display_msg
```

the first item passed to a function is stored in the $_[0] element of the @_ array

Figure 7-3   The Temp-Employment script

 As you learned in Chapter 3, the backslash (\) before a dollar sign ($) tells the Perl interpreter to ignore the dollar sign's special meaning and simply treat the symbol verbatim.

When arguments are passed to a user-defined function, Perl stores the arguments in a special array named @_. As you learned in Chapter 4, an array is composed of scalar variables, each having the same name but a different index. Recall that you use the array name to refer to a scalar variable contained in an array, but you replace the @ in the name with a $, and you follow the name with the scalar variable's index enclosed in square brackets ([]). For example, $_[0] refers to the first scalar variable contained in the @_ array, $_[1] refers to the second scalar variable, and $_[2] refers to the third scalar variable.

When the display_msg function is called, Perl stores the argument passed to the function—either "Minimum hourly rate is \$5.75.", or "Maximum hourly rate is \$10.25.", or "The hourly rate is valid."—in the $_[0] variable. Notice that the $_[0] variable appears in the print "$_[0]\n"; statement, which is the fifth line in the display_msg function definition shown in Figure 7-3. The print "$_[0]\n"; statement sends the contents of the $_[0] variable and a newline character to the browser.

As you learned earlier, user-defined functions allow large and complex scripts to be broken into small and manageable tasks. Although the script you view in the next section is not large or complex, it can be used to demonstrate the concept of assigning major tasks to user-defined functions.

Example 3–The O'Rourke Sales Script

Figure 7-4 shows the O'Rourke Sales script, which processes two sales amounts submitted using a form. Notice that all of the tasks performed by the script are assigned to user-defined functions. The statements that call the user-defined functions are shaded in the figure.

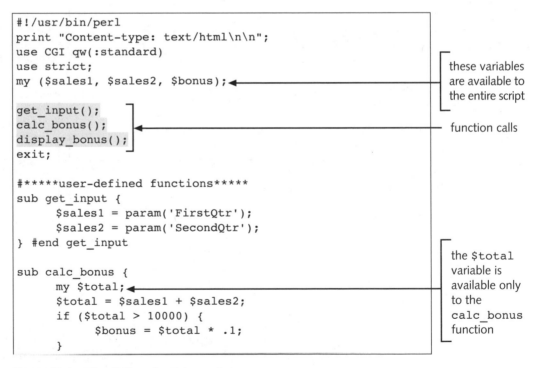

Figure 7-4 The O'Rourke Sales script

```
        else {
                $bonus = $total * .05;
        }
} #end calc_bonus

sub display_bonus {
        print "<HTML>\n";
        print "<HEAD><TITLE>O'Rourke Sales</TITLE></HEAD>\n";
        print "<BODY>\n";
        print "<H2>Bonus: \$$bonus<BR>\n";
        print "</BODY></HTML>\n";
} #end display_bonus
```

Figure 7-4   The O'Rourke Sales script (continued)

Study the main section's code. The statement `my ($sales1, $sales2, $bonus);` declares three scalar variables named `$sales1`, `$sales2`, and `$bonus`. The next statement, `get_input();`, calls the `get_input` function, which assigns the form data to the `$sales1` and `$sales2` variables. Notice that the `get_input` function can access the `$sales1` and `$sales2` variables declared in the main section of the script. This is because all variables declared in the main section of a script are available to the main section and to any functions defined within the script.

The next statement listed in the main section, `calc_bonus();`, calls the `calc_bonus` function to calculate a bonus amount. Notice that the `calc_bonus` function declares a variable named `$total`. Unlike the variables declared in the main section of a script, variables declared within a user-defined function are available only to the function in which they are declared. In this case, for example, only the `calc_bonus` function has access to the `$total` variable.

The next statement listed in the main section, `display_bonus();`, calls the `display_bonus` function, which creates a Web page that displays the bonus amount calculated by the `calc_bonus` function. The last statement in the main section, `exit;`, terminates the script.

Study closely the `get_input` and `calc_bonus` function definitions. Notice that the functions assign values to the variables declared in the main section of the script. The `get_input` function, for example, assigns the form data to the `$sales1` and `$sales2` variables, and the `calc_bonus` function assigns the result of a calculation to the `$bonus` variable. Many programmers consider it poor programming when a user-defined function assigns a value to a variable declared in the main section of a script. They feel that doing so makes the script difficult to understand and debug, because it is not always obvious where the variable gets its value. In the next section, you view another version of the O'Rourke Sales script. In the new version, the values of the main section variables are changed in the main section rather than in a user-defined function.

Example 4–Another Version of the O'Rourke Sales Script

Figure 7-5 shows another version of the O'Rourke Sales script. The lines of code that differ from the original version (shown in Figure 7-4) are shaded in the figure.

```perl
#!/usr/bin/perl
print "Content-type: text/html\n\n";
use CGI qw(:standard);
use strict;
my ($sales1, $sales2, $bonus);

($sales1, $sales2) = get_input();
$bonus = calc_bonus();                              ←——————— function calls
display_bonus();
exit;

#*****user-defined functions*****
sub get_input {
     return param('FirstQtr'), param('SecondQtr');
} #end get_input

sub calc_bonus {
     my ($total, $bonus_amt);
     $total = $sales1 + $sales2;
     if ($total > 10000) {
          $bonus_amt = $total * .1;
     }
     else {
          $bonus_amt = $total * .05;
     }
     return $bonus_amt;
} #end calc_bonus

sub display_bonus {
     print "<HTML>\n";
     print "<HEAD><TITLE>O'Rourke Sales</TITLE></HEAD>\n";
     print "<BODY>\n";
     print "<H2>Bonus: \$$bonus<BR>\n";
     print "</BODY></HTML>\n";
} #end display_bonus
```

Figure 7-5   Another version of the O'Rourke Sales script

Notice that the `get_input` function in the new version of the script contains a `return` statement rather than two assignment statements. The `return` statement returns two values to the calling statement, which is the statement `($sales1, $sales2) = get_input();` in the new version of the script. (Recall that the calling statement in the original version was the statement `get_input();`.) The

($sales1, $sales2) = get_input(); statement assigns the two values returned by the get_input function to the $sales1 and $sales2 variables. Notice that both variables are assigned their values in the main section of the script, rather than in the user-defined section. Assigning the values in the main section makes it obvious where the $sales1 and $sales2 variables get their values. If the script needs to be modified at a later date, you (or another programmer) will not need to search the entire script to locate the origin of the values.

The calc_bonus function shown in Figure 7-5 also contains a return statement. In this case, however, the return statement returns only one value to the calling statement—the value stored in the $bonus_amt variable. Notice that the calling statement in the new version of the script is $bonus = calc_bonus(); rather than calc_bonus();. The $bonus = calc_bonus(); statement assigns the calc_bonus function's return value to the $bonus variable. Here again, a statement in the main section of the script, rather than one located in a user-defined function, is responsible for changing the $bonus variable's value.

You will use user-defined functions in the International Coffees script that you create in this chapter. Before doing so, however, you view the International Coffees form and the dynamic Web pages that the script will create.

THE INTERNATIONAL COFFEES FORM AND DYNAMIC WEB PAGES

International Coffees uses the form shown in Figure 7-6 to gather comments about the coffees it sells. As indicated in the figure, the form contains three elements that allow the user to enter his or her name, e-mail address, and comments. The elements are named Name, Email, and Comments.

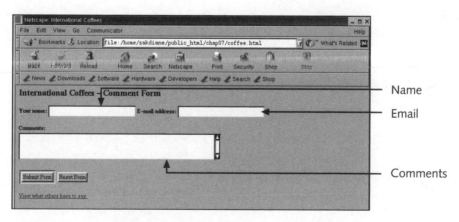

Figure 7-6   International Coffees form

When the user clicks the Submit Form button, the International Coffees script should verify that the user completed the three input areas on the form. If one or more of the input areas is blank, the script should display a dynamic Web page similar to the one shown in Figure 7-7.

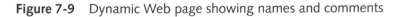

Figure 7-7   Dynamic Web page displayed when an incomplete form is submitted

If none of the input areas on the form is blank, then the script should save the form data (name, e-mail address, and comments) to a file named comments.txt, and then display a dynamic Web page similar to the one shown in Figure 7-8.

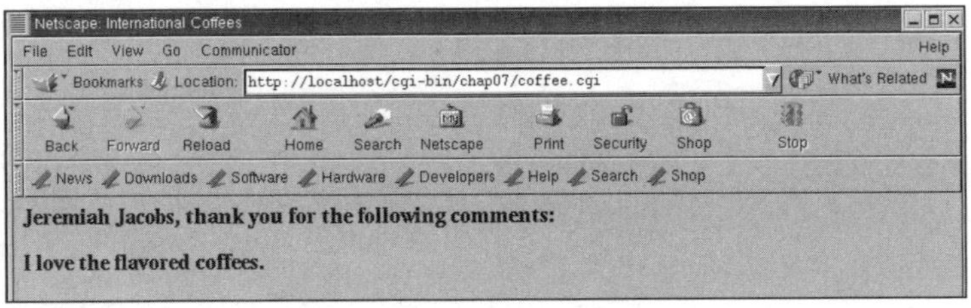

Figure 7-8   Dynamic Web page acknowledging receipt of the form

When the user clicks the "View what others have to say" link on the International Coffees form, the script should display a dynamic Web page that lists the names and comments stored in the comments.txt file. A sample Web page is shown in Figure 7-9.

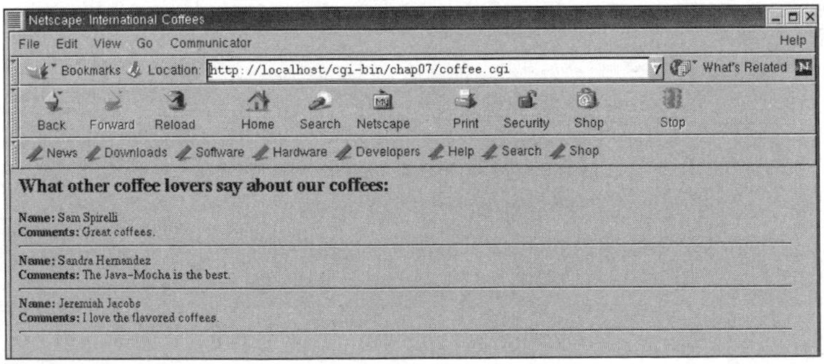

Figure 7-9   Dynamic Web page showing names and comments

Before you begin planning the script that will process the form data and create the three dynamic Web pages, you view the HTML code used to create the International Coffees form.

To view the HTML code used to create the International Coffees form:

1. Open the coffee.html file in a text editor. The file is contained in the public_html/chap07 directory. Figure 7-10 shows the contents of the file.

```
<!coffee.html>
<HTML>
<HEAD><TITLE>International Coffees</TITLE></HEAD>
<BODY>
<H1>International Coffees - Comment Form</H1>
<FORM ACTION="http://yourservername/cgi-bin/chap07/coffee.cgi" METHOD=POST>

<B>Your name:      </B> <INPUT TYPE=text NAME=Name  SIZE=30>
<B>E-mail address:</B> <INPUT TYPE=text NAME=Email SIZE=30><BR>
<P><B>Comments:</B><BR>
<TEXTAREA NAME=Comments ROWS=4 COLS=70 WRAP=Virtual></TEXTAREA></P>

<P><INPUT TYPE=submit VALUE="Submit Form">
   <INPUT TYPE=reset  VALUE="Reset Form"></P>

<A HREF="http://yourservername/cgi-bin/chap07/coffee.cgi">
View what others have to say
</FORM></BODY></HTML>
```

Figure 7-10   HTML code used to create the International Coffees form

The TEXTAREA tag creates a large text box in which you can enter several lines of text.

The <FORM> tag's ACTION and METHOD properties indicate that the coffee.cgi script will process the form data, and that the form data will be sent using the POST method. Additionally, the <A> tag's HREF property links the text "View what others have to say" to the coffee.cgi script.

2. Change yourservername in the <FORM> tag's ACTION property and in the <A> tag's HREF property to the name of your server.

3. Save the coffee.html document, and then close the document.

Now you can begin planning the International Coffees script.

PLANNING THE INTERNATIONAL COFFEES SCRIPT

Figure 7-11 shows the input, output, and algorithm for the International Coffees script. Notice that the script's input is the form data (name, e-mail address, and comments), and its output is a file that contains the form data, and three different dynamic Web pages.

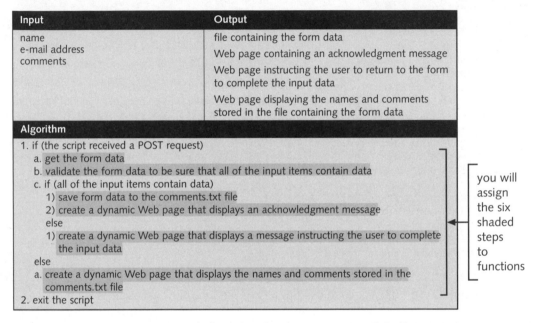

Input	Output
name e-mail address comments	file containing the form data
	Web page containing an acknowledgment message
	Web page instructing the user to return to the form to complete the input data
	Web page displaying the names and comments stored in the file containing the form data

Algorithm

1. if (the script received a POST request)
   a. get the form data
   b. validate the form data to be sure that all of the input items contain data
   c. if (all of the input items contain data)
      1) save form data to the comments.txt file
      2) create a dynamic Web page that displays an acknowledgment message
      else
      1) create a dynamic Web page that displays a message instructing the user to complete the input data
   else
   a. create a dynamic Web page that displays the names and comments stored in the comments.txt file
2. exit the script

you will assign the six shaded steps to functions

Figure 7-11　Input, output, and algorithm for the International Coffees script

Each of the six steps shaded in the algorithm will be assigned to a separate function. The six functions will be named `get_input`, `validate_input`, `save_to_file`, `create_acknowledgment_page`, `create_error_page`, and `create_comments_page`.

Before you begin coding the International Coffees algorithm, you learn about environment variables. You will need to use an environment variable to code the first step in the algorithm.

ENVIRONMENT VARIABLES

Environment variables are a series of hidden *keys* and *values* that the Web server sends to a CGI script when the script is run. You can use environment variables to learn more about the server, the user, and the user's browser. Perl stores the environment variables in a special hash named `%ENV`. Listed in Figure 7-12 are the *keys* corresponding to the more commonly used environment variables. Also listed in the figure is both a description and example of the value stored in each environment variable.

Name	Value	Example
CONTENT_LENGTH	number of bytes passed from the server	45
GATEWAY_INTERFACE	version of the CGI used by the server	CGI/1.1
HTTP_ACCEPT	MIME types accepted by the browser	image/gif, image/jpeg, and so on
HTTP_HOST	server's host name	course.com
HTTP_USER_AGENT	name and version of the user's browser	Mozilla/4.0(compatible; MSIE 5.01; Windows NT 5.0)
QUERY_STRING	values sent using the GET method	Hours=40&Rate=5
REMOTE_ADDR	visitor's IP address	127.0.0.1
REMOTE_HOST	visitor's host name	microsoft.com
REQUEST_METHOD	type of request (GET or POST) sent to a script	GET
SCRIPT_NAME	relative path name of the CGI	/cgi-bin/chap07/bonus.cgi
SERVER_NAME	server's host name, DNS alias, or IP address	localhost
SERVER_PORT	port number where browser's request was sent	80
SERVER_PROTOCOL	name and version of the protocol	HTTP/1.1
SERVER_SOFTWARE	name and version of the server software	Apache /1.3.12

Figure 7-12   List of commonly used environment variables

You will use the REQUEST_METHOD environment variable to code the first step in the International Coffees algorithm. As Figure 7-12 shows, the REQUEST_METHOD environment variable stores the type of request (GET or POST) sent to a script. You begin coding the International Coffees script in the next section.

CODING THE INTERNATIONAL COFFEES SCRIPT

On your computer's disk is a partially completed script for International Coffees. To complete the script, you need to finish coding the main section, and also enter the function definitions for two of the six user-defined functions: `get_input` and `validate_input`. The function definitions for the remaining user-defined functions (`save_to_file`, `create_acknowledgment_page`, `create_error_page`, and `create_comments_page`) have already been entered in the script.

To complete the main section of the International Coffees script:

1. Open the coffee.cgi file in a text editor. The file is contained in the cgi-bin/chap07 directory. Figure 7-13 shows the contents of the partially completed script. (**Important note**: If you are using a Windows system, the shebang line will say `#!C:/Perl/bin/perl.exe`. Also, "chap07/comments.txt" will appear as the filename in the two **open** statements.)

```
#!/usr/bin/perl
#coffee.cgi - saves form data to a file, and creates
#three different dynamic Web pages
print "Content-type: text/html\n\n";
use CGI qw(:standard);

#prevent Perl from creating undeclared variables
use strict;

#declare variables
my ($name, $email, $comments, $data_ok);


exit;

#*****user-defined functions*****

sub save_to_file {
     open(OUTFILE, ">>", "comments.txt")
          or die "Error opening comments.txt for save. $!, stopped";
     print OUTFILE "$name|$email|$comments\n";
     close(OUTFILE);
} #end save_to_file

sub create_acknowledgment_page {
     print "<HTML>\n";
     print "<HEAD><TITLE>International Coffees</TITLE></HEAD>\n";
     print "<BODY>\n";
     print "<H2>$name, thank you for the following \n";
     print "comments:<BR><BR>$comments\n";
     print "</H2></BODY></HTML>\n";
} #end create_acknowledgment_page

sub create_error_page {
     print "<HTML>\n";
     print "<HEAD><TITLE>International Coffees</TITLE></HEAD>\n";
     print "<BODY>\n";
     print "<H2>Please return to the form and \n";
     print "complete all items.</H2>\n";
     print "</BODY></HTML>\n";
} #end create_error_page

sub create_comments_page {
     my (@records, $name_field, $email_field, $com_field);

     open(INFILE, "<", "comments.txt")
          or die "Error opening comments.txt. $!, stopped";
```

Figure 7-13   Partially completed coffee.cgi script

```
    print "<HTML>\n";
    print "<HEAD><TITLE>International Coffees</TITLE></HEAD>\n";
    print "<BODY>\n";
    print "<H2>What other coffee lovers say \n";
    print "about our coffees:</H2>\n";
    @records = <INFILE>;
    close(INFILE);
    foreach my $rec (@records) {
        chomp($rec);
        ($name_field, $email_field, $com_field) = split(/\|/, $rec);
        print "<B>Name:</B> $name_field<BR>\n";
        print "<B>Comments:</B> $com_field<BR>\n";
        print "<HR>";
    }
    print "</BODY></HTML>\n";
} #end create_comments_page
```

Figure 7-13   Partially completed coffee.cgi script (continued)

2. If necessary, change the shebang line to reflect the location of the Perl interpreter on your system.

3. If necessary, add the **–debug** pragma to the use CGI qw(:standard);
   statement.

   Step 1 in the algorithm shown in Figure 7-11 is to determine whether a
   POST request was sent to the script.

4. In the blank line immediately above the **exit;** statement, type **if
   ($ENV{'REQUEST_METHOD'} eq "POST") {** and press **Enter**.

   If a POST request was sent to the script, it means that the user clicked the
   Submit Form button on the International Coffees form. (You can refer back
   to Figure 7-10 to verify that the METHOD property in the <FORM> tag
   is set to POST.) In that case, you need to get the form data; you will use a
   user-defined function named **get_input** to perform this task. You can call
   the get_input function using either the statement get_input(); or the
   statement ($name, $email, $comments) = get_input();. If you use
   the former statement, the **get_input** function will be responsible for assigning the appropriate values to the $name, $email, and $comments variables,
   which are declared in the main section of the script. If you use the latter
   statement, the main section will be responsible for changing the values of its
   variables. You will use the latter statement, because it makes the script easier
   to understand and debug.

5. Press **Tab**, if necessary, to indent the line. Type **($name, $email,
   $comments) = get_input();** and press **Enter**.

   Next, you need to verify that the three input items contain data. This task will be
   performed by the **validate_input** user-defined function. The function will
   return the value "Y" if all of the input items contain data; otherwise, the function

will return the value "N". The script will store the function's return value in the $data_ok variable, which is declared in the main section of the script.

6. Press the **Tab** key, if necessary, to indent the line. Type **$data_ok = validate_input();** and press **Enter**.

You also could have called the `validate_input` function using the statement `validate_input();`. In that case, the function would be responsible for assigning the appropriate value to the $data_ok variable declared in the main section.

If the $data_ok variable contains the value "Y", it means that the three input items contain data. In that case, the script should save the form data to the comments.txt file and then create the acknowledgment Web page shown earlier in Figure 7-8. These tasks will be handled by the save_to_file and create_acknowledgment_page user-defined functions. However, if the $data_ok variable does not contain the value "Y", it means that at least one of the input items is blank. In that case, the script should create the error Web page shown earlier in Figure 7-7. This task will be handled by the create_error_page user-defined function.

7. Enter the additional code shaded in Figure 7-14.

```perl
#!/usr/bin/perl
#coffee.cgi - saves form data to a file, and creates
#three different dynamic Web pages
print "Content-type: text/html\n\n";
use CGI qw(:standard);

#prevent Perl from creating undeclared variables
use strict;

#declare variables
my ($name, $email, $comments, $data_ok);

if ($ENV{'REQUEST_METHOD'} eq "POST") {
    ($name, $email, $comments) = get_input();
    $data_ok = validate_input();
    if ($data_ok eq "Y") {
        save_to_file();
        create_acknowledgment_page();
    }
    else {
        create_error_page();
    }
}

exit;
```

Figure 7-14   Additional code entered in the script

If the script did not receive a POST request, it means that the user clicked the "View what others have to say" link rather than the Submit Form button. In that case, the script should call the `create_comments_page` function to create the Web page shown earlier in Figure 7-9.

When you click a link that is associated with a CGI script, the REQUEST_METHOD environment variable is automatically set to GET.

8. Enter the additional code shaded in Figure 7-15, which shows the completed main section of the script.

```perl
#!/usr/bin/perl
#coffee.cgi - saves form data to a file, and creates
#three different dynamic Web pages
print "Content-type: text/html\n\n";
use CGI qw(:standard);

#prevent Perl from creating undeclared variables
use strict;

#declare variables
my ($name, $email, $comments, $data_ok);

if ($ENV{'REQUEST_METHOD'} eq "POST") {
    ($name, $email, $comments) = get_input();
    $data_ok = validate_input();
    if ($data_ok eq "Y") {
        save_to_file();
        create_acknowledgment_page();
    }
    else {
        create_error_page();
    }
}
else {
    create_comments_page();
}
exit;
```

Figure 7-15   Completed main section of the script

9. Save the coffee.cgi document.

Recall that in addition to completing the main section of the script, you also need to enter the function definitions for the `get_input` and `validate_input` functions.

7

To enter the missing function definitions, which will complete the script:

1. In the blank line below the comment #*****user-defined functions*****, type **sub get_input {** and press **Enter**.

2. Press the **Tab** key, if necessary, to indent the line. Type **return param('Name'), param('Email'), param('Comments');** and press **Enter**.

3. Press the **Backspace** key, if necessary, to remove the indentation. Type **}** **#end get_input** and press **Enter** twice.

   Now enter the function definition for the `validate_input` function.

4. Enter the `validate_input` function definition, which is shaded in Figure 7-16. Figure 7-16 shows the completed user-defined functions section of the script.

```
#*****user-defined functions*****
sub get_input {
      return param('Name'), param('Email'), param('Comments');
} #end get_input

sub validate_input {
      my $valid = "Y";
      if ($name eq "" or $email eq "" or $comments eq "") {
            $valid = "N";
      }
      return $valid;
} #end validate_input

sub save_to_file {
      open(OUTFILE, ">>", "comments.txt")
            or die "Error opening comments.txt for save. $!, stopped";
      print OUTFILE "$name|$email|$comments\n";
      close(OUTFILE);
} #end save_to_file

sub create_acknowledgment_page {
      print "<HTML>\n";
      print "<HEAD><TITLE>International Coffees</TITLE></HEAD>\n";
      print "<BODY>\n";
      print "<H2>$name, thank you for the following \n";
      print "comments:<BR><BR>$comments\n";
      print "</H2></BODY></HTML>\n";
} #end create_acknowledgment_page

sub create_error_page {
      print "<HTML>\n";
      print "<HEAD><TITLE>International Coffees</TITLE></HEAD>\n";
      print "<BODY>\n";
      print "<H2>Please return to the form and \n";
```

Figure 7-16   Completed user-defined functions section of the script

```
        print "complete all items.</H2>\n";
        print "</BODY></HTML>\n";
} #end create_error_page

sub create_comments_page {
    my (@records, $name_field, $email_field, $com_field);

    open(INFILE, "<", "comments.txt")
            or die "Error opening comments.txt. $!, stopped";

    print "<HTML>\n";
    print "<HEAD><TITLE>International Coffees</TITLE></HEAD>\n";
    print "<BODY>\n";
    print "<H2>What other coffee lovers say \n";
    print "about our coffees:</H2>\n";
    @records = <INFILE>;
    close(INFILE);
    foreach my $rec (@records) {
            chomp($rec);
            ($name_field, $email_field, $com_field) = split(/\|/, $rec);
            print "<B>Name:</B> $name_field<BR>\n";
            print "<B>Comments:</B> $com_field<BR>\n";
            print "<HR>";
    }
    print "</BODY></HTML>\n";
} #end create_comments_page
```

Figure 7-16   Completed user-defined functions section of the script (continued)

> 5. Save the coffee.cgi document.

Now test the coffee.cgi script to make sure that it is working correctly.

To test the coffee.cgi script:

1. *If you are using a UNIX system*, open a terminal window, if necessary. Make the cgi-bin/chap07 directory the current directory, and then change the coffee.cgi file permissions to **755**. Also change the file permissions for the comments.txt file, which is contained in the cgi-bin/chap07 directory, to **666**.

    If you are using a Windows system, open a Command Prompt window, and then make the cgi-bin\chap07 directory the current directory.

2. Type **perl -c coffee.cgi** and press **Enter** to check the script for syntax errors. If necessary, correct any syntax errors in the script before continuing to the next step.

    You will not be able to test the script by executing it using the -w switch, because the first selection structure in the script refers to the REQUEST_METHOD environment variable, whose value is set by the Web server. You will need to test the script by executing it from the browser.

3. Start your Web browser, then use the browser's File menu to open the cof-fee.html document. The file is contained in the public_html/chap07 directory. A form similar to the one shown earlier in Figure 7-6 appears on the screen.

First, complete and then submit the form.

4. Enter **Jeremiah Jacobs** in the Your name text box, **jj@server.com** in the E-mail address text box, and **I love the flavored coffees.** in the Comments text area. Click the **Submit Form** button. If necessary, click the **Continue Submission** button. The script saves the form data to the comments.txt file, and then displays an acknowledgment Web page similar to the one shown earlier in Figure 7-8.

Next, verify that the form data you entered was saved to the comments.txt file.

5. Return to the form, then click the **View what others have to say** link. The script displays a Web page similar to the one shown earlier in Figure 7-9. The Web page lists the names and comments contained in the comments.txt file, and includes the form data you entered in Step 4. (The first two records were already included in the comments.txt file.)

Now verify that the script displays the appropriate Web page when the user submits an incomplete form.

6. Return to the form. Click the **Reset Form** button, and then click the **Submit Form** button. If necessary, click the **Continue Submission** button. The script displays a Web page similar to the one shown earlier in Figure 7-7. The Web page advises the user to return to the form and complete all items.

In Chapter 5, you learned how to open a data file and read its contents into an array. As was mentioned in the chapter, you should assign only the contents of small files to an array. You should not assign the contents of a large file to an array, because it will consume too much of the computer's internal memory. Before you can learn how to read a data file without first assigning its contents to an array, you need to learn about the while and until statements in Perl.

THE while AND until STATEMENTS

As you learned in Chapter 4, you use the repetition structure, also called a loop, to instruct the computer to repeat a block of instructions either a specified number of times or until some condition is met. Recall that Perl provides several statements that you can use to code a loop. You learned how to use the foreach and for statements in Chapter 4. In this chapter, you learn how to use the while and until statements. The syntax and examples of the while and until statements are shown in Figure 7-17.

Syntax of the while statement	Syntax of the until statement

while (*condition*) {
    one or more statements to be
    processed as long as the condition
    is true
}
	until (*condition*) {
	    one or more statements to be
	    processed until the condition is true
	}

Example of the while **statement**	**Example of the** until **statement**

`my ($x, @nums);`
`@nums = (5000, 200, 100, 3);`
`$x = 0;`
`while ($x < 4) {`
`    print "$nums[$x]\n";`
`    $x = $x + 1;`
`}`
 	
Result
5000
200
100
3
	`my ($x, @nums);`
	`@nums = (5000, 200, 100, 3);`
	`$x = 0;`
	`until ($x == 4) {`
	`    print "$nums[$x]\n";`
	`    $x = $x + 1;`
	`}`
	
	Result
	5000
	200
	100
	3

Figure 7-17   Syntax and examples of the while and until statements

You use the while statement to repeat a block of instructions *while* a condition is true. The example of the while statement shown in Figure 7-17, for instance, repeats the loop instructions as long as (or while) the $x variable contains a value that is less than the number 4. The loop stops when the $x variable contains the number 4.

You use the until statement, on the other hand, to repeat a block of instructions *until* a condition becomes true. The example of the until statement shown in Figure 7-17, for instance, repeats the loop instructions until the $x variable contains the number 4.

In the next section, you modify the International Coffees script so that it uses the while statement to read the records from the comments.txt file and display the names and comments on a Web page.

Using the while Statement in the International Coffees Script

In the International Coffees script, the **create_comments_page** function opens the comments.txt file for input, and uses the `@records = <INFILE>;` statement to assign the contents of the file to the `@records` array. The function then uses the `close(INFILE);` statement to close the file immediately after the records are read. Depending on the number of customers submitting comments, it is possible that, over time, the comments.txt file could become quite large and consume a considerable amount of the computer's internal memory if saved to an array. In the next set of steps, you remove the `@records` array from the **create_comments_page** function. Rather than opening the comments.txt file and assigning its contents to an array, and then closing the file before processing each record, the function will simply open the file, process each record while the file remains open, and then close the file. The function will use the `while` statement to handle the processing task.

To modify the `create_comments_page` function:

1. Open the coffee.html file in a text editor.

2. Change the filename in the first line from coffee.html to **coffee2.html**.

3. Modify the <FORM> tag's ACTION property and the <A> tag's HREF property to refer to the **coffee2.cgi** script. Save the document as **coffee2.html**, then close the document.

4. Open the coffee.cgi file in a text editor. Change the filename in the second line from coffee.cgi to **coffee2.cgi**, then save the document as **coffee2.cgi**.

5. Remove the `@records,` entry from the variable declaration statement, which is located immediately below the `create_comments_page` function header. The statement should now say `my ($name_field, $email_field, $com_field);`.

6. Change the `@records = <INFILE>;` statement to `while (<INFILE>) {`. As you learned in Chapter 5, `<INFILE>` tells the computer to read each record from the file whose *filehandle* is INFILE; in this case, the file is the comments.txt file. The `while (<INFILE>) {` instruction indicates that the computer should repeat the `while` loop's instructions as long as (or while) there are records to read. In other words, repeat the loop instructions for each record in the file.

   The comments.txt file will need to remain open while the `while` statement is processing the records.

7. Delete the line containing the `close(INFILE);` statement from the script. Insert a blank line above the `print "</BODY></HTML>\n";` statement, which is located immediately above the `} #end create_comments_page` function footer, then type **close(INFILE);** in the blank line.

   Now that you are using the `while` statement to process the records in the comments.txt file, you no longer need the `foreach` statement.

8. Delete the line containing the `foreach my $rec (@records) {` instruction.

   Each time the angle operator (<>) reads a record, it temporarily stores the record in a special variable named $_.

9. Modify the `chomp` and `split` functions as shown in Figure 7-18.

```
sub create_comments_page {
    my ($name_field, $email_field, $com_field);

    open(INFILE, "<", "comments.txt")
        or die "Error opening comments.txt. $!, stopped";

    print "<HTML>\n";
    print "<HEAD><TITLE>International Coffees</TITLE></HEAD>\n";
    print "<BODY>\n";
    print "<H2>What other coffee lovers say \n";
    print "about our coffees:</H2>\n";
    while (<INFILE>) {
        chomp($_);
        ($name_field, $email_field, $com_field) = split(/\|/, $_);
        print "<B>Name:</B> $name_field<BR>\n";
        print "<B>Comments:</B> $com_field<BR>\n";
        print "<HR>";
    }
    close(INFILE);
    print "</BODY></HTML>\n";
} #end create_comments_page
```

change from
$rec to $_

Figure 7-18   Modified `create_comments_page` function

7

   10. Save the coffee2.cgi document.

Now test the modified script from the browser.

To test the modified script from the browser:

   1. Return to your browser. Use the browser's File menu to open the coffee2.html file.

   2. Click the **View what others have to say** link. The script displays a Web page similar to the one shown earlier in Figure 7-9.

   3. Close your browser and any open windows.

CHAPTER SUMMARY

□ User-defined functions allow a programmer to avoid writing and testing the same code more than once. They also allow large and complex scripts to be broken into small and manageable tasks.

□ A function is a block of code that begins with the Perl keyword **sub**.

□ A function's code is processed only when the function is called, or invoked. You call (invoke) a function by including its name and arguments (if any) in a statement.

□ Every function performs a specific task and then returns one or more values to the statement that called it. The calling statement can either make use of or ignore the function's return value(s).

❑ You can use the `length` function to determine the number of characters contained in a scalar variable. The syntax of the `length` function is **length(*variable*)**, where *variable* is the name of a scalar variable.

❑ A function definition is composed of a function header, function body, and function footer.

❑ The `return` statement is used in a function body to return one or more values to the statement that called the function. The syntax of the `return` statement is **return *expression*;**, where *expression* represents the one or more values you want returned to the calling statement.

❑ When a function body does not contain a `return` statement, the function returns the value of the last statement it processes.

❑ You can use the `exit` statement to terminate a script.

❑ When arguments are passed to a user-defined function, Perl stores the arguments in a special array named `@_`.

❑ Many programmers consider it poor programming to let a user-defined function assign a value to a variable declared in the main section.

❑ Environment variables are a series of hidden *keys* and *values* that the Web server sends to a CGI script when the script is run. Perl stores the environment variables in a special hash named `%ENV`.

❑ You use the `while` statement to repeat one or more instructions while a condition is true.

❑ You use the `until` statement to repeat one or more instructions until a condition becomes true.

❑ The angle operator temporarily stores each record it reads, one at a time, in the `$_` variable.

REVIEW QUESTIONS

1. A function is a block of code that begins with the Perl keyword
   _____.

   a. `block`

   b. `function`

   c. `func`

   d. `sub`

2. The code for a user-defined function _____.

   a. must be entered in the same file as the calling statement

   b. can be entered in the same file as the calling statement

   c. can be entered in a file separate from the calling statement

   d. both b and c

3. Which of the following statements calls a user-defined function named `calc_netpay`, and assigns the function's return value to the `$net` variable?

   a. `calc_netpay();`

   b. `calc_netpay() = $net;`

   c. `$net = calc_netpay();`

   d. `calc_netpay($net);`

4. Which of the following statements calls a user-defined function named `calc_taxes`, and assigns the function's return values to the `$federal` and `$state` variables?

   a. `($federal, $state) = calc_taxes();`

   b. `$federal, $state = calc_taxes();`

   c. `calc_taxes() = ($federal, $state);`

   d. both a and b

5. The `return` statement is required in a function definition.

   a. true

   b. false

6. The _____ function terminates a script.

   a. `end`

   b. `exit`

   c. `halt`

   d. `stop`

7. Perl stores the arguments passed to a user-defined function in an array named

   _____.

   a. `@_`

   b. `_@`

   c. `$_`

   d. `%ENV`

8. Variables declared in the main section of a script are available to the main section and to any functions defined within the script.

   a. true

   b. false

9. Which of the following statements determines the number of characters stored in the $email variable, and then assigns the result to the $num_char variable?

   a. $num_char = len($email);

   b. $num_char = length($email);

   c. $num_char = num($email);

   d. $num_char = size($email);

10. Environment variables are stored in a hash named _____.

   a. @_

   b. %_

   c. %ENV

   d. None of the above.

11. What are the two reasons that programmers create user-defined functions?

12. List the three parts of a function definition.

13. When the angle operator (<>) reads a record, it temporarily stores the record in the _____ variable.

14. The first argument passed to a user-defined function is stored in a scalar variable named _____.

15. When you click a link that is associated with a CGI script, the REQUEST_METHOD is automatically set to _____.

16. Write a statement that prints the method used to send form data.

17. Write a **return** statement that returns the result of multiplying the contents of the $hours variable by the contents of the $rate variable.

18. Write a **return** statement that returns the contents of the $name and $age variables.

19. Write a function header for a user-defined function named **display_errors**.

20. Write a **while** loop that prints the numbers 1 through 5.

HANDS-ON PROJECTS

Project 1

In this project, you modify the International Coffees script so that the **create_error_page** function lists the input items that were left blank on the form.

   a. Open the coffee.html file in a text editor. The file is contained in the public_html/chap07 directory.

   b. Change the filename in the first line from coffee.html to c07ex1.html.

   c. Modify the <FORM> tag's ACTION property and the <A> tag's HREF property to refer to the c07ex1.cgi script.

d. Save the document as c07ex1.html.

e. Open the comments.txt file in a text editor. The file is contained in the cgi-bin/chap07 directory. Save the document as c07ex1.txt, then close the document.

f. Open the coffee.cgi file in a text editor. The file is contained in the cgi-bin/chap07 directory.

g. Change the filename in the second line from coffee.cgi to c07ex1.cgi.

h. Change the filename in the two **open** statements and in the two **die** functions from comments.txt to c07ex1.txt.

i. Save the document as c07ex1.cgi.

j. Modify the script so that the **validate_input** function records in an array the items that were left blank on the form.

k. Modify the script so that the **create_error_page** function lists the input items that were left blank on the form. (Recall that you stored the items in an array in Step j.) Change the message displayed by the function to "Please return to the form and complete the following items."

l. Save the c07ex1.cgi document.

m. *If you are using a UNIX system*, change the c07ex1.cgi file permissions to 755. Also change the c07ex1.txt file permissions to 666.

n. Test the script from the command line using the -c switch.

o. Open the c07ex1.html document in your Web browser. Enter Robert Lee as the name, then click the Submit Form button. If necessary, click the Continue Submission button. The Web page that appears on the screen should advise the user to return to the form to complete the E-mail and Comments sections.

Project 2

In this project, you modify the International Coffees script so that the **get_input** and **validate_input** functions assign values to the variables declared in the main section of the script. (Although many programmers consider it poor programming to code a script in this manner, many do not. Therefore, you might see this type of coding in scripts written by other programmers.)

a. Open the coffee.html file in a text editor. The file is contained in the public_html/chap07 directory.

b. Change the filename in the first line from coffee.html to c07ex2.html.

c. Modify the <FORM> tag's ACTION property and the <A> tag's HREF property to refer to the c07ex2.cgi script.

d. Save the document as c07ex2.html.

e. Open the comments.txt file in a text editor. The file is contained in the cgi-bin/chap07 directory. Save the document as c07ex2.txt, then close the document.

f. Open the coffee.cgi file in a text editor. The file is contained in the cgi-bin/chap07 directory.

g. Change the filename in the second line from coffee.cgi to c07ex2.cgi.

h. Change the filename in the two **open** statements and in the two **die** functions from comments.txt to c07ex2.txt.

i. Save the document as c07ex2.cgi.

j. Modify the script so that the **get_input** and **validate_input** functions assign the appropriate values to the variables declared in the main section of the script.

k. Save the c07ex2.cgi document.

l. *If you are using a UNIX system*, change the c07ex2.cgi file permissions to 755. Also change the c07ex2.txt file permissions to 666.

m. Test the script from the command line using the –c switch.

n. Open the c07ex2.html document in your Web browser. Enter Suman Habiva as the name, suman@rs.com as the e-mail address, and "I really love your coffee. Your service is great also." as the comments. Click the Submit Form button. If necessary, click the Continue Submission button. The acknowledgment Web page appears on the screen.

o. Return to the form. Click the "View what others have to say" link. The Web page listing the names and comments appears on the screen.

p. Return to the form. Click the Reset Form button, then click the Submit Form button. If necessary, click the Continue Submission button. A Web page advising you to return to the form to complete all items appears on the screen.

Project 3

In this project, you modify the International Coffees script so that it assigns the form data to an array, rather than to three variables.

a. Open the coffee.html file in a text editor. The file is contained in the public_html/chap07 directory.

b. Change the filename in the first line from coffee.html to c07ex3.html.

c. Modify the <FORM> tag's ACTION property and the <A> tag's HREF property to refer to the c07ex3.cgi script.

d. Save the document as c07ex3.html.

e. Open the comments.txt file in a text editor. The file is contained in the cgi-bin/chap07 directory. Save the document as c07ex3.txt, then close the document.

f. Open the coffee.cgi file in a text editor. The file is contained in the cgi-bin/chap07 directory.

g. Change the filename in the second line from coffee.cgi to c07ex3.cgi.

h. Change the filename in the two **open** statements and in the two **die** functions from comments.txt to c07ex3.txt.

i. Save the document as c07ex3.cgi.

j. Change the **my ($name, $email, $comments, $data_ok);** statement to **my ($data_ok, @input_items);**. Modify the statement that calls the **get_input** function so that it assigns the function's return values to the **@input_items** array.

k. Modify the **validate_input**, **save_to_file**, and **create_ acknowledgment_page** functions so that each refers to the data stored in the **@input_items** array, rather than to the data stored in the **$name**, **$email**, and **$comments** variables.

l. Save the c07ex3.cgi document.

m. *If you are using a UNIX system*, change the c07ex3.cgi file permissions to 755. Also change the c07ex3.txt file permissions to 666.

n. Test the script from the command line using the –c switch.

o. Open the c07ex3.html document in your Web browser. Enter Pamela Hernandez as the name, ph@server.com as the e-mail address, and "The Hazelnut is my favorite." as the comments. Click the Submit Form button. If necessary, click the Continue Submission button. The acknowledgment Web page appears on the screen.

p. Return to the form. Click the "View what others have to say" link. The Web page listing the names and comments appears on the screen.

q. Return to the form. Click the Reset Form button, then click the Submit Form button. If necessary, click the Continue Submission button. A Web page advising you to return to the form to complete all items appears on the screen.

Project 4

In this project, you modify the International Coffees script so that it uses the **foreach** statement to read and process each record stored in the data file.

a. Open the coffee2.html file in a text editor. The file is contained in the public_html/chap07 directory.

b. Change the filename in the first line from coffee2.html to c07ex4.html.

c. Modify the <FORM> tag's ACTION property and the <A> tag's HREF property to refer to the c07ex4.cgi script.

d. Save the document as c07ex4.html.

e. Open the comments.txt file in a text editor. The file is contained in the cgi-bin/chap07 directory. Save the document as c07ex4.txt, then close the document.

f. Open the coffee2.cgi file in a text editor. The file is contained in the cgi-bin/chap07 directory.

g. Change the filename in the second line from coffee2.cgi to c07ex4.cgi.

h. Change the filename in the two **open** statements and in the two **die** functions from comments.txt to c07ex4.txt.

i. Save the document as c07ex4.cgi.

j. Modify the script so that the **create_comments_page** function uses the **foreach** statement, rather than the **while** statement, to read and process each record contained in the c07ex4.txt file.

k. Save the c07ex4.cgi document.

l. *If you are using a UNIX system*, change the c07ex4.cgi file permissions to 755. Also change the c07ex4.txt file permissions to 666.

m. Test the script from the command line using the -c switch.

n. Open the c07ex4.html document in your Web browser. Click the "View what others have to say" link. The Web page listing the names and comments appears on the screen.

Project 5

In this project, you modify the Super Bowl script that you created in Chapter 6 so that it uses user-defined functions and a **while** statement.

a. Copy the supbowl.html file from the public_html/chap06 directory to the public_html/chap07 directory. Rename the file c07ex5.html.

b. Copy the supbowl.cgi file from the cgi-bin/chap06 directory to the cgi-bin/chap07 directory. Rename the file c07ex5.cgi.

c. Open the c07ex5.html file in a text editor. Change the filename in the first line from supbowl.html to c07ex5.html.

d. Modify the <FORM> tag's ACTION property to refer to the c07ex5.cgi script, which is contained in the cgi-bin/chap07 directory.

e. Save the c07ex5.html document.

f. Open the survey.txt file in a text editor. The file is contained in the cgi-bin/chap07 directory. Save the document as c07ex5.txt, then close the document.

g. Open the c07ex5.cgi file in a text editor. Change the filename in the second line from supbowl.cgi to c07ex5.cgi.

h. *If you are using a UNIX system*, change the filename argument in the two **open** statements from "survey.txt" to "c07ex5.txt".

   If you are using a Windows system, change the filename argument in the two **open** statements from "chap06/survey.txt" to simply "c07ex5.txt".

i. Change the filename in the two **die** functions from survey.txt to c07ex5.txt.

j. Save the c07ex5.cgi document.

k. Modify the script so that it uses two user-defined functions named `process_input_data` and `display_error_page`.

l. The `process_input data` function should store the records contained in the c07ex5.txt file in an array, but it should use a `while` statement, rather than a `foreach` statement, to process the records. Modify the function appropriately.

m. Save the c07ex5.cgi document.

n. *If you are using a UNIX system*, change the c07ex5.cgi file permissions to 755. Also change the c07ex5.txt file permissions to 666.

o. Test the script from the command line, using both valid and invalid data.

p. *If you are using a Windows system*, return to the c07ex5.cgi document in your text editor. Change the filename argument in the two **open** statements from "c07ex5.txt" to "chap07/c07ex5.txt", then save the c07ex5.cgi document.

q. Open the c07ex5.html file in your browser. Test the script using both valid and invalid data.

Project 6

In this project, you modify the Juniper Printers script that you created in Chapter 4 so that it uses user-defined functions.

a. Copy the juniper.html file from the public_html/chap04 directory to the public_html/chap07 directory. Rename the file c07ex6.html.

b. Copy the juniper.cgi file from the cgi-bin/chap04 directory to the cgi-bin/chap07 directory. Rename the file c07ex6.cgi.

c. Open the c07ex6.html file in a text editor. Change the filename in the first line from juniper.html to c07ex6.html.

d. Modify the <FORM> tag's ACTION property to refer to the c07ex6.cgi script, which is contained in the cgi-bin/chap07 directory.

e. Save the c07ex6.html document.

f. Open the c07ex6.cgi file in a text editor. Change the filename in the second line from juniper.cgi to c07ex6.cgi.

g. Modify the script so that it uses two user-defined functions named `get_form_data` and `create_web_page`.

h. Save the c07ex6.cgi document.

i. *If you are using a UNIX system*, change the c07ex6.cgi file permissions to 755.

j. Test the script from the command line.

k. Open the c07ex6.html file in your browser and test the script.

7

CASE PROJECTS

1. Create an HTML form and a script for Washington Middle School. Name the form c07case1.html and save it in the public_html/chap07 directory. Name the script c07case1.cgi and save it in the cgi-bin/chap07 directory. The form should allow the user to enter a temperature in either Fahrenheit or Celsius. The CGI script that processes the form data should convert a Fahrenheit temperature to a Celsius temperature, and vice versa. The script should display both the temperature entered by the user and the converted temperature on a Web page. Be sure to use at least one user-defined function in the script. (*Hint:* The following formula converts a Fahrenheit temperature to a Celsius temperature: 5 / 9 * (Fahrenheit temperature - 32). The following formula converts a Celsius temperature to a Fahrenheit temperature: Celsius temperature * 9 / 5 + 32.)

2. Create an HTML form and a script for the Allenton Township water department. Name the form c07case2.html and save it in the public_html/chap07 directory. Name the script c07case2.cgi and save it in the cgi-bin/chap07 directory. The form should allow the user to enter a customer's current and previous water meter readings. The CGI script that processes the form data should calculate the amount due, based on a charge of $1.75 per 1000 gallons of water used. (For example, if the current and previous readings are 14000 and 7500 gallons, respectively, the amount due is $11.38.) Display the current and previous water meter readings and the amount due on a Web page. Display the amount due with a dollar sign and two decimal places. Be sure to use at least one user-defined function in the script.

8

STRING MANIPULATION

In this chapter, you will:

- ◆ Convert a string to uppercase letters using the uc function
- ◆ Convert a string to lowercase letters using the lc function
- ◆ Return, replace, or insert text using the substr function
- ◆ Use the index function to locate a string within another string
- ◆ Replace text using the transliteration operator
- ◆ Use the binding operators
- ◆ Perform pattern matching using the matching operator
- ◆ Include metacharacters in a search pattern
- ◆ Replace text using the substitution operator

Many times, a script will need to manipulate the data it receives from a server to get the data in the format it requires. For example, a script may need to remove a dollar sign from a number entered on a form. Or, it may need to convert a state abbreviation from lowercase letters to uppercase letters. Perl provides built-in functions and operators that you can use to perform these and other data manipulation tasks. You learn how to use these built-in functions and operators in this chapter. First you learn about the functions, and then you learn about the operators.

THE uc AND lc FUNCTIONS

As you learned in Chapter 6, string comparisons in Perl are case sensitive. In other words, the string "Y" is not the same as the string "y" when both strings are compared by a computer, because both strings are stored in the computer's internal memory using different ASCII values. A problem occurs when you need to include a string, entered by the user on a form, in a comparison. The problem occurs because you cannot control the case in which the user enters the string.

The ASCII values associated with the characters on your keyboard are listed in Appendix D.

You can use the logical operators you learned about in Chapter 6 to solve the string comparison problem. For example, to determine if the $answer variable does or does not contain the string "Y" in either uppercase or lowercase, you can use either the *condition* (`$answer eq "Y" or $answer eq "y"`) or the *condition* (`$answer ne "Y" and $answer ne "y"`) in an `if` or `while` statement.

Rather than using a logical operator when comparing two strings that contain letters of the alphabet, you also can use a function that temporarily converts one or both of the strings to either uppercase or lowercase before the comparison is made. In Perl, you use the **uc function** to temporarily convert the letters in a string to uppercase, and you use the **lc function** to temporarily convert the letters to lowercase. (uc stands for uppercase, and lc stands for lowercase.) Figure 8-1 shows the syntax and purpose of the uc and lc functions, and examples of using each function.

The uc and lc functions affect only characters that represent letters of the alphabet, as these are the only characters that have uppercase and lowercase forms. The functions have no effect on numbers and special characters—such as the dollar sign ($) and percent sign (%).

The uc and lc functions temporarily store in memory a copy of the variable's contents in either uppercase or lowercase while the function is being processed.

The parentheses in the uc and lc functions are optional. In other words, the statement `$name = uc($name);` is equivalent to the statement `$name = uc $name;`. Both statements produce the same result.

Perl also has a function named `ucfirst` that converts only the first character in a string to uppercase. You also can combine the `ucfirst` function with the `lc` function. For example, assuming the $state variable contains the string "aLABAMA", the statement `print ucfirst(lc($state));` will print "Alabama".

Syntax	Purpose
uc(*string*)	convert *string* to uppercase
lc(*string*)	convert *string* to lowercase
Examples	**Results**

Example 1
`if (uc($answer) eq "Y") {`
      one or more statements to be
      processed when the condition
      evaluates to true
`}`
	temporarily converts the contents of the $answer variable to uppercase, then compares the uppercase value to the uppercase letter "Y"

Example 2
`while (lc($item) ne "done") {`
      one or more statements to be
      processed when the condition
      evaluates to true
`}`
	temporarily converts the contents of the $item variable to lowercase, then compares the lowercase value to the lowercase word "done"

Example 3 `$name = uc($name);`	changes the string stored in the $name variable to uppercase
Example 4 `$emp = lc($name);`	assigns, to the $emp variable, the lowercase version of the string stored in the $name variable

Figure 8-1   Syntax, purpose, and examples of the uc and lc functions

8

In the first example shown in Figure 8-1, the uc function temporarily converts the contents of the $answer variable to uppercase. The if statement's *condition* compares the result of the conversion to the uppercase letter "Y". The *condition* will evaluate to true if the contents of the $answer variable is either the letter "Y" or the letter "y", because the letter "Y" is the uppercase equivalent of both letters.

Notice that the *condition* compares the uppercase equivalent of one string to the uppercase equivalent of another string. For the uc function to work correctly when comparing strings, both strings included in the comparison must be uppercase. In other words, the *condition* (uc($answer) eq "y") will not work correctly. The *condition* always will evaluate to false, because the uppercase version of a letter is never equal to its lowercase counterpart.

In the second example shown in Figure 8-1, the lc function temporarily converts the contents of the $item variable to lowercase. The while statement's *condition* compares the result of the conversion to the lowercase word "done". The *condition* will evaluate to true if the contents of the $item variable is the word "done", entered in any case—for example, "done", "DONE", "doNe", and so on.

Notice that the *condition* in this instance compares the lowercase equivalent of one string to the lowercase equivalent of another string. For the lc function to work correctly, both strings included in the comparison must be lowercase.

You also can use the uc and lc functions to assign the uppercase and lowercase versions of a string to a variable, as shown in the last two examples in Figure 8-1. The $name = uc($name); statement shown in Example 3, for instance, temporarily converts the contents of the $name variable to uppercase, and then assigns the converted value to the $name variable. The contents of the $name variable will be uppercase after this statement is processed. Similarly, the statement shown in Example 4, $emp = lc($name);, temporarily converts the contents of the $name variable to lowercase, and then assigns the converted value to the $emp variable. After this statement is processed, the $name variable will contain the original string, and the $emp variable will contain the lowercase equivalent of the string.

You also can use the substr function to manipulate strings in Perl.

THE substr FUNCTION

You can use the **substr function** to return a portion of a string contained in another string. You also can use the substr function to replace one or more characters in a string with other characters, and to insert one or more characters within a string. Figure 8-2 shows three versions of the substr function's syntax, along with the purpose and examples of using each version.

As Figure 8-2 indicates, you use version 1 of the syntax to return one or more characters from a string. You use version 2 to replace one or more characters in a string with other characters, and version 3 to insert one or more characters within a string. In versions 1 and 2 of the syntax, *length* is the number of characters you want to return or replace, beginning with the character located in position *start* in the *string*. The first character in a string is located in position 0, the second character is in position 1, and so on. Notice that, if *length* is omitted in versions 1 and 2 of the syntax, the function returns or replaces all characters from the *start* position through the end of the *string*. Also notice that, when using version 3 of the syntax to insert characters within a string, *length* is always the number 0.

Study closely each of the examples shown in Figure 8-2. Begin with the four examples of the version 1 syntax, which is used to return characters from a string. In Example 1, the statement $first = substr($name, 0, 4); assigns the string "John" to the $first variable, because "John" is the first four characters stored in the $name variable. In Example 2, the statement $last = substr($name, 5, 6); assigns the string "Smitty" to the $last variable. In this case, "Smitty" is the six characters, beginning with the character in position 5, stored in the $name variable. Notice that the statement $last = substr($name, 5);, which is shown in Example 3, also assigns the string "Smitty" to the $last variable. Recall that when you omit the *length* from syntax version 1, the substr function returns all characters from the *start* position (in this case, position 5) through the end of the *string*. The code shown in Example 4 in Figure 8-2 prints the contents of the $part variable, but only if the string "X" is located in position 3 in the variable.

Syntax versions	Purpose
Version 1 – return characters **substr**(*string*, *start*, *length*)	Return *length* number of characters from *string* beginning at position *start*. If *length* is omitted, the function returns all characters from the *start* position through the end of the *string*.
Version 2 – replace characters **substr**(*string*, *start*, *length*) = *replacementstring*	Replace *length* number of characters in *string* with *replacementstring*, beginning at position *start* in *string*. If *length* is omitted, the function replaces all characters from the *start* position through the end of *string*.
Version 3 – insert characters **substr**(*string*, *start*, **0**) = *insertionstring*	Insert *insertionstring* within *string*, beginning at position *start* in *string*.

Examples of syntax version 1	Results

Example 1
`$name = "John Smitty";`
`$first = substr($name, 0, 4);`
	assigns John to the `$first` variable

Example 2
`$name = "John Smitty";`
`$last = substr($name, 5, 6);`
	assigns Smitty to the `$last` variable

Example 3
`$name = "John Smitty";`
`$last = substr($name, 5);`
	assigns Smitty to the `$last` variable

Example 4
`if (substr($part, 3, 1) eq "X") {`
`    print "$part\n";`
`}`
	prints the contents of the `$part` variable if the letter X is in position 3 in the variable (in other words, if X is the fourth character in the variable)

Examples of syntax version 2	Results

Example 5
`$name = "Pat Jeffrey";`
`substr($name, 0, 3) = "Patty";`
	replaces Pat with Patty; the `$name` variable now stores Patty Jeffrey

Example 6
`$name = "Pat Jeffrey";`
`substr($name, 4) = "Carr";`
	replaces Jeffrey with Carr; the `$name` variable now stores Pat Carr

Examples of syntax version 3	Results

Example 7
`$price = "45";`
`substr($price, 0, 0) = "\$";`
	inserts a dollar sign in position 0 in the `$price` variable; the `$price` variable now stores $45

Example 8
`$location = "Chicago IL";`
`substr($location, 7, 0) = ",";`
	inserts a comma in position 7 in the `$location` variable; the `$location` variable now stores Chicago, IL

Figure 8-2   Three versions of the `substr` function's syntax along with the purpose and examples of each version

Next, study the two examples of the version 2 syntax, which is used to replace characters in a string with other characters. The `substr($name, 0, 3) = "Patty";` statement shown in Example 5 replaces "Pat", which is the first three characters in the `$name` variable, with "Patty"; the `$name` variable will contain "Patty Jeffrey" after the statement is processed. The `substr($name, 4) = "Carr";` statement shown in Example 6 replaces all of the characters in the `$name` variable, beginning with the character located in position 4, with "Carr"; the `$name` variable will contain " Pat Carr" after the statement is processed. Recall that when you omit the *length* from syntax version 2, the `substr` function replaces all characters from the *start* position (in this case, position 4) through the end of the *string*.

Finally, study the two examples of the version 3 syntax, which is used to insert characters within a string. The `substr($price, 0, 0) = "\$";` statement shown in Example 7 inserts a dollar sign in position 0 in the `$price` variable; the variable will contain $45 after the statement is processed. The `substr($location, 7, 0) = ",";` statement shown in Example 8 inserts a comma in position 7 in the `$location` variable. The `$location` variable will contain the string "Chicago, IL" after the statement is processed.

As you learned in Chapter 3, the backslash (\) alerts Perl to ignore the special meaning of the dollar sign and simply treat the dollar sign verbatim.

Next, learn about the `index` function, which is used to search for one string within another string.

THE index FUNCTION

You can use the **index function** to search a string to determine if it contains another string. Figure 8-3 shows the syntax and purpose of the `index` function. It also shows several examples of using the function.

The `index` function searches for the *substring* in the *string*, starting with the character in position *start* in the *string*. If you omit the *start* argument, the function begins the search with the first character in the *string*; in other words, it begins the search with the character in position 0. If the *substring* is not contained within the *string*, the function returns the number –1. However, if the *substring* is contained within the *string*, the `index` function returns a number that is greater than or equal to zero. The number indicates the beginning position of the first occurrence of the *substring* within the *string*, beginning at position *start*.

Perl also has a function named `rindex` that returns the position of the last occurrence of the *substring* within the *string*, beginning at position *start*.

Syntax	Purpose
index(*string*, *substring*, *start*)	Return the position of the first occurrence of the *substring* within the *string*, beginning with position *start* in the *string*. If you omit the *start* argument, the function begins the search with the first character in the *string*.

Examples	Results

Example 1
`$num = "15%";`
`$percent = index($num, "%");`
	assigns the number 2 to the `$percent` variable

Example 2
`$num = "15";`
`$dollar = index($num, "\$");`
	assigns the number -1 to the `$dollar` variable

Example 3
`$msg = "Have a really good day!";`
`$word = index($msg, "good");`
	assigns the number 14 to the `$word` variable

Example 4
`$msg = "Have a really good day!";`
`$word = index($msg, "Good");`
	assigns the number 1 to the `$word` variable

Example 5
`$address = "Chicago, IL, 60614";`
`$comma = index($address, ",");`
	assigns the number 7 to the `$comma` variable

Example 6
`$address = "Chicago, IL, 60614";`
`$comma = index($address, ",", 8);`
	assigns the number 11 to the `$comma` variable

Example 7
`$n = "Sue+Smith";`
`substr($n, index($n, "+"), 1) = " ";`
	replaces the plus sign in the `$n` variable with a space; the `$n` variable now stores "Sue Smith"

Figure 8-3   Syntax, purpose, and examples of the index function

The `index` function in Example 1 searches for the percent sign in the `$num` variable, beginning with the first character in the variable. The function returns the number 2, because the percent sign is located in position 2 in the `$num` variable. The `$percent = index($num, "%");` statement assigns the `index` function's return value to the `$percent` variable.

The `$dollar = index($num, "\$");` statement in Example 2 assigns the number –1 to the `$dollar` variable, because the `$num` variable does not contain the dollar sign. Recall that if the *substring* is not contained within the *string*, the `index` function returns –1.

Examples 3 and 4 in Figure 8-3 search for the strings "good" and "Good", respectively, in the `$msg` variable. Notice that the `$word = index($msg, "good");` statement in Example 3 returns the number 14, which indicates that the string "good" begins in position 14 in the

$msg variable. The $word = index($msg, "Good"); statement in Example 4, on the other hand, returns –1, which indicates that the string "Good" is not contained in the $msg variable. (Recall that string comparisons in Perl are case sensitive.)

Examples 5 and 6 in Figure 8-3 search the $address variable for a comma. In Example 5, the search begins with the first character in the $address variable. (Recall that if you omit the *start* argument, the index function begins the search with the first character in the *string*.) The $comma = index($address, ","); statement in Example 5 assigns the number 7 to the $comma variable. In Example 6, the search begins with the character located in position 8 in the $address variable—the space character. In this case, the $comma = index($address, ",", 8); statement in Example 6 assigns the number 11 to the $comma variable.

You also can use the index function together with the substr function. The substr($n, index($n, "+"), 1) = " "; statement shown in Example 7, for instance, uses the index function to locate the plus sign in the $n variable. It then uses the substr function to replace the plus sign with a space. After the statement is processed, the $n variable will contain the string "Sue Smith" rather than "Sue+Smith".

In addition to providing functions for string manipulation, Perl also provides operators that you can use to manipulate strings. In the next section, you learn about the transliteration operator and the "contains" operator.

THE TRANSLITERATION AND "CONTAINS" OPERATORS

You can use the Perl **transliteration operator** to replace a character in a string with a different character. Many Perl programmers refer to the transliteration operator as simply the **tr operator** or the **tr/// operator**. In this book, the transliteration operator will be referred to as the tr/// operator, because this will help you remember that three forward slashes are required in the operator's syntax.

The transliteration operator also is called the translation operator.

Figure 8-4 shows the syntax and purpose of the tr/// operator. For now, do not worry if you do not fully understand the syntax. The syntax will become clearer as you view examples of using the operator.

A common error made when entering the tr/// operator is to forget the final slash (/). The Perl interpreter will display a syntax error message if the tr/// operator does not contain three forward slashes.

Syntax and purpose	
Syntax	
string =~ **tr**/*searchlist*/*replacementlist*/*modifier*	
Purpose	
replace characters in or delete characters from a string	

Parts	Description
string	*String*, which is required, is the string whose contents should be searched.
=~	The "contains" operator is required.
searchlist	*Searchlist*, which is required, is the one or more characters you want to search for in the *string*.
replacementlist	*Replacementlist*, which is optional, is the one or more characters that will replace the characters listed in the *searchlist*.
modifier	*Modifier*, which is optional, modifies the task performed by the tr/// operator and can be d, c, or s. The purpose of each *modifier* is listed below.
	Modifier Purpose
	d Delete found but unreplaced characters
	c Complement the *searchlist*
	s Squash duplicate replaced characters to a single character

Figure 8-4   Syntax and purpose of the tr/// operator

The tr/// operator scans the contents of *string*, character by character, and then replaces each occurrence of a character found in the *searchlist* with the corresponding character from the *replacementlist*. As Figure 8-4 indicates, you can use a *modifier* to modify the task performed by the tr/// operator. The modifier can be d, c, or s. You will learn more about the *modifier* when you view examples of using the tr/// operator.

You use the tr/// operator together with the **"contains" operator**, which is an equal sign followed by a tilde (=~). The "contains" operator is referred to as a **binding operator** in Perl, because it binds (connects) the string that appears on the left side of the operator to the expression that appears on the right side; in this case, for example, it binds the *string* to the tr/// operator. When used in this manner, the "contains" operator tells the tr/// operator to search the *string* to determine if it contains any of the characters listed in the *searchlist*.

One way to remember that the tilde comes after the equal sign in the "contains" operator is to think of the tilde as a tail that follows the equal sign. You can also associate the t in tilde with the t in tail.

Perl also provides another binding operator, called the "does not contain" operator. You learn about the "does not contain" operator later in this chapter.

Figure 8-5 shows examples of using the `tr///` operator without a *modifier*.

Examples	Results

Example 1
`$state = "Ca";`
`$state =~ tr/a-z/A-Z/;`
	replaces the lowercase letters in the `$state` variable with uppercase letters; the variable now contains CA

Example 2
`$phone = "555-1212";`
`$phone =~ tr/0-9/*/;`
	replaces the numbers in the `$phone` variable with asterisks; the variable now contains ***-****

Example 3
`$password = "Berry";`
`$password =~ tr/a-z/p-za-o/;`
	replaces the lowercase letters a through k in the `$password` variable with the lowercase letters p through z, and replaces the lowercase letters l through z with the lowercase letters a through o; the variable now contains Btggn

Example 4
`$item = "ax34B";`
`$item =~ tr/a-zA-Z/A-Za-z/;`
	replaces the lowercase letters in the `$item` variable with uppercase letters, and replaces the uppercase letters with lowercase letters; the variable now contains AX34b

Example 5
`$name = "Bob+Trent";`
`$name =~ tr/+/ /;`
	replaces the plus sign in the `$name` variable with a space; the variable now contains Bob Trent

Example 6
`$letters = "ACBA";`
`$letters =~ tr/AXB/135/;`
	replaces the letter A in the `$letters` variable with the number 1, the letter X with the number 3, and the letter B with the number 5; the variable now contains 1C51

Example 7
`$add = "Chicago,IL,60614";`
`$x = ($add =~ tr/,/ /);`
	replaces the commas in the `$add` variable with a space (the variable now contains Chicago IL 60614), then assigns the number 2 (which is the number of commas replaced) to the `$x` variable

Figure 8-5   Examples of using the `tr///` operator without a *modifier*

The `$state =~ tr/a-z/A-Z/;` statement shown in Example 1 replaces the lowercase letters a through z in the `$state` variable with the uppercase letters A through Z. The lowercase letter a will be replaced with the uppercase letter A, the lowercase letter b with the uppercase letter B, and so on. Notice that you use a hyphen (-) to specify a range of values. Also notice that the `tr///` operator contains three forward slashes, which is required by its syntax. The `$state` variable will contain the string "CA" after the statement is processed.

 When using the hyphen to specify a range of values, the value on the left side of the hyphen must have a lower ASCII value than the value on the right side of the hyphen. For example, you must use a-z, and not z-a, to specify the lowercase letters of the alphabet.

The $phone =~ tr/0-9/*/; statement in Example 2 scans the contents of the $phone variable to see if the variable contains any numbers. If a number is found, it is replaced with an asterisk ("). The $phone variable will contain the string "***-****" after the statement is processed.

The $password =~ tr/a-z/p-za-o/; statement in Example 3 changes the value stored in the $password variable from "Berry" to "Btggn". It does so by replacing the 26 lowercase letters a through z with the 11 lowercase letters p through z and the 15 lowercase letters a through o. The letter a will be replaced with the letter p, the letter b with the letter q, and so on.

The $item =~ tr/a-zA-Z/A-Za-z/; statement in Example 4 replaces the lowercase letters in the $item variable with uppercase letters, and vice versa. The $item variable will contain the string "AX34b" after the statement is processed.

The $name =~ tr/+/ /; statement in Example 5 changes the value stored in the $name variable from "Bob+Trent" to "Bob Trent". It does so by replacing the plus sign with a space.

The $letters =~ tr/AXB/135/; statement in Example 6 replaces the letter A in the $letters variable with the number 1, the letter X with the number 3, and the letter D with the number 5. The $letters variable will contain the string "1C51" after the statement is processed. Notice that the letter C remains as is, because it is not listed in the *searchlist*.

Finally, the $x = ($add =~ tr/,/ /); statement in Example 7 shows how you can determine the number of characters replaced by the tr/// operator. The statement first replaces each comma in the $add variable with a space. It then assigns the number of characters replaced—in this case, 2—to the $x variable.

Figure 8-6 shows examples of using the tr/// operator with a *modifier*.

Examples	Results
Example 1 $price = "\$5,600,000"; $price =~ tr/$,//d;	Deletes any dollar signs and commas from the contents of the $price variable; the variable will contain the string "5600000" after the statement is processed
Example 2 $msg = "T.J.\tCompany"; $msg =~ tr/\t./ /d;	replaces the tab character (\t) with a space, and deletes the period; the $msg variable will contain the string "TJ Company" after the statement is processed
Example 3 $course = "CIS100"; $course =~ tr/A-Z/*/c;	complements the *searchlist* by replacing all characters that are <u>not</u> the uppercase letters A through Z with an asterisk; the $course variable will contain the string "CIS***" after the statement is processed
Example 4 $name = "Bob Jones"; $name =~ tr/ //s;	squashes the 10 spaces in the $name variable down to one space; the variable will contain the string "Bob Jones" after the statement is processed

Figure 8-6   Examples of using the tr/// operator with a *modifier*

The **d** *modifier* included in the $price =~ tr/$,//d; statement in Example 1 tells the tr/// operator to delete any dollar signs and commas from the contents of the $price variable. The variable will contain the string "5600000" after the statement is processed. Notice that the tr/// operator in Example 1 does not include a *replacementlist*, which is optional in the syntax. However, it does include the *searchlist* and the three forward slashes, which are required.

The $msg =~ tr/\t./ /d; statement in Example 2 shows how you can use one tr/// operator to perform two operations: a replacement and a deletion. Notice that the tr/// operator's *searchlist* contains two characters—a tab (\t) and a period. However, its *replacementlist* contains only one character—a space. The tr/// operator will replace the tab character (\t), which is the first character listed in the *searchlist*, with the space character contained in the *replacementlist*. The **d** *modifier* then will delete the period from the $msg variable, because the period does not have a corresponding entry in the *replacementlist*. The $msg variable will contain the string "TJ Company" after the statement is processed.

The **c** *modifier* included in the $course =~ tr/A-Z/*/c; statement in Example 3 tells the tr/// operator to replace with an asterisk (*) all characters that are not the uppercase letters A through Z. The $course variable will contain the string "CIS***" after the statement is processed.

The **s** *modifier* included in the $name =~ tr/ //s; statement in Example 4 tells the tr/// operator to squash the 10 spaces contained in the $name variable down to one space—in other words, replace the 10 spaces with one space. The $name variable will contain the string "Bob Jones" after the statement is processed.

Next, you learn about the match operator.

THE MATCH OPERATOR

As you can with the **index** function, you can use the Perl **match operator** to determine if one string is contained within another string. Many Perl programmers refer to the match operator as simply the **m operator** or the **m// operator**. In this book, the match operator will be referred to as the **m//** operator, because this will help you remember that two forward slashes are required in the operator's syntax. Figure 8-7 shows the syntax, purpose, and examples of the **m//** operator.

Study the examples shown in Figure 8-7. The ($name =~ m/Pete/) *condition* included in the **if** statement shown in Example 1 scans the $name variable to see if it contains the *searchpattern*, which is Pete. Unlike the **index** function—which returns either a number that indicates the starting position of *substring* within *string*, or the number -1 if *substring* is not located within *string*—the **m//** operator typically returns either the value **true** (if *searchpattern* is contained in *string*) or the value **false** (if *searchpattern* is not contained in *string*). In this case, the **m//** operator returns the value **true** because the *searchpattern* (Pete) is contained in the $name variable. As a result, the **print** statement in the **if** clause will print the string "Yes" on the screen.

Syntax and purpose	
Syntax *string bindingOperator* **m/***searchpattern***/***modifier* Purpose determine if one string (the *searchpattern*) is contained within another string	

Parts	Description
string	*String*, which is required, is the string whose contents should be searched.
bindingOperator	A binding operator—either the "contains" operator (=~) or the "does not contain" operator (!~)—is required.
searchpattern	*Searchpattern*, which is required, is the one or more characters you want to search for in the *string*.
modifier	*Modifier*, which is optional, modifies the task performed by the m/ / operator. The most commonly used *modifiers* and their purposes are listed below. Modifier Purpose i Ignore case when performing search g Perform a global search

Examples	Results

Example 1
`$name = "Peter Peterson";`
`if ($name =~ m/Pete/) {`
`    print "Yes";`
`}`
	prints the string "Yes", because the string "Pete" is contained in the $name variable

Example 2
`$name = "Peter Peterson";`
`if ($name =~ m/pete/) {`
`    print "Yes";`
`}`
	nothing is printed, because the string "pete" is not contained in the $name variable

Example 3
`$name = "Peter Peterson";`
`if ($name =~ m/pete/i) {`
`    print "Yes";`
`}`
	prints the string "Yes", because, ignoring case, the string "pete" is contained in the $name variable

Example 4
`$name = "Peter Peterson";`
`if ($name !~ m/Jeff/) {`
`    print "Yes";`
`}`
	prints "Yes", because the string "Jeff" is not contained in the $name variable

Example 5
`$x = "ton,tin,Toll,atom";`
`@items = ($x =~ m/to/gi);`
`$size = @items;`
`print "$size";`
	prints the number 3, because, ignoring case, the string "to" appears three times in the $x variable

Figure 8-7   Syntax, purpose, and examples of the m/ / operator

8

Notice that the *searchpattern* (Pete) appears twice in the $name variable: it appears in the first name and in the last name. The m// operator stops searching for the *searchpattern* after it finds the first match. In this case, it will stop searching after it finds the first occurrence of the string "Pete".

The ($name =~ m/pete/) *condition* shown in Example 2's if statement searches for the *searchpattern* (pete) in the $name variable. In this case, the *condition* evaluates to false, because the string "pete" is not contained in the $name variable. (Recall that string comparisons in Perl are case sensitive.) Therefore, the print statement in the if clause is not processed.

You can perform a case insensitive search by including the i *modifier* at the end of the m// operator, as shown in Example 3 in Figure 8-7. The i stands for "ignore case." Example 3's code will print the string "Yes" on the screen, because, ignoring case, the *searchpattern* (pete) is contained in the $name variable.

Earlier, you learned about the "contains" operator, which is an equal sign followed by a tilde (=~). Recall that the "contains" operator is one of the binding operators in Perl. The other binding operator is the **"does not contain" operator**, and is represented by a bang symbol followed by a tilde, like this: !~. Unlike the "contains" operator, which you use to determine if a *searchpattern* is contained in a *string*, the "does not contain" operator is used to determine if a *searchpattern* is not contained in a *string*. The *condition* shown in Example 4's if statement, ($name !~ m/Jeff/), uses the "does not contain" operator to determine if the *searchpattern* (Jeff) is not contained in the $name variable. In this case, the *condition* will evaluate to true, and the print statement will print the string "Yes" on the screen.

In addition to using the m// operator to determine if a *searchpattern* is contained within a *string*, you also can use the m// operator to determine the number of times a *searchpattern* occurs in a *string*. To use the m// operator in this manner, you include the g modifier at the end of the operator, and you assign the operator's return value to an array, as shown in Example 5 in Figure 8-7. The g stands for "global" and indicates that the m// operator should continue searching for the *searchpattern* even after a match has been found. Assigning the m// operator's return value to an array tells the Perl interpreter to return a list of values that match the *searchpattern*, rather than returning the value true or false. The @items = ($x =~ m/to/gi); statement in Example 5, for instance, will assign three values to the @items array: the "to" from the word "ton", the "To" from the word "Toll", and the "to" from the word "atom". The $size = @items; statement assigns the size of the @items array—in other words, the number of scalar variables contained in the array—to the $size variable. In this case, the statement assigns the number 3, which is the number of times the *searchpattern* (to) occurs in the $x variable. The last statement in Example 5, print "$size";, simply prints the number 3 on the screen.

Recall that you learned how to determine the size of an array in Chapter 6.

The m// operator's *searchpattern* can include special characters called metacharacters.

Using Metacharacters in a Search Pattern

Figure 8-8 lists the most commonly used **metacharacters** and describes the purpose of each. You can use the metacharacters in the m// operator's *searchpattern*, and also in the s/// operator's *searchpattern*. You learn about the s/// (substitution) operator in the next section.

Metacharacter	Matches a single character
.	any character except the newline
[*set*]	any single character in the *set* (for example, [a-z] matches any lower-case letter)
[^*set*]	any single characer not in the set (for example, [^a-z] matches any character that is not a lowercase letter)
\d	one digit (same as [0-9])
\D	a non-digit (same as [^0-9])
\w	an alphanumeric character (same as [a-zA-Z0-9_])
\W	a non-alphanumeric character (same as [^a-zA-Z0-9_])
Metacharacter	**Matches whitespace characters**
\s	a whitespace character (space, tab, return, and newline)
\S	a non-whitespace character
\n	a newline character
\r	a return
\t	a tab
Metacharacter	**Matches boundary characters**
\b	a word boundary
\B	a non-word boundary
^	beginning of a string
$	end of a string
Metacharacter	**Matches repeated characters**
x?	zero or one of *x*
x*	zero or more of *x*
x+	one or more of *x*
x{*min,max*}	at least *min* of *x*, but not more than *max* of *x* (*max* is optional)
pattern1|*pattern2*	either *pattern1* or *pattern2*

Figure 8-8   Most commonly used metacharacters and their purposes

The metacharacters can be grouped into four major categories, as shown in Figure 8-8. The first category contains the metacharacters that are used in a *searchpattern* to match a single character. For example, you use the \d metacharacter to match a digit (number), and the \D metacharacter to match a non-digit. The second category shown in

8

Figure 8-8 contains the metacharacters that are used to match whitespace characters, such as the return (\r) and newline (\n) characters. The third category contains the metacharacters that are used to match boundary characters. Included in this category are the caret (^) and dollar sign ($), which are used to match the beginning and end of a string, respectively. The last category shown in Figure 8-8 contains the metacharacters that are used in a *searchpattern* to match repeated characters. For example, to determine if a string contains a series of one or more 9s, you use the *searchpattern* 9+.

A detailed discussion of each of the metacharacters listed in Figure 8-8 is beyond the scope of this book. However, you can learn more about each of the metacharacters listed in the figure by completing Hands-on Project 7 at the end of this chapter.

Figure 8-9 shows examples of using a metacharacter in the m// operator's *searchpattern*.

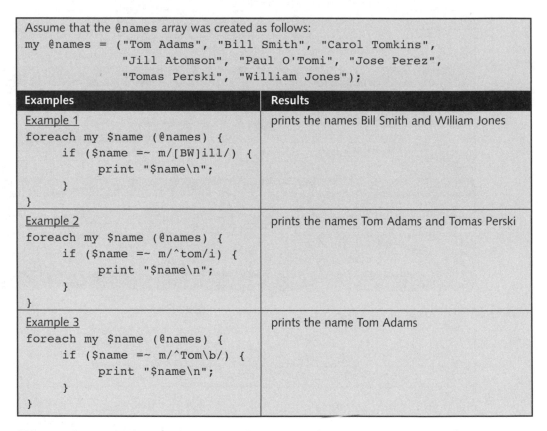

Assume that the @names array was created as follows:
```
my @names = ("Tom Adams", "Bill Smith", "Carol Tomkins",
             "Jill Atomson", "Paul O'Tomi", "Jose Perez",
             "Tomas Perski", "William Jones");
```

Examples	Results
Example 1 ```foreach my $name (@names) {` ` if ($name =~ m/[BW]ill/) {` ` print "$name\n";` ` }` `}```	prints the names Bill Smith and William Jones
Example 2 ```foreach my $name (@names) {` ` if ($name =~ m/^tom/i) {` ` print "$name\n";` ` }` `}```	prints the names Tom Adams and Tomas Perski
Example 3 ```foreach my $name (@names) {` ` if ($name =~ m/^Tom\b/) {` ` print "$name\n";` ` }` `}```	prints the name Tom Adams

Figure 8-9 Examples of using a metacharacter in the m// operator's *searchpattern*

The [BW]ill *searchpattern* in Example 1 in Figure 8-9 includes the [*set*] metacharacter. Recall from Figure 8-8 that the [*set*] metacharacter tells the m// operator to match any single character in the *set*. In this case, the *searchpattern* indicates that the m// operator should search the contents of the @names array for either the string "Bill" or the string "Will". Two names in the @names array match the [BW]ill *searchpattern*: Bill Smith and William Jones.

The ^tom *searchpattern* in Example 2 includes the ^ metacharacter, which is listed in the boundary characters category in Figure 8-8. The ^ metacharacter tells the m// operator that, for a match to occur, the *searchpattern* must be located at the beginning of the *string*. Two names in the @names array match the ^tom *searchpattern*: Tom Adams and Tomas Perski. (Recall that the i modifier tells the m// operator to ignore the case when performing the search.)

The ^Tom\b *searchpattern* in Example 3 includes two boundary metacharacters: ^ and \b. Recall that the ^ metacharacter indicates that the *searchpattern* must be located at the beginning of the *string*. The \b metacharacter indicates that the *searchpattern* also must be followed by a **word boundary character**, which is a character that you might expect to find at the end of a word. Examples of word boundary characters include the period, comma, and space. In this case, only the name Tom Adams matches the ^Tom\b *searchpattern*. A match occurs because the name Tom Adams begins with the three characters "Tom" followed by a word boundary character—in this case, a space. Notice that the name Tomas Perski does not match the ^Tom\b *searchpattern*. Although the name Tomas Perski begins with the three characters "Tom", the characters are not followed by a word boundary character; rather, they are followed by the letter "a". Letters, numbers, and the underscore (_) are not considered word boundary characters.

One popular use for the m// operator in a script is to verify the format of an e-mail address sent from the server. As you may already know, a valid e-mail address begins with one or more letters, numbers, underscores, or hyphens, followed by an at sign (@), followed by one or more letters, numbers, underscores, or hyphens, followed by a period, followed by one or more letters, numbers, underscores, or hyphens. Examples of correctly formatted e-mail addresses include rrr3@micro.com and jrs-co@cd.edu. Examples of incorrectly formatted e-mail addresses include janwhite.gov and paul@nwu. Figure 8-10 shows the m// operator you could use to verify the format of an e-mail address stored in the $email variable.

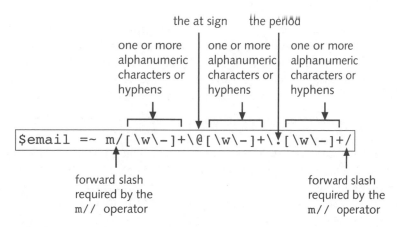

Figure 8-10 m// operator used to verify the format of an e-mail address

Notice that the pattern [\w\-]+ appears three times in the *searchpattern* shown in Figure 8-10. The [\w\-]+ pattern tells the m// operator to search for one or more alphanumeric characters (\w) or hyphens (\-). Similarly, the \@ and \. patterns tell the m// operator to search for the at sign and period, respectively.

 As indicated in the description of the \w metacharacter shown in Figure 8-8, an alphanumeric character is a letter, number, or underscore.

Notice that a backslash appears before the hyphens, the at sign, and the period in Figure 8-10. As you may remember from several of the examples shown earlier in Figure 8-5, the hyphen has a special meaning when performing a search; recall that it is used to specify a range of values. To search for the hyphen character itself, you must precede it with a backslash, which tells the Perl interpreter to ignore the character's special meaning. Similarly, the backslash that precedes the at sign tells the Perl interpreter to search for the at sign itself, rather than for the name of an array. Finally, the backslash before the period tells the Perl interpreter to ignore the period's special meaning. Recall from Figure 8-8 that the period is used to search for any character except the newline.

The last operator you learn about in this chapter is the substitution operator.

THE SUBSTITUTION OPERATOR

You can use the Perl **substitution operator** to replace one or more characters in a string with other characters, or to remove one or more characters from a string. The substitution operator is most times referred to as simply the **s operator** or the **s/// operator**. In this book, the substitution operator will be referred to as the s/// operator, because this will help you remember that three forward slashes are required in the operator's syntax. Figure 8-11 shows the syntax, purpose, and examples of the s/// operator.

The $name =~ s/Jan/Janice/; statement in Example 1 replaces the first occurrence of "Jan" with "Janice" in the $name variable. The $name variable will contain the string "Janice Jantos" after the statement is processed. To replace all occurrences of "Jan" with "Janice", you use the $name =~ s/Jan/Janice/g; statement shown in Example 2. After this statement is processed, the $name variable contains the string "Janice Janicetos".

The $item =~ s/\r\n/ /; statement shown in Example 3 replaces the return and newline character combination (\r\n) with a space. The $item variable will contain the string "Red Chair" after the statement is processed. The $rate =~ s/%//; statement in Example 4 deletes the percent sign from the $rate variable. Notice that the s/// operator in Example 4 does not contain a *replacementlist*, which is optional in the syntax. It does, however, contain a *searchpattern* and three forward slashes, which are required.

Syntax and purpose	
Syntax *string* =~ **s**/*searchpattern*/*replacementlist*/*modifier* Purpose replace characters in or delete characters from a string	

Parts	Description
string	*String*, which is required, is the string whose contents should be searched.
=~	The "contains" operator is required.
searchpattern	*Searchpattern*, which is required, is the one or more characters you want to search for in the *string*.
replacementlist	*Replacementlist*, which is optional, is the one or more characters that will replace the characters listed in the *searchpattern*.
modifier	*Modifier*, which is optional, modifies the task performed by the s/// operator. The most commonly used *modifiers* and their purposes are listed below. Modifier Purpose i Ignore case when performing search g Perform a global search

Examples	Results
Example 1 $name = "Jan Jantos"; $name =~ s/Jan/Janice/;	replaces the first "Jan" in the $name variable with "Janice"; the $name variable now stores "Janice Jantos"
Example 2 $name = "Jan Jantos"; $name =~ s/Jan/Janice/g;	replaces each "Jan" in the $name variable with "Janice"; the $name variable now stores "Janice Janicetos"
Example 3 $item = "Red\r\nChair"; $item =~ s/\r\n/ /;	replaces the return and newline character combination (\r\n) with a space; the $item variable now stores "Red Chair"
Example 4 $rate = "45%"; $rate =~ s/%//;	deletes the percent sign from the $rate variable, the variable now stores "45"
Example 5 $name = "\t\tBob\tNoel"; $name =~ s/^\t+//;	deletes the tab characters from the beginning of the string stored in the $name variable; the variable now stores "Bob\tNoel"
Example 6 $name = " Bob Noel "; $name =~ s/^ +//; $name =~ s/ +$//;	deletes the leading and trailing spaces from the $name variable; the variable now stores "Bob Noel"

Figure 8-11   Syntax, purpose, and examples of the s/// operator

8

The /^\t+/ *searchpattern* in Example 5 contains three of the metacharacters listed in Figure 8-8: ^, \t, and +. Recall that the ^ metacharacter indicates that the *searchpattern* must be located at the beginning of the *string*. The \t metacharacter represents the tab character, and the + metacharacter indicates one or more of the preceding character; in this case, it indicates one or more of the tab character. The $name =~ s/^\t+//; statement will delete the two tab characters located at the beginning of the string stored in the $name variable. The characters are deleted rather than replaced, simply because the s/// operator does not contain a *replacementlist*. Notice that the statement will not delete the tab character that appears between the words "Bob" and "Noel".

The $name =~ s/^ +//; statement in Example 6 contains two of the metacharacters listed in Figure 8-8: ^ and +. The ^ metacharacter indicates the beginning of the *string*, and the + metacharacter indicates one or more of the preceding character in the *string*. Put simply, the $name =~ s/^ +//; statement tells the computer to delete the leading space characters from the string stored in the $name variable.

The $name =~ s/ +$//; statement in Example 6 also contains two of the metacharacters listed in Figure 8-8: + and $. This statement tells the computer to delete the trailing space characters from the string stored in the $name variable.

You will use the tr///, s///, and =~ operators to manipulate the form data (customer name, e-mail address, and comments) sent to the International Coffees script, which you created in Chapter 7. You also will use the m// and !~ operators to validate the e-mail address sent to the script.

THE INTERNATIONAL COFFEES FORM AND SCRIPT

Figure 8-12 shows the International Coffees form from Chapter 7. As indicated in the figure, the form contains three elements that allow the user to enter his or her name, e-mail address, and comments. The two text box elements are named Name and Email, and the text area element is named Comments.

When entering the information on the form, it is possible that the user might inadvertently press the spacebar after typing his or her name or e-mail address. Or, he or she might press the Enter key when entering the comments. Currently, the International Coffees script will save the extra spaces and return key in the comments.txt file. In the next set of steps, you modify the script to handle these errors.

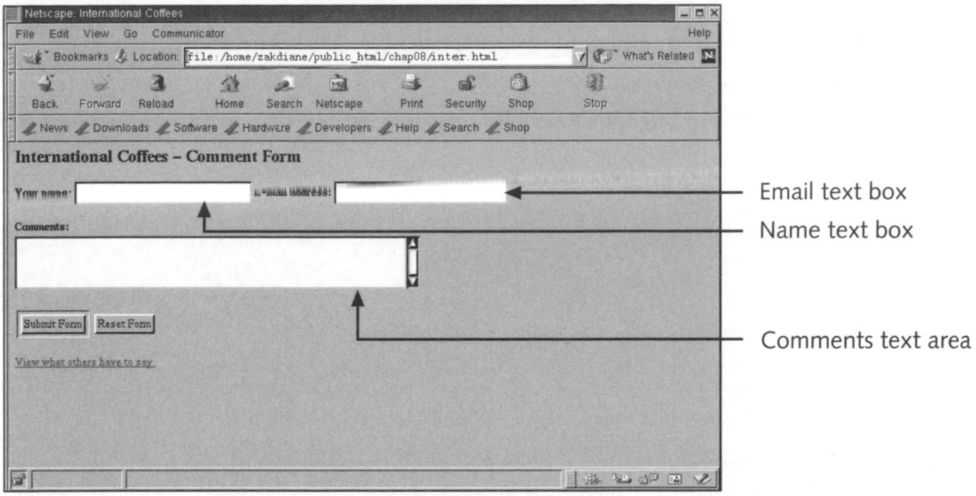

Figure 8-12   International Coffees form

To modify the International Coffees script:

1. Open the inter.cgi file in a text editor. The file is contained in the cgi-bin/chap08 directory. The inter.cgi file is the same as the coffee.cgi file that you created in Chapter 7.

2. If necessary, change the shebang line to reflect the location of the Perl interpreter on your system.

3. If necessary, add the **-debug** pragma to the **use CGI qw(:standard);** statement.

   First, enter the instructions to create and call a user-defined function named **format_input**. The function will be responsible for removing the leading and trailing spaces from the name and e-mail address entries. It also will be responsible for removing any leading and trailing whitespace characters from the comments entry. If the user presses the Enter key when entering his or her comments—for example, if he or she types a sentence and then presses the Enter key before typing the next sentence—the computer will enter an invisible return and newline character (\r\n) within the comments. The **format_input** function will be responsible for replacing, with a space character, the return and newline characters that appear within the comments.

4. Enter the statement that calls the **format_input** function. Also enter the **format_input** function definition. The code you are to enter is shaded in Figure 8-13. (Figure 8-13 does not show the entire script.)

```perl
#!/usr/bin/perl
#inter.cgi - saves form data to a file, and creates
#three different dynamic Web pages
print "Content-type: text/html\n\n";
use CGI qw(:standard);

#prevent Perl from creating undeclared variables
use strict;

#declare variables
my ($name, $email, $comments, $data_ok);

if ($ENV{'REQUEST_METHOD'} eq "POST") {
    ($name, $email, $comments) = get_input();
    ($name, $email, $comments) = format_input();
    $data_ok = validate_input();
    if ($data_ok eq "Y") {
        save_to_file();
        create_acknowledgment_page();
    }
    else {
        create_error_page();
    }
}
else {
    create_comments_page();
}
exit;

#*****user-defined functions*****
sub get_input {
    return param('Name'), param('Email'), param('Comments');
} #end get_input

sub format_input {
    #declare and assign values to temporary variables
    my ($n, $e, $c);
    ($n, $e, $c) = ($name, $email, $comments);
    #remove leading and trailing spaces from name
    $n =~ s/^ +//;
    $n =~ s/ +$//;
    #remove leading and trailing spaces from e-mail address
    $e =~ s/^ +//;
    $e =~ s/ +$//;
    #remove leading and trailing whitespace characters
```

your shebang line might be different

you might need to use the −debug pragma in this statement

Figure 8-13   `format_input` function call and definition entered in the script

```
        #from comments
        $c =~ s/^\s+//;
        $c =~ s/\s+$//;
        #replace return and newline combination within comments
        #with a space
        $c =~ tr/\r\n/ /;
        #remove extra spaces from within comments
        $c =~ tr/ //s;
        return $n, $e, $c;
} #end format_input

sub validate_input {
```

Figure 8-13   `format_input` function call and definition entered in the script (continued)

Notice that the statements contained in the `format_input` function change the values stored in the function's variables only; they do not change the values stored in any of the variables declared in the main section of the script. As you learned in Chapter 7, many programmers consider it poor programming when a user-defined function changes the contents of a variable declared in the main section of a script.

Next, modify the **validate_input** function so that it verifies the format of the e-mail address received from the script.

5. Locate the **validate_input** function in the script, then make the modifications shaded in Figure 8-14.

```
sub validate_input {
    my $valid = "Y";
    my $errormsg;
    if ($name eq "" or $email eq "" or $comments eq "") {
        $valid = "N";
        $errormsg = "complete all items";
    }
    elsif ($email !~ m/[\w\-]+\@[\w\-]+\.[\w\-]+/) {
        $valid = "N";
        $errormsg = "enter a valid e-mail address";
    }
    return $valid, $errormsg;
} #end validate_input
```

Figure 8-14   Modifications made to the `validate_input` function

Notice that the **validate_input** function now returns two values rather than one value. You will need to modify the statement that calls the function so that it can receive two values.

6. Change the my ($name, $email, $comments, $data_ok); statement in the main section of the script to **my ($name, $email, $comments, $data_ok, $msg);**.

7. Change the $data_ok = validate_input(); statement in the main section of the script to **($data_ok, $msg) = validate_input();**.

The last change you need to make is in the **create_error_page** function.

8. Locate the **create_error_page** function in the script. Change the print "complete all items.</H2>\n"; statement to **print "$msg.</H2>\n";**.

9. Save the inter.cgi document.

Figure 8-15 shows the completed International Coffees script. Statements that were added to or changed from the original script are shaded in the figure.

```perl
#!/usr/bin/perl
#inter.cgi - saves form data to a file, and creates
#three different dynamic Web pages
print "Content-type: text/html\n\n";
use CGI qw(:standard);

#prevent Perl from creating undeclared variables
use strict;

#declare variables
my ($name, $email, $comments, $data_ok, $msg);

if ($ENV{'REQUEST_METHOD'} eq "POST") {
        ($name, $email, $comments) = get_input();
        ($name, $email, $comments) = format_input();
        ($data_ok, $msg) = validate_input();
        if ($data_ok eq "Y") {
                save_to_file();
                create_acknowledgment_page();
        }
        else {
                create_error_page();
        }
}
else {
        create_comments_page();
}
exit;
```

Figure 8-15   Completed International Coffees script

```
#*****user-defined functions*****
sub get_input {
      return param('Name'), param('Email'), param('Comments');
} #end get_input

sub format_input {
      #declare and assign values to temporary variables
      my ($n, $e, $c);
      ($n, $e, $c) = ($name, $email, $comments);
      #remove leading and trailing spaces from name
      $n =~ s/^ +//;
      $n =~ s/ +$//;
      #remove leading and trailing spaces from e-mail address
      $e =~ s/^ +//;
      $e =~ s/ +$//;
      #remove leading and trailing whitespace characters
      #from comments
      $c =~ s/^\s+//;
      $c =~ s/\s+$//;
      #replace return and newline combination within comments
      #with a space
      $c =~ tr/\r\n/ /;
      #remove extra spaces from within comments
      $c =~ tr/ //s;
      return $n, $e, $c;
} #end format_input

sub validate_input {
      my $valid = "Y";
      my $errormsg;
      if ($name eq "" or $email eq "" or $comments eq "") {
            $valid = "N";
            $errormsg = "complete all items";
      }
      elsif ($email !~ m/[\w\-]+\@[\w\-]+\.[\w\-]+/) {
            $valid = "N";
            $errormsg = "enter a valid e-mail address";
      }
      return $valid, $errormsg;
} #end validate_input
```

Figure 8-15   Completed International Coffees script (continued)

```
sub save_to_file {
     open(OUTFILE, ">>", "comments.txt")
          or die "Error opening comments.txt for save. $!, stopped";
     print OUTFILE "$name|$email|$comments\n";
     close(OUTFILE);
} #end save_to_file

sub create_acknowledgment_page {
     print "<HTML>\n";
     print "<HEAD><TITLE>International Coffees</TITLE></HEAD>\n";
     print "<BODY>\n";
     print "<H2>$name, thank you for the following \n";
     print "comments:<BR><BR>$comments\n";
     print "</H2></BODY></HTML>\n";
} #end create_acknowledgment_page

sub create_error_page {
     print "<HTML>\n";
     print "<HEAD><TITLE>International Coffees</TITLE></HEAD>\n";
     print "<BODY>\n";
     print "<H2>Please return to the form and \n";
     print "$msg.</H2>\n";
     print "</BODY></HTML>\n";
} #end create_error_page

sub create_comments_page {
     my (@records, $name_field, $email_field, $com_field);
     open(INFILE, "<", "comments.txt")
          or die "Error opening comments.txt. $!, stopped";

     print "<HTML>\n";
     print "<HEAD><TITLE>International Coffees</TITLE></HEAD>\n";
     print "<BODY>\n";
     print "<H2>What other coffee lovers say \n";
     print "about our coffees:</H2>\n";
     @records = <INFILE>;
     close(INFILE);
```

Figure 8-15 Completed International Coffees script (continued)

```
    foreach my $rec (@records) {
        chomp($rec);
        ($name_field, $email_field, $com_field) = split(/\|/, $rec);
        print "<B>Name:</B> $name_field<BR>\n";
        print "<B>Comments:</B> $com_field<BR>\n";
        print "<HR>";
    }
    print "</BODY></HTML>\n";
} #end create_comments_page
```

Figure 8-15   Completed International Coffees script (continued)

Important note: If you are using a Windows system, "chap08/comments.txt" will appear as the filename argument in the two **open** statements.

Now test the inter.cgi script to make sure that it is working correctly.

To test the inter.cgi script:

1. *If you are using a UNIX system*, open a terminal window, if necessary. Make the cgi-bin/chap08 directory the current directory, and then change the inter.cgi file permissions to **755**. Also change the file permissions for the comments.txt file, which is contained in the cgi-bin/chap08 directory, to **666**.

   If you are using a Windows system, open a Command Prompt window, and then make the cgi-bin\chap08 directory the current directory.

2. Type **perl –c inter.cgi** and press **Enter** to check the script for syntax errors. If necessary, correct any syntax errors in the script before continuing to the next step.

   Recall that you will not be able to test the script by executing it using the –w switch, because the first selection structure in the script uses the REQUEST_METHOD environment variable, whose value is set by the Web server. You will need to test the script by executing it from the browser.

3. Open the inter.html document in a text editor. The file is contained in the public_html/chap08 directory. Change yourservername in the <FORM> and <A> tags to the name of your server, then save the inter.html document.

4. Start your Web browser, then use the browser's File menu to open the inter.html document.

   First, complete and then submit the form.

5. Enter **Jeremiah Jacobs** in the Name text box, **jj@server.com** in the E-mail address text box, and **I love the flavored coffees.** in the Comments text area. Click the **Submit Form** button. If necessary, click the **Continue**

Submission button. The script saves the form data to the comments.txt file, and then displays an acknowledgment Web page.

Now verify that the script removes the leading and trailing spaces from the text entered in the Name and E-mail address text boxes and the Comments text area. Also verify that the script removes the return and newline characters from the text entered in the Comments area.

6. Return to the form. Enter three spaces before the name Jeremiah Jacobs in the Name text box. Also enter several spaces after the e-mail address jj@server.com in the E-mail address text box. Position the insertion point after the period in the Comments text area. Press **Enter** twice, then type **Great** and press **Enter** three times. Type **coffee!** and press **Enter**. Click the **Submit Form** button. If necessary, click the **Continue Submission** button. The script saves the form data to the comments.txt file, and then displays an acknowledgment Web page.

7. Open the comments.txt file in a text editor. The file is located in the cgi-bin/chap08 directory. The file contains the records shown in Figure 8-16. (The first two records were already entered in the file.)

Nancy Patelli|nan@ccc.gov|Great coffees.
Jerry Rogers|jr@aws.com|The best coffee I have tasted so far.
Jeremiah Jacobs|jj@server.com|I love the flavored coffees.
Jeremiah Jacobs|jj@server.com|I love the flavored coffees. Great coffee!

Figure 8-16   Records contained in the comments.txt file

8. Close the comments.txt file.

9. Return to the form in your browser. Click the **View what others have to say** link to display the records on a Web page. A Web page similar to the one shown in Figure 8-17 appears.

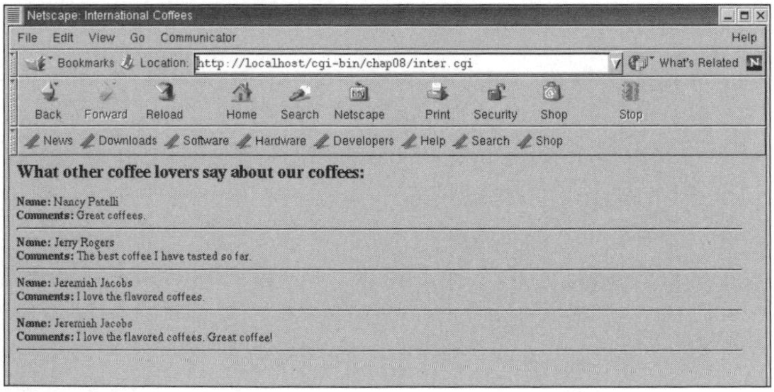

Figure 8-17   Web page showing the records contained in the comments.txt file

Now verify that the script displays the appropriate Web page when the user enters an e-mail address whose format is not valid.

10. Return to the form. Change the e-mail address to **jjserver.com** and then click the **Submit Form** button. If necessary, click the **Continue Submission** button. The script displays a Web page containing the message "Please return to the form and enter a valid e-mail address."

11. Close your browser and any open windows.

CHAPTER SUMMARY

❑ The `uc` function temporarily converts the letters in a string to uppercase.

❑ The `lc` function temporarily converts the letters in a string to lowercase.

❑ You can use the `substr` function to return a portion of a string contained in another string. You also can use it to replace one or more characters in a string with other characters, and to insert one or more characters within a string.

❑ You can use the `index` function to search a string to determine if it contains another string. The `index` function returns a number that indicates the beginning position of the *substring* within the *string*. If the *substring* is not contained within the *string*, the function returns the number -1.

❑ You can use the `tr///` (transliteration) operator to replace a character in a string with a different character, or to delete a character from a string.

❑ You can use the `m//` (match) operator to determine if one string is contained within another string. The operator returns the value `true` if the *searchpattern* is contained in the *string*. It returns the value `false` if the *searchpattern* is not contained in the *string*. If you assign the `m//` operator's return value to an array, the operator returns a list of values that match the *searchpattern*.

❑ The *searchpattern* entered in the `m//` and `s///` operators can include special characters called metacharacters. The metacharacters are divided into four major categories. The first category contains the metacharacters that are used in a *searchpattern* to match a single character. The second category contains the metacharacters that are used to match whitespace characters. The third category contains the metacharacters that are used to match boundary characters. The fourth category contains the metacharacters that are used to match repeated characters.

❑ You can use the `s///` (substitution) operator to replace one or more characters in a string with other characters, or to delete one or more characters from a string.

REVIEW QUESTIONS

1. You can use the _____ function to convert lowercase letters to uppercase letters.

   a. `uc`

   b. `ucase`

   c. `up`

   d. `upper`

2. Which of the following statements assigns to the `$pos` variable the starting position of the *substring* "day" within the string "Sunday"?

   a. `$pos = index("Sunday", "day", 0);`

   b. `$pos = index("Sunday", "day", 3);`

   c. `$pos = index("Sunday", "day");`

   d. All of the above.

3. Which of the following is a binding operator?

   a. `=`

   b. `!=`

   c. `=~`

   d. `~=`

4. Which of the following statements replaces the first occurrence of the string "Jan" in the `$msg` variable with the string "January"?

   a. `$msg = r/Jan/January/;`

   b. `$msg ~= r/Jan/January/;`

   c. `$msg = s/Jan/January/;`

   d. `$msg =~ s/Jan/January/;`

5. Which of the following statements assigns the first three characters contained in the $item variable to the $prefix variable?

   a. $prefix = substr($item, 3);

   b. $prefix = substr($item, 3, 0);

   c. $prefix = substr($item, 0, 3);

   d. $prefix = substr($item, 1, 3);

6. Assume the string "John Paulos" is stored in the $name variable. Which of the following statements changes the contents of the $name variable to "Joan Paulos"?

   a. substr($name, 0, 4) = "Joan";

   b. substr($name, 2, 1) = "a";

   c. $name =~ s/John/Joan/;

   d. All of the above.

7. Assume the @words array contains these words: dog, cat, bird, cap, bike, bobcat, and Canada. Which of the following loops will print the words cat, cap, bobcat, and Canada?

   a.
   ```
   foreach my $word (@words) {
           if ($word =~ m/ca/i) {
                   print "$word\n";
           }
   }
   ```

   b.
   ```
   foreach my $word (@words) {
           if ($word =~ m/ca/) {
                   print "$word\n";
           }
   }
   ```

   c.
   ```
   foreach my $word (@words) {
           if ($word =~ m/Ca/) {
                   print "$word\n";
           }
   }
   ```

   d. All of the above.

8

8. Assume the `@words` array contains these words: dog, cat, bird, cap, bike, bobcat, and Canada. Which of the following loops will print only the words cat and cap?

a.
```
foreach my $word (@words) {
        if ($word =~ m/^ca/i) {
                print "$word\n";
        }
}
```

b.
```
foreach my $word (@words) {
        if ($word =~ m/^ca/) {
                print "$word\n";
        }
}
```

c.
```
foreach my $word (@words) {
        if ($word =~ m/^Ca/) {
                print "$word\n";
        }
}
```

d.
```
foreach my $word (@words) {
        if ($word =~ m/^ca) {
                print "$word\n";
        }
}
```

9. Assume the `@names` array contains the following names: John Jones, Carol Smith, Peter Smith, Kristen Smithson, and Paula Hau. Which of the following loops will print only the names Carol Smith and Peter Smith?

a.
```
foreach my $name (@names) {
        if ($name =~ m/smith$/i) {
                print "$name\n";
        }
}
```

b.
```
foreach my $name (@names) {
        if ($name =~ m/Smith$/) {
                print "$name\n";
        }
}
```

c.
```
foreach my $name (@names) {
        if ($name =~ m/Smith\b/) {
                print "$name\n";
        }
}
```

d. All of the above.

10. Assume the @nums array contains the following numbers: 35, 67.05, 2, 9, and 5.5. Which of the following loops will print only the whole numbers (35, 2, and 9)?

    a. ```
    foreach my $num (@nums) {
            if ($num !~ m/\./) {
                    print "$num\n";
            }
    }
    ```

    b. ```
    foreach my $num (@nums) {
            if ($num !~ m/./) {
                    print "$num\n";
            }
    }
    ```

    c. ```
    foreach my $num (@nums) {
            if ($num =~ m/\./) {
                    print "$num\n";
            }
    }
    ```

    d. None of the above.

11. Write a statement that uses the `lc` function to change the contents of the `$code` variable to lowercase.

12. Write a statement that uses the `tr///` operator to replace any tab character contained in the `$notes` variable with a space.

13. Write a statement that uses the `tr///` operator to remove any percent sign (%) from the `$rate` variable.

14. Write a statement that uses the `s///` operator to replace all occurrences of the string "Party Time" in the `$msg` variable with the string "Party Time Inc". Perform a case insensitive comparison.

15. Assume that a company's employee numbers contain five characters. The third character in the employee number is either the number 1 or the number 2. A 1 indicates that the employee is full-time, and a 2 indicates that he or she is part time. Write a statement that uses the `substr` function to assign the third character from the `$empnum` variable to the `$status` variable.

16. Write a statement that uses the `substr` function to change the name Tom Jeffries, which is stored in the `$name` variable, to Thomas Jeffries.

17. Assume the @phonenums array contains the following phone numbers: 111-222-2222, 112-555-1111, 111-555-1212, 333-555-1212. Write a `foreach` loop that will print only the phone numbers with an area code of 111. Use the `m//` operator.

18. Rewrite the loop from Question 17 so that it prints only phone numbers whose area code is not 222.

**8**
    ```

19. Assume the **$msg** variable contains four sentences, each ending with a period followed by one or more spaces. Write a statement that will separate each sentence with one space only. Use the **tr///** operator.

20. Write the two statements to remove the leading and trailing spaces from the contents of the **$employee** variable.

HANDS-ON PROJECTS

Project 1

In this project, you modify the International Coffees script so that the **format_input** function uses the **s///** operator to remove the return and newline characters and the extra spaces from within the comments field.

    a. Open the inter.html file in a text editor. The file is contained in the public_html/chap08 directory.

    b. Change the filename in the first line from inter.html to c08ex1.html.

    c. Modify the <FORM> tag's ACTION property and the <A> tag's HREF property to refer to the c08ex1.cgi script.

    d. Save the document as c08ex1.html.

    e. Open the c08ex1.ori file in a text editor. The file is contained in the cgi-bin/chap08 directory. Save the file as c08ex1.txt.

    f. Open the inter.cgi file in a text editor. The file is contained in the cgi-bin/chap08 directory.

    g. Change the filename in the second line from inter.cgi to c08ex1.cgi.

    h. Change the filename in the two **open** statements and in the two **die** functions from comments.txt to c08ex1.txt.

    i. Save the document as c08ex1.cgi.

    j. Modify the script so that the **format_input** function uses the **s///** operator to remove the return and newline characters and the extra spaces from within the comments field.

    k. Save the c08ex1.cgi document.

    l. *If you are using a UNIX system*, change the c08ex1.cgi file permissions to 755. Also change the c08ex1.txt file permissions to 666.

    m. Test the script from the command line using the -c switch.

    n. Open the c08ex1.html document in your Web browser. Type Jennifer Smith followed by two spaces in the Your name text box. Type three spaces followed by ar@cw.gov in the E-mail address text box. Type the string "I love " (without the quotation marks, but with two spaces after each word) and press Enter twice. Then type the string "your coffee.   " (without the quotation marks, but with four spaces after the period). Click the Submit Form button. If necessary, click the Continue Submission button. The acknowledgment Web page appears on the screen.

o. Return to the form and click the View what others have to say link. The comments Web page appears on the screen.

Project 2

In this project, you modify the Bonus Calculator script, which you created in Chapter 3, so that the script can handle a sales amount entered with a dollar sign and/or a comma. The script also should be able to handle bonus rates entered in various formats.

a. Copy the bonus.html file from the public_html/chap03 directory to the public_html/chap08 directory. Rename the file c08ex2.html.

b. Copy the bonus.cgi file from the cgi-bin/chap03 directory to the cgi-bin/chap08 directory. Rename the file c08ex2.cgi.

c. Open the c08ex2.html file in a text editor. Change the filename in the first line from bonus.html to c08ex2.html.

d. Modify the <FORM> tag to refer to the c08ex2.cgi script, which is contained in the cgi-bin/chap08 directory.

e. Save the c08ex2.html document.

f. Open the c08ex2.cgi file in a text editor. Change the filename in the second line from bonus.cgi to c08ex2.cgi.

g. Modify the script so that it removes any leading and trailing spaces from the input data.

h. Modify the script so that it can handle a sales amount entered with a dollar sign and/or comma. (*Hint:* Use the **tr///** operator to remove these characters from the number.)

i. Modify the script so that it can handle a bonus rate entered as a whole number, a floating-point number, and a number with a percent sign   for example, 5, .05, 5.0, 5.0%, and 5%.

j. Save the c08ex2.cgi document.

k. *If you are using a UNIX system,* change the c08ex2.cgi file permissions to 755.

l. Test the script from the command line using the -c and -w switches. (Be sure to try each of the different variations for the sales amount and bonus rate.)

m. Open the c08ex2.html document in your Web browser. Enter Kareem Patel as the name. Enter 4,000,000 as the sales amount. Enter 1.2% as the bonus rate. Click the Submit button. If necessary, click the Continue Submission button. The Web page should show that the bonus amount is $48000, the sales amount is $4000000, and the bonus rate is 1.2%.

Project 3

In this project, you modify the Juniper Printers registration script, which you created in Chapter 4, so that it removes any commas from the name entry. The script also will determine if the serial number entry is correct.

    a. Copy the juniper.html file from the public_html/chap04 directory to the public_html/chap08 directory. Rename the file c08ex3.html.

    b. Copy the juniper.cgi file from the cgi-bin/chap04 directory to the cgi-bin/chap08 directory. Rename the file c08ex3.cgi.

    c. Open the c08ex3.html file in a text editor. Change the filename in the first line from juniper.html to c08ex3.html.

    d. Modify the <FORM> tag to refer to the c08ex3.cgi script, which is contained in the cgi-bin/chap08 directory.

    e. Save the c08ex3.html document.

    f. Open the c08ex3.cgi file in a text editor. Change the filename in the second line from juniper.cgi to c08ex3.cgi.

    g. Modify the script so that it removes any leading and trailing spaces from the name and serial number.

    h. Modify the script so that it removes any commas from the name entry.

    i. To be valid, the serial number must contain seven characters: three numbers, followed by two letters, followed by two numbers. Modify the script so that it validates the serial number. Use the uc function to convert the serial number to uppercase before performing the validation. Display an appropriate error Web page if the serial number is not valid.

    j. Save the c08ex3.cgi document.

    k. *If you are using a UNIX system*, change the c08ex3.cgi file permissions to 755.

    l. Test the script from the command line using the -c and -w switches.

    m. Open the c08ex3.html document in your Web browser. Enter Phil Washington, Jr. as the name and 123AX45 as the serial number. Click the Submit Registration button. If necessary, click the Continue Submission button. The acknowledgment Web page should appear on the screen.

    n. Return to the registration form. Enter 34ABC11 as the serial number. Click the Submit Registration button. If necessary, click the Continue Submission button. The error Web page should appear on the screen.

    o. Return to the registration form. Enter 123AX345 as the serial number. Click the Submit Registration button. If necessary, click the Continue Submission button. The error Web page should appear on the screen.

Project 4

In this project, you create a script that allows the user to change the area codes stored in a file.

a. Open the codes.ori file in a text editor. The file is contained in the cgi-bin/chap08 directory. The file contains seven records. Each record is composed of two fields: a name and a phone number. Notice that two of the records have area code 111.

b. Save the file as c08ex4a.txt.

c. Open the codes.cgi file in a text editor. The file is contained in the cgi-bin/chap08 directory.

d. Change the filename in the second line from codes.cgi to c08ex4.cgi, then save the document as c08ex4.cgi.

e. Study the script's existing code. Notice that the script allows the user to input the old area code and the new area code.

f. Modify the script so that it removes any leading and trailing spaces from the two input items.

g. Modify the script so that it reads each record in the codes.txt file and changes the area code in the appropriate records. The script then should save each record in a file named c08ex4b.txt.

h. Save the c08ex4.cgi document.

i. *If you are using a UNIX system*, change the c08ex4.cgi file permissions to 755.

j. Test the script from the command line using the -c switch.

k. Test the script from the command line using the -w switch. Replace area code 111 with 999.

l. Open the c08ex4b.txt file in a text editor. The two records with area code 111 should now have area code 999.

Project 5

In this project, you create a script that displays a name entered using the format "last, first" as "first last".

a. Open the name.cgi file in a text editor. The file is contained in the cgi-bin/chap08 directory.

b. Change the filename in the second line from name.cgi to c08ex5.cgi, then save the document as c08ex5.cgi. Notice that the script allows the user to enter a name. The name will be entered using the format "last, first".

c. The script should display the name using the format "first last". In other words, the name "Wells, Jason" should be displayed as "Jason Wells". Complete the script appropriately.

d. Save the c08ex5.cgi document.

e. *If you are using a UNIX system*, change the c08ex5.cgi file permissions to 755.

8

f. Test the script from the command line using the -c switch.

g. Test the script from the command line using the -w switch.

Project 6

In this project, you create a script that displays as a string a date entered using a numeric format.

a. Open the date.cgi file in a text editor. The file is contained in the cgi-bin/chap08 directory.

b. Change the filename in the second line from date.cgi to c08ex6.cgi, then save the document as c08ex6.cgi. Notice that the script allows the user to enter a date. The date will be entered using numbers and forward slashes. The month and day numbers can be entered using one or two digits, and the year number can be entered using either two or four digits. In other words, July 5th of 2004 can be entered as 07/05/2004, 7/5/2004, 07/5/04, and so on.

c. The script should display the date entered by the user as a string. For example, the date 7/05/04 should be displayed as July 5, 2004. Notice that, if the year number contains only two digits, you should append the number 20 to the beginning of the year number. Complete the script appropriately.

d. Save the c08ex6.cgi document.

e. *If you are using a UNIX system*, change the c08ex6.cgi file permissions to 755.

f. Test the script from the command line using the -c switch.

g. Test the script from the command line using the -w switch. The following dates should display April 9, 2004: 4/9/04, 4/9/2004, 04/9/04, 04/09/2004, and 4/09/04.

Project 7

In this project, you experiment with the **m//** operator.

a. Open the c08ex7.cgi file in a text editor. The file is contained in the cgi-bin/chap08 directory. The file contains 21 **print** statements that will allow you to experiment with the different metacharacters listed in Figure 8-8.

b. Delete the # sign from the beginning of the first **print** statement, then save the c08ex7.cgi document.

c. *If you are using a UNIX system*, change the c08ex7.cgi file permissions to 755.

d. Test the script from the command line using the -w switch. What did the **print** statement display? Why did it display these array elements and not the others?

e. Enter a # sign at the beginning of the first **print** statement, then delete the # sign from the beginning of the second **print** statement. Save the c08ex7.cgi document, then test the script from the command line using the -w switch.

What did the `print` statement display? Why did it display these array elements and not the others?

f. Use the procedure from Step e to test each `print` statement entered in the script.

CASE PROJECTS

1. Create an HTML form and a script for Lakeside University. Name the form c08case1.html and save it in the public_html/chap08 directory. Name the script c08case1.cgi and save it in the cgi-bin/chap08 directory. The form should allow the user to select one of four department names: Accounting, Communications, Computer Information Systems, and Mathematics. The c08case1.cgi script should display on a Web page the name of the selected department and the names of the faculty members working in the department. The faculty member names and their employee numbers are stored in the c08case1.ori file, which is contained in the cgi-bin/chap08 directory. Open the c08case1.ori file in a text editor, then save the file as c08case1.txt. The employee numbers contained in the file are composed of either six or seven characters. The first three or four characters represent the department code: ACCO is the code for the Accounting department, COMM for the Communications department, CIS for the Computer Information Systems department, and MATH for the Mathematics department.

2. Each salesperson at Bobcat Motors is assigned a code that consists of two characters. The first character is either the letter F or the letter P. The letter F indicates that a salesperson is a full-time employee, and the letter P indicates that he or she is a part-time employee. The second character is either a 1 or a 2. A 1 indicates that the salesperson sells new cars, and a 2 indicates that he or she sells used cars. The salesperson names and codes are stored in the c08case2.ori file, which is contained in the cgi-bin/chap08 directory. Open the c08case2.ori file in a text editor, then save the file as c08case2.txt. The file contains 10 records. Each record is composed of two fields: the salesperson's code and his or her name. Create an HTML form and a script for Bobcat Motors. Name the form c08case2.html and save it in the public_html/chap08 directory. Name the script c08case2.cgi and save it in the cgi-bin/chap08 directory. The form should allow the user to display on a Web page one of the following listings:

1) the names of full-time salespeople

2) the names of part-time salespeople

3) the names of salespeople who sell new cars

4) the names of salespeople who sell used cars

5) the names of full-time salespeople who sell new cars

6) the names of full-time salespeople who sell used cars

7) the names of part-time salespeople who sell new cars

8) the names of part-time salespeople who sell used cars

9

DBM DATABASES

In this chapter, you will:

♦ Create and open a DBM database
♦ Add a record to a DBM database
♦ Modify and delete a record in a DBM database
♦ Determine whether a DBM database contains a specific *key*
♦ Close a DBM database
♦ Concatenate strings
♦ Create a "here" document

Most businesses store information about their employees, customers, and inventory in databases. A **database** is simply a collection of data that is stored in a disk file and organized so that its contents can be easily accessed, managed, and updated. You can create a database using a software package such as Oracle, Microsoft Access, Sybase, or MySQL, and then use the Perl DBI (Database Interface) module, along with the appropriate DBD (Database Driver) file, to manipulate the database. You also can use one of the Perl DBM (Database Management) modules to create and manipulate a special type of database, called a DBM database. In this chapter, you learn about DBM databases, because they are easy to create and use, and are the standard database type in Perl. Additionally, you learn how to concatenate strings and create a "here" document.

THE JEFFREY SIKES BAND FORM

The Jeffrey Sikes Band has been playing the blues for over 10 years and has developed a large following. Recently, the band's manager, Chris Thompson, has received numerous requests for information about the band's future appearances. Rather than responding separately to each request, Chris has decided to include the information in a monthly newsletter, which he will send to fans who sign up on the band's mailing list. To be included on the mailing list, you need simply to visit the band's Web site and complete the form shown in Figure 9-1.

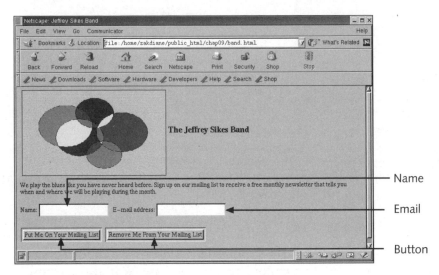

Figure 9-1   The Jeffrey Sikes Band form

As Figure 9-1 indicates, the form contains two text boxes named Name and Email, and two submit buttons named Button. You use the Put Me On Your Mailing List button to record your name and e-mail address on the band's mailing list, and you use the Remove Me From Your Mailing List button to remove your name and e-mail address from the list. Now view the HTML code used to create the form.

To view the HTML code used to create the Jeffrey Sikes Band form:

1. Open the band.html file in a text editor. The file is contained in the public_html/chap09 directory. Figure 9-2 shows the contents of the file.

The   text shown in the document is the nonbreaking space character and is used to display a blank space on a Web page.

```
<!band.html>
<HTML>
<HEAD><TITLE>Jeffrey Sikes Band</TITLE></HEAD>
<BODY BGCOLOR=silver>
<H1><IMG SRC="band.gif" ALIGN=middle HSPACE=5>The Jeffrey Sikes Band</H1>
<FORM ACTION="http://yourservername/cgi-bin/chap09/band.cgi" METHOD=POST>
<FONT SIZE=4>
We play the blues like you have never heard before. Sign up on our
mailing list to receive a free monthly newsletter that tells you
when and where we will be playing during the month.
<P>Name: <INPUT TYPE=text NAME=Name>  
E-mail address: <INPUT TYPE=text NAME=Email></P>
<INPUT TYPE=submit Name=Button VALUE="Put Me On Your Mailing List">
<INPUT TYPE=submit Name=Button VALUE="Remove Me From Your Mailing List">
</FONT></FORM></BODY></HTML>
```

Figure 9-2   HTML code used to create the Jeffrey Sikes Band form

The <FORM> tag indicates that the band.cgi script will process the form data. The form data includes the Name and Email *keys* and their corresponding *values*. It also includes the Button *key* and either the *value* "Put Me On Your Mailing List" or the *value* "Remove Me From Your Mailing List".

2. Change yourservername in the <FORM> tag to the name of your server.

3. Save the band.html document, and then close the document.

When the user clicks the Put Me On Your Mailing List button, the band.cgi script should save the user's name and e-mail address in a database, and then display a Web page similar to the one shown in Figure 9-3.

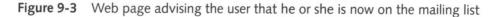

Figure 9-3   Web page advising the user that he or she is now on the mailing list

When the user clicks the Remove Me From Your Mailing List button, the band.cgi script should determine whether the user's information appears in the database. If the information is contained in the database, the script should remove the information from the database and then display a Web page similar to the one shown in Figure 9-4. However, if the user's information is not contained in the database, the script should display a Web page similar to the one shown in Figure 9-5.

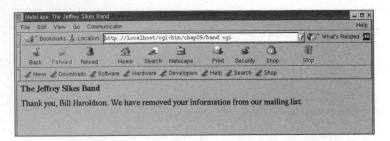

Figure 9-4 Web page advising the user that he or she has been removed from the mailing list

Figure 9-5 Web page advising the user that he or she is not on the mailing list

Now that you know what information will be passed to the server and what information to include on the dynamic Web pages, you can begin completing the band.cgi script, which will process the form data.

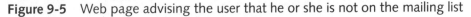

PLANNING AND CODING THE JEFFREY SIKES BAND SCRIPT

Figure 9-6 shows the input and output for the Jeffrey Sikes Band script. It also shows the algorithm for the main section of the script, and the algorithms for two user-defined functions named **add** and **remove**.

In Hands-on Project 1 at the end of this chapter, you modify the band.cgi script so that it removes any leading and trailing spaces from the name and e-mail address received from the server. You also enter the code to verify the format of the e-mail address.

Input	Output
button choice	mailing list database containing the name and e-mail address
name	Web page advising the user that he or she is now on the mailing list
e-mail address	Web page advising the user that his or her information has been removed from the mailing list
	Web page advising the user that he or she is not on the mailing list

Algorithms

main section
1. assign input items to variables
2. determine which submit button was selected
   a. if (the button choice is "Put Me On Your Mailing List")
      1) call the add function
   else
   a. if (the button choice is "Remove Me From Your Mailing List")
      1) call the remove function
3. exit the script

add function
1. open the mailing list database
2. add the user's record (name and e-mail address) to the database
3. close the database
4. create a dynamic Web page that advises the user that he or she is now on the mailing list

remove function
1. open the mailing list database
2. determine whether the user's e-mail address is in the database
   a. if (the user's e-mail address is in the database)
      1) delete the user's record (name and e-mail address) from the database
      2) assign the message "Thank you, *username*. We have removed your information from our mailing list." to the $msg variable
   else
   a. assign the message "You are not on our mailing list." to the $msg variable
3. close the database
4. create a dynamic Web page that displays the contents of the $msg variable

Figure 9-6   Input, output, and algorithms for the Jeffrey Sikes Band script

 As you learned in Chapter 5, a field is a single item of information about a person, place, or thing, and a record is one or more related fields that contain all of the necessary data about a specific person, place, or thing.

Notice that the main section of the script calls either the **add** function or the **remove** function, depending on which submit button the user clicked. The **add** function performs four tasks when it is called. First, it opens the mailing list database.

It then adds the user's record, which consists of two fields (a name and an e-mail address), to the database. After adding the record to the database, the **add** function closes the database, and then creates a Web page that advises the user that he or she is now on the mailing list.

Like the **add** function, the **remove** function also performs four tasks when it is called. First, it opens the mailing list database. It then determines whether the user's e-mail address appears in the database. If the e-mail address is in the database, the user's record is removed from the database and the message "Thank you, *username*. We have removed your information from our mailing list." is assigned to the **$msg** variable. (*Username* in the message will be replaced with the name of the user.) However, if the user's e-mail address is not in the database, the message "You are not on our mailing list." is assigned to the **$msg** variable. The **remove** function then closes the database and displays the contents of the **$msg** variable on a Web page.

On your computer's disk is a partially completed script for the Jeffrey Sikes Band. In the next set of steps, you open the script and finish coding the main section's algorithm.

To finish coding the main section's algorithm in the band.cgi script:

1. Open the band.cgi script in a text editor. The file is contained in the cgi-bin/chap09 directory.

2. If necessary, change the shebang line to reflect the location of the Perl interpreter on your system.

3. If necessary, add the **–debug** pragma to the **use CGI qw(:standard);** statement.

4. Enter the code shaded in Figure 9-7.

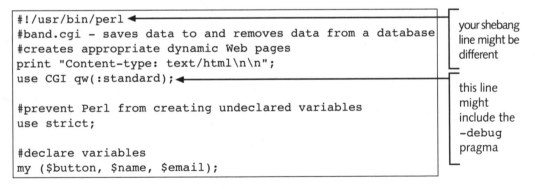

```
#!/usr/bin/perl
#band.cgi - saves data to and removes data from a database
#creates appropriate dynamic Web pages
print "Content-type: text/html\n\n";
use CGI qw(:standard);

#prevent Perl from creating undeclared variables
use strict;

#declare variables
my ($button, $name, $email);
```

your shebang line might be different

this line might include the –debug pragma

Figure 9-7   Additional code entered in the script's main section

```
#assign values to variables
$button = param('Button');
$name = param('Name');
$email = param('Email');

if ($button eq "Put Me On Your Mailing List") {
     add();
}
elsif ($button eq "Remove Me From Your Mailing List") {
     remove();
}
exit;

#*****user-defined functions*****
```

the band.cgi document contains additional code below this line

Figure 9-7   Additional code entered in the script's main section (continued)

5. Save the band.cgi document.

Next, you begin coding the **add** function. The first step in the function's algorithm (shown earlier in Figure 9-6) is to open the mailing list database. As mentioned earlier, you learn about DBM databases in this chapter, because they are easy to create and use, and are the standard database type in Perl.

CREATING AND OPENING A DBM DATABASE

For a script to create or open a DBM database using the **tie** function, which you learn about in this chapter, it must contain a **use** statement that specifies the name of a Perl DBM module. As you learned in Chapter 2, a module is simply a collection of prewritten code stored in a file. Examples of Perl DBM modules include ODBM_File.pm, NDBM_File.pm, and SDBM_File.pm. In this chapter, you use the SDBM_File.pm module, because it is included in the standard Perl distribution for both the UNIX and Windows operating systems. To use the module to create and/or open a DBM database, you simply include the statement **use SDBM_File;** in a script.

The O, N, and S before DBM in the module names stand for "Old", "New", and "Simple", respectively.

Recall that you do not include the ".pm" part of the module name in the **use** statement.

It is a good programming practice to plan a database before you begin creating it. Planning a database involves listing the fields to include in each record, and then identifying the primary key in the list. The **primary key** is the field whose contents uniquely identify each record in the database. In the case of the mailing list database, you could use either of the two fields—name or e-mail address—as the primary key. However, the better choice is the e-mail address field, because it is possible for more than one fan to have the same name.

 Although the primary key in most databases is one field only, it can be two or more fields. For example, you could use a combination of a last name field and a first name field as the primary key. When a primary key contains more than one field, it often is referred to as a combined or compound primary key.

You need to identify the primary key field because of the way the DBM modules store records in a DBM database. The modules store the records on disk using a *key/value* format, similar to the way data is stored in a hash in the computer's internal memory. The *key* is the data entered in each record's primary key field, and the *value* is the data entered in the remaining fields in the record. The *key/value* format allows the computer to distinguish between a record's *key* and its *value*, and allows you to access a *value* simply by referring to its *key* in a script.

You use the **tie function** to create and open a DBM database on disk. The syntax of the **tie** function is shown in Figure 9-8. (For now, do not worry if you do not fully understand the syntax. The syntax will become clearer as you view examples of using the function.)

Syntax
tie(*hash, module, filename, flag, mode*)

Parts	Description
hash	*Hash* is required and is the name of the hash to tie to a DBM database.
module	*Module* is required and is the name of a DBM module.
filename	*Filename* is required and is the name of the database file to create and/or open on your computer's disk.
flag	*Flag* is required and controls how the database is opened. The valid *flags* and their purposes are listed below. (**Note**: The *flags* are defined in the Fcntl.pm module.) *flag* Purpose O_RDONLY Open the database for reading only O_WRONLY Open the database for writing only O_RDWR Open the database for both reading and writing O_CREAT Create the database if it does not exist
mode	*Mode* is required and specifies the file permissions for databases created as a result of using the O_CREAT *flag*. Typically, *mode* is the number 0666 if the O_CREAT *flag* is used; otherwise, *mode* is the number 0.

Figure 9-8   Syntax of the **tie** function

You also can use the `dbmopen` function to create and open a DBM database; however, the `tie` function supersedes the `dbmopen` function.

As Figure 9-8 shows, the `tie` function requires five arguments: *hash*, *module*, *filename*, *flag*, and *mode*. The `tie` function creates and opens a DBM database on disk by binding (or tying) the database to a hash in the computer's internal memory. The *hash* argument contains the name of the hash, and the *filename* argument contains the name of the database.

The *module* argument in the `tie` function specifies the DBM module to use to create, open, and manage the database. The *flag* argument controls how the database is opened. Notice that you use the `O_RDONLY` *flag* to open the database for reading only. You use the `O_WRONLY` *flag* to open the database for writing only, and the `O_RDWR` *flag* to open the database for both reading and writing. The `O_CREAT` *flag* tells the computer to create the database if it does not already exist. As noted in Figure 9-8, the *flags* are defined in the Fcntl.pm module. ("Fcntl" stands for "file control.")

The *mode* argument in the `tie` function specifies the file permissions for newly created databases—those created as a result of using the `O_CREAT` *flag*. Typically, *mode* is the number 0666 if the `O_CREAT` *flag* is used, and the number 0 if it is not used. (A *mode* of 0666 allows a file to be written to and read from.)

If you do not include the `O_CREAT` *flag* in the `tie` function, the function will fail if it tries to open a nonexistent database. The function also can fail for other reasons—such as trying to write to a disk that is full. You can use the `die` function, which you learned about in Chapter 5, to display a message and then exit a script when the `tie` function fails. Figure 9-9 shows examples of using the `tie` and `die` functions to create and open a DBM database.

9

Examples and results

Example 1

```
tie(%teams, "SDBM_File", "scores", O_RDWR, 0)
        or die "Error: $!\n";
```

Result

opens the scores database for both reading and writing, and ties the database to the %teams hash; displays an error message and exits the script if the tie function fails

Example 2

```
tie(%emps, "SDBM_File", "employ", O_CREAT|O_RDWR, 0666)
        or die "Error: $!\n";
```

Result

creates the employ database, if necessary, and then opens the database for both reading and writing; the database is tied to the %emp hash; displays an error message and exits the script if the tie function fails

Example 3

```
tie(%inv, "SDBM_File", "items", O_RDONLY, 0)
        or die "Error: $!\n";
```

Result

opens the items database for reading only, and ties the database to the %inv hash; displays an error message and exits the script if the tie function fails

Figure 9-9   Examples of using the tie and die functions to create and open a DBM database

The tie function in Example 1 opens the scores database for both reading and writing, and it ties the database to a hash named %teams. If the tie function fails, the die function displays an error message and then exits the script.

Notice that the *flag* argument in Example 2's tie function contains two *flags* separated by a pipe symbol (|). The O_CREAT *flag* tells the function to create the employ database if the database does not already exist, and the O_RDWR *flag* tells the function to open the employ database for both reading and writing. Notice that the *mode* argument is 0666 rather than simply 0; this is because the tie function contains the O_CREAT flag. Example 2's tie function ties the employ database to the %emps hash. The die function in the example displays an error message and then exits the script if the tie function fails.

Example 3's tie function opens the items database for reading only, and it ties the database to the %inv hash. If the tie function fails, the die function in the example displays an error message and then exits the script.

In the next set of steps, you use the tie function in the band.cgi script to open the mailing list database.

To tie a database named maillist to a hash named %mail:

1. Position the insertion point in the blank line below either the use CGI qw(:standard); statement or the use CGI qw(:standard -debug); statement.

   As you learned earlier, for a script to create or open a DBM database using the tie function, it must contain a use statement that specifies the name of a Perl DBM module.

2. Type **use SDBM_File;** and press **Enter**.

   Recall that the *flags* used in the tie function are defined in the Fcntl.pm module. To use the *flags*, you will need to include the module in the script.

3. Type **use Fcntl;** and press **Enter**.

   Next, declare the %mail hash variable, which will be tied to the maillist database.

4. Position the insertion point in the blank line below the comment #declare variable in the add function. Press **Tab**, if necessary, to indent the line, then type **my %mail;** and press **Enter**.

5. Position the insertion point in the blank line below the comment #open database, add record, close database in the add function. Press **Tab**, if necessary, to indent the line, then type **tie(%mail, "SDBM_File", "maillist", O_CREAT|O_RDWR, 0666)** and press **Enter**.

6. Press **Tab**, if necessary, to indent the line below the tie function. (You may need to press Tab more than once.). Type **or die "Error opening maillist. $!, stopped";** and press **Enter**.

7. Save the band.cgi document.

Step 2 in the add function's algorithm is to add the user's record to the database.

ADDING A RECORD TO AND MODIFYING A RECORD IN A DBM DATABASE

You add a record to a DBM database by adding a *key/value* pair to the hash that is tied to the database, and you modify a record by modifying the *value* corresponding to an existing *key* in the tied hash. It is necessary to use the tied hash to add and modify records because you cannot make changes directly to a DBM database on disk; rather, you can make changes to the database only through its tied hash. Any changes made to a tied hash are automatically recorded in the database.

As you learn later in this chapter, a tied hash also is necessary when using the untie function to delete a record from a DBM database.

Figure 9-10 shows examples of statements that you could use to add or modify a record in a DBM database.

Examples
Note: For the following examples, assume that the employ database is tied to the `%emps` hash, and that the invent database is tied to the `%inv` hash.
<u>Example 1</u> `$emps{HR} = 95;` <u>Result</u> If the HR *key* is not contained in the `%emps` hash, the statement adds a record that consists of the *key* HR and the *value* 95 to the employ database; otherwise, it assigns the *value* 95 to the existing HR *key* in the database.
<u>Example 2</u> `$emps{$dept} = $num;` <u>Result</u> If the `$dept` *key* is not contained in the `%emps` hash, the statement adds a record that consists of the `$dept` *key* and the `$num` *value* to the employ database; otherwise, it assigns the `$num` *value* to the existing `$dept` *key* in the database.
<u>Example 3</u> `$inv{$partnum} = "$name,$price";` <u>Result</u> If the *key* stored in the `$partnum` variable is not contained in the `%inv` hash, the statement adds a record that consists of the `$partnum` *key* and the `$name,$price` *value* to the invent database; otherwise, it assigns the `$name,$price` *value* to the existing `$partnum` *key* in the database.

Figure 9-10   Examples of statements that either add or modify a record

Notice that the three statements shown in Figure 9-10 can be used to either add a new record to the database or modify an existing record in the database. Whether the statement adds a new record or modifies an existing record depends on the record's *key*. If the record's *key* does not appear in the tied hash, the statement adds the record to the database; otherwise, it simply changes the *value* assigned to the existing *key* in the database.

Now that you know how to add a record to a DBM database, you can code Step 2 in the **add** function's algorithm. Recall that Step 2 is to add the user's name (*value*) and e-mail address (*key*) to the mailing list database.

To add the user's name and e-mail address to the mailing list database:

1. The insertion point should be positioned in the blank line below the **die** function in the user-defined **add** function.

2. Press **Tab** or **Backspace**, if necessary, to align the insertion point with the word "tie" in the **tie** function.

3. Type **$mail{$email} = $name;** and press **Enter**.

4. Save the band.cgi document.

Step 3 in the **add** function's algorithm is to close the database, and Step 4 is to create a dynamic Web page that advises the user that he or she is now on the mailing list. To complete the **add** function, you just need to enter the code for Step 3; Step 4's code is already entered in the function.

CLOSING A DBM DATABASE

You close a DBM database by removing (or untying) the tie that binds the database to the hash. You untie a database using the **untie function**. The syntax of the **untie** function is **untie(**_hash_**)**, where _hash_ is the name of the hash tied to the database. For example, the statement **untie(%mail);** unties (or closes) the maillist database, which is tied to the **%mail** hash.

 You also can use the **dbmclose** function to close a DBM database; however, the **untie** function supersedes the **dbmclose** function.

To complete the **add** function in the band.cgi script:

1. Type the additional line of code shaded in Figure 9-11, which shows the completed **add** function.

```
sub add {
    #declare variable
    my %mail;

    #open database, add record, close database
    tie(%mail, "SDBM_File", "maillist", O_CREAT|O_RDWR, 0666)
        or die "Error opening maillist. $!, stopped";
    $mail{$email} = $name;
    untie(%mail);

    #create Web page
    print "<HTML>\n";
    print "<HEAD><TITLE>The Jeffrey Sikes Band</TITLE></HEAD>\n";
    print "<BODY BGCOLOR=silver>\n";
    print "<FONT SIZE=5>\n";
    print "<H1>The Jeffrey Sikes Band</H1>\n";
    print "Thank you, $name. We will send the monthly \n";
    print "newsletter to $email.\n";
    print "</FONT></BODY></HTML>\n";
} #end add
```

Figure 9-11   Completed add function

2. Save the band.cgi document.

Before coding the **remove** function, you test the **add** function to make sure that it is working correctly.

To test the **add** function in the band.cgi script:

1. *If you are using a UNIX system*, open a terminal window, if necessary. Make the cgi-bin/chap09 directory the current directory, and then change the band.cgi file permissions to **755**.

   If you are using a Windows system, open a Command Prompt window, and then make the cgi-bin\chap09 directory the current directory.

2. Type **perl –c band.cgi** and press **Enter** to check the script for syntax errors. If necessary, correct any syntax errors in the script before continuing to the next step.

3. Type **perl –w band.cgi** and press **Enter**. When the offline mode message appears, type **Button=Put+Me+On+Your+Mailing+List** and press **Enter**.

4. Type **Name=Jackie** and press **Enter**, then type **Email=jc@pop.com** and press **Enter**.

5. Press **Ctrl+d** (UNIX), or press **Ctrl+z** and then press **Enter** (Windows), to indicate that you are finished entering the data.

   The **add** function tells the computer to open the maillist database. At this point, the database does not exist, so the computer creates it for you. After the database is created and opened, the **add** function adds the user's name and e-mail address to the database. It then closes the database and displays the message "Thank you, Jackie. We will send the monthly newsletter to jc@pop.com."

6. *If you are using a UNIX system*, type **ls** (the letters l and s) and then press **Enter** to display a listing of the files contained in the cgi-bin/chap09 directory.

   If you are using a Windows system, type **dir** and then press **Enter** to display a listing of the files contained in the cgi-bin\chap09 directory.

Notice that the file listing includes two files named maillist.dir and maillist.pag. Both files were created by the **tie** function and contain the *key* and *value* information for each record stored in the maillist database.

 You will not be able to read the contents of the maillist.dir and maillist.pag files by opening them in a text editor, because the information is stored in the files in binary format rather than in ASCII format.

Next, you begin completing the code for the **remove** function.

COMPLETING THE remove FUNCTION'S CODE

Figure 9-12 shows the algorithm for the **remove** function. (The algorithm was shown earlier in Figure 9-6.)

---

remove function
1. open the mailing list database
2. determine whether the user's e-mail address is in the database
   a. if (the user's e-mail address is in the database)
      1) delete the user's record (name and e-mail address) from the database
      2) assign the message "Thank you, *username*. We have removed your information from our mailing list." to the $msg variable
   else
   a. assign the message "You are not on our mailing list." to the $msg variable
3. close the database
4. create a dynamic Web page that displays the contents of the $msg variable

---

Figure 9-12   remove function's algorithm

The first step in the algorithm is to open the mailing list database. You will not need to enter the code for this step, because the **remove** function in the script already contains the appropriate **tie** function.

Step 2 in the algorithm is to determine whether the user's e-mail address is contained in the database. You can use the **exists** function to make the determination.

Determining Whether a Specific Key is Contained in a DBM Database

You can use the **exists function** to determine if a specific *key* is contained in a DBM database. To do so, you use the syntax **exists($*hash*{*key*})**, where *hash* is the name of the hash tied to the database, and *key* is the specific *key* you are searching for. For example, you can use the function **exists($mail{$email})** in an if statement to determine whether a specific e-mail address appears in the maillist database. (Recall that the maillist database is tied to the **%mail** hash.)

You also can use the **exists** function to determine if a specific *key* is contained in a hash that is not tied to a database.

The **exists** function returns **true** if the *key* is contained in the database (or hash); otherwise, it returns **false**.

To determine if a specific e-mail address is contained in the maillist database:

1. Return to the band.cgi document in your text editor. Position the insertion point in the blank line below the comment #determine if user's information is in the database in the remove function.

2. Press **Tab**, if necessary, to indent the line, then type **if (exists($mail{$email})) {** and press **Enter**.

If the user's e-mail address appears as a *key* in the maillist database, you need to delete the user's record (name and e-mail address) from the database, and then assign an appropriate message to the $msg variable. You learn how to delete a record from a DBM database in the next section.

Deleting a Record From a DBM Database

You use the **delete function** to delete a record from a DBM database. The syntax of the delete function is **delete($*hash*{*key*})**, where *hash* is the name of the hash tied to the database, and *key* is the *key* that identifies the record you want to delete. For example, to delete a user's name and e-mail address from the maillist database, which is tied to the %mail hash, you use the statement delete($mail{$email});.

To delete a record from the maillist database:

1. Press **Tab** to indent the line in the if clause. (You may need to press Tab more than once.)

2. Type **delete($mail{$email});** and press **Enter**.

3. Save the band.cgi document.

In addition to deleting the user's record from the database, recall that you also need to assign a message to the $msg variable. The message you need to assign is fairly long, and will not fit conveniently on one line in most text editors. The easiest way to assign a long message to a variable is to use string concatenation.

CONCATENATING STRINGS

Connecting (or linking) strings together is called **concatenating**. In Perl, you concatenate strings with the concatenation operator, which is a period (.). Figure 9-13 shows examples of using the Perl concatenation operator in a statement.

Examples	Results

Example 1
`$first = "Jerry";`
`$last = "Nuerburg";`
`$full = $first . " " . $last;`
	concatenates the contents of the `$first` variable, a space, and the contents of the `$last` variable, and then assigns the result (Jerry Nuerburg) to the `$full` variable

Example 2
`$part1 = "It is a beautiful";`
`$part2 = " day today!";`
`$sentence = $part1 . $part2;`
	concatenates the contents of the `$part1` variable and the contents of the `$part2` variable, and then assigns the result (It is a beautiful day today!) to the `$sentence` variable

Example 3
`$msg = "Thank you for";`
`$msg = $msg . " calling.";`
	concatenates the contents of the `$msg` variable and the string " calling.", and then assigns the result (Thank you for calling.) to the `$msg` variable

Figure 9-13   Examples of using the Perl concatenation operator

The two concatenation operators shown in Example 1 concatenate the contents of the `$first` variable, a space, and the contents of the `$last` variable. The statement containing the concatenation operators assigns the result (Jerry Nuerburg) to the `$full` variable.

The concatenation operator shown in Example 2 in Figure 9-13 concatenates the contents of the `$part1` variable and the contents of the `$part2` variable. The statement containing the concatenation operator assigns the result (It is a beautiful day today!) to the `$sentence` variable. Finally, the concatenation operator in Example 3 concatenates the contents of the `$msg` variable with the string " calling.". The statement containing the concatenation operator assigns the result (Thank you for calling.) to the `$msg` variable.

You will use the concatenation operator to assign the message "Thank you, $name. We have removed your information from our mailing list." to the `$msg` variable.

To assign the appropriate message to the `$msg` variable:

1. Type the additional lines of code shaded in Figure 9-14

9

```
sub remove {
    #declare variables
    my (%mail, $msg);

    #open database
    tie(%mail, "SDBM_File", "maillist", O_RDWR, 0)
        or die "Error opening maillist. $!, stopped";

    #determine if user's information is in the database
    if (exists($mail{$email})) {
        delete($mail{$email});
        $msg = "Thank you, $name. We have removed your ";
        $msg = $msg . "information from our mailing list.";
    }

    #close database
    untie(%mail);

    #create Web page
    print "<HTML>\n";
    print "<HEAD><TITLE>The Jeffrey Sikes Band</TITLE></HEAD>\n";
    print "<BODY BGCOLOR=silver>\n";
    print "<FONT SIZE=5>\n";
    print "<H1>The Jeffrey Sikes Band</H1>\n";
    print "$msg\n";
    print "</FONT></BODY></HTML>\n";
} #end remove
```

Figure 9-14   Additional lines of code entered in the `remove` function

> If the user's e-mail address is not in the database, the `remove` function should assign the message "You are not on our mailing list." to the `$msg` variable.

2. Position the insertion point immediately below the `if` clause's closing brace (}), then type **else {** and press **Enter**.

3. Press **Tab**, if necessary, to indent the line. (You may need to press Tab more than once.)

4. Type **$msg = "You are not on our mailing list.";** and press **Enter**.

5. Press **Tab** or **Backspace**, if necessary, to align the insertion point with the word "else".

6. Type **}** (a closing brace), which marks the end of the `else` clause.

7. Save the band.cgi document.

The last two steps in the `remove` function's algorithm are to close the database and then create a dynamic Web page that displays the contents of the `$msg` variable. Notice that the `remove` function already contains the code for both of these steps. The completed band.cgi script is shown in Figure 9-15.

```perl
#!/usr/bin/perl
#band.cgi - saves data to and removes data from a database
#creates appropriate dynamic Web pages
print "Content-type: text/html\n\n";
use CGI qw(:standard);
use SDBM_File;
use Fcntl;

#prevent Perl from creating undeclared variables
use strict;

#declare variables
my ($button, $name, $email);

#assign values to variables
$button = param('Button');
$name = param('Name');
$email = param('Email');
if ($button eq "Put Me On Your Mailing List") {
    add();
}
elsif ($button eq "Remove Me From Your Mailing List") {
    remove();
}
exit;

#*****user-defined functions*****
sub add {
    #declare variable
    my %mail;

    #open database, add record, close database
    tie(%mail, "SDBM_File", "maillist", O_CREAT|O_RDWR, 0666)
        or die "Error opening maillist. $!, stopped";
    $mail{$email} = $name;
    untie(%mail);

    #create Web page
    print "<HTML>\n";
    print "<HEAD><TITLE>The Jeffrey Sikes Band</TITLE></HEAD>\n";
    print "<BODY BGCOLOR=silver>\n";
    print "<FONT SIZE=5>\n";
    print "<H1>The Jeffrey Sikes Band</H1>\n";
    print "Thank you, $name. We will send the monthly \n";
    print "newsletter to $email.\n";
    print "</FONT></BODY></HTML>\n";
} #end add
```

Figure 9-15   Completed band.cgi script

9

```
sub remove {
    #declare variables
    my (%mail, $msg);

    #open database
    tie(%mail, "SDBM_File", "maillist", O_RDWR, 0)
        or die "Error opening maillist. $!, stopped";

    #determine if user's information is in the database
    if (exists($mail{$email})) {
        delete($mail{$email});
        $msg = "Thank you, $name. We have removed your ";
        $msg = $msg . "information from our mailing list.";
    }
    else {
        $msg = "You are not on our mailing list.";
    }

    #close database
    untie(%mail);

    #create Web page
    print "<HTML>\n";
    print "<HEAD><TITLE>The Jeffrey Sikes Band</TITLE></HEAD>\n";
    print "<BODY BGCOLOR=silver>\n";
    print "<FONT SIZE=5>\n";
    print "<H1>The Jeffrey Sikes Band</H1>\n";
    print "$msg\n";
    print "</FONT></BODY></HTML>\n";
} #end remove
```

Figure 9-15   Completed band.cgi script (continued)

Now test the script to make sure the **remove** function is working correctly.

To test the script's **remove** function:

1. *If you are using a UNIX system*, return to the UNIX command prompt. Verify that the cgi-bin/chap09 directory is the current directory.

   If you are using a Windows system, return to the Command Prompt window. Verify that the cgi-bin\chap09 directory is the current directory.

2. Type **perl –c band.cgi** and press **Enter** to check the script for syntax errors. If necessary, correct any syntax errors in the script before continuing to the next step.

3. Type **perl -w band.cgi** and press **Enter**. When the offline mode message appears, type **Button=Remove+Me+From+Your+Mailing+List** and press **Enter**.

4. Type **Name=Jackie** and press **Enter**, then type **Email=jc@pop.com** and press **Enter**.

5. Press **Ctrl+d** (UNIX), or press **Ctrl+z** and then press **Enter** (Windows), to indicate that you are finished entering the data.

   The **remove** function opens the maillist database, which was created in an earlier set of steps. It then deletes the jc@pop.com e-mail address and its corresponding name from the database, and displays the message "Thank you, Jackie. We have removed your information from our mailing list." Verify that the name and e-mail address were deleted from the database.

6. Type **perl -w band.cgi** and press **Enter**. When the offline mode message appears, type **Button=Remove+Me+From+Your+Mailing+List** and press **Enter**.

7. Type **Name=Jackie** and press **Enter**, then type **Email=jc@pop.com** and press **Enter**.

8. Press **Ctrl+d** (UNIX), or press **Ctrl+z** and then press **Enter** (Windows). The **remove** function displays the message "You are not on our mailing list".

   Now test the script using your Web browser.

To use your browser to test the band.cgi script:

1. *If you are using a Windows system*, return to the band.cgi document in your text editor. Change the filename argument in the two **tie** functions from "maillist" to "chap09/maillist", then save the band.cgi document.

2. *If you are using a UNIX system*, change the maillist.dir and maillist.pag file permissions to 666.

3. Start your Web browser, then use the File menu to open the band.html file.

   Begin by adding a record to the database.

4. Type **Bill Haroldson** in the Name text box. Type **wjh@blue.com** in the E-mail address text box. Click the **Put Me On Your Mailing List** button. A Web page similar to the one shown earlier in Figure 9-3 appears on the screen.

In Chapter 10, you learn how to e-mail the newsletter to fans on the mailing list.

   Now delete the record you just added.

5. Click the browser's **Back** button to return to the form. Click the **Remove Me From Your Mailing List** button. A Web page similar to the one shown earlier in Figure 9-4 appears on the screen.

Next, verify that the record was deleted from the database.

6. Click the browser's **Back** button to return to the form. Click the **Remove Me From Your Mailing List** button. A Web page similar to the one shown earlier in Figure 9-5 appears on the screen.

7. Close your browser and any open windows.

As you learned in Chapter 2, a CGI script written in Perl can use various methods to generate HTML output. Examples of these methods include the `print` and `printf` functions and "here" documents. You learned how to use the `print` and `printf` functions in Chapter 2 and Chapter 3, respectively. In this chapter, you learn how to use "here" documents.

CREATING A "HERE" DOCUMENT

Most CGI scripts contain a lot of `print` statements, because their output typically is HTML code. Typing multiple `print` statements in a script can be tedious, not to mention time-consuming. A **"here" document** allows you to use one `print` statement to print a block of HTML code in a script. In other words, it allows you to replace multiple `print` statements with just one `print` statement. Figure 9-16 shows the syntax and an example of a "here" document. The example shows how you can use a "here" document, rather than multiple `print` statements, in the band.cgi script's `add` function.

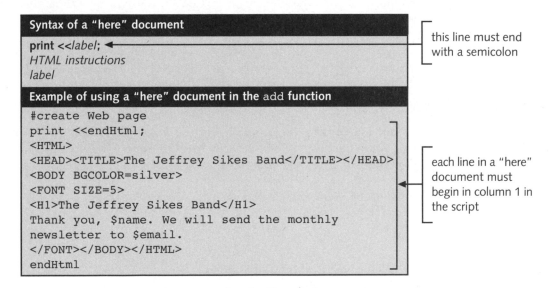

Syntax of a "here" document
print <<_label_; ◄────   this line must end
HTML instructions   with a semicolon
label

```
#create Web page
print <<endHtml;
<HTML>
<HEAD><TITLE>The Jeffrey Sikes Band</TITLE></HEAD>
<BODY BGCOLOR=silver>
<FONT SIZE=5>
<H1>The Jeffrey Sikes Band</H1>
Thank you, $name. We will send the monthly
newsletter to $email.
</FONT></BODY></HTML>
endHtml
```

Example of using a "here" document in the add function

each line in a "here" document must begin in column 1 in the script

Figure 9-16   Syntax and an example of a "here" document

The syntax of a "here" document begins with a `print` statement that contains the keyword `print` followed by a space, two less than symbols (`<<`), a *label*, and a semicolon. It ends with a line that contains only the *label*, which must be identical to the *label* used in the `print` statement. The *label* can be one or more words; however, if you use more than one word, you must enclose the *label* in either double or single quotation marks. The *label* used in the example shown in Figure 9-16 is `endhtml`.

 If you enclose the *label* in double quotation marks, or if you leave the *label* unquoted, Perl performs variable interpolation on any variable names that appear in the "here" document. To prevent variable interpolation from occurring in a "here" document, you must enclose the label in single quotation marks.

Between the **print** `<<`*label***;** line and the *label* line, you enter the HTML code that you want to print on a Web page. Notice in the example shown in Figure 9-16 that the HTML code does not include any `print` statements. The `print` statements are not necessary, because the "here" document's syntax tells the computer to print everything from "here" (**print** `<<`*label***;**) to "here" (*label*). The HTML code included in the "here" document will be printed verbatim.

As Figure 9-16 indicates, each line of code in a "here" document, including the **print** `<<`*label***;** and *label* lines, must begin in column 1 in the script; otherwise, the "here" document will not work correctly. In Hands-on Project 2 at the end of this chapter, you will modify the **add** and **remove** functions in the Jeffrey Sikes Band script so that each function uses a "here" document.

 Technically, only the *label* line must begin in column 1 in a script for a "here" document to work correctly. In other words, the other lines in a "here" document can begin in any column in a script. However, keep in mind that the HTML code in a "here" document is printed verbatim. If the lines begin in column 10 in the script, they also will begin in column 10 when the resulting Web page's source code is viewed in a browser.

9

CHAPTER SUMMARY

- A database is a collection of data that is stored in a disk file and organized so that its contents can be easily accessed, managed, and updated.

- You can use one of the Perl DBM (Database Management) modules to create and manipulate a DBM database. Examples of DBM modules include SDBM_File.pm, ODBM_File.pm, and NDBM_File.pm.

- The data contained in a DBM database is stored on disk using a *key/value* format.

- You use the Perl `tie` function to create and open a DBM database. The syntax of the `tie` function is **tie**(*hash, module, filename, flag, mode*). The *flag* argument values (`O_CREAT`, `O_RDONLY`, `O_WRONLY`, and `O_RDWR`) are defined in the

Fcntl module. If the `tie` function contains the `O_CREAT` *flag*, then the *mode* argument is usually the number 0666; otherwise, it is the number 0.

❑ You can use the `die` function to display a message and then exit a script when the `tie` function fails.

❑ You use the syntax *$hash{key}* = *value*; to add a record to and modify a record in a DBM database. In the syntax, *hash* is the name of the hash tied to the database, *key* is the data contained in the record's primary key field, and *value* is the data contained in the remaining fields in the record. You also use the syntax to add and modify a *key/value* pair in a hash that is not tied to a database.

❑ You use the `untie` function to close a DBM database. The syntax of the `untie` function is **untie(*hash*)**, where *hash* is the name of the hash used in the `tie` function.

❑ The SDBM_File module creates two files for the database. One of the files has a "dir" extension on its filename, and the other has a "pag" extension.

❑ You can use the `exists` function to determine if a DBM database contains a specific *key*. The syntax of the `exists` function is **exists($*hash{key}*)**. You also can use the function to determine if a hash that is not tied to a database contains a specific *key*.

❑ You use the `delete` function to remove a record from a DBM database. The syntax of the `delete` function is **delete($*hash{key}*)**. You also can use the function to delete a *key/value* pair from a hash that is not tied to a database.

❑ The string concatenation operator in Perl is the period (.).

❑ You can use a "here" document to send HTML code to the browser.

REVIEW QUESTIONS

1. Which of the following functions binds a hash to a DBM database?

   a. `bind`

   b. `bindhash`

   c. `tie`

   d. `hashtie`

2. You use the _____ function to determine if a DBM database contains a specific *key*.

   a. `exist`

   b. `find`

   c. `found`

   d. None of the above.

3. Which of the following statements opens a DBM database named citystate for both reading and writing?

   a. `open("citystate", "<<", ">");`

   b. `opendb(%city, "SDBM_File", "citystate", READWR, 0);`

   c. `tie(%city, "SDBM File", "citystate", RDWR);`

   d. `tie(%city, "SDBM_File", "citystate", O_RDWR, 0);`

4. Which of the following statements writes the *key* "Atlanta" and the *value* "GA" to a DBM database named citystate? The database is tied to the `%city` hash.

   a. `%city{GA} = "Atlanta";`

   b. `$citystate{Atlanta} = "GA";`

   c. `$city{Atlanta} = "GA";`

   d. None of the above.

5. Which of the following statements closes the citystate database, which is tied to the `%city` hash?

   a. `close(citystate);`

   b. `unbind(%city);`

   c. `untie($city);`

   d. `untie(%city);`

6. If the `tie` function does not contain the **O_CREAT** *flag*, the number _____ is used in the function's *mode* argument.

   a. 0 (zero)

   b. 1 (one)

   c. 0666

   d. None of the above.

7. The _____ module contains the definition of the **O RDONLY** *flag*

   a. Fcntl

   b. Fcntrl

   c. Filectrl

   d. Filecon

8. Which of the following statements removes the "Atlanta" *key* and its corresponding *value* from the citystate database, which is tied to the `%city` hash?

   a. `delete(%city{Atlanta});`

   b. `delete($city{Atlanta});`

   c. `delete($citystate{Atlanta});`

   d. None of the above.

9

9. Which of the following statements concatenates the contents of the `$first` variable, a space, and the contents of the `$last` variable, and then assigns the result to the `$name` variable?

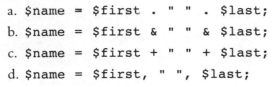

a. `$name = $first . " " . $last;`

b. `$name = $first & " " & $last;`

c. `$name = $first + " " + $last;`

d. `$name = $first, " ", $last;`

10. When a database is tied to a hash, changes made to the hash are automatically reflected in the database.

a. true

b. false

11. A collection of data that is stored in a disk file and organized so that its contents can be easily accessed, managed, and updated is called a _____.

12. Write a Perl statement that uses the `tie` function to open a DBM database named payroll. The statement should bind the database to a hash named `%pay`. The database should be opened for both reading and writing, and created if it does not exist.

13. Write the statement to add the "1234" *key* and the *value* "450.67" to the payroll database opened in Question 12.

14. Write the statement to add the "2222" *key* and the *value* "500" to the payroll database opened in Question 12.

15. Write the statement to delete the "1234" *key* and the *value* "450.67" from the payroll database opened in Question 12.

16. Write the statement to increase, by 10%, the *value* corresponding to the "2222" *key* in the payroll database opened in Question 12.

17. Write a selection structure that determines whether the payroll database opened in Question 12 contains the "1234" *key*. If it does, print the *value* corresponding to the *key*; otherwise, print the message "This key is not in the database."

18. Write a statement that closes the payroll database opened in Question 12.

19. Assume that the `$city`, `$state`, and `$zip` variables contain the strings "Darien", "IL", and "60561", respectively. Write a Perl statement that uses the variables and the concatenation operator to assign the string "Darien, IL 60561" to the `$address2` variable.

20. The SDBM_File module saves the database information in two files. One file has a dir extension on its filename, and the other has a _____ extension.

HANDS-ON PROJECTS

Project 1

In this project, you modify the Jeffrey Sikes Band script so that it removes any leading and trailing spaces from the name and address input data, and also verifies that the input data is not blank. The script also should verify that the e-mail address is in the correct format.

a. Open the band.html file in a text editor. The file is contained in the public_html/chap09 directory.

b. Change the filename in the first line from band.html to c09ex1.html.

c. Modify the <FORM> tag to refer to the c09ex1.cgi script.

d. Save the document as c09ex1.html.

e. Open the band.cgi file in a text editor. The file is contained in the cgi-bin/chap09 directory.

f. Change the filename in the second line from band.cgi to c09ex1.cgi.

g. *If you are using a UNIX system*, change the filename argument in the two `tie` functions from "maillist" to "c09ex1".
If you are using a Windows system, change the filename argument in the two `tie` functions from "chap09/maillist" to simply "c09ex1".

h. Change the filename in the two `die` functions from maillist to c09ex1.

i. Save the document as c09ex1.cgi.

j. Modify the script so that it removes the leading and trailing spaces from the name and e-mail address passed to the script. Perform this task before a record is added to or deleted from the database.

k. Modify the script so that it displays an appropriate Web page if the name and/or e-mail address passed to the script are blank. Perform this task before a record is added to or deleted from the database.

l. The script should verify that the e-mail address sent to the script is the correct format before adding a record to or deleting a record from database. Modify the script appropriately.

m. Save the c09ex1.cgi document.

n. *If you are using a UNIX system*, change the c09ex1.cgi file permissions to 755.

o. Test the script from the command line using the –c and –w switches.

p. *If you are using a UNIX system*, change the file permissions for the c09ex1.dir and c09ex1.pag files to 666.

9

q. *If you are using a Windows system*, return to the c09ex1.cgi script. Change the filename argument in the two **tie** functions from "c09ex1" to "chap09/c09ex1", then save the c09ex1.cgi document.

r. Open the c09ex1.html document in your Web browser. Test the script using both valid and invalid data.

Project 2

In this project, you include two "here" documents in the Jeffrey Sikes Band script.

a. Open the band.html file in a text editor. The file is contained in the public_html/chap09 directory.

b. Change the filename in the first line from band.html to c09ex2.html.

c. Modify the <FORM> tag to refer to the c09ex2.cgi script.

d. Save the document as c09ex2.html.

e. Open the band.cgi file in a text editor. The file is contained in the cgi-bin/chap09 directory.

f. Change the filename in the second line from band.cgi to c09ex2.cgi.

g. *If you are using a UNIX system*, change the filename argument in the two **tie** functions from "maillist" to "c09ex2".
If you are using a Windows system, change the filename argument in the two **tie** functions from "chap09/maillist" to simply "c09ex2".

h. Change the filename in the two **die** functions from maillist to c09ex2.

i. Save the document as c09ex2.cgi.

j. Modify the **add** function so that it uses the "here" document shown in Figure 9-16. (Remember that each line of code in a "here" document must begin in column 1.)

k. Modify the **remove** function so that it uses a "here" document.

l. Save the c09ex2.cgi document.

m. *If you are using a UNIX system*, change the c09ex2.cgi file permissions to 755.

n. Test the script from the command line using the –c and –w switches.

o. *If you are using a UNIX system*, change the file permissions for the c09ex2.dir and c09ex2.pag files to 666.

p. *If you are using a Windows system*, return to the c09ex2.cgi script. Change the filename argument in the two **tie** functions from "c09ex2" to "chap09/c09ex2", then save the c09ex2.cgi document.

q. Open the c09ex2.html document in your Web browser. Test the script using both valid and invalid data.

Project 3

In this project, you modify the International Coffees script that you created in Chapter 8 so that it saves the form data to a DBM database rather than to a text file.

   a. Copy the inter.html file from the public_html/chap08 directory to the public_html/chap09 directory. Rename the file c09ex3.html.

   b. Copy the inter.cgi file from the cgi-bin/chap08 directory to the cgi-bin/chap09 directory. Rename the file c09ex3.cgi.

   c. Open the c09ex3.html file in a text editor. Change the filename in the first line from inter.html to c09ex3.html.

   d. Modify the <FORM> and <A> tags to refer to the c09ex3.cgi script, which is contained in the cgi-bin/chap09 directory.

   e. Save the c09ex3.html document.

   f. Open the c09ex3.cgi file in a text editor. Change the filename in the second line from inter.cgi to c09ex3.cgi.

   g. Modify the script so that it saves the form data to and retrieves the form data from a DBM database named c09ex3. (*Hint*: Use the e-mail address as the *key*, and the name and comments as the *value*. Example 3 in Figure 9-10 shows you how to save a *value* that contains more than one field. Use the pipe symbol as the field separator.)

   h. Save the c09ex3.cgi document.

   i. *If you are using a UNIX system*, change the c09ex3.cgi file permissions to 755.

   j. Test the script from the command line using the -c switch.

   k. Open the c09ex3.html document in your Web browser.

   l. Add three records to the database, then use the View what others have to say link to display the records on a Web page.

Project 4

In this project, you create a script that uses a DBM database to store credit card names and account numbers.

   a. Open the credit.html file in a text editor. The file is contained in the public_html/chap09 directory. The document creates a form that contains two text boxes and two submit buttons. You use the two text boxes to enter a credit card name and account number. You use one of the submit buttons to record the credit card information in a DBM database, and the other to display the information on a Web page.

   b. Change the filename in the first line from credit.html to c09ex4.html.

   c. Change yourservername in the <FORM> tag to the name of your server.

   d. Save the document as c09ex4.html.

9

e. Create a script that will process the form data. Name the script c09ex4.cgi and save it in the cgi-bin/chap09 directory. If the user clicked the Enter Data button on the form, the script should store the form data in a DBM database named c09ex4, and then display a Web page that advises the user that the information has been entered in the database. Remove any leading and trailing spaces from the data before saving it to the database, and save the credit card name using uppercase letters. Verify that none of the input data is blank before saving the data to the database. If the user clicked the Display Data button on the form, the script should display the contents of the c09ex4 database on a Web page.

f. Save the c09ex4.cgi document.

g. *If you are using a UNIX system*, change the c09ex4.cgi file permissions to 755.

h. Test the script from the command line using the –c and –w switches.

i. *If you are using a UNIX system*, change the c09ex4.dir and c09ex4.pag file permissions to 666.

j. *If you are using a Windows system*, return to the c09ex4.cgi script. Change the filename argument in the two `tie` functions from "c09ex4" to "chap09/c09ex4", then save the c09ex4.cgi document.

k. Open the c09ex4.html document in your Web browser. Enter the following three credit card names and account numbers in the database: Horizon, 123–456, Petries, 45–6789, Bells, 1–23–67.

l. Display the contents of the database on a Web page.

Project 5

In this project, you create a script for Candles Unlimited. The script stores product information in a DBM database.

a. Open the candle.html file in a text editor. The file is contained in the public_html/chap09 directory. The document creates a form that contains three text boxes and two submit buttons. You use the three text boxes to enter the product information (code, name, and price). You use the Save submit button to record the product information in a DBM database, and the Delete button to delete the product information from the database.

b. Change the filename in the first line from candle.html to c09ex5.html.

c. Change yourservername in the <FORM> tag to the name of your server.

d. Save the document as c09ex5.html.

e. Create a script that will process the form data. Name the script c09ex5.cgi and save it in the cgi-bin/chap09 directory. If the user clicked the Save button on the form, the script should store the form data in a DBM database named c09ex5. (*Hint:* Use the product code as the *key*, and the product name and price as the *value*. Example 3 in Figure 9-10 shows you how to save a *value* that contains more than one field.) Remove any leading and trailing spaces from the data before saving it to the database. Also remove any dollar signs from the price, and save the product code and name using uppercase letters. If the user clicked the Delete button on the form, the script should delete the product information from the database. (Keep in mind that the user may enter the product code using uppercase and/or lowercase letters.) Display appropriate Web pages advising the user of the status of his or her request.

f. Save the c09ex5.cgi document.

g. *If you are using a UNIX system,* change the c09ex5.cgi file permissions to 755.

h. Test the script from the command line using the –c and –w switches.

i. *If you are using a UNIX system,* change the c09ex5.dir and c09ex5.pag file permissions to 666.

j. *If you are using a Windows system,* return to the c09ex5.cgi script. Change the filename argument in the two **tie** functions from "c09ex5" to "chap09/c09ex5", then save the c09ex5.cgi document.

k. Open the c09ex5.html document in your Web browser. Use the form to enter the following product information:

Code	Name	Price
FL234	Floral	$5
TA589	Tapered	7.50
WE999	Wedding	10
MI222	Mini	4

l. Use the form to delete the MI222 candles from the database.

Project 6

In this project, you create a form and script for Candles Unlimited. You use the c09ex5 database that you created in Hands-on Project 5.

a. Create an HTML form that allows the user to enter a product code. Name the form c09ex6.html and save it in the public_html/chap09 directory.

b. Create a script that will process the product code received from the server. Name the script c09ex6.cgi and save it in the cgi-bin/chap09 directory. The script should locate the product code in the c09ex5 database, which you created in Hands-on Project 5, and then display the name and price of the product on a Web page. (Keep in mind that the user may enter the product code using uppercase and/or lowercase letters.)

c. Save the c09ex6.cgi document.

d. *If you are using a UNIX system,* change the c09ex6.cgi file permissions to 755.

e. Test the script from the command line using the –c and –w switches.

f. *If you are using a Windows system*, return to the c09ex6.cgi script. Change the filename argument in the **tie** function from "c09ex5" to "chap09/c09ex5", then save the c09ex6.cgi document.

g. Open the c09ex6.html document in your Web browser. Use the form to display the name and price of the WE999 and TA589 candles.

Case Projects

1. Create an HTML form and a script that a student can use to keep track of the college courses that he or she has completed, and the grade earned in each course. Name the form c09case1.html and save it in the public_html/chap09 directory. Name the script c09case1.cgi and save it in the cgi-bin/chap09 directory. The form should allow the student to enter a course code (for example, CIS100) and the grade earned in the course. Include an "Add" submit button, a "Remove" submit button, and a "Display Courses" submit button on the form. If the student clicks the "Add" submit button, the c09case1.cgi script should add the course information to a DBM database named c09case1. If the student clicks the "Remove" submit button, the script should remove the course information from the c09case1 database. If the student clicks the "Display Courses" submit button, the script should display the contents of the c09case1 database on a Web page.

2. Create an HTML form and a script for Books Online. Name the form c09case2.html and save it in the public_html/chap09 directory. Name the script c09case2.cgi and save it in the cgi-bin/chap09 directory. The form should allow the user to enter a five-digit account number and a password that must include from six to 10 characters. Include a "Create Account" submit button and a "Tell Me My Password" submit button on the form. If the user enters an account number and a password, and then clicks the "Create Account" submit button, the c09case2.cgi script should add the account number and the password to a DBM database named c09case2. Use the **tr///** operator, which you learned about in Chapter 8, to encrypt the password before saving it to the database. If the user enters an account number and then clicks the "Tell Me My Password" submit button, the script should display the user's password (unencrypted) on a Web page.

10

HIDDEN FIELDS AND E-MAIL

In this chapter, you will:

♦ Create a form using a CGI script
♦ Include a selection list in a form
♦ Use a hidden field to pass information from one script to another
♦ Send an e-mail message using a script

s you learned in Chapter 1, when you request a document using your Web browser, the browser looks for the Web server specified in the URL. If the browser is able to locate the server, it opens a connection, or *session*, between the server and your computer, and then submits your request to the server. The request may require the server to transmit the contents of a static Web page, or process the code in a CGI script. After the server fulfills your request, the connection to the server is closed and the server maintains no information about the session. Each time your computer's browser needs something from the server, it must make a new, independent request.

In many cases, you need the server to remember information about the current session, so that the information can be used in a subsequent session. For example, a Web site that allows you to order products must remember each item ordered so that an invoice can be prepared when you finish shopping. Similarly, a Web site that allows you to select a language to use when displaying the site's Web pages should remember your selection while you are browsing the site, and also when you return to the site a week later.

Hidden fields and cookies are techniques that you can use to retain information that normally would be lost at the end of a session. In this chapter, you learn how to use hidden fields; cookies are covered in Chapter 11. Also in this chapter, you learn how to use a script to send an e-mail message.

THE SUN TRAVEL WEB PAGES

You can use Sun Travel's Web site to request a vacation brochure. To do so, you enter your name and e-mail address on the Brochure Request form, as shown in Figure 10-1.

Figure 10-1   Brochure Request form

Typically, you also would enter your mailing address on the form. The mailing address information was omitted to keep the script that processes the form data simple.

Notice that the Brochure Request form contains two text boxes named Name and Email, and one submit button. Now view the HTML code used to create the form.

To view the HTML code used to create the Brochure Request form:

1. Open the sun.html file in a text editor. The file is contained in the public_html/chap10 directory. Figure 10-2 shows the contents of the file.

```
<!sun.html>
<HTML>
<HEAD><TITLE>Sun Travel</TITLE></HEAD>
<BODY>
<H1>Sun Travel Brochure Request</H1><HR>
<FORM ACTION="http://yourservername/cgi-bin/chap10/sun1.cgi" METHOD=POST>

<TABLE>
<TR><TD>Name:</TD><TD>
    <INPUT TYPE=text NAME=Name SIZE=25></TD></TR>
<TR><TD>E-mail address:</TD><TD>
    <INPUT TYPE=text NAME=Email SIZE=25></TD></TR>
</TABLE>

<BR><INPUT TYPE=submit VALUE="Send Me A Brochure">
</FORM></BODY></HTML>
```

Figure 10-2   HTML code used to create the Brochure Request form

The <FORM> tag indicates that the sun1.cgi script will process the form data, which includes the Name and Email *keys* and their corresponding *values*.

2. Change yourservername in the <FORM> tag to the name of your server.

3. Save the sun.html document, and then close the document.

When you click the Send Me A Brochure button on the Brochure Request form, the browser should send the form data to the first of two Sun Travel scripts. The script, named sun1.cgi, should process the form data and also display the Brochure Listing form shown in Figure 10-3.

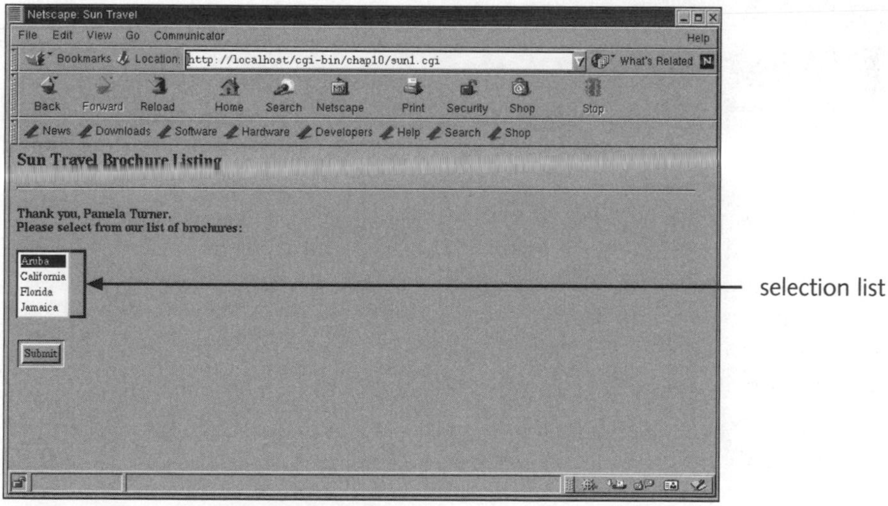

Figure 10-3   Brochure Listing form

As Figure 10-3 indicates, the Brochure Listing form contains a form element called a selection list. A **selection list** is a list box from which the user can select a particular value or set of values. It is a good idea to use a selection list rather than a text box when you have a fixed set of possible values, because most users prefer selecting a value to typing it. Selection lists also help maintain data integrity, because they allow the user to enter only valid information.

Keep in mind that the connection to the server is closed after the Brochure Listing form is displayed, and the server maintains no information about the session. In other words, the server does not keep track of (or remember) the user's name and e-mail address that it received during the session.

When you click the Submit button on the Brochure Listing form, the browser should send the brochure selection (Aruba, California, Florida, or Jamaica) to the second Sun Travel script, which is named sun2.cgi. You also want the browser to send the user's name and e-mail address, because the sun2.cgi script will need the information to e-mail an appropriate acknowledgment message to the user, and also display a Web page similar to the one shown in Figure 10-4. (The Web page assumes that the user, Pamela Turner, selected Jamaica in the selection list before clicking the Submit button.)

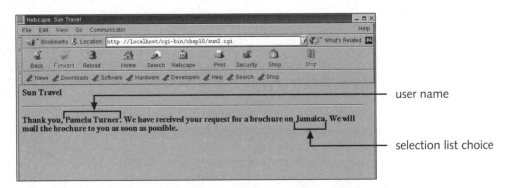

Figure 10-4 Web page acknowledgment

At this point, you may be wondering how you can get the browser to send the user's name and e-mail address to the sun2.cgi script, when neither entry appears in an element on the Brochure Listing form. You can do so by including two hidden fields on the form: one to store the user's name, and the other to store the e-mail address. The browser passes the values stored in a hidden field together with the values stored in the other elements on a form.

In the next section, you begin completing the first Sun Travel script, which is named sun1.cgi.

PLANNING AND CODING THE SUN1.CGI SCRIPT

Figure 10-5 shows the input, output, and algorithm for the first Sun Travel script, which is named sun1.cgi.

Input	Output
name e-mail address	Brochure Listing form
Algorithm	

1. assign input items to variables
2. create the Brochure Listing form, which should
   a. display the name
   b. allow the user to select a brochure from a list of available brochures
   c. record the name and e-mail address in hidden fields	

Figure 10-5   Input, output, and algorithm for the sun1.cgi script

 In Hands-on Project 1 at the end of this chapter, you modify the sun1.cgi script so that it removes any leading and trailing spaces from the name and e-mail address received from the server. You also enter the code to verify the format of the e-mail address.

The sun1.cgi script's input is the user's name and e-mail address, which are entered on the Brochure Request form and passed by the browser to the script; its output is the Brochure Listing form. According to Step 2 in the algorithm, the Brochure Listing form should display the user's name, and also allow the user to select a brochure from a list of available brochures. Additionally, the Brochure Listing form should record the user's name and e-mail address in hidden fields; doing so allows the browser to pass the information to the sun2.cgi script.

On your computer system is a partially completed script named sun1.cgi. In the next set of steps, you open the script and begin completing its code.

To begin completing the sun1.cgi script:

1. Open the sun1.cgi script in a text editor. The file is contained in the cgi–bin/chap10 directory.

2. If necessary, change the shebang line to reflect the location of the Perl interpreter on your system.

3. If necessary, add the **-debug** pragma to the `use CGI qw(:standard);` statement.

    Recall that the script's output is a form—more specifically, the Brochure Listing form. The <FORM> tag included in the script indicates that the sun2.cgi script will process the Brochure Listing form's data.

10

4. Change yourservername in the <FORM> tag to the name of your server.

Notice that the entire <FORM> tag is enclosed in double quotation marks, with the value assigned to the ACTION property enclosed in single quotation marks. The different quotation marks are necessary to differentiate the outer quoted string from the inner one.

The first step in the algorithm shown in Figure 10-5 is to assign the input items to variables.

5. Enter the code shaded in Figure 10-6.

```perl
#!/usr/bin/perl
#sun1.cgi - displays a dynamic Web page listing available brochures
print "Content-type: text/html\n\n";
use CGI qw(:standard);

#prevent Perl from creating undeclared variables
use strict;

#declare and assign values to variables
my ($name, $email);
$name = param('Name');
$email = param('Email');

#create Brochure Listing form
print "<HTML>\n";
print "<HEAD><TITLE>Sun Travel</TITLE></HEAD>\n";
print "<BODY>\n";
print "<FORM
        ACTION='http://yourservername/cgi-bin/chap10/sun2.cgi'
        METHOD=POST>\n";
print "<!hidden fields>\n";

print "<H1>Sun Travel Brochure Listing</H1><HR>\n";
print "<H3>Thank you, $name.<BR>\n";
print "Please select from our list of brochures:</H3>\n";
print "<SELECT NAME=Brochure SIZE=4>\n";
print "<OPTION VALUE=Aruba SELECTED>Aruba\n";
print "<OPTION VALUE=California>California\n";
print "<OPTION VALUE=Florida>Florida\n";
print "<OPTION VALUE=Jamaica>Jamaica\n";
print "</SELECT><BR><BR>\n";

print "<INPUT TYPE=submit VALUE=Submit>\n";
print "</FORM></BODY></HTML>\n";
```

your shebang line might be different

this line might include the –debug pragma

your server name will appear here

creates the Brochure Listing form

Figure 10-6   Additional code entered in the sun1.cgi script

You use the HTML <SELECT>, <OPTION>, and </SELECT> tags to include a selection list element on a Web page. By default, a selection list allows the user to select only one item in the list. To allow the user to select multiple items, you include the MULTIPLE property in the SELECT tag. In Hands-on Project 2 at the end of this chapter, you modify the sun1.cgi script so that it allows the user to select more than one brochure from the listing of available brochures.

6. Save the sun1.cgi document.

Step 2 in the algorithm is to create the Brochure Listing form. Most of the code for Step 2 is already entered in the sun1.cgi script. Before you can complete the step, you need to learn how to create a hidden field.

Creating a Hidden Field in a Script

A hidden field is similar to any other form element in that it has both a *key* and a *value*. The *key* and *value* associated with a hidden field are passed to the server together with the *keys* and *values* of the other elements on the form. Unlike other form elements, however, a hidden field is not visible on the form.

Although a hidden field is not visible on the form, its HTML tag is visible when you view the form's source code.

You can use a hidden field in a form created by a CGI script to save information that would be lost when the connection to the server is closed. For example, you can use hidden fields in the Brochure Listing form created by the sun1.cgi script to save the user's name and e-mail address, which were passed to the script. Figure 10-7 shows the syntax and examples of including a hidden field in a form created by a CGI script.

Syntax
print "<INPUT TYPE=hidden NAME=*name* VALUE=*value*>\n";
Examples
Example 1
print "<INPUT TYPE=hidden NAME=H_zip VALUE=60514>\n";
Example 2
print "<INPUT TYPE=hidden NAME=H_hours VALUE=$hours>\n";
Example 3
print "<INPUT TYPE=hidden NAME=H_name VALUE='Ann Smith'>\n";
Example 4
print "<INPUT TYPE=hidden NAME=H_state VALUE='$state'>\n";

Figure 10-7   Syntax and examples of including a hidden field in a form created by a CGI script

10

It is not necessary to begin a hidden field's name with the letter H followed by an underscore. However, using this naming convention helps to distinguish the hidden fields from the other elements in the form.

The `print "<INPUT TYPE=hidden NAME=H_zip VALUE=60514>\n";` statement in Example 1 creates a hidden field whose *key* and *value* are H_zip and 60514, respectively. Similarly, Example 2's statement, `print "<INPUT TYPE=hidden NAME=H_hours VALUE=$hours>\n";`, creates a hidden field whose *key* is H_hours and whose *value* is the contents of the `$hours` variable. If the *value* assigned to a hidden field contains a space, or if it may contain a space, you enclose the *value* in single quotation marks, as shown in both Example 3 (`'Ann Smith'`) and Example 4 (`'$state'`) in Figure 10-7.

You will use two hidden fields in the sun1.cgi script. One hidden field will store the name received by the script, and the other will store the e-mail address. You are storing this information in hidden fields so that the browser can pass the information to the sun2.cgi script when the user clicks the Submit button on the Brochure Listing form.

To finish coding the sun1.cgi script, and then test the script from the command line:

1. Position the insertion point in the blank line below the `print "<!hidden fields>\n";` statement.

   It is a standard practice to put all hidden fields in one place, typically at the beginning of the form.

2. Type the two statements shaded in Figure 10-8, which shows the completed sun1.cgi script.

```
#!/usr/bin/perl
#sun1.cgi - displays a dynamic Web page listing available brochures
print "Content-type: text/html\n\n";
use CGI qw(:standard);

#prevent Perl from creating undeclared variables
use strict;

#declare and assign values to variables
my ($name, $email);
$name = param('Name');
$email = param('Email');

#create Brochure Listing form
print "<HTML>\n";
print "<HEAD><TITLE>Sun Travel</TITLE></HEAD>\n";
print "<BODY>\n";
print "<FORM
        ACTION='http://yourservername/cgi-bin/chap10/sun2.cgi'
        METHOD=POST>\n";
```

Figure 10-8   Completed sun1.cgi script

```
print "<!hidden fields>\n";
print "<INPUT TYPE=hidden NAME=H_name VALUE='$name'>\n";
print "<INPUT TYPE=hidden NAME=H_email VALUE=$email>\n";

print "<H1>Sun Travel Brochure Listing</H1><HR>\n";
print "<H3>Thank you, $name.<BR>\n";
print "Please select from our list of brochures:</H3>\n";
print "<SELECT NAME=Brochure SIZE=4>\n";
print "<OPTION VALUE=Aruba SELECTED>Aruba\n";
print "<OPTION VALUE=California>California\n";
print "<OPTION VALUE=Florida>Florida\n";
print "<OPTION VALUE=Jamaica>Jamaica\n";
print "</SELECT><BR><BR>\n";

print "<INPUT TYPE=submit VALUE=Submit>\n";
print "</FORM></BODY></HTML>\n";
```

Figure 10-8   Completed sun1.cgi script (continued)

3. Save the sun1.cgi script.

4. *If you are using a UNIX system*, open a terminal window, if necessary. Make the cgi-bin/chap10 directory the current directory, and then change the sun1.cgi file permissions to **755**.

   If you are using a Windows system, open a Command Prompt window, and then make the cgi-bin\chap10 directory the current directory.

5. Type **perl –c sun1.cgi** and press **Enter** to check the script for syntax errors. If necessary, correct any syntax errors in the script before continuing to the next step.

6. Type **perl –w sun1.cgi** and press **Enter**. When the offline mode message appears, type **Name=Helen+Jonas** and press **Enter**, then type **Email=hj@job.com** and press **Enter**.

7. Press **Ctrl+d** (UNIX), or press **Ctrl+z** and then press **Enter** (Windows), to indicate that you are finished entering the data. See Figure 10-9. (Figure 10-9 shows the output in a terminal window in UNIX. The output will look similar if you are using a Command Prompt window in Windows.)

10

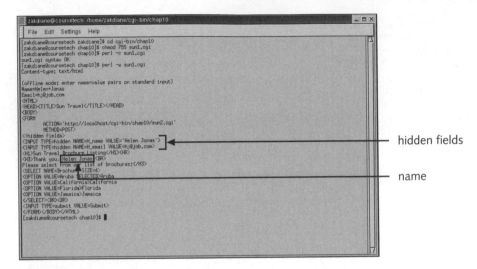

hidden fields

name

Figure 10-9   Result of executing the sun1.cgi script using the -w switch

Next, you complete the sun2.cgi script.

PLANNING AND CODING THE SUN2.CGI SCRIPT

Figure 10-10 shows the input, output, and algorithm for the second Sun Travel script, which is named sun2.cgi.

Input	Output
brochure selection name e-mail address	Web page containing an acknowledgment message E-mail containing an acknowledgment message
Algorithm	
1. assign input items to variables 2. create a dynamic Web page that displays an acknowledgment message, which should include the brochure selection and name 3. send an e-mail message that acknowledges receipt of the brochure request and includes the brochure selection and name	

Figure 10-10   Input, output, and algorithm for the sun2.cgi script

Notice that the sun2.cgi script's input is the brochure selection, as well as the user's name and e-mail address. The output is an acknowledgment message displayed on a Web page and also sent to the user by e-mail.

On your computer system is a partially completed script named sun2.cgi. In the next set of steps, you open the script and begin completing its code.

To begin completing the sun2.cgi script:

1. Open the sun2.cgi script in a text editor. The file is contained in the cgi-bin/chap10 directory.

2. If necessary, change the shebang line to reflect the location of the Perl interpreter on your system.

3. If necessary, add the **-debug** pragma to the **use CGI qw(:standard);** statement.

   The first step in the sun2.cgi script's algorithm is to assign the input items to variables.

4. Enter the code shaded in Figure 10-11, then save the sun2.cgi document.

```perl
#!/usr/bin/perl  ◄────────────────────────────────
#sun2.cgi - displays a dynamic Web page and sends e-mail that
#acknowledges the request for information

print "Content-type: text/html\n\n";
use CGI qw(:standard);  ◄───────────────────────

#prevent Perl from creating undeclared variables
use strict;

#declare variables
my ($brochure, $name, $email, $msg);

#assign input items to variables
$brochure = param('Brochure');
$name = param('H_name');
$email = param('H_email');

#create message
$msg = "Thank you, $name. We have received your request for a \n";
$msg = $msg . "brochure on $brochure. We will mail the brochure \n";
$msg = $msg . "to you as soon as possible.";

#create Web page acknowledgment
print "<HTML>\n";
print "<HEAD><TITLE>Sun Travel</TITLE></HEAD>\n";
print "<BODY>\n";
print "<H1>Sun Travel</H1><HR>\n";
print "<H2>$msg</H2>\n";
print "</BODY></HTML>\n";

#send e-mail acknowledgment
```

your shebang line might be different

this line might include the –debug pragma

10

Figure 10-11   Additional code entered in the sun2.cgi script

Step 2 in the sun2.cgi script's algorithm is to create a dynamic Web page that displays an acknowledgment message. The code for Step 2 is already entered in the sun2.cgi script.

Step 3 in the algorithm is to e-mail an acknowledgment message to the user. Before learning how to send an e-mail message using a script, you will test the sun2.cgi script to see if it is working correctly.

To test the sun2.cgi script:

1. *If you are using a UNIX system*, return to the UNIX command prompt. The cgi-bin/chap10 directory should be the current directory. Change the sun2.cgi file permissions to **755**.

   If you are using a Windows system, return to the Command Prompt window. The cgi-bin\chap10 directory should be the current directory.

2. Type **perl –c sun2.cgi** and press **Enter** to check the script for syntax errors. If necessary, correct any syntax errors in the script before continuing to the next step.

3. Type **perl –w sun2.cgi** and press **Enter**. When the offline mode message appears, type **Brochure=Aruba** and press **Enter**. Type **H_name=Helen+Jonas** and press **Enter**, then type **H_email=hj@job.com** and press **Enter**.

4. Press **Ctrl+d** (UNIX), or press **Ctrl+z** and then press **Enter** (Windows), to indicate that you are finished entering the data. See Figure 10-12.

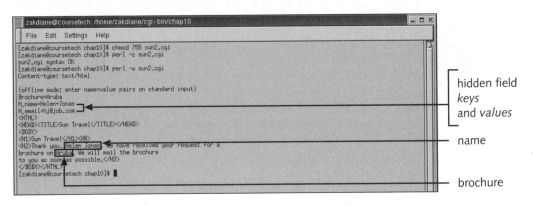

Figure 10-12   Result of executing the sun2.cgi script using the -w switch

Now test the Sun Travel Web site using your Web browser.

5. Start your Web browser. Use the browser's File menu to open the sun.html file.

6. Type **Pamela Turner** in the Name text box, then type **pam@jrc.com** in the E-mail address text box. Click the **Send Me A Brochure** button. If necessary, click the **Continue Submission** button. A Web page similar to the one shown earlier in Figure 10-3 appears on the screen.

7. Click **Jamaica** in the selection list, then click the **Submit** button. If necessary, click the **Continue Submission** button. A Web page similar to the one shown earlier in Figure 10-4 appears on the screen.

8. Close your browser.

Next, you learn how to send e-mail from a script.

Important note: Before you can complete the following section, the Mail::Sendmail module must be installed on your computer system. If you are not sure whether the module has been installed, type whereis Sendmail.pm at the UNIX command prompt. If you are using a Windows system, click Start, point to Search, click For Files or Folders, type Sendmail.pm in the Search for files or folders named text box, and then click the Search Now button. (The Read This Before You Begin section contains the instructions for installing the Mail::Sendmail module.)

USING A SCRIPT TO SEND E-MAIL

Many Perl programmers have created e-mail routines that simplify the process of sending e-mail from a script. One such routine is contained in a platform-independent module named Mail::Sendmail. To use the e-mail routine contained in the module, you simply follow the procedure outlined in Figure 10-13.

10

Procedure for using the Mail::Sendmail module in a CGI script	
1. enter the use `Mail::Sendmail;` statement 2. create a hash and assign a *value* to each *key* listed below 3. enter the `sendmail(`*hash*`);` statement, where *hash* is the name of the hash created in Step 2	
key	*value*
`To`	recipient's e-mail address
`From`	sender's e-mail address
`Subject`	message subject (will appear in the e-mail's Subject line)
`Smtp`	sender's SMTP server (for example, 'course.com')
`Message`	message to send to the recipient

Figure 10-13   Mail::Sendmail procedure

The Mail::Sendmail module was written by Milivoj Ivkovic.

SMTP, which stands for "Simple Mail Transfer Protocol," is the protocol used when sending and receiving e-mail.

For a script to use the e-mail routine contained in the Mail::Sendmail module, it must include the use Mail::Sendmail; statement. The e-mail routine requires you to store the e-mail information in a hash, using the *keys* To, From, Subject, Smtp, and Message. Notice that you assign the recipient's e-mail address to the To *key*, and the sender's e-mail address to the From *key*. You assign the subject of the e-mail message to the Subject *key*, and the name of the sender's SMTP server to the Smtp *key*. Lastly, you assign the e-mail message itself to the Message *key*.

After assigning the appropriate *values* to the *keys* listed in Figure 10-13, you then tell the script to actually send the e-mail using a statement that follows the syntax **sendmail(***hash***);**. In the syntax, *hash* is the name of the hash containing the e-mail information. You will use the Mail::Sendmail module in the sun2.cgi script to send the user an acknowledgment message.

To complete the sun2.cgi script, then test the script:

1. Return to the sun2.cgi document in your text editor. In the blank line below the use CGI qw(:standard); or use CGI qw(:standard -debug); statement, type **use Mail::Sendmail;** and press **Enter**.

2. Change the my ($brochure, $name, $email, $msg); statement to **my ($brochure, $name, $email, $msg, %mail);**.

3. Enter the additional lines of code shaded in Figure 10-14, which shows the completed sun2.cgi script. Be sure to replace 'your e-mail address' with your e-mail address enclosed in single quotation marks. Also replace 'your SMTP server' with the name of your SMTP server enclosed in single quotation marks.

```
#!/usr/bin/perl
#sun2.cgi - displays a dynamic Web page and sends e-mail that
#acknowledges the request for information

print "Content-type: text/html\n\n";
use CGI qw(:standard);
use Mail::Sendmail;

#prevent Perl from creating undeclared variables
use strict;

#declare variables
my ($brochure, $name, $email, $msg, %mail);

#assign input items to variables
$brochure = param('Brochure');
$name = param('H_name');
$email = param('H_email');
```

Figure 10-14   Completed sun2.cgi script

```
#create message
$msg = "Thank you, $name. We have received your request for a \n";
$msg = $msg . "brochure on $brochure. We will mail the brochure \n";
$msg = $msg . "to you as soon as possible.";

#create Web page acknowledgment
print "<HTML>\n";
print "<HEAD><TITLE>Sun Travel</TITLE></HEAD>\n";
print "<BODY>\n";
print "<H1>Sun Travel</H1><HR>\n";
print "<H2>$msg</H2>\n";
print "</BODY></HTML>\n";

#send e-mail acknowledgment
$mail{To} = $email;
$mail{From} = 'your e-mail address';
$mail{Subject} = 'Travel Information';
$mail{Smtp} = 'your SMTP server';
$mail{Message} = $msg;
sendmail(%mail);
```

Figure 10-14   Completed sun2.cgi script (continued)

10

4. Save the sun2.cgi document.

5. *If you are using a UNIX system*, return to the UNIX command prompt. The cgi–bin/chap10 directory should be the current directory.

   If you are using a Windows system, return to the Command Prompt window. The cgi–bin\chap10 directory should be the current directory.

6. Type **perl –c sun2.cgi** and press **Enter** to check the script for syntax errors. If necessary, correct any syntax errors in the script before continuing to the next step.

   Important note: If you do not have an e-mail account, you will not be able to complete the following steps. You can obtain a free e-mail account from a number of sources on the Web—such as hotmail.com and yahoo.com.

7. Connect to the Internet, if necessary. Start your Web browser. Use the browser's File menu to open the sun.html file.

8. Type your name in the Name text box, then type your e-mail address in the E-mail address text box. Click the **Send Me A Brochure** button. If necessary, click the **Continue Submission** button.

9. When the Brochure Listing form appears on the screen, click **Florida** in the selection list, then click the **Submit** button. If necessary, click the **Continue Submission** button. The sun2.cgi script displays the acknowledgment Web page on the screen, and also e-mails you an acknowledgment message.

10. Check your e-mail account to verify that you received the appropriate e-mail from the script.

11. Close your browser and any open windows.

CHAPTER SUMMARY

❑ A selection list is a list box from which the user can select a particular value or set of values.

❑ You can use a hidden field to pass information from one CGI script to another.

❑ Like other form elements, a hidden field has a *key* and a *value*. The *key* and *value* associated with a hidden field are passed to the server just like any other *key* and *value*.

❑ Unlike other form elements, a hidden field does not appear on the form.

❑ You can use the Mail::Sendmail module to send e-mail from a script. To use the module, the script must contain the statement **use Mail::Sendmail;**.

❑ You enter the information you want to send by e-mail in a hash, using the *keys* To, From, Subject, Smtp, and Message. You send the e-mail using a statement that follows the syntax **sendmail(***hash***);**.

REVIEW QUESTIONS

1. Assume you use your browser to request a static Web page from the server. After the server delivers the page to the browser, the connection between your computer and the server is closed.

   a. true

   b. false

2. Which of the following form elements can be used to display a set of predefined choices on a form?

   a. check boxes

   b. option buttons

   c. selection list

   d. All of the above.

3. A hidden field is so named because it does not appear on the form and its HTML tag is invisible in the form's source code.

   a. true

   b. false

4. Which of the following creates a hidden field named H_book and assigns the contents of the `$title` variable to it?

   a. `print "<INPUT TYPE=hidden NAME=H_book VALUE=$title>\n";`

   b. `print "<INPUT TYPE=hidden NAME=H_book VALUE="$title">\n";`

   c. `print "<INPUT TYPE=hidden NAME=H_book VALUE='$title'>\n";`

   d. `print "<INPUT TYPE=hidden KEY=H_book VALUE=$title>\n";`

5. Which of the following creates a hidden field named H_age and assigns the number 25 to it?

   a. `print "<INPUT TYPE=hidden KEY=H_age VALUE=25>\n";`

   b. `print "<INPUT TYPE=hidden KEY=H_age VALUE="25">\n";`

   c. `print "<INPUT TYPE=hidden NAME=H_age VALUE=25>\n";`

   d. Both a and b.

6. You can use the _____ module to send e-mail from a script.

   a. Mail::Sendmail

   b. Sendmail::Mail

   c. Mail_Sendmail

   d. Sendmail_Mail

7. When using the module from Question 6, which of the following statements actually sends the e-mail? (Assume the hash that contains the information is named `%mailinfo`).

   a. `mail{%mailinfo};`

   b. `send{%mailinfo};`

   c. `sendmail[%mailinfo];`

   d. None of the above.

8. When using the module from Question 6, which of the following statements assigns the sender's e-mail address to the %mailinfo hash? The e-mail address is stored in the `$add` variable.

   a. `$mailinfo{From}=$add;`

   b. `$mailinfo{Sender}=$add;`

   c. `%mailinfo{From}=$add;`

   d. `%mailinfo{Sender}=$add;`

10

9. When using the module from Question 6, which of the following *keys* is associated with the e-mail message itself?

    a. `Email`

    b. `Emsg`

    c. `Message`

    d. `Msg`

10. The name of a hidden field must begin with the letter H followed by an underscore.

    a. true

    b. false

11. Why is it a good idea to use a selection list rather than a text box when you have a fixed set of possible values?

12. A _____ is a list box from which the user can select one or more values.

13. In what way does a hidden field differ from other form elements?

14. Write a Perl statement that creates a hidden field whose *key* and *value* are H_city and Boston, respectively.

15. Write a Perl statement that creates a hidden field whose *key* and *value* are H_city and San Diego, respectively.

16. Write a Perl statement that creates a hidden field whose *key* is H_city and whose *value* is the contents of the `$city` variable.

17. Assume you are using the module from Question 6 to send e-mail from a script. Write the statement to assign the e-mail message, which is stored in the `$msg` variable, to the appropriate *key* in the `%mail` hash.

18. Assume you are using the module from Question 6 to send e-mail from a script. Write the statement to assign the subject, which is stored in the `$subject` variable, to the appropriate *key* in the `%mail` hash.

19. Assume you are using the module from Question 6 to send e-mail from a script. Write the statement to send the e-mail message. The e-mail information is stored in a hash named `%email`.

20. What does SMTP stand for?

HANDS-ON PROJECTS

Project 1

In this project, you modify the first Sun Travel script so that it removes any leading and trailing spaces from the name and e-mail address entered on the Brochure Request form. The script also should verify that the input data is not blank, and that the e-mail address is in the correct format.

a. Open the sun.html file in a text editor. The file is contained in the public_html/chap10 directory.

b. Change the filename in the first line from sun.html to c10ex1.html.

c. Modify the <FORM> tag to refer to the c10ex1.cgi script.

d. Save the document as c10ex1.html.

e. Open the sun1.cgi file in a text editor. The file is contained in the cgi-bin/chap10 directory.

f. Change the filename in the second line from sun1.cgi to c10ex1.cgi.

g. Save the document as c10ex1.cgi.

h. Modify the script so that it removes the leading and trailing spaces from the name and e-mail address passed to the script.

i. Modify the script so that it displays an appropriate Web page if the name and/or e-mail address passed to the script are blank, or if the e-mail address is not in the correct format.

j. Save the c10ex1.cgi document.

k. *If you are using a UNIX system*, change the c10ex1.cgi file permissions to 755.

l. Test the script from the command line using the –c and –w switches.

m. Connect to the Internet, if necessary, then open the c10ex1.html document in your Web browser. Test the Sun Travel Web site using both valid and invalid data.

10

Project 2

In this project, you modify the first Sun Travel script so that it allows the user to select more than one brochure from the selection list. You also modify the second Sun Travel script to accommodate this change.

a. Open the sun.html file in a text editor. The file is contained in the public_html/chap10 directory.

b. Change the filename in the first line from sun.html to c10ex2.html.

c. Modify the <FORM> tag to refer to the c10ex2a.cgi script.

d. Save the document as c10ex2.html.

e. Open the sun1.cgi file in a text editor. The file is contained in the cgi-bin/chap10 directory.

f. Change the filename in the second line from sun1.cgi to c10ex2a.cgi.

g. Change the filename in the <FORM> tag from sun2.cgi to c10ex2b.cgi.

h. Save the document as c10ex2a.cgi.

i. Include the MULTIPLE property in the <SELECT> tag. (*Hint*: Simply insert the word MULTIPLE between the NAME and SIZE properties.)

j. Save the c10ex2a.cgi document.

k. Open the sun2.cgi file in a text editor. The file is contained in the cgi-bin/chap10 directory.

l. Change the filename in the second line from sun2.cgi to c10ex2b.cgi, then save the document as c10ex2b.cgi.

m. Modify the script so that it accepts one or more *values* for the Brochure *key*.

n. Modify the message assigned to the $msg variable so that it lists each of the brochures requested by the user.

o. Save the c10ex2b.cgi document.

p. *If you are using a UNIX system*, change the c10ex2a.cgi file permissions to 755. Also change the c10ex2b.cgi file permissions to 755.

q. Test the c10ex2b.cgi script from the command line using the –c switch.

r. Connect to the Internet, if necessary, then open the c10ex2.html document in your Web browser and test the Sun Travel Web site. (*Hint*: To select multiple items in a selection list, you might need to press and hold down the Ctrl key as you click each item you want to select. To deselect an item, you might need to press and hold down the Ctrl key as you click the item.)

Project 3

In this project, you use a hidden field to store the background color chosen by the user.

a. Open the color.html file in a text editor. The file is contained in the public_html/chap10 directory. The document displays a Web page that allows the user to select one of four different colors. The selected color will be used as the background color when displaying pages on the Maribeth Designs Web site.

b. Change the filename in the first line from color.html to c10ex3.html.

c. Change yourservername in the <FORM> tag to the name of your server.

d. Save the document as c10ex3.html.

e. Open the color1.cgi file in a text editor. The file is contained in the cgi-bin/chap10 directory. Change the filename in the second line from color1.cgi to c10ex3a.cgi. Change yourservername in the <FORM> tag to the name of your server.

f. Save the document as c10ex3a.cgi.

g. Declare a variable to store the color choice, then assign the value received from the server to the variable.

h. Modify the script so that it saves the color choice in a hidden field. Also complete the BGCOLOR property in the <BODY> tag.

i. Save the c10ex3a.cgi document.

j. Open the color2.cgi file in a text editor. Change the filename in the second line from color2.cgi to c10ex3b.cgi.

k. Save the document as c10ex3b.cgi.

l. Declare a variable to store the color choice, then assign the value received from the server to the variable.

m. Complete the BGCOLOR property in the <BODY> tag.

n. Save the c10ex3b.cgi document.

o. *If you are using a UNIX system*, change the c10ex3a.cgi file permissions to 755. Also change the c10ex3b.cgi file permissions to 755.

p. Test the scripts from the command line using the –c switch.

q. Open the c10ex3.html document in your Web browser and test the Maribeth Designs Web site.

Project 4

In this project, you modify the Jeffrey Sikes Band script that you created in Chapter 9. The script will now e-mail a message to fans who sign up on the band's mailing list.

a. Copy the band.html file from the public_html/chap09 directory to the public_html/chap10 directory. Rename the file c10ex4.html.

b. Copy the band.cgi file from the cgi-bin/chap09 directory to the cgi-bin/chap10 directory. Rename the file c10ex4.cgi.

c. Open the c10ex4.html file in a text editor. Change the filename in the first line from band.html to c10ex4.html.

d. Modify the <FORM> tag to refer to the c10ex4.cgi script, which is contained in the cgi-bin/chap10 directory.

e. Save the c10ex4.html document.

f. Open the c10ex4.cgi file in a text editor. Change the filename in the second line from band.cgi to c10ex4.cgi.

g. *If you are using a UNIX system*, change the filename argument in the two `tie` functions from "maillist" to "c10ex4".

If you are using a Windows system, change the filename argument in the two `tie` functions from "chap09/maillist" to simply "c10ex4".

h. Change the filename in the two `die` functions from maillist to c10ex4.

i. Save the c10ex4.cgi document.

j. The script should send an appropriate e-mail message when a fan signs up on the band's mailing list. Modify the script appropriately.

k. Save the c10ex4.cgi document.

l. *If you are using a UNIX system*, change the c10ex4.cgi file permissions to 755.

m. Test the script from the command line using the –c and –w switches.

n. *If you are using a UNIX system*, change the file permissions for the c10ex4.dir and c10ex4.pag files to 666.

o. *If you are using a Windows system*, return to the c10ex4.cgi script in your text editor. Change the filename argument in the two **tie** functions from "c10ex4" to "chap10/c10ex4", then save the c10ex4.cgi document.

p. Connect to the Internet, if necessary, then open the c10ex4.html document in your Web browser. Test the script by adding your name and e-mail address to the mailing list.

Project 5

In this project, you modify the International Coffees script that you created in Chapter 8. The script will now e-mail a message to the customer.

a. Copy the inter.html file from the public_html/chap08 directory to the public_html/chap10 directory. Rename the file c10ex5.html.

b. Copy the inter.cgi file from the cgi-bin/chap08 directory to the cgi-bin/chap10 directory. Rename the file c10ex5.cgi.

c. Open the c10ex5.html file in a text editor. Change the filename in the first line from inter.html to c10ex5.html.

d. Modify the <FORM> tag's ACTION property and the <A> tag's HREF property to refer to the c10ex5.cgi script, which is contained in the cgi-bin/chap10 directory.

e. Save the c10ex5.html document.

f. Open the c10ex5.ori file in a text editor. The file is contained in the cgi-bin/chap10 directory. Save the file as c10ex5.txt, then close the file.

g. Open the c10ex5.cgi file in a text editor. Change the filename in the second line from inter.cgi to c10ex5.cgi.

h. *If you are using a UNIX system*, change the filename argument in the two **open** functions from "comments.txt" to "c10ex5.txt".

If you are using a Windows system, change the filename argument in the two **open** functions from "chap08/comments.txt" to "chap10/c10ex5.txt".

i. Change the filename in the two **die** functions from comments.txt to c10ex5.txt.

j. Save the c10ex5.cgi document.

k. Modify the script so that it e-mails an acknowledgment message to the customer. E-mail the message after displaying the acknowledgment Web page.

l. Save the c10ex5.cgi document.

m. *If you are using a UNIX system*, change the c10ex5.cgi file permissions to 755. Also change the c10ex5.txt file permissions to 666.

n. Test the script from the command line using the –c switch.

o. Connect to the Internet, if necessary, then open the c10ex5.html document in your Web browser. Type your name and e-mail address in the Your name and E-mail address text boxes. Type the comment "Your coffee is good, but pretty expensive." in the Comments text area. Click the Submit Form button. If necessary, click the Continue Submission button. The acknowledgment Web page appears on the screen, and an acknowledgment message is e-mailed to you.

Project 6

In this project, you learn how to use the Mail::Sendmail module to record information in a log file.

a. Open the email.html file in your text editor. The file is contained in the public_html/chap10 directory.

b. Change the filename in the first line from email.html to c10ex6.html.

c. Change yourservername in the <FORM> tag to the name of your server.

d. Save the document as c10ex6.html.

e. Open the email.cgi file in a text editor. Change the filename in the second line from email.cgi to c10ex6.cgi.

f. Save the document as c10ex6.cgi.

g. Assign your e-mail address and server's name to the **$mail{From}** and **$mail{Smtp}** variables, respectively.

h. In the blank line below the **sendmail(%mail);** statement, enter an **open** function that opens a data file named c10ex6.log for append. If the file cannot be opened, display an appropriate message and then exit the script.

The Mail::Sendmail module records a summary of each e-mail request in a variable named **$Mail::Sendmail::log**. The summary includes the information assigned to the **To**, **From**, **Subject**, and **Smtp** *keys*, as well as the date the message was sent and the port number used to send the message.

i. Below the statement you entered in Step h, enter a statement that prints the contents of the **$Mail::Sendmail::log** variable to the c10ex6.log file. Then enter a statement to close the c10ex6.log file.

j. Save the c10ex6.cgi document.

k. *If you are using a UNIX system*, change the c10ex6.cgi file permissions to 755.

l. Test the script from the command line using the –c and –w switches.

m. *If you are using a UNIX system*, change the file permissions for the c10ex6.log file to 666.

n. *If you are using a Windows system*, return to the c10ex6.cgi script in your text editor. Change the filename argument in the **open** function from "c10ex6.log" to "chap10/c10ex6.log", then save the c10ex6.cgi document.

10

o. Connect to the Internet, if necessary, and then open the c10ex6.html document in your Web browser. Test the script twice, using both a valid and an invalid e-mail address.

p. Open the c10ex6.log file in a text editor. The file contains a summary of your e-mail requests.

CASE PROJECTS

1. Create an HTML form and a script that Jason's Cycle Shop can use to keep track of the names and addresses of customers requesting a catalog. Name the form c10case1.html and save it in the public_html/chap10 directory. Name the script c10case1.cgi and save it in the cgi-bin/chap10 directory. The HTML form should allow the user to enter his or her name, street address, city, state, and ZIP code. It also should allow the user to select one of four different catalogs: Cumberland ATV, Polar ATV, Solaris Motorcycle, and Timber Motorcycle. Use a selection list to display the catalog choices. Include a submit button on the form. When the user clicks the submit button, a CGI script should display an acknowledgment message to the customer. It also should e-mail a message to Jerry Kreter, who is in charge of mailing the catalogs. Include the customer's name and address information, as well as the name of the catalog, in the message. (Address the message to Jerry Kreter, but send it to your e-mail address.)

2. Create an HTML form and two scripts for Jerrod Accessories Online. Name the form c10case2.html and save it in the public_html/chap10 directory. Name the scripts c10case2a.cgi and c10case2b.cgi, and save them in the cgi-bin/chap10 directory. The HTML form should contain five check boxes labeled Gold Bracelet, Silver Bracelet, Diamond Necklace, Ruby Earrings, and Pearl Ring. The form also should contain a submit button and a reset button. When the customer clicks the submit button, the c10case2a.cgi script should display a form that allows the customer to enter his or her name, street address, city, state, and ZIP code. The form created by the script also should contain a submit button. When the customer clicks the submit button, the c10case2b.cgi script should display a Web page that contains the customer's name and address information. The Web page also should list the items purchased by the customer.

CHAPTER

11

COOKIES

In this chapter, you will:

♦ Learn the difference between temporary and persistent cookies
♦ Create a cookie
♦ Send a cookie to a Web browser
♦ Access the information stored in a cookie

In Chapter 10, you learned how to use hidden fields to save information that normally would be lost at the end of a session between a Web browser and a Web server. In addition to saving the information in a hidden field, you also can save the information in a cookie.

You may have heard or read some of the common misconceptions about cookies—for example, that cookies can contain viruses, or that they can gain access to the private information stored on your computer system. However, the truth is that a cookie is simply a piece of text; it is not a program, so it cannot pass a virus to your computer or read from your computer's hard disk. A cookie can contain only as much information about you as you disclose on the Web site that creates the cookie. For example, a cookie can contain your e-mail address only if you disclose that information when completing an online form. Similarly, a Web site can retrieve only the information stored in its own cookies. A Web site does not have access to information stored in another site's cookie files, or in any other files stored on your computer's hard disk. In this chapter, you learn how to create and manipulate cookies in a script.

USING A COOKIE

A **cookie** is a piece of data that a Web server can store on your computer, either in RAM (Random Access Memory) or on the hard disk, depending on the life span of the cookie. A cookie allows a Web site to remember something about you, such as the data you entered on a form or the number of times you visited the site. When you return to the site in a future session, the cookie can be retrieved and the appropriate action taken. For example, a Web site can store your name in a cookie on your first visit to the site. When you return to the Web site at a later date, the site can use the information in the cookie to display a customized message, such as "Welcome back, Kareem Menard!"

 Most of your computer's internal memory is composed of RAM (Random Access Memory) chips, which can be both written to and read from.

 Cookies are commonly used in shopping cart applications to store an ID that identifies a customer's record in a database. Cookies also are used to store user's preferences, such as the language and background color to use when displaying a Web page.

Every cookie contains a *key* and a *value*, and can contain optional information, such as an expiration date. A cookie can be either temporary or persistent. A **temporary cookie**, also called a **session cookie**, is stored in your computer's RAM and exists only while the browser is open; it is erased from the computer's internal memory when you close the browser. A **persistent cookie**, on the other hand, is stored in a text file on your computer's hard disk, where it remains (or persists) even when you close the browser. Persistent cookies have an expiration date that tells your browser when the cookie should be deleted.

 Netscape stores persistent cookies in a file named cookies.txt. The file typically is contained in the Netscape directory. Internet Explorer 5 stores each persistent cookie in a separate file and begins each file name with your username; the individual files are contained in the Cookies directory.

Your browser keeps track of all the cookies sent to it by a particular server. When you enter a URL in your browser, the browser searches your computer's RAM and hard disk for any cookies belonging to the server. It then contacts the server and transmits the cookies (if any) to the server along with the URL.

The CGI.pm module, which you learned about in Chapter 2, contains functions that allow you to easily create and retrieve cookies in a script. First learn how to create a cookie.

 Recall that the CGI.pm module also contains the `param` function, which is used to parse the data passed to a script.

Creating a Cookie

The CGI.pm module provides the **cookie function** for creating a cookie. Figure 11-1 shows the basic syntax of the **cookie** function.

Syntax

cookie(-name => *key*,
       -value => *value*,
       -path => *path*,
       -expires => *expires*);

Parts	Description
key	*Key*, which is required, is the name of the *value* listed in the –value argument and can be a string, number, or scalar variable.
value	*Value*, which is required, is the value of the cookie and can be a string, number, scalar variable, array, or hash.
path	*Path*, which is optional, indicates the scripts to which the cookie will be sent. If you omit the –path argument, the cookie is sent to all scripts on the server.
expires	*Expires*, which is optional, indicates when the cookie will expire. If you omit the –expires argument, the cookie expires when the browser is closed. The valid *expires* settings are listed below. Setting The cookie will expire +*n*s in *n* seconds +*n*m in *n* minutes +*n*h in *n* hours +*n*d in *n* days now immediately +*n*M in *n* months +*n*Y in *n* years

11

Figure 11-1   Basic syntax of the **cookie** function used to create a cookie

 As you will learn later in this chapter, you also use the **cookie** function to access the data stored in a cookie.

The **cookie** function also has optional arguments named **–domain** and **–secure**. You use the **–domain** argument to specify the domain for which the cookie is valid. The default domain is the domain of the script that creates the cookie. When used, the **–secure** argument is set to the number 1 to indicate that a secure connection, such as SSL, is needed for the cookie to be transmitted. SSL stands for Secure Sockets Layer and is a protocol for transmitting private documents using the Internet.

Notice that the **cookie** function has four arguments named **–name**, **–value**, **–path**, and **–expires**; only the **–name** and **–value** arguments are required. The => operator in the syntax is called the **"corresponds to" operator** and is used to associate each argument with a value. For example, the "corresponds to" operator associates the **–name** argument with the cookie's *key*, and the **–value** argument with the cookie's *value*.

You also can use a comma in place of the "corresponds to" operator in the cookie function. In other words, you can use "**-name,** *key*" rather than "**-name =>** *key*" to match the **–name** argument with the *key*. However, most Perl programmers use the "corresponds to" operator.

You use the **–path** argument, which is optional, to indicate the scripts that are allowed to receive the cookie. For example, the argument **-path => "/cgi-bin"** directs the server to send the cookie to all scripts contained in the "/cgi-bin" directory. The cookie also will be sent to scripts contained in subdirectories of the "/cgi-bin" directory, such as the "/cgi-bin/chap11" and "/cgi-bin/payroll" directories.

The **–expires** argument is optional when creating a temporary (or session) cookie; however, it is required when creating a persistent cookie. The **–expires** argument indicates the period after which the cookie will expire. For example, to create a cookie that expires 10 days after it is created, you use the argument **-expires => "+10d"**.

Figure 11-2 shows three examples of using the **cookie** function to create a cookie. As the examples indicate, you assign the **cookie** function's return value to a scalar variable. Scalar variables that contain cookie information often are referred to as cookie variables.

Examples
Example 1
| ```
$C_color = cookie(-name => "Color",
                  -value => "gray",
                  -path => "/cgi-bin/chap11");
``` |
| Example 2 |
| ```
$C_id = cookie(-name    => "Id",
               -value    => "$id",
               -path     => "/cgi-bin",
               -expires  => "+3M");
``` |
| Example 3 |
| ```
$C_record = cookie(-name    => "Record",
                   -value    => "@record",
                   -path     => "/cgi-bin/chap11",
                   -expires  => "+7d");
``` |

Figure 11-2   Examples of using the **cookie** function to create a cookie

It is not necessary to begin a cookie variable's name with the letter C followed by an underscore. However, using this naming convention helps to distinguish the scalar variables that contain cookies from the other scalar variables in the script.
```

The statement shown in Example 1 in Figure 11-2 uses the **cookie** function to create a cookie whose *key* is "Color" and whose *value* is "gray"; it then assigns the cookie to a variable named **$C_color**. The **-path** argument in the **cookie** function indicates that the cookie should be sent to each script contained in the "/cgi-bin/chap11" directory and its subdirectories. Notice that the **cookie** function does not contain the **-expires** argument; as a result, the cookie will expire when the browser is closed.

Example 2's statement uses the **cookie** function to create a cookie whose *key* is "Id" and whose *value* is the contents of the **$id** variable; it then assigns the cookie to a variable named **$C_id**. In this case, the **-path** argument in the **cookie** function indicates that the cookie should be sent to each script contained in the "/cgi-bin" directory and its subdirectories. The **-expires** argument specifies that the cookie will expire three months from its creation date.

Example 3's statement uses the **cookie** function to create a cookie whose *key* is "Record" and whose *value* is the contents of the **@record** array; it then assigns the cookie to a variable named **$C_record**. The **-path** argument in the **cookie** function indicates that the cookie should be sent to each script contained in the "/cgi-bin/chap11" directory and its subdirectories. The **-expires** argument specifies that the cookie will expire seven days after it was created.

 Your browser is constantly performing maintenance on its cookies. Every time you open your browser, the cookies are read in from disk, and every time you close your browser, temporary (or session) cookies are discarded from the computer's memory, and persistent cookies that have expired are deleted from the computer's hard disk.

After creating a cookie and assigning it to a variable, you then use the **header** function to send the cookie to the browser.

Sending a Cookie to the Browser

The CGI.pm module provides the **header** function for sending one or more cookies to a browser. Figure 11-3 shows two versions of the **header** function's syntax. The figure also shows examples of using each syntax version to send one or more cookies to a browser.

11

Syntax

Version 1 – used to send one cookie to a browser

print header(-cookie => *variable*);

Version 2 – used to send multiple cookies to a browser

print header(-cookie => [*variable1, variable2...variableN*]);

Important note: In addition to sending the cookie (or cookies) to the browser, the header function also sends the statement `print "Content-type: text/html\n\n";`. As a result, you do not enter the `print "Content-type: text/html\n\n";` statement in a script that uses the `header` function.

Examples

Version 1 example
```
print header(-cookie => $C_color);
```

Version 2 example
```
print header(-cookie => [$C_id, $C_record]);
```

Figure 11-3   Syntax versions and examples of the `header` function

As Figure 11-3 indicates, you use the Version 1 syntax to send one cookie to the browser, and the Version 2 syntax to send multiple cookies. Notice that, if you have more than one cookie to send, you enclose the names of the cookie variables in square brackets ([]), using a comma to separate one name from the next.

The `print header(-cookie => $C_color);` statement shown in Version 1's example sends one cookie—the cookie whose information is stored in the `$C_color` variable—to the browser. The `print header(-cookie => [$C_id, $C_record]);` statement shown in Version 2's example, on the other hand, sends two cookies to the browser. The information for one of the cookies is stored in the `$C_id` variable, and the information for the other is stored in the `$C_record` variable.

Pay particular attention to the Important note shown in Figure 11-3. In addition to sending any cookie information to the browser, the `header` function also sends the statement `print "Content-type: text/html\n\n";`. As a result, you do not enter the `print "Content-type: text/html\n\n";` statement in a script that uses the `header` function.

If you mistakenly enter the `print "Content-type: text/html\n\n";` statement above the `header` function in a script, the `header` function will not be able to send the cookies to the browser, because all cookies must be sent before the Content-type header line is processed. If you enter the `print "Content-type: text/html\n\n";` statement below the `header` function in a script, the text "Content-type: text/html" will appear on the Web page.

Next you learn how to access the information stored in a cookie.

Accessing the Information Stored in a Cookie

When you enter a URL in your browser, the browser searches your computer's RAM and hard disk for any cookies that belong to the server and are associated with the URL's path. It then contacts the server and transmits the cookies (if there are any) to the server along with the URL. Recall that any form data also is transmitted to the server at this time. If the URL is associated with a script, the server sends the cookie and form data to the script for processing.

Similar to the way you use the **param** function in a script to access form data, you use the **cookie** function in a script to access cookie data. Figure 11-4 shows this version of the **cookie** function's syntax. The figure also shows examples of using the syntax to access the data stored in the cookies created in Figure 11-2.

Syntax
cookie(*key*)
Examples
Example 1
`$color = cookie('Color');` `print "<BODY BGCOLOR=$color>\n";`
Example 2
`$custid = cookie('Id');` `print "Customer id: $custid \n";`
Example 3
`@custrec = split(/ /, cookie('Record'));` `foreach my $rec (@custrec) {` `    print "$rec \n";` `}`

Figure 11-4   Syntax and examples of using the **cookie** function to access cookie data

 You can enclose the *key* in either single quotation marks or double quotation marks; however, most Perl programmers use single quotation marks.

The `$color = cookie('Color');` statement in Example 1 in Figure 11-4 assigns the *value* of the **Color** *key* to the **$color** variable. In this case, the statement assigns the *value* "gray", which is the *value* that was associated with the **Color** *key* when the cookie was created. (You can refer back to Example 1 in Figure 11-2 to verify the *key* and *value*.) The `print "<BODY BGCOLOR=$color>\n";` statement uses the contents of the **$color** variable to set the background color for the Web page generated by the script.

The $custid = cookie('Id'); statement in Example 2 assigns the *value* of the Id *key* to the $custid variable, and the print "Customer id: $custid
\n"; statement displays the contents of the variable on a Web page. If the *value* associated with the Id *key* is "ABC2", then "ABC2" will be assigned to the variable and then displayed on the screen.

As you may remember from Example 3 in Figure 11-2, the *value* associated with the Record *key* is an array. The @custrec = split(/ /, cookie('Record')); statement in Example 3 in Figure 11-4 splits (or divides) the *value* associated with the Record *key* into separate elements based on the space character, and then assigns the elements to the @custrec array. The foreach loop then prints each element on the screen.

Now that you know how to create a cookie and send it to the browser, and also access the information stored in a cookie, you can begin completing the Jubilee Book Club scripts.

THE JUBILEE BOOK CLUB WEB PAGES

On the first day of each month, the Jubilee Book Club displays on its Web site the name of the book that its members should read during the month. Figure 11-5 shows the Jubilee Book Club's home page.

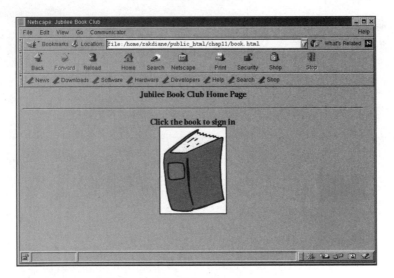

Figure 11-5   Jubilee Book Club's home page

Notice that the home page directs the user to click the book image to sign in. Now view the HTML code used to create the home page.

To view the HTML code used to create the Jubilee Book Club's home page:

1. Open the book.html file in a text editor. The file is contained in the public_html/chap11 directory. Figure 11-6 shows the contents of the file.

```
<!book.html>
<HTML>
<HEAD><TITLE>Jubilee Book Club</TITLE></HEAD>
<BODY>
<H1 ALIGN=center>Jubilee Book Club Home Page</H1><HR>
<H2 ALIGN=center>Click the book to sign in<BR>
<A HREF="http://yourservername/cgi-bin/chap11/book1.cgi">
<IMG SRC=book.jpg></A></H2>
</BODY></HTML>
```

Figure 11-6   HTML code used to create the Jubilee Book Club home page

The <A> tag indicates that the book1.cgi script will be executed when the user clicks the book image on the home page.

2. Change yourservername in the <A> tag to the name of your server.

3. Save the book.html document, and then close the document.

When the user clicks the book image on the book club's home page, the book1.cgi script should display a sign-in form similar to the one shown in Figure 11-7. If this is the first time the user has visited the Jubilee Book Club's Web site, the Name text box on the form should be blank, as shown in the figure. However, if the user has visited the site previously, his or her name should automatically appear in the Name text box. For this to happen, you will need to save the user's name in a cookie, and then retrieve the cookie whenever the user returns to the site.

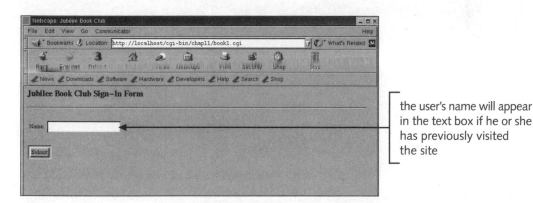

the user's name will appear in the text box if he or she has previously visited the site

Figure 11-7   Sign-in form displayed when the user clicks the book image

When the user clicks the Submit button on the sign-in form, the name entered on the form will be sent to a script named book2.cgi for processing. The book2.cgi script will be responsible for saving the name in a cookie on the user's computer system, and then displaying a Web page similar to the one shown in Figure 11-8. Notice that the Web page contains the user's name, as well as the name and author of the book.

![Netscape browser window titled "Jubilee Book Club" at http://localhost/cgi-bin/chap11/book2.cgi showing "Hello, Janice Wiseman! The book of the month is" and "The Case of the Missing Dagger by H.T. Sims"](netscape-window)

Figure 11-8   Web page displayed when the user signs in

First you will complete the book2.cgi script, which saves the user's name in a cookie. You then will complete the book1.cgi script, which retrieves the cookie information.

PLANNING AND CODING THE book2.cgi SCRIPT

Figure 11-9 shows the input, output, and algorithm for the book2.cgi script.

Input	Output
user's name entered on the sign-in form	cookie containing the user's name
	Web page containing the user's name and the book information
Algorithm	
1. store the user's name in a cookie	
2. create a dynamic Web page that contains the user's name and the book information	

Figure 11-9   Input, output, and algorithm for the book2.cgi script

In Hands-on Project 1 at the end of this chapter, you modify the book2.cgi script so that it removes any leading and trailing spaces from the user's name before the name is saved to a cookie. The modified script also will verify that the user entered a name.

As Figure 11-9 indicates, the script's input is the user's name, which he or she enters on the sign-in form. The output is a cookie containing the user's name, and a Web page containing the user's name and the book information.

On your computer system is a partially completed book2.cgi script. In the next set of steps, you open the script and complete its code.

To complete the book2.cgi script:

1. Open the book2.cgi script in a text editor. The file is contained in the cgi-bin/chap11 directory.

2. If necessary, change the shebang line to reflect the location of the Perl interpreter on your system.

3. If necessary, add the -debug pragma to the use CGI qw(:standard); statement.

   The first step in the algorithm shown in Figure 11-9 is to store the user's name in a cookie. To do so, you first use the **cookie** function to create the cookie, and then use the **header** function to send the cookie to the browser.

4. Enter the code shaded in Figure 11-10, which shows the completed book2.cgi script. (The code for Step 2 in the algorithm is already entered in the script.)

```perl
#!/usr/bin/perl
#book2.cgi - displays a Web page containing the user's
#name and the book information
use CGI qw(:standard);

#prevent Perl from creating undeclared variables
use strict;

#declare variables
my ($name, $C_name);

#assign input to variable
$name = param('Name');

#create cookie
$C_name = cookie(-name => "Name",
                 -value => "$name",
                 -path => "/cgi-bin/chap11",
                 -expires => "+6M");

#send cookie to browser
print header(-cookie => $C_name);

#create Web page
print "<HTML>\n";
print "<HEAD><TITLE>Jubilee Book Club</TITLE></HEAD>\n";
print "<BODY>\n";
print "<H1 ALIGN=center>Hello, $name!<BR>\n";
print "The book of the month is</H1><HR>\n";
print "<H2 ALIGN=center><FONT COLOR=red>\n";
print "<I>The Case of the Missing Dagger</I>\n";
print "<BR>by H.T. Sims\n";
print "</FONT></H2>\n";
print "</BODY></HTML>\n";
```

your shebang line might be different

this line might include the –debug pragma

Figure 11-10   Completed book2.cgi script

11

Notice that the book2.cgi script does not contain the `print "Content-type: text/html\n\n";` line. Recall that the `header` function sends the Content-type header line to the browser for you.

5. Save the book2.cgi document.

The `cookie` function shown in Figure 11-10 creates a cookie whose *key* is "Name" and whose *value* is the contents of the `$name` variable. (The `$name` variable gets its value from the text box element on the sign-in form.) The `-path` argument in the `cookie` function indicates that the cookie should be sent to scripts contained in the "/cgi-bin/chap11" directory and its subdirectories. The `-expires` argument specifies that the cookie will expire six months from its creation date.

Each time the user visits the Jubilee Book Club Web site, the book2.cgi script will create the Name cookie and then send it to the user's browser. The browser will save the Name cookie to the hard disk on the user's computer, overwriting the existing Name cookie (if necessary) and also updating the expiration date. If the user does not return to the Web site within six months of the expiration date, the Name cookie information will be removed from the computer's hard disk.

You could have chosen any expiration period for the cookie.

Next, you complete the book1.cgi script.

PLANNING AND CODING THE book1.cgi SCRIPT

Figure 11-11 shows the input, output, and algorithm for the book1.cgi script.

Input	Output
value stored in the cookie whose key is Name	sign-in form
Algorithm	
1. assign the Name cookie's value to a variable	
2. create the sign-in form, which should	
a. allow the user to enter his or her name	
b. display the user's name if this is his or her second or subsequent visit to the site	

Figure 11-11   Input, output, and algorithm for the book1.cgi script

As Figure 11-11 indicates, the script's input is the value stored in the cookie whose key is Name; recall that the cookie is created and sent to the browser by the book2.cgi script. The output is the sign-in form shown earlier in Figure 11-7.

On your computer system is a partially completed book1.cgi script. In the next set of steps, you open the script and complete its code.

To complete the book1.cgi script:

1. Open the book1.cgi script in a text editor. The file is contained in the cgi-bin/chap11 directory.

2. If necessary, change the shebang line to reflect the location of the Perl interpreter on your system.

3. If necessary, add the **–debug** pragma to the use CGI qw(:standard); statement.

4. Change yourservername in the <FORM> tag to the name of your server.

   The first step in the algorithm shown in Figure 11-11 is to assign the **Name** cookie's value to a variable.

5. In the blank line below the comment **#retrieve Name cookie**, type **$name = cookie('Name');** and press **Enter**.

   The second step in the algorithm is to create the sign-in form. Most of the code for this step is already entered in the script. To complete the script, you need only to modify the VALUE property of the <INPUT> tag that creates the Name text box.

6. Make the modification shaded in Figure 11-12, which shows the completed book1.cgi script.

11

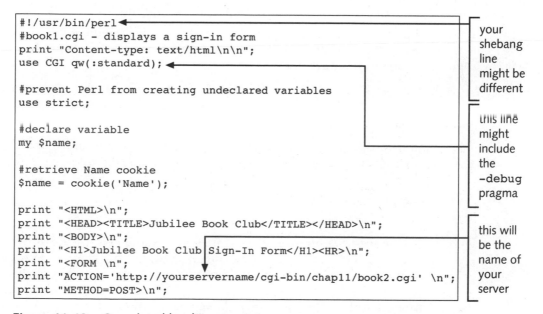

```
#!/usr/bin/perl                                              your
#book1.cgi - displays a sign-in form                         shebang
print "Content-type: text/html\n\n";                         line
use CGI qw(:standard);                                       might be
                                                             different
#prevent Perl from creating undeclared variables
use strict;                                                  this line
                                                             might
#declare variable                                            include
my $name;                                                    the
                                                             -debug
#retrieve Name cookie                                        pragma
$name = cookie('Name');

print "<HTML>\n";
print "<HEAD><TITLE>Jubilee Book Club</TITLE></HEAD>\n";     this will
print "<BODY>\n";                                            be the
print "<H1>Jubilee Book Club Sign-In Form</H1><HR>\n";       name of
print "<FORM \n";                                            your
print "ACTION='http://yourservername/cgi-bin/chap11/book2.cgi' \n";  server
print "METHOD=POST>\n";
```

Figure 11-12   Completed book1.cgi script

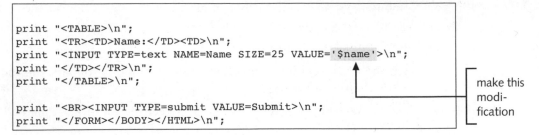

```
print "<TABLE>\n";
print "<TR><TD>Name:</TD><TD>\n";
print "<INPUT TYPE=text NAME=Name SIZE=25 VALUE='$name'>\n";
print "</TD></TR>\n";
print "</TABLE>\n";

print "<BR><INPUT TYPE=submit VALUE=Submit>\n";
print "</FORM></BODY></HTML>\n";
```

make this modification

Figure 11-12   Completed book1.cgi script (continued)

The single quotation marks around the $name variable in the VALUE property are necessary, because the variable typically will contain a space between the user's first and last names. If you do not include the single quotation marks, the text box will display the user's first name only.

7. Save the book1.cgi document.

Now test the book1.cgi and book2.cgi scripts to determine if they are working correctly.

To test the book1.cgi and book2.cgi scripts:

1. *If you are using a UNIX system*, open a terminal window, if necessary. Make the cgi-bin/chap11 directory the current directory, and then change the book1.cgi and book2.cgi file permissions to **755**.

   If you are using a Windows system, open a Command Prompt window, and then make the cgi-bin\chap11 directory the current directory.

2. Type **perl –c book1.cgi** and press **Enter** to check the book1.cgi script for syntax errors. If necessary, correct any syntax errors in the script before continuing to the next step.

3. Type **perl –c book2.cgi** and press **Enter** to check the book2.cgi script for syntax errors. If necessary, correct any syntax errors in the script before continuing to the next step.

4. Start your Web browser. Use the browser's File menu to open the book.html file.

5. Click the book image on the Jubilee Book Club's home page. A sign-in form similar to the one shown earlier in Figure 11-7 appears on the screen. Notice that the Name text box is empty, because this is the first time you have visited the book club's site.

6. Type **Janice Wiseman** in the Name text box, then click the **Submit** button. If necessary, click the **Continue Submission** button. Depending on how it is configured, your browser may display a message informing you that a cookie is being sent to your computer system. If necessary, click the appropriate button to accept the cookie. A Web page similar to the one shown earlier in Figure 11-8 appears on the screen.

7. Close your browser.

8. Start your Web browser again. Use the browser's File menu to open the book.html file.

9. Click the book image on the Jubilee Book Club's home page. The sign-in form appears on the screen, but this time the Name text box contains the name Janice Wiseman.

10. Close your browser and any open windows.

CHAPTER SUMMARY

- A cookie is a piece of data that a Web server can store on your computer, either in RAM (Random Access Memory) or on the hard disk, depending on the life span of the cookie.

- A cookie cannot pass a virus to your computer or read from your computer's hard disk.

- A cookie can contain only as much information about you as you disclose on the Web site that creates the cookie.

- Every cookie contains a *key* and a *value*, and can contain optional information, such as a path and an expiration date.

- A temporary cookie, also called a session cookie, is stored in your computer's RAM and is erased from the computer's internal memory when you close the browser.

- A persistent cookie is stored in a text file on your computer's hard disk. Persistent cookies have an expiration date that tells your browser when the cookie should be deleted.

- Like form data, cookies are sent along with the URL you are requesting.

- You use the `cookie` function, which is defined in the CGI.pm module, to create a cookie. You also use the `cookie` function to access the data stored in a cookie.

- When using the `cookie` function to create a cookie, you must specify the `-name` and `-value` arguments.

- The `=>` operator is called the "corresponds to" operator.

- The `-path` argument in the `cookie` function determines which scripts receive the cookie.

- The `-expires` argument in the `cookie` function indicates the expiration period for the cookie.

- You use the `header` function, which is defined in the CGI.pm module, to send one or more cookies to a browser.

- The `header` function sends the cookie information and the Content-type header line to the browser. Consequently, you do not enter the `print "Content-type: text/html\n\n";` statement in a script that uses the `header` function.

11

REVIEW QUESTIONS

1. A cookie can send a virus to your computer system.

    a. true

    b. false

2. A cookie can read any file stored on your computer's hard disk.

    a. true

    b. false

3. You can use a cookie to _____.

    a. keep track of the items a customer purchased

    b. keep track of the number of times a user visits a Web site

    c. record the information entered on a form

    d. All of the above.

4. In addition to sending one or more cookies to the browser, the `header` function also sends the statement _____.

    a. `print "Content-type: text/html\n\n";`

    b. `use CGI qw(:standard);`

    c. `use strict;`

    d. All of the above.

5. Session cookies are _____.

    a. stored in your computer's internal memory

    b. stored on your computer's hard disk

    c. removed when you close your browser

    d. Both a and c.

6. Which type of cookie remains on your computer's hard disk until its expiration date?

    a. persistent

    b. session

    c. temporary

    d. Both a and c.

7. You can use the _____ function to create a cookie.

    a. `cookies`

    b. `create`

    c. `create_cookie`

    d. None of the above.

8. You can use the _____ function to access the data stored in a cookie.

   a. access

   b. cookie

   c. data

   d. None of the above.

9. Which functions are defined in the CGI.pm module?

   a. cookie

   b. header

   c. param

   d. All of the above.

10. Which of the following `cookie` function arguments tells the browser to remove the cookie after 30 minutes?

    a. expires => "+30m"

    b. -expires => "+30m"

    c. expires => "+30M"

    d. -expires <= "+30M"

11. Where are session cookies stored?

12. Which two arguments are required when using the `cookie` function to create a cookie?

13. Write the statement to create a temporary cookie whose *key* is "Number" and whose *value* is the contents of the `$part_num` variable. The cookie should be passed to the scripts contained in the "/cgi-bin/chap11" directory. Assign the cookie to a variable named `$C_num`.

14. Modify the statement from Question 13 so that it creates a persistent cookie that will expire two years from its creation date.

15. Write the statement to send the cookie created in Question 14 to the browser.

16. Write the statement to retrieve the cookie created in Question 14. Assign the cookie's value to the `$part` variable.

17. Write the statement to send three cookies to the browser. The cookies are stored in variables named `$C_name`, `$C_email`, and `$C_age`.

18. The "corresponds to" operator looks like this: _____

19. Write the `cookie` function argument that tells the browser to delete the cookie immediately.

20. Write the `cookie` function argument that tells the browser to delete the cookie in 24 hours.

HANDS-ON PROJECTS

Project 1

In this project, you modify the second Jubilee Book Club script so that it removes any leading and trailing spaces from the name entered on the sign-in form. The script also should verify that the user entered a name.

    a. Open the book.html file in a text editor. The file is contained in the public_html/chap11 directory.

    b. Change the filename in the first line from book.html to c11ex1.html.

    c. Modify the <A> tag to refer to the c11ex1a.cgi script.

    d. Save the document as c11ex1.html.

    e. Open the book1.cgi file in a text editor. The file is contained in the cgi-bin/chap11 directory.

    f. Change the filename in the second line from book1.cgi to c11ex1a.cgi.

    g. Change the filename in the <FORM> tag from book2.cgi to c11ex1b.cgi.

    h. Save the document as c11ex1a.cgi.

    i. Open the book2.cgi file in a text editor. The file is contained in the cgi-bin/chap11 directory.

    j. Change the filename in the second line from book2.cgi to c11ex1b.cgi, then save the document as c11ex1b.cgi.

    k. Modify the script so that it removes the leading and trailing spaces from the name passed to the script.

    l. Modify the script so that it displays an appropriate Web page if the name passed to the script is blank.

    m. Save the c11ex1b.cgi document.

    n. *If you are using a UNIX system*, change the c11ex1a.cgi and c11ex1b.cgi file permissions to 755.

    o. Test the c11ex1b.cgi script from the command line using the -c switch.

    p. Open the c11ex1.html file in your Web browser, then test the Jubilee Book Club Web site using both valid and invalid data.

Project 2

In this project, you modify the sign-in form created by the first Jubilee Book Club script. The form will now allow the user to also enter his or her e-mail address. You also modify the second Jubilee Book Club script so that it saves the e-mail address in a cookie.

    a. Open the book.html file in a text editor. The file is contained in the public_html/chap11 directory.

b. Change the filename in the first line from book.html to c11ex2.html.

c. Modify the <A> tag to refer to the c11ex2a.cgi script.

d. Save the document as c11ex2.html.

e. Open the book1.cgi file in a text editor. The file is contained in the cgi-bin/chap11 directory.

f. Change the filename in the second line from book1.cgi to c11ex2a.cgi.

g. Change the filename in the <FORM> tag from book2.cgi to c11ex2b.cgi.

h. Save the document as c11ex2a.cgi.

i. Modify the script so that it displays another text box on the sign-in form. The new text box should allow the user to enter his or her e-mail address. Also modify the script so that it retrieves the cookie that stores the e-mail address.

j. Save the c11ex2a.cgi document.

k. Open the book2.cgi file in a text editor. The file is contained in the cgi-bin/chap11 directory.

l. Change the filename in the second line from book2.cgi to c11ex2b.cgi.

m. Save the document as c11ex2b.cgi.

n. Modify the script so that it saves the user's e-mail address to a persistent cookie.

o. Save the c11ex2b.cgi document.

p. *If you are using a UNIX system*, change the c11ex2a.cgi and c11ex2b.cgi file permissions to 755.

q. Test the scripts from the command line using the -c switch.

r. Open the c11ex2.html file in your Web browser, then test the Jubilee Book Club Web site.

Project 3

In this project, you modify the Sun Travel scripts from Chapter 10 so that they use cookies rather than **hidden** fields.

a. Copy the sun.html file from the public_html/chap10 directory to the public_html/chap11 directory. Rename the file c11ex3.html.

b. Copy the sun1.cgi file from the cgi-bin/chap10 directory to the cgi-bin/chap11 directory. Rename the file c11ex3a.cgi.

c. Copy the sun2.cgi file from the cgi-bin/chap10 directory to the cgi-bin/chap11 directory. Rename the file c11ex3b.cgi.

d. Open the c11ex3.html file in a text editor. Change the filename in the first line from sun.html to c11ex3.html.

e. Modify the <FORM> tag to refer to the c11ex3a.cgi script, which is contained in the cgi-bin/chap11 directory.

11

f. Save the c11ex3.html document.

g. Open the c11ex3a.cgi file in a text editor. Change the filename in the second line from sun1.cgi to c11ex3a.cgi.

h. Modify the <FORM> tag to refer to the c11ex3b.cgi script, which is contained in the cgi-bin/chap11 directory.

i. Modify the c11ex3a.cgi script so that it uses two temporary cookies rather than two hidden fields.

j. Save the c11ex3a.cgi document.

k. Open the c11ex3b.cgi file in a text editor.

l. Change the filename in the second line from sun2.cgi to c11ex3b.cgi.

m. Modify the c11ex3b.cgi script so that it retrieves the appropriate cookie information.

n. Save the c11ex3b.cgi document.

o. *If you are using a UNIX system*, change the c11ex3a.cgi and c11ex3b.cgi file permissions to 755.

p. Test the scripts from the command line using the -c switch.

q. Connect to the Internet, if necessary, then open the c11ex3.html document in your Web browser and test the Sun Travel Web site.

Project 4

In this project, you use a cookie to store the background color chosen by the user.

a. Open the color.html file in a text editor. The file is contained in the public_html/chap11 directory. The document displays a Web page that allows the user to select one of four different colors. The selected color will be used as the background color when displaying pages on the Maribeth Designs Web site.

b. Change the filename in the first line from color.html to c11ex4.html.

c. Change yourservername in the <FORM> tag to the name of your server.

d. Save the document as c11ex4.html.

e. Open the color1.cgi file in a text editor. The file is contained in the cgi-bin/chap11 directory. Change the filename in the second line from color1.cgi to c11ex4a.cgi. Also change yourservername in the <FORM> tag to the name of your server.

f. Save the document as c11ex4a.cgi.

g. Modify the script so that it saves the color choice in a temporary cookie. Also complete the BGCOLOR property in the <BODY> tag.

h. Save the c11ex4a.cgi document.

i. Open the color2.cgi file in a text editor. The file is contained in the cgi-bin/chap11 directory. Change the filename in the second line from color2.cgi to c11ex4b.cgi.

j. Save the document as c11ex4b.cgi.

k. Declare a variable to store the color choice, then assign a value to the variable.

l. Complete the BGCOLOR property in the <BODY> tag.

m. Save the c11ex4b.cgi document.

n. *If you are using a UNIX system*, change the c11ex4a.cgi and c11ex4b.cgi file permissions to 755.

o. Test the scripts from the command line using the -c switch.

p. Open the c11ex4.html document in your Web browser and test the Maribeth Designs Web site.

Project 5

In this project, you use a cookie to keep track of the number of times a user visits the Jubilee Book Club Web site.

a. Open the book.html file in a text editor. The file is contained in the public_html/chap11 directory.

b. Change the filename in the first line from book.html to c11ex5.html.

c. Change the <A> tag to refer to the c11ex5.cgi script.

d. Save the document as c11ex5.html.

e. Create a script that uses a cookie to keep track of the number of times the user visits the Jubilee Book Club Web site. The cookie should expire in six months and be available only to scripts stored in the /cgi-bin/chap11 directory. The script also should display a message that contains the number of visits made by the user. Name the script c11ex5.cgi and save it in the cgi-bin/chap11 directory.

f. *If you are using a UNIX system*, change the c11ex5.cgi file permissions to 755.

g. Test the script from the command line using the -c switch.

h. Open the c11ex5.html document in your Web browser and test the script.

11

Project 6

In this project, you use a cookie to keep track of the items purchased by a customer.

a. Open the shop.html file in a text editor. The file is contained in the public_html/chap11 directory.

b. Change the filename in the first line from shop.html to c11ex6.html.

c. Change yourservername in the <FORM> tag to the name of your server.

d. Save the document as c11ex6.html.

e. Create a script that uses a cookie to keep track of the items purchased by a customer. The script should display the items purchased on a Web page. Name the script c11ex6.cgi and save it in the cgi-bin/chap11 directory. (*Hint*: Each time the user clicks the Purchase This Basket button, assign the cookie's current values to an array, and then add the current purchase to the array.)

f. *If you are using a UNIX system*, change the c11ex6.cgi file permissions to 755.

g. Test the script from the command line using the –c switch.

h. Open the c11ex6.html document in your Web browser and test the script.

CASE PROJECTS

1. Create an HTML form and two scripts for Quilts Inc. Name the form c11case1.html and save it in the public_html/chap11 directory. Name the two scripts c11case1a.cgi and c11case1b.cgi, and save them in the cgi-bin/chap11 directory. The HTML form should allow the user to enter his or her name, street address, city, state, and ZIP code. Include a submit button on the form. When the user clicks the submit button, the c11case1a.cgi script should save the customer information in a DBM database named customers. Use the customer's name as the *key*. The c11case1a.cgi script also should save the customer name to a temporary cookie. Additionally, the c11case1a.cgi script should display a form that allows the user to select one of four different catalogs: Baby, Country Prints, Solid Color, and Special Occasion. Include a submit button on the form. When the user clicks the submit button, the c11case1b.cgi script should display on a Web page the customer information and the name of the catalog requested by the customer.

2. Create an HTML form and two scripts for Jarrod Accessories Online. Name the form c11case2.html and save it in the public_html/chap11 directory. Name the scripts c11case2a.cgi and c11case2b.cgi, and save them in the cgi-bin/chap11 directory. The HTML form should contain five check boxes labeled Gold Bracelet, Silver Bracelet, Diamond Necklace, Ruby Earrings, and Pearl Ring. The form also should contain a submit button and a reset button. When the customer clicks the submit button, the c11case2a.cgi script should display a form that allows the customer to enter his or her name, street address, city, state, and ZIP code. The form created by the script also should contain a submit button. When the customer clicks the submit button, the c11case2b.cgi script should display a Web page that contains the customer's name and address information. The Web page also should list the items purchased by the customer. (Use a temporary cookie to allow the two scripts to communicate.)

12

REDIRECTION

It is not uncommon for documents on the Web to be moved from one location to another. In most cases, you will use a "document has moved" Web page to forward the user to the document's new address. A "document has moved" Web page informs the visitor that the document that he or she is requesting has been relocated, and typically includes a link to the document's new URL.

Sometimes, however, you may prefer to automatically forward the visitor's browser to a document's new address, either immediately or after a few seconds have elapsed. You can do so by including a META tag in an HTML document. Or, you can use either the Location header or the Refresh header in a CGI script. In this chapter, you learn how to redirect a browser using the Location and Refresh headers. (You can learn how to include a META tag in an HTML document by completing Hands-on Project 1 at the end of this chapter.)

Redirecting a Browser

You can use either the Location header or the Refresh header in a script to redirect a browser to another location. The **Location header** redirects the browser immediately, whereas the **Refresh header** waits a specified number of seconds before performing the redirection.

Figure 12-1 shows the syntax and an example of the Location and Refresh headers. In each syntax, *url* is the URL of the document to which the browser should be sent; the document can be an HTML file or a CGI script file. *Seconds* in the Refresh header's syntax is the number of seconds the computer will wait before redirecting the browser.

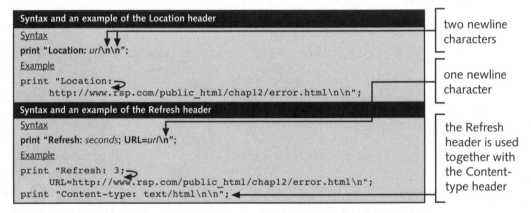

Syntax and an example of the Location header

Syntax
print "Location: *url***\n\n";**

Example
`print "Location:`
`    http://www.rsp.com/public_html/chap12/error.html\n\n";`

two newline characters

one newline character

Syntax and an example of the Refresh header

Syntax
print "Refresh: *seconds***; URL=**url**\n";**

Example
`print "Refresh: 3;`
`    URL=http://www.rsp.com/public_html/chap12/error.html\n";`
`print "Content-type: text/html\n\n";`

the Refresh header is used together with the Content-type header

Figure 12-1   Syntax and an example of the Location and Refresh headers

Notice that Location begins with an uppercase letter L, and Refresh begins with an uppercase letter R.

As Figure 12-1 indicates, both headers begin with the Perl `print` function, whose task is to send the text enclosed in quotation marks to the browser; both headers end with a semicolon, because they are Perl statements. Notice that two newline characters follow the *url* in the Location header's syntax. The first newline character identifies the end of the Location header, and ensures that the header appears on a line by itself. The second newline character inserts a blank line below the header, and signals the browser that it has reached the end of the header information. A script whose task is to redirect the user's browser will contain a Location header rather than a Content-type header. Unlike the Location header, the Refresh header contains one newline character rather than two newline characters. Only one newline character is necessary because the Refresh header is used together with the Content-type header, which contains the newline character that marks the end of the header information.

You also can enter the Refresh header after the Content-type header rather than before it. If you do so, then the Content-type header will contain one newline character, and the Refresh header will contain two newline characters.

Both examples shown in Figure 12-1 tell the computer to redirect the user's browser to the Web page located at http://www.rsp.com/public_html/chap12/error.html. However, the Location header tells the computer to perform the redirection immediately, and the Refresh header tells it to perform the redirection after three seconds have elapsed.

You will use a Refresh header in the next section, and a Location header later in the chapter.

Using a Refresh Header

On your computer system are two HTML documents and a CGI script currently used by Fulton Enterprises. In the next set of steps, you observe how these files currently interact with each other.

1. Open the fulton1.html file in a text editor. The file is contained in the public_html/chap12 directory.

   The <A> tag indicates that the fulton.cgi script will be executed when the user clicks the Catalog Department link.

2. Change yourservername in the <A> tag to the name of your server.

3. Save the fulton1.html document, then close the document.

4. Open the fulton.cgi file in a text editor. The file is contained in the cgi-bin/chap12 directory.

5. If necessary, change the shebang line to reflect the location of the Perl interpreter on your system.

   The <A> tag in the script indicates that the fulton2.html document will be displayed when the user clicks the Click here to be redirected to the document's new location link.

6. Change yourservername in the <A> tag to the name of your server, then save the document.

7. *If you are using a UNIX system*, open a terminal window, if necessary. Make the cgi-bin/chap12 directory the current directory, and then change the fulton.cgi file permissions to **755**.

8. Start your Web browser. Use the browser's File menu to open the fulton1.html document. A Web page similar to the one shown in Figure 12-2 appears on the screen.

12

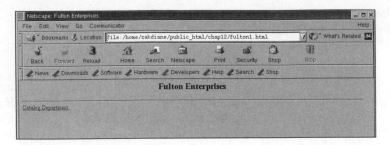

Figure 12-2   Web page created by the fulton1.html file

9. Click **Catalog Department**. The <A> tag associated with the Catalog Department link tells the computer to execute the fulton.cgi script, which displays a Web page similar to the one shown in Figure 12-3.

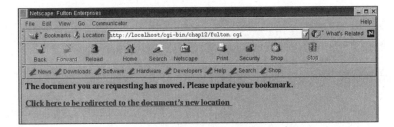

Figure 12-3   Web page displayed by the fulton.cgi script

The Web page informs you that the document that you are requesting has moved, and it advises you to update your bookmark. The Web page also includes a link that you can use to be redirected to the document's new location.

10. Click **Click here to be redirected to the document's new location**. The <A> tag associated with the link tells the computer to process the HTML code contained in the fulton2.html document. A Web page similar to the one shown in Figure 12-4 appears on the screen. In this case, the Web page simply informs you that you have reached the document's new location.

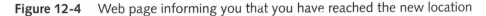

Figure 12-4   Web page informing you that you have reached the new location

In addition to providing a link to the document's new location, you also can have the fulton.cgi script automatically forward a visitor to the new location. To do so, you need simply to include a Refresh header in the script.

To include a Refresh header in the fulton.cgi script:

1. Return to the fulton.cgi document in your text editor.

2. In the blank line above the Content-type header, type **print "Refresh: 3; URL=http://yourservername/public_html/chap12/fulton2.html\n";**. (Be sure to replace yourservername with the name of your server.)

3. Change the `print  "</H2>\n";` statement to **print "You will be taken to the new location in 3 seconds.</H2>\n";**.

4. Change the `print "Click here to be redirected to the document's new location</A>\n";` statement to **print "Click here if you are not redirected in 3 seconds</A>\n";**.

5. Save the fulton.cgi document.

   Figure 12-5 shows the completed fulton.cgi script. The modifications you made to the script are shaded in the figure. (The Refresh header is entered on one line in the script.)

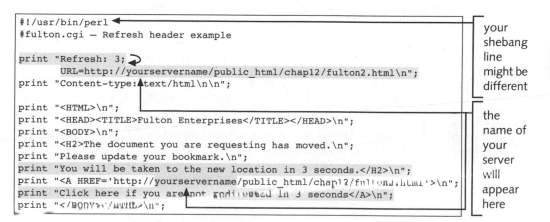

Figure 12-5   Completed fulton.cgi script

6. Return to your Web browser. Use the browser's File menu to open the fulton1.html document. A Web page similar to the one shown earlier in Figure 12-2 appears on the screen.

7. Click **Catalog Department**. A Web page similar to the one shown earlier in Figure 12-3 appears on the screen.

8. Rather than using the link, simply wait three seconds. After the three seconds have elapsed, a Web page similar to the one shown earlier in Figure 12-4 appears on the screen.

9. Minimize your browser.

Next, learn how to include a Location header in a script.

Using a Location Header

On your computer system are an HTML document and a CGI script currently used by Cara Antiques. In the next set of steps, you observe how both files currently interact with each other.

1. Open the cara1.html file in a text editor. The file is contained in the public_html/chap12 directory.

   The document creates a form that contains one text box in which the user enters his or her name. The <FORM> tag indicates that the cara.cgi script will process the form data.

2. Change yourservername in the <FORM> tag to the name of your server.

3. Save the cara1.html document, then close the document.

4. Open the cara.cgi file in a text editor. The file is contained in the cgi-bin/chap12 directory.

5. If necessary, change the shebang line to reflect the location of the Perl interpreter on your system, then save the document.

   The code entered in the cara.cgi document is shown in Figure 12-6. Notice that the code creates a Web page that displays a "Hello" message and the user's name.

```
#!/usr/bin/perl          ◄                    your shebang line might be
#cara.cgi - Location header example           different
print "Content-type: text/html\n\n";
use CGI qw(:standard);
use strict;

#declare and assign value to variable
my $name;
$name = param('Name');

#create Hello page

print "<HTML>\n";
print "<HEAD><TITLE>Cara Antiques</TITLE></HEAD>\n";
print "<BODY>\n";
print "<H1 ALIGN=center>Cara Antiques<HR>\n";
print "Hello, $name!</H1></BODY></HTML>";
```

Figure 12-6   Code contained in the cara.cgi document

6. *If you are using a UNIX system*, open a terminal window, if necessary. Make the cgi-bin/chap12 directory the current directory, and then change the cara.cgi file permissions to **755**.

7. Restore your browser, which you minimized in an earlier set of steps. Use the browser's File menu to open the cara1.html document. A Web page similar to the one shown in Figure 12-7 appears on the screen.

Figure 12-7   Web page created by the cara1.html file

8. Type **Bob** in the Name text box, then click the **Submit** button. The computer executes the cara.cgi script, which displays a Web page similar to the one shown in Figure 12-8.

Figure 12-8   Web page displayed by the cara.cgi script

9. Press the **Back** button to return to the form. Click the **Reset** button, then click the **Submit** button. A Web page similar to the one shown in Figure 12-8 appears, but this time the "Hello" message does not include a name.

Rather than displaying the "Hello" Web page when the user clicks the Submit button without entering a name, you should display an error Web page that advises the user to return to the form to complete it. You can create the error page by including the appropriate HTML code in the cara.cgi script, or you can use the Location header to automatically forward the user to an existing HTML document. You will use a Location header to forward the user to the cara2.html document, which is contained in the public-html/chap12 directory on your computer system.

To include a Location header in the cara.cgi script:

1. Return to the cara.cgi document in your text editor.

2. In the blank line below the `#create Hello page` comment, type **if ($name ne "")** { and press **Enter**.

3. Position the insertion point below the last statement in the script, then type } (the closing brace) to end the `if` clause and press **Enter**.

4. Type **else {** and press **Enter**.

5. Press **Tab** to indent the line, then type **print "Location: http://yourservername/public_html/chap12/cara2.html\n\n";** and press **Enter**. (Be sure to replace yourservername with the name of your server.)

6. Type } (the closing brace) to end the `else` clause and press **Enter**.

   The Content-type header, which currently appears as the third line in the document, is necessary only in the `if` clause in the script, because that is the only clause that sends HTML output to the browser.

7. Move the Content-type header from its current location to the blank line above the `print "<HTML>\n";` statement in the `if` clause. Also, indent the statements within the `if` clause. Save the cara.cgi document. Figure 12-9 shows the completed cara.cgi script. Modifications you made to the script are shaded in the figure. (The Location header is entered on one line in the script.)

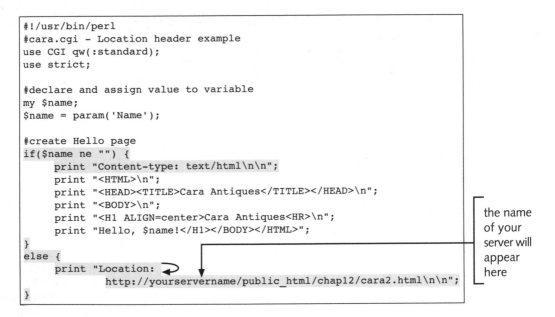

```perl
#!/usr/bin/perl
#cara.cgi - Location header example
use CGI qw(:standard);
use strict;

#declare and assign value to variable
my $name;
$name = param('Name');

#create Hello page
if($name ne "") {
    print "Content-type: text/html\n\n";
    print "<HTML>\n";
    print "<HEAD><TITLE>Cara Antiques</TITLE></HEAD>\n";
    print "<BODY>\n";
    print "<H1 ALIGN=center>Cara Antiques<HR>\n";
    print "Hello, $name!</H1></BODY></HTML>";
}
else {
    print "Location:
            http://yourservername/public_html/chap12/cara2.html\n\n";
}
```

the name of your server will appear here

Figure 12-9   Completed cara.cgi script

8. Return to your Web browser. Use the browser's File menu to open the cara1.html document. A Web page similar to the one shown earlier in Figure 12-7 appears on the screen.

9. Type **Bob** in the Name text box, then click the **Submit** button. The computer executes the cara.cgi script, which displays a Web page similar to the one shown earlier in Figure 12-8.

10. Press the **Back** button to return to the form. Click the **Reset** button, then click the **Submit** button. The script redirects your browser to the error Web page shown in Figure 12-10.

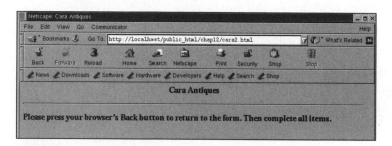

Figure 12-10 Error Web page

11. Close your browser and any open windows.

CHAPTER SUMMARY

❏ You can use the Location header or the Refresh header in a CGI script to redirect the user's browser to another location.

❏ The Location header redirects the browser immediately. The Refresh header waits until a specified number of seconds have elapsed before redirecting the browser.

❏ The syntax of the Location header is **print "Location:** *url*\n\n"**;**, where *url* is the URL of the document to which the browser should be sent.

❏ The syntax of the Refresh header is **print "Refresh:** *seconds***; URL=***url*\n"**;**. In the syntax, *url* is the URL of the document to which the browser should be sent, and *seconds* is the number of seconds to wait before the redirection occurs. The Refresh header is used together with the Content-type header.

REVIEW QUESTIONS

1. You can use a CGI script to redirect a browser to another location.

   a. true

   b. false

2. Which of the following can be used to redirect a browser?

   a. a META tag in an HTML document

   b. a Location header in a CGI script

   c. a Refresh header in a CGI script

   d. All of the above.

3. The _____ header tells the computer to redirect the user's browser after a specified number of seconds have elapsed.

   a. Content-type

   b. Location

   c. Redirect

   d. Refresh

4. Which of the following headers can you use to redirect the user's browser immediately?

   a. Content-type

   b. Location

   c. Redirect

   d. Both b and c.

5. Which of the following headers is used together with the Content-type header?

   a. Location

   b. Redirect

   c. Refresh

   d. All of the above.

6. Which of the following statements tells the computer to redirect the user's browser immediately?

   a. `"Redirect: 0; URL=http://yourservername/public_html/toms.html\n";`

   b. `print "Refresh: 0; URL=http://yourservername/public_html/toms.html\n";`

   c. `print "Location: http://yourservername/public_html/toms.html\n\n";`

   d. Both b and c.

7. Write a Location header that directs the user's browser to the following URL: http://yourservername/cgi-bin/chap12/pay.cgi.

8. Write a Location header that directs the user's browser to the following URL: http://yourservername/public_html/chap12/harper.html.

9. Write a Refresh header that tells the computer to wait five seconds before redirecting the browser to the following URL: http://yourservername/cgi-bin/chap12/pay.cgi.

10. Write a Refresh header that tells the computer to wait 10 seconds before redirecting the browser to the following URL: http://yourservername/public_html/chap12/harper.html.

HANDS-ON PROJECTS

Project 1

In this project, you learn how to include a META tag in an HTML document.

a. Open the fulton1.html file in a text editor. The file is contained in the public_html/chap12 directory.

b. Change the filename in the first line from fulton1.html to c12ex1.html.

c. Remove the <A> tag from the document.

The syntax of the META tag used to redirect the browser is
<META HTTP-EQUIV="Refresh" CONTENT="*seconds***; URL=***url***">**,
where *seconds* is the number of seconds to wait before the browser is redirected to the *url*.

d. Insert <META HTTP-EQUIV="Refresh" CONTENT="5; URL=fulton2.html"> between the <HEAD> and <TITLE> tags.

e. Save the document as c12ex1.html.

f. Open the c12ex1.html file in your Web browser. After three seconds, your browser will be redirected to the fulton2.html document.

Project 2

In this project, you modify the Jackson Elementary School script from Chapter 2 so that it uses the Refresh header to redirect the user's browser to the jackson.html file.

a. Copy the jackson.gif file from the public_html/chap02 directory to the public_html/chap12 directory.

b. Copy the jackson.html file from the public_html/chap02 directory to the public_html/chap12 directory. Rename the file c12ex2.html.

c. Copy the jackson.cgi file from the cgi-bin/chap02 directory to the cgi-bin/chap12 directory. Rename the file c12ex2.cgi.

d. Open the c12ex2.html file in a text editor. Change the filename in the first line from jackson.html to c12ex2.html.

e. Modify the <A> tags to refer to the c12ex2.cgi script, which is contained in the cgi-bin/chap12 directory.

12

f. Save the c12ex2.html document.

g. Open the c12ex2.cgi file in a text editor. Change the filename in the second line from jackson.cgi to c12ex2.cgi.

h. Above the Content-type header, enter a Refresh header that directs the user's browser to the c12ex2.html page after five seconds.

i. Save the c12ex2.cgi document.

j. *If you are using a UNIX system*, change the c12ex2.cgi file permissions to 755.

k. Open the c12ex2.html file in your Web browser. The Jackson Elementary School Web page appears on the screen.

l. Click Alabama. A Web page appears and displays the message "The capital of Alabama is Montgomery." After five seconds, the browser is redirected to the Jackson Elementary School Web page.

Project 3

In this project, you modify the Patton Industries script from Chapter 3 so that it verifies that the user completed the required entries on the form. The modified script will use a Location header to redirect the user's browser to an error Web page if one or more form entries are blank.

a. Copy the bonus.html file from the public_html/chap03 directory to the public_html/chap12 directory. Rename the file c12ex3a.html.

b. Copy the bonus.cgi file from the cgi-bin/chap03 directory to the cgi-bin/chap12 directory. Rename the file c12ex3.cgi.

c. Open the c12ex3a.html file in a text editor. Change the filename in the first line from bonus.html to c12ex3a.html.

d. Modify the <FORM> tag to refer to the c12ex3.cgi script, which is contained in the cgi-bin/chap12 directory.

e. Save the c12ex3a.html document.

f. Open the c12ex3.cgi file in a text editor. Change the filename in the second line from bonus.cgi to c12ex3.cgi.

g. Modify the script so that it verifies that the form data is complete. (Be sure to remove any leading and trailing spaces from the form data.) If one or more entries are blank, use a Location header to redirect the browser to the c12ex3b.html file, which is contained in the public_html/chap12 directory.

h. Move the Content-type header from its current location to the appropriate location in the script.

i. Save the c12ex3.cgi document.

j. *If you are using a UNIX system*, change the c12ex3.cgi file permissions to 755.

k. Open the c12ex3a.html file in your Web browser. The Bonus Calculator Web page appears on the screen.

l. Click the Submit button. If necessary, click the Continue Submission button. A Web page advising you to return to the form should appear on the screen.

m. Return to the form. Enter John as the name, 1000 as the sales, and .05 as the rate. Click the Submit button. If necessary, click the Continue Submission button. A Web page showing the salesperson's name, bonus amount, sales amount, and bonus rate should appear on the screen.

Project 4

In this project, you modify the Patton Industries script from Hands-on Project 3 so that it lists (on the error Web page) the form entries that were left blank.

a. Open the c12ex3a.html file in a text editor. Change the filename in the first line from c12ex3a.html to c12ex4.html.

b. Modify the <FORM> tag to refer to the c12ex4a.cgi script.

c. Save the document as c12ex4.html.

d. Open the c12ex3.cgi file in a text editor. Change the filename in the second line from c12ex3.cgi to c12ex4a.cgi, then save the document as c12ex4a.cgi.

e. Modify the script so that it stores, in an array, the entries that were left blank on the form. (*Hint*: Store the entries in a *key=value* format. For example, if the Salesperson text box is empty, store the entry as Error=Salesperson.)

f. Use string concatenation, which you learned about in Chapter 8, to concatenate the array entries into one string. Modify the Location header to pass the string along with the URL.

g. Modify the Location header so that it redirects the browser to a script named c12ex4b.cgi, which you will save in the cgi-bin/chap12 directory.

h. Save the c12ex4a.cgi document.

i. Create a script named c12ex4b.cgi. Save the script in the cgi-bin/chap12 directory. The script should create an error Web page that lists the information passed to the script.

j. *If you are using a UNIX system*, change the c12ex4a.cgi and c12ex4b.cgi file permissions to 755.

k. Open the c12ex4.html file in your Web browser. The Bonus Calculator Web page appears on the screen.

l. Enter your name in the Salesperson name text box, then click the Submit button. If necessary, click the Continue Submission button. A Web page advising you to return to the form to complete the sales and bonus rate entries should appear on the screen.

12

Project 5

In this project, you modify the Juniper Printers script from Chapter 4 so that it verifies that the user completed the required entries on the form. The modified script will use a Location header to redirect the user's browser to an error Web page if one or more form entries are blank.

a. Copy the juniper.html file from the public_html/chap04 directory to the public_html/chap12 directory. Rename the file c12ex5a.html.

b. Copy the juniper.cgi file from the cgi-bin/chap04 directory to the cgi-bin/chap12 directory. Rename the file c12ex5.cgi.

c. Open the c12ex5a.html file in a text editor. Change the filename in the first line from juniper.html to c12ex5a.html.

d. Modify the <FORM> tag to refer to the c12ex5.cgi script, which is contained in the cgi-bin/chap12 directory.

e. Save the c12ex5a.html document.

f. Open the c12ex5.cgi file in a text editor. Change the filename in the second line from juniper.cgi to c12ex5.cgi.

g. Modify the script so that it verifies that the name and serial number entries are complete. (Be sure to remove any leading and trailing spaces from both entries.) If the name and serial number entries are blank, use a Location header to redirect the browser to the c12ex5b.html file, which is contained in the public_html/chap12 directory.

h. Move the Content-type header from its current location to the appropriate location in the script.

i. Save the c12ex5.cgi document.

j. *If you are using a UNIX system*, change the c12ex5.cgi file permissions to 755.

k. Open the c12ex5a.html file in your Web browser. The Product Registration Form appears on the screen.

l. Click the Submit Registration button. If necessary, click the Continue Submission button. A Web page advising you to return to the form should appear on the screen.

m. Return to the form. Enter Carol Thompkins as the name and 34A as the serial number. Click the Submit Registration button. If necessary, click the Continue Submission button. A Web page acknowledging receipt of the form should appear on the screen.

Project 6

In this project, you modify the Juniper Printers script from Hands-on Project 5 so that it lists (on the error Web page) the form entries that were left blank.

a. Open the c12ex5a.html file in a text editor. Change the filename in the first line from c12ex5a.html to c12ex6.html.

b. Modify the <FORM> tag to refer to the c12ex6a.cgi script.

c. Save the document as c12ex6.html.

d. Open the c12ex5.cgi file in a text editor. Change the filename in the second line from c12ex5.cgi to c12ex6a.cgi, then save the document as c12ex6a.cgi.

e. Modify the script so that it stores, in an array, the text box entries that were left blank on the form. (*Hint*: Store the entries in a *key=value* format. For example, if the Name text box is empty, store the entry as Error=0. Likewise, if the Serial number text box is empty, store the entry as Error=1.)

f. Use string concatenation, which you learned about in Chapter 8, to concatenate the array entries into one string. Modify the Location header to pass the string along with the URL.

g. Modify the Location header so that it redirects the browser to a script named c12ex6b.cgi, which you will save in the cgi-bin/chap12 directory.

h. Save the c12ex6a.cgi document.

i. Create a script named c12ex6b.cgi. Save the script in the cgi-bin/chap12 directory. The script should create an error Web page that lists the information passed to the script.

j. *If you are using a UNIX system*, change the c12ex6a.cgi and c12ex6b.cgi file permissions to 755.

k. Open the c12ex6.html file in your Web browser. The Product Registration Form appears on the screen.

l. Click the Submit Registration button. If necessary, click the Continue Submission button. A Web page advising you to return to the form to complete the name and serial number entries should appear on the screen.

m. Return to the form. Enter Ned Yardley as the name and 123B as the serial number. Click the Submit Registration button. If necessary, click the Continue Submission button. A Web page acknowledging receipt of the form should appear on the screen.

12

CASE PROJECTS

1. Create two HTML documents and a script for Phoenix Industries. Name the HTML documents c12case1a.html and c12case1b.html, and save them in the public_html/chap12 directory. Name the script c12case1.cgi and save it in the cgi-bin/chap12 directory. The c12case1a.html document should display a form that allows the user to enter his or her name, street address, city, state, and ZIP code. Include a submit button and a reset button on the form. When the user clicks the submit button, the c12case1.cgi script should verify that the form data is complete before displaying the data on a Web page. If one or more form entries are blank, the script should redirect the user's browser to the c12case1b.html document, which should advise the user to return to the form to complete all entries.

2. Create an HTML document, a script, and a text file for Henderson Products. Name the HTML document c12case2.html and save it in the public_html/chap12 directory. Name the script c12case2.cgi and save it in the cgi-bin/chap12 directory. Name the text file c12case2.txt and save it in the cgi-bin/chap12 directory. Enter only the number 0 in the text file. (If you are using a UNIX system, be sure to change the text file permissions to 666.) The c12case2.html document should display a link labeled "Click here". When the user clicks the link, the c12case2.cgi script should display one of three phrases, depending on the value stored in the c12case2.txt file. The phrases are "A stitch in time saves nine.", "Measure twice, cut once.", and "Look before you leap." For example, when the script is executed the first time, the phrase "A stitch in time saves nine." will appear on the screen. After displaying the appropriate phrase, the script should change the contents of the text file from the number 0 to the number 1. The script should include a Refresh header that tells the computer to execute the script again. (Refresh the screen every three seconds.) When the script is executed the second time, it will display the "Measure twice, cut once." phrase, because the value stored in the text file is the number 1. After all three phrases are displayed, use a Location header to redirect the user's browser to the c12case2.html document.

A

UNIX COMMANDS

Tasks	Type the following after the UNIX command prompt	Examples
change the current directory	**cd** *path* (*path* is the path to the directory)	`cd cgi-bin/chap01`
change the file permissions	**chmod** *permissions filename*	`chmod 755 first.cgi`
change to your home directory	**cd**	`cd`
copy a file from the current directory to the current directory	**cp** *source destination*	`cp sun.html c01ex1.html`
create a subdirectory in the current directory	**mkdir** *directoryname*	`mkdir chap01`
delete a file from the current directory	**rm** *filename*	`rm first.cgi`
delete an empty subdirectory from the current directory	**rmdir** *directoryname*	`rmdir chap01`
delete a subdirectory and its files from the current directory	**rm -r** *directoryname*	`rm -r chap01`
determine the location of a file on your UNIX system	**find** *start* **-name** *filename* (*start* is the starting directory for the search, and *filename* is the name of the file you want to find)	`find /cgi-bin -name pay.cgi`
determine the location of the Perl interpreter on your UNIX system	**whereis perl**	`whereis perl`
display a help screen	*command* **--help**	`date --help`
display the contents of a text file	**cat** *filename*	`cat comments.txt`
display the contents of a large text file, one screen at a time	**more** *filename* (Press the spacebar to view the next screen. Press q to exit.)	`more inter.cgi`

Tasks	Type the following after the UNIX command prompt	Examples
display the manual page for a UNIX command	**man** *command* (If the manual page contains more than a screen of information, you will need to press the spacebar to view the next screen. Press q to exit.)	`man ls`
display the names and file permissions of files contained in the current directory	**ls -l**	`ls -l`
display the names of files contained in the current directory	**ls**	`ls`
display the path to the current directory	**pwd**	`pwd`
move a file from the current directory to another directory	**mv** *file destination*	`mv sun.html /home/jp/chap02`
rename a file in the current directory	**mv** *oldname newname*	`mv pay.cgi payroll.cgi`

B

USING THE GEDIT TEXT EDITOR

Figure B-1 shows the gedit text editor with the first.cgi script from Chapter 1 loaded for editing.

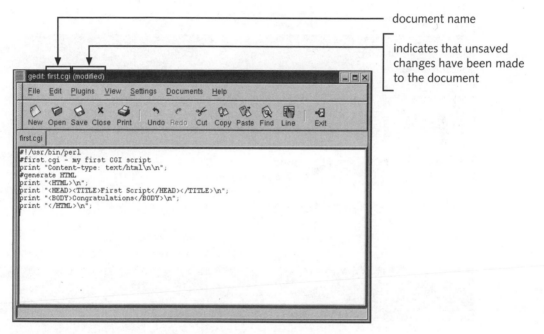

document name

indicates that unsaved changes have been made to the document

Figure B-1   gedit text editor containing the first.cgi script

As Figure B-1 indicates, the editor's title bar displays the name of the document being edited and whether unsaved changes have been made to the document.

Figure B-2 shows a listing of commands available in gedit. The commands are split into six groups as follows: starting and exiting; opening, saving, and printing a document; marking, unmarking, cutting, copying, and pasting text; inserting and deleting a character; moving the cursor; and other.

Starting and exiting	Procedure
start gedit	1. Log on to your UNIX system. Depending on how your system is configured, the system may be in a text-mode environment or a graphical environment. 2. If the system is in a text-mode environment, type startx after the command prompt and press Enter. 3. Click the Main Menu button (the footprint) on the Gnome panel, point to Programs, point to Applications, and then click gedit. (You also can click the Main Menu button, and then click Run. When the Run Program dialog box appears, type gedit in the text box and then click the Run button.)
exit gedit	click the Exit button on the toolbar
Opening, saving, and printing a document	**Procedure**
open (read text from) an existing document	1. click the Open button on the toolbar 2. select the appropriate file 3. click the OK button
save the current document	To save the document using its current name: 1. click the Save button on the toolbar To save the document using a new name: 1. click File on the menu bar 2. click Save As 3. type the filename in the Selection text box 4. click the OK button
print the current document	1. click the Print button on the toolbar 2. click the Print button on the Print Preview dialog box's toolbar
Marking, unmarking, cutting, copying, and pasting text	**Procedure**
mark/unmark a block of text	1. use your mouse to select (highlight) the block of text 2. to unmark the text, simply click an area of the document
cut text	1. mark the block of text to be cut 2. click the Cut button on the toolbar
copy text	1. mark the block of text to be copied 2. click the Copy button on the toolbar 3. position the cursor to where you want the text copied 4. click the Paste button on the toolbar
paste text	1. cut or copy the text to be pasted 2. position the cursor to where you want the text pasted 3. click the Paste button on the toolbar

Figure B-2   Listing of gedit commands

Inserting and deleting a character	Procedure
insert a character	1. position the cursor to where you want the character inserted 2. type the character
delete the current character	press the Delete key
delete the previous character	press the Backspace key
insert a Tab character at the current cursor position	press the Tab key
Moving the cursor	**Procedure**
move cursor up, down, right, and left	press the appropriate arrow key
move cursor to beginning of line	press the Home key
move cursor to end of line	press the End key
move cursor to next page	press the Pg Dn (or Page Down) key
move cursor to previous page	press the Pg Up (or Page Up) key
Other	**Procedure**
search the file for a string of characters	1. click the Find button on the toolbar 2. type the text in the Search for text box 3. click the Find button
display the help screens	1. click Help on the menu bar 2. click Help

Figure B-2   Listing of gedit commands (continued)

APPENDIX C

USING THE PICO TEXT EDITOR

Figure C-1 shows the pico text editor with the first.cgi script from Chapter 1 loaded for editing.

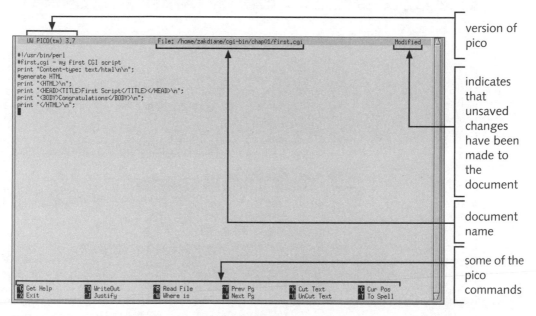

version of pico

indicates that unsaved changes have been made to the document

document name

some of the pico commands

Figure C-1   Pico text editor containing the first.cgi script

As Figure C-1 indicates, the editor's status line displays the version of pico that you are using, the name of the document being edited, and whether unsaved changes have been made to the document. Listed at the bottom of the editor are the commands you use to perform common tasks, such as opening and saving a file. The caret (^) in each command indicates the Ctrl key. For example, to exit the pico text editor, you press and hold down the Ctrl key as you type the letter x.

Figure C-2 shows a listing of commands available in pico. The commands are split into six groups as follows: starting and exiting; opening, saving, and printing a document; marking, unmarking, cutting, copying, and pasting text; inserting and deleting a character; moving the cursor; and other.

Starting and exiting	Procedure
start pico	1. Log on to your UNIX system. Depending on how your system is configured, the system may be in a text-mode environment or a graphical-mode environment. 2. If the system is in a graphical-mode environment, open a terminal window. 3. Type pico after the UNIX command prompt and press Enter.
exit pico	press ^x

Opening, saving, and printing a document	Procedure
open (read text from) an existing document	1. press ^r 2. type the filename 3. press Enter or 1. press ^r 2. press ^t to see a listing of files 3. use the arrow keys to select a file 4. press Enter
save the current document	1. press ^o 2. type the filename, if necessary 3. press Enter
print the current document	1. return to the UNIX command prompt 2. type lp *filename*, where *filename* is the name (and path, if necessary) of the file to print 3. press Enter

Marking, unmarking, cutting, copying, and pasting text	Procedure
mark/unmark a block of text	1. position the cursor on the first character to include in the block 2. press ^^ (press and hold down the Ctrl key as you type the caret) 3. use the arrow keys to highlight the remaining characters in the block 4. to unmark the text, press ^^ again
cut text	1. mark the block of text to be cut 2. press ^k to cut the marked text or 1. position the cursor somewhere in the line to be cut 2. press ^k to cut the line containing the cursor

Figure C-2   Listing of pico commands

Marking, unmarking, cutting, copying, and pasting text	Procedure
copy text	1. mark the block of text to be copied 2. press ^k to cut the marked text, then immediately press ^u to paste the text in its current location 3. position the cursor to where you want the text copied, then press ^u to paste the text in this location
paste text	1. position the cursor to where you want the text pasted 2. press ^u
Inserting and deleting a character	**Procedure**
insert a character	1. position the cursor to where you want the character inserted 2. type the character
delete the current character	press the Delete key
delete the previous character	press the Backspace key
insert a Tab character at the current cursor position	press the Tab key
Moving the cursor	**Procedure**
move cursor up, down, right, and left	press the appropriate arrow key
move cursor to beginning of line	press the Home key
move cursor to end of line	press the End key
move cursor to next page	press ^v
move cursor to previous page	press ^y
Other	**Procedure**
search the file for a string of characters	1. press ^w 2. type the string of characters 3. press Enter
display the help screens	press ^g
refresh the display	press ^l (the letter l)
left-justify the current paragraph	press ^j
spell check the document	press ^t

Figure C-2   Listing of pico commands (continued)

D

ASCII CODES

Character	ASCII	Binary	Character	ASCII	Binary
SPACE	32	00100000	>	62	00111110
!	33	00100001	?	63	00111111
"	34	00100010	@	64	01000000
#	35	00100011	A	65	01000001
$	36	00100100	B	66	01000010
%	37	00100101	C	67	01000011
&	38	00100110	D	68	01000100
'	39	00100111	E	69	01000101
(	40	00101000	F	70	01000110
)	41	00101001	G	71	01000111
*	42	00101010	H	72	01001000
+	43	00101011	I	73	01001001
'	44	00101100	J	74	01001010
–	45	00101101	K	75	01001011
.	46	00101110	L	76	01001100
/	47	00101111	M	77	01001101
0	48	00110000	N	78	01001110
1	49	00110001	O	79	01001111
2	50	00110010	P	80	01010000
3	51	00110011	Q	81	01010001
4	52	00110100	R	82	01010010
5	53	00110101	S	83	01010011
6	54	00110110	T	84	01010100
7	55	00110111	U	85	01010101
8	56	00111000	V	86	01010110
9	57	00111001	W	87	01010111
:	58	00111010	X	88	01011000
;	59	00111011	Y	89	01011001
<	60	00111100	Z	90	01011010
=	61	00111101	[	91	01011011

Character	ASCII	Binary	Character	ASCII	Binary
\	92	01011100	n	110	01101110
]	93	01011101	o	111	01101111
^	94	01011110	p	112	01110000
_	95	01011111	q	113	01110001
`	96	01100000	r	114	01110010
a	97	01100001	s	115	01110011
b	98	01100010	t	116	01110100
c	99	01100011	u	117	01110101
d	100	01100100	v	118	01110110
e	101	01100101	w	119	01110111
f	102	01100110	x	120	01111000
g	103	01100111	y	121	01111001
h	104	01101000	z	122	01111010
i	105	01101001	{	123	01111011
j	106	01101010	|	124	01111100
k	107	01101011	}	125	01111101
l	108	01101100	~	126	01111110
m	109	01101101	DELETE	127	01111111

Index